THE CONCENTRATION
OF ECONOMIC POWER

DAVID LYNCH

THE CONCENTRATION
OF ECONOMIC POWER

COLUMBIA UNIVERSITY PRESS

NEW YORK · MORNINGSIDE HEIGHTS

TO M. E. L.

CONTENTS

TABLES

CHAPTER I

INTRODUCTION

IN ADDITION to undertaking the arduous task of readjusting to the conditions of a peacetime economy during the postwar period, the people of the United States must, perforce, grapple with the momentous problems which in 1938 were responsible for the creation of the Temporary National Economic Committee (TNEC). Idle factories, unemployment, social unrest, maldistribution of income, hoarded savings, concentration of economic power, and monopolistic control of industrial activities—all these problems are intricately and delicately interrelated. Upon the success or the failure to find an effective solution to these great problems may depend the future of free economic and political institutions—liberal captitalism and representative democracy.

The war which broke out in Europe in September, 1939, and our entrance into it after the attack on Pearl Harbor temporarily have obscured the imminence of these problems and have created an unprecedented period of industrial expansion and full employment. But in due time the issues will have to be met, and because of the war and the tremendous dislocations which are in process the adjustments which will have to be made may be more urgent, more trying, and of greater magnitude. That leaders in a position to understand the implications of present-day economic trends are deeply disturbed is evidenced by the character of their remarks, which are strikingly similar to those of President Roosevelt on April 29, 1938, when he requested the Congress to conduct a study of the concentration of economic power in American industry and the effect of that concentration upon the decline of competition. At that time the President said, "the liberty of a democracy is not safe if the people tolerate the growth of private power to a point where it becomes stronger than their democratic state itself. . . . Concentration of economic power . . . and the resulting unemployment of labor and capital are inescapable problems for a modern 'private enterprise' democracy." [1]

[1] S. Doc. 173, 75th Cong., 3d sess.

Displaying the same concern for the future of free institutions, the president of the United States Chamber of Commerce recently said:

Small and medium-sized businesses are the backbone of our people's capitalism. We must make it possible for them to exist and to grow. They cannot live if the weight and bulk of Big Business can be used to stunt or crush small competitors. . . . We must demonstrate our faith in free economy by making it truly free, and right of way for small enterprise is at the core of that freedom. . . . Instinctively Americans know that the doom of small business would be the doom of their cherished free economy. . . . In a people's capitalism of the American variety it [monopoly] is not a capitalist device but an *anti*-capitalist tendency. It runs counter to the ideals and the interests of a democratic competitive economy.[2]

A similar view was expressed in July, 1943, by the Secretary of Commerce:

The business structure is imperiled whenever small business is driven by concentration of private power into a less and less independent position. Unfortunately that has been happening. But, fortunately, it is not too late to call a halt to dangerous tendencies toward concentration of wealth and power and of markets in the monopolistic control of a relatively few number of private enterprises.[3]

Many such opinions have been voiced by statesmen, business leaders, and men of public affairs since the work of the TNEC was completed; the following, by a prominent business journal and the chairman of the Senate Small Business Committee, are representative:

Democracy can only exist in a capitalistic system in which the life of the individual is controlled by the laws of supply and demand. If capitalism is to be saved we must . . . prevent small business from being shattered and destroyed by the war.[4]

Small business for many years has been waging a losing fight against its big competitors. The growing concentration of economic control and the extension of monopolistic practices has become appalling.[5]

These apprehensions and warnings are based on an understanding of the fact that little has occurred to alter the complex pattern of forces, practices, and institutions which culminated in the economic collapse of 1929 and in the long period of underemployment which was terminated only by the feverish activities of war. With the return

2 Extracted from Johnston, *America Unlimited*, pp. 156, 157–158, 161, 177.
3 U. S. Department of Commerce, *390 Bills, a Digest of Proposals Considered in Congress in Behalf of Small Business, 1933–1942*, p. 1.
4 *The Magazine of Wall Street*, LXXI (October 31, 1942), 61–62.
5 Senator James E. Murray, *Hearings before the Special Committee to Study and Survey the Problems of American Small Business Enterprises*, U. S. Senate, 76th Cong., 1st sess., Part 1, 1942, p. 2.

of peace many aspects of the pattern remain, and the resulting maladjustments may be aggravated by new dislocations created by the war and by further concentration of economic power which the war itself appears to have accentuated.

THE WARTIME DRIFT TOWARD GREATER ECONOMIC CONCENTRATION

Scarcely had the TNEC completed its work when trends of a momentous character were under way, accelerating the tempo and increasing the extent of concentration within the economy. War had broken out in Europe, necessitating the mobilization of industrial resources for national defense. Eventually this country itself was plunged into the conflict, requiring the subordination of many peacetime objectives to the prosecution of the war. The necessity for immediate action, the fact that modern warfare requires increasing quantities of the products of heavy and mass production industries, and measures of wartime expediency have resulted in the awarding of defense contracts and the utilization of productive resources in a manner injurious to small business and accentuating the trend to industrial giantism. Moreover, it appears that the disruption of normal markets, the allocation of supplies, the regulation of prices, the restriction of man power, and other dislocations inherent in a wartime economy have dealt more severely with small enterprisers. Great shifts have taken place within the economy—shifts toward greater concentration of economic power—many of which probably will outlast the war.

No comprehensive survey of this great movement has been made, but a few studies have been undertaken, the results of which suggest the character of the trend. Even before the entrance of the United States into the war the placing of defense contracts served to augment the growth of bigness in industry and to intensify the struggle for survival by small concerns. By 1941 the pattern of defense contracts which, with modifications, was to remain for the duration of the war had been established. It is reported that in that year fifty-six firms, less than one-half of 1 percent of the manufacturing establishments of the country, were awarded 75 percent of all the contracts. Concentration was even more marked within this group, however, inasmuch as six corporations held 31 percent of the total.[6] Between June, 1940, and

---

[6] *Business Week*, August 2, 1941, p. 32; see also Murray, "Has Small Business a Future," *Vital Speeches*, IX (May 15, 1943), 473–477.

March, 1943, more than 100 million dollars worth of prime war-supply contracts were awarded. Seventy percent of these were held by the leading 100 corporations; 10 corporations held 32 percent, and the leading 50 held 60 percent.

Studies by the United States Department of Commerce during 1943–1944 throw additional light on this trend toward industrial concentration.[7] After Pearl Harbor the total number of firms in business declined precipitously. Despite the wartime industrial boom, the number of firms which discontinued operations was greater than that replaced by new entries; it is estimated that the number in business in 1943 was nearly 17 percent less than in 1941. There are numerous indications that the relative importance of small business has declined during the war period and that the dominance of big business has become more marked. Between 1938 and 1942 it appears that the total number of workers employed by 95 percent of the nation's corporations (the smallest) declined 23 percent, whereas those employed by 5 percent of the corporations (the largest) increased 22 percent. A related study indicates that between January 1, 1941, and January 1, 1943, business firms employing fewer than 125 workers each experienced an increase in employment of 1 percent and an increase in the value of their product (attributable principally to price increases) of 16 percent; during the same period, however, the increase in employment by the large establishments employing more than 125 workers was 62 percent and the increase in the value of the product, 96 percent.[8]

These portentous trends are but scattered manifestations of a wartime drift toward greater economic concentration. A product of the apprehension thus created has been the "small business movement," which recently has attracted the attention of the country. Champions of small business, fearful of its fate and of the effects of the war upon the small entrepreneur, point to the indispensable role of small enterprisers in a capitalistic democracy. It is claimed that small business is the seedbed of new ideas and the yeast of a dynamic industrialism and that its maintenance is essential to wide opportunities of consumer choice—the prerequisites of a free economy, where

[7] Bowen, "The Impact of the War upon Smaller Manufacturing Plants," *Survey of Current Business*, XXIII (July and September, 1943), 19 ff.; and "Trends in the Business Population," *Survey of Current Business*, XXIV (March, 1944), 8–13.
[8] See also A. Ford Hinrichs, *Hearings before the Special Committee to Study and Survey the Problems of American Small Business Enterprises*, U. S. Senate, 76th Cong., 1st sess., Part 1, pp. 30–39.

each may buy according to his means and his tastes. Moreover, it is maintained that an economy in which small business plays a vital role is more flexible, that it more readily adapts itself to change, and that it effects a wider distribution of income and encourages individual enterprise.

Three aspects of the problem of concentration are more vital than the issues thus far raised: monopoly exploitation, the relation of monopoly to full employment, and the threat of concentration to democratic institutions. Little need be said of the interest which society at large has in preventing great industrial combinations from exacting too high a tribute for their control over the market place. The historic antitrust movement is an expression of that interest. Perhaps even more fundamental is the impact of monopoly and economic concentration upon the capitalistic economy. By contributing to the concentration of wealth and income, it undermines the foundation of the economic system by increasing the tendency to hoard, thereby accentuating the imbalance between savings and investment with resultant catastrophies such as occurred in 1929. There is growing doubt whether the capitalistic system, predicated as it is on the assumption of relatively free competition, can continue to function under increasing domination by monopoly. Equally serious is the impact of monopoly upon democratic institutions. Free enterprise and free institutions are not unrelated, and the diffusion of economic power would seem to be indispensable to an effective democracy.

Concern over the trend toward greater concentration during the war has been manifested by the so-called small business movement and has resulted in the organization of numerous governmental agencies to represent the public interest. Late in 1940 the Senate Small Business Committee was created,[9] and in the middle of 1941 a similar committee was organized by the House of Representatives.[10] A Small Business Section was established in the Department of Justice, a Small Business Division in the Department of Commerce, and the Smaller War Plants Corporation in the War Production Board. The activities of these agencies have been directed to a common purpose—that of re-enforcing the position of small enterprise and of retarding the trend toward concentration. They have undertaken to

[9] The Special Committee to Study and Survey the Problems of Small Business Enterprises, created by S. Res. 298, 76th Cong.
[10] The Select Committee to Conduct a Study and Investigation of the National Defense Program in Its Relation to Small Business in the United States, created by H. Res. 294, 77th Cong.

hold hearings and to suggest remedial legislation, to engage in research with respect to the problems of small business, to effect a wider
distribution of war contracts, to encourage subcontracting by the large
corporations among smaller firms, to render financial assistance to
small enterprisers, to offer counsel and to provide services to small
business in order to enhance its capacity for survival, to maintain
effective vigilance over monopolistic and unfair trade practices particularly harmful to small business, and to plan for an orderly conversion to a peacetime economy least harmful to small enterprise and
least conducive to monopoly.

Thus, because of the dislocations created by the war there has developed a renewed interest in the problems which concerned the
TNEC. Moreover, recent disclosures relating to controls instituted
by international cartels have revealed both their harmful effects to
domestic consumers and their interference with the national defense
program. Not only will monopoly and the concentration of economic
power be fundamental in the economic readjustments which will
have to be made, but the all-important task of achieving and maintaining full employment in a peacetime, free-enterprise economy will,
in all probability, once more become the foremost problem of our
time. These were the issues to which the TNEC devoted its labors;
consequently, its findings and its recommendations will be pertinent
to many of the major issues which will arise.

THE SCOPE OF THIS STUDY

The literature relating to the work of the Temporary National
Economic Committee is not extensive, and that pertaining to the
hearings is quite limited. A few articles have been published in current periodicals and professional journals. The most comprehensive
works are the Final Report of the Executive Secretary [11] and a volume
sponsored by the National Association of Manufacturers.[12] These
two publications, however, relate almost exclusively to the forty-three
monographs published by the TNEC. Although such contributions
are valuable, the monographs, unfortunately perhaps, played an
unimportant role in the final deliberations and recommendations
of the Committee. There is need, therefore, for a similar work to assemble and interpret the many thousands of pages of testimony be-

[11] Final Report of the Executive Secretary to the Temporary National Economic Committee, 77th Cong., 1st sess.
[12] Scoville and Sargent, *Fact and Fancy in the T.N.E.C. Monographs.*

fore the TNEC. Such will be the purpose of this study in which an endeavor will be made to: (1) analyze the political and economic forces which resulted in the creation of the TNEC; (2) describe the composition of the Committee and examine briefly the background, qualifications, and predilections of its members; (3) set forth the initial purposes of the Committee and define the character of its assignment; (4) give an account of the activities of the TNEC and present a concise outline of the hearings; (5) report what the testimony reveals concerning the structure of the American economy; (6) assemble the Committee's findings relating to concentration of economic power and the extent to which such concentration characterizes the economy; (7) ascertain the role which monopoly plays in American economic life and discover the methods by which it is implemented; (8) reveal the devices by which public authority and legal institutions are exploited for the advantage of special-interest groups; (9) recount briefly various disclosures made by the TNEC; (10) discover what can be learned about the nature and the cause of the Great Depression and what may be done to achieve full employment; (11) assemble the various recommendations made either to or by the Committee for economic reconstruction; (12) present an over-all appraisal of the work of the TNEC; and (13) evaluate, in general, the role of congressional investigations and their contributions to American economic and political life.

CHAPTER II

CREATION OF THE TEMPORARY NATIONAL ECONOMIC COMMITTEE

ON APRIL 29, 1938, President Franklin D. Roosevelt sent a message to the Congress calling attention to the growing concentration of economic power and its threat to the democratic way of life, to free private enterprise, and to human liberty.[1] In this message he requested the legislative branch to conduct an exhaustive hearing to determine the character and the social consequences of this trend. Specifically the President said, "There should be a thorough study of the concentration of economic power in American industry and the effect of that concentration upon the decline of competition."

The decision on the part of the Chief Executive to make such a request came only after a period of public and private discussion and represented the culmination of many forces and circumstances generating both from problems immediately demanding solution and from economic attitudes dating even to antiquity. The economic crisis of 1937, popularly known as the recession, created the major complex forces which led to the demand for a "monopoly investigation." Nevertheless, deep rooted in the folkways of Western peoples is the distrust and fear of monopoly.

EVENTS LEADING TO THE PRESIDENT'S MONOPOLY MESSAGE

To trace the events which led to the request for a temporary national economic committee would require a review of the evolution of opinions and attitudes from the early market places to the distressing years following 1929. The TNEC, like all social agencies, evolved from a variety of experiences and associations. It is a product of ancient antimonopoly sentiment as old as civilization itself. Rome, under Emperor Zeno (A. D. 483), had its Sherman Act.[2] Concepts of

---

[1] Message from the President of the United States Transmitting Recommendations Relative to the Strengthening and Enforcement of Antitrust Laws, S. Doc. 173, 75th Cong., 3d sess.
[2] Hearings before the Temporary National Economic Committee, Part 5, p. 1658.

"just price" and "reasonable" value as well as the condemnation of engrossing, regrating, and forestalling characterized medieval thinking. Antimonopoly sentiment played an important part in the outbursts against the British Crown between 1597 and 1640, ending in the beheading of Charles I; it was a fundamental factor in generating and accentuating the horrors of the French Revolution. By the close of the seventeenth century the common-law doctrine against monopoly, conspiracy, and restraint of trade had become established in England.

Despite the fact that the British common law became the basis of American jurisprudence and however much antimonopoly sentiment became established as part of American folklore, monopolies and monopolistic trends grew in magnitude and significance in the New World. Legislators became convinced that something stronger was necessary to cope with the problem, and in 1890 the Sherman Act was passed, declaring every contract, combination, or conspiracy in restraint of trade to be illegal. However, after fifty years of monopoly regulation under this Act, during which time public prosecutors followed one another in a kaleidoscopic sequence of action, despair, resolve, apathy, hostility, and zeal, monopolies continued to grow, quite unmolested.[3] In 1914 the Sherman Act was strengthened by the passage of the Clayton Act; at the same time the Federal Trade Commission was created to prevent unfair methods of competition. Following this there was rather vigorous administration of the antitrust laws. During the decade between 1920 and 1930, however, their administration hit a low ebb, and the weapon of monopoly litigation fell into virtual disuse.[4]

When the Great Depression followed the boom years of the late twenties, the fifty years of American experience under the Sherman Act seemed to have revealed two basic facts: (1) that the American people repeatedly had voiced their opposition to monopoly and monopolistic devices, and (2) that the great combinations, which they feared,

[3] In a prophetic moment nearly half a century ago Finley Peter Dunne epitomized what came near being the country's policy with respect to monopoly; his famous Mr. Dooley said: "Iv all th' gr-reat evils now threatenin' th' body politic an' th' pollytical bodies, these crool organizations an' combinations iv capital is perhaps th' best example iv what upright an' arnest business men can do whin they are let alone. They cannot be stamped out be laws or th' decisions iv coorts, or hos-tile ligislachion which is too frindly. Their desthruction cannot be accomplished be dimagogues.

"Th' thrusts are heejous monsthers built up be th' inlightened intherprise iv th' men that have done so much to advance pro-gress in our beloved counthry. On wan hand I wud stamp thim undher fut; on th' other hand not so fast."

[4] See Temporary National Economic Committee Monograph No. 16.

had come to play an increasingly dominant role in the national economy. These facts, the antimonopoly tradition, dating from centuries past, and the rise of giantism in industry, lent their weight in the creation of a Temporary National Economic Committee.

THE GREAT DEPRESSION

The Great Depression was responsible for numerous studies which sought to explain the behavior of the economic system. Ultimately the studies by Berle and Means,[5] Chamberlain,[6] the Brookings Institution,[7] Joan Robinson,[8] the Department of Agriculture,[9] Keynes,[10] the National Resources Committee,[11] and the Works Progress Administration [12] were all significant contributions preliminary to the adoption of the resolution creating the Temporary National Economic Committee. From these contributions there emerged the belief that the breakdown of the capitalistic system which occurred after 1929 was related to industrial concentration, to the breakdown of consumer purchasing power, to the behavior of inflexible prices, to the inequalities of income distribution, and to the increasing trend toward monopolistic [13] organization of economic life. These studies, among others, represented milestones of the thinking of the early thirties.

CONCENTRATION OF ECONOMIC POWER

Chapter III of *The Modern Corporation and Private Property,* written by Berle and Means, bore the title "Concentration of Economic Power." It is scarcely a coincidence that Section I of the President's message of April 29, 1938, bore the caption, "The Growing Concentration of Economic Power." In that now-famous work of Berle and Means it is shown that substantially all the major production in American industry was carried on under the corporate form of organization. But concentration did not cease there. Not only had the Adam Smith type of individualistic enterpriser all but passed from the scene, but also there was marked concentration even among corporations. Out of more than 300,000 nonfinancial corporations it was found that less than seven-hundredths of 1 percent controlled

5 Berle and Means, *The Modern Corporation and Private Property.*
6 Chamberlain, *The Theory of Monopolistic Competition.*
7 Moulton, *Income and Economic Progress.*
8 Robinson, *The Economics of Imperfect Competition.*
9 *Industrial Prices and Their Relative Inflexibility,* S. Doc. 13, 74th Cong., 1st sess., 1935.
10 Keynes, *General Theory of Employment, Interest, and Money.*
11 *Consumer Incomes in the United States.*
12 *Price Dispersion and Industrial Activity, 1928–1938.*
13 "Monopolistic" is used here in the broader sense to include oligopoly and monopolistic competition.

nearly half the corporate wealth. In other words, "nearly half of the corporate wealth in the United States" is in the control of two hundred corporations, and the largest, the American Telephone and Telegraph Company, "controls more wealth than is contained within the borders of twenty-one of the states of the country." Moreover, the large corporations were growing more rapidly than the small; in fact, their growth was from two to three times as fast. The authors set forth two significant conclusions relating directly to the problems later studied by the TNEC.

1. Competition has changed in character and the principles applicable to present conditions are radically different from those which apply when the dominant competing units are smaller and more numerous. The principles of duopoly have become more important than those of free competition.[14]

2. A society in which production is governed by blind economic forces is being replaced by one in which production is carried under the ultimate control of a handful of individuals. The economic power in the hands of a few persons who control a giant corporation is a tremendous force which can harm or benefit a multitude of individuals.[15]

MONOPOLISTIC COMPETITION

Following soon after the publication of *The Modern Corporation and Private Property* came Chamberlain's *The Theory of Monopolistic Competition* and the work of Joan Robinson. Chamberlain's technique, like that of Robinson, added realism and precision to economic analysis; they presented a value theory adaptable to actual conditions of the market, where neither the idealized concept of pure competition nor that of pure monopoly generally is applicable. Chamberlain's assertion that "because most prices involve monopoly elements, it is monopolistic competition that most people think of in connection with the simple word 'competition'" brought a new approach to theoretical analysis. Probably for the first time the full importance of duopoly and oligopoly (monopolistic competition) was recognized as a force in economic life. As Chamberlain stated, "competitive theory is unreal in large part because it fails truly to represent the forces at work in the economic system." Here, then, is another milestone which led up to the President's message of April 29, Section III of which was devoted to "The Decline of Competition and Its Effects on Employment."

[14] Berle and Means, *The Modern Corporation and Private Property*, p. 45. By permission of The Macmillan Company, publishers.
[15] *Ibid.*, p. 46.

INFLEXIBLE PRICES

In 1935 Gardiner Means, economic adviser to the Secretary of Agriculture, submitted an interesting study emphasizing the "widespread presence in our economy of inflexible, administered prices which have produced highly disruptive effects" and were responsible for the collapse of the system of laissez faire.[16] Means described two essentially different types of markets in operation: first, the traditional market where supply and demand are brought into equilibrium by a flexible price, and second, the administered market where "production" and demand are equated through the mechanism of an administered price. The author called attention to the growing concentration of corporate power and emphasized the fact that this trend has by its very nature destroyed the free market and seriously disorganized the economic system. Two sets of prices were found to exist side by side. One set, flexible prices, as typified by agricultural products, adjusted themselves to the impact of falling demand during the depression by appropriate changes; the other set, the administered or inflexible prices, as typified by the prices for farm implements, forced the impact of falling demand to be accommodated by a reduction in production. In fact, between 1929 and 1934 prices for twenty leading agricultural implements declined on the average only 6 percent; yet production and employment declined 80 percent. These great adjustments in production, instead of in price, aggravated the already acute problem of unemployment and were seen by some scholars as a major cause of the depression itself. When President Roosevelt asked Congress for an investigation of industrial concentration, he said:

One of the primary causes of our present difficulties lies in the disappearance of price competition in many industrial fields. . . . Managed industrial prices mean fewer jobs. It is no accident that in industries like cement and steel where prices have remained firm in the face of falling demand, pay rolls have shrunk as much as 40 or 50 percent in recent months. Nor is it mere chance that in most competitive industries where prices adjust themselves quickly to falling demand, pay rolls and employment have been far better maintained.

INEQUALITIES OF DISTRIBUTION

By 1935 the Brookings Institution had completed and published four notable books which, too, prepared the way for the TNEC investigations: Nourse, *America's Capacity to Produce,* and Moulton,

16 *Industrial Prices and Their Relative Inflexibility,* S. Doc. 13, 74th Cong., 1st sess., 1935.

America's Capacity to Consume, The Formation of Capital, and *Income and Economic Progress.* This study was directed to the question why the economic machine had broken down as it did in the late twenties. The authors of these volumes concluded that the collapse was by no means due to the incapacity of the productive mechanism to sustain a high prosperity such as was experienced in 1929, nor was it due to the incapacity of the population to consume the fruits of the industrial machine. A chapter entitled "The Primary Source of Economic Difficulty" indicated that the distribution of income among consumers was startlingly unequal; that the wants of people were far from satisfied, even in the best years; that market demand was less than productive capacity; that the proportion of the national income saved was large and constantly increasing; and that money savings did not automatically become new investments. In another chapter, "Price Stabilization in Relation to Progress," the authors found that while industrial efficiency had increased materially, wholesale prices had scarcely reflected this change. In other words, price stabilization by industrial combinations, by cartels, and by trade associations had defeated the gains of technological efficiency. As a result, incomes were denied to the masses, restricting their capacity to purchase, and a surplus was syphoned off to the wealthy owners of the productive regime who in turn failed to find profitable employment for their savings.

The Brookings Institution found wide inequalities in the distribution of income. By their calculations one-tenth of 1 percent of the families at the top of the economic scale received substantially as much as the total income of the 42 percent of the families at the bottom and 60 percent of American families received incomes insufficient to supply the basic necessities of life. It was found that the wealthy 10 percent saved 86 percent of the nation's savings and that the poorest 80 percent saved but 2 percent of the total.

It is evident that considerations such as these were given more than casual attention by those close to the Administration in Washington. By the time the President sent his message to Congress the National Resources Committee had initiated, and they were nearing completion, two important studies: *Consumer Incomes in the United States* [17] and *The Structure of the American Economy.*[18] The former, more

[17] U. S., National Resources Committee, *Consumer Incomes in the United States—Their Distribution in 1935–36.*
[18] U.S., National Resources Committee, *The Structure of the American Economy.*

exhaustive than the Brookings study of income distribution, arrived at similar conclusions, but seemed to indicate that the spread between the rich and the poor had widened. The latter study produced additional evidence of corporate concentration and of inflexible price structures.

UNDERCONSUMPTION THEORIES OF THE INDUSTRIAL CRISIS

There was developing in the minds of both laymen and professional economists a school of thought which attributed the recurrence of depressions to the failure of capitalism to place purchasing power in the hands of the great masses of the population in quantities sufficient to enable them to purchase the abundance of goods which modern industrialism brings to the market place. Underconsumption theories are not new, and they have enjoyed increasing support following each of the recent economic crises.[19] Sometimes the thesis has appeared in very naïve form, sometimes it has been championed by professional economists, at times by politicians, and at times it has appeared as an overproduction or oversavings theory. Hobson,[20] in 1922, found maldistribution and oversavings the root of the capitalistic trade cycle. Professor Douglas,[21] in 1935, presented evidence that such conditions contributed to the Great Depression. He found that wages did not keep pace with the production of labor and that prices failed to fall with lowered labor costs.

Thus, the underconsumption theory, both in its naïve and in its sophisticated forms, was enjoying a popularity in and out of New Deal circles prior to the creation of the TNEC. Leaders were becoming increasingly aware of the role which purchasing power plays in the economic organization. The fact that insufficient purchasing power is distributed to consumers came to be recognized as a primary force in the generation of depressions. According to this view, maldistribution of income results in the concentration of savings, which, in turn, creates forced hoarding, and capital fails to find profitable employment; hoarded income thus becomes lost to the economic stream, and the industrial spiral turns downward.

19 The author, in an unpublished manuscript, has traced the origins of the underconsumption theory back to the seventeenth century: Laffemas (1598), Montchretien (1615), Petty (1662), Von Schroetter (1686), Barbon (1690), Cary (1695), Mandeville (1705), and Von Hopken—all stated the theory in crude form before it was set forth almost in modern dress by Lauderdale in 1804. Following Lauderdale, Robert Owen, Sismondi, Malthus, Rodbertus, and Marx might be catalogued as underconsumptionists.
20 Hobson, *Economics of Unemployment.*
21 Douglas, *Controlling Depressions,* pp. 55–58.

The marked influence of the writings and theories of Mr. Keynes cannot be ignored in this connection.[22] It is evident that Keynes is in some respects an underconsumptionist. He accepts the principle of effective demand as the chief determinant of output. He would agree that concentrated savings and the resultant hoarding is deflationary; furthermore, he sees maldistribution of income as a force in generating depressions.[23]

Advisers to the Administration held no monopoly on this viewpoint. In 1932 the chief adviser to the party of the opposition gave voice to opinions which were almost Marxian in their implications:

Today, however, events are proving that a wider distribution of wealth is essential to the solvency and success of capitalistic industrialism itself, on the simple grounds that it is obviously self-defeating for western industrialism to get itself in position to produce vast quantities of goods unless, at the same time, it sees to it that there are vast masses of potential consumers ready with money to buy and leisure in which to enjoy the goods that the high-powered industrial machine produces.

. . .

Unless we can bring millions upon millions of men and women into position to buy the lavish output of western industrialism, even our existing investment in its marvelous productive facilities will become a permanently frozen asset.

. . .

A too great concentration of wealth means money in the hands of those who will invest it in producer goods . . . it is the absence of an adequate and dependable market for consumer goods that is stalling the economic machine of the west.[24]

That the same views were current among high New Dealers is illustrated by the following statement of a prominent Administration economist in a publication which went to the press before the TNEC hearings were complete:

Both theoretical analysis and the statistical material more recently published by the National Resources Planning Board in its studies of distribution and utilization of consumer income, show clearly the way in which increases in the proportion of income in the upper income brackets may tend to increase the proportion of income saved. Unless offsetting factors simultaneously increase the willingness to invest, or unless the Federal

22 Keynes, *General Theory of Employment, Interest, and Money.*
23 This superficial treatment of the Keynesian doctrine should not be allowed to conceal the fact that his writings in all their refinement posed problems which might very well have challenged the proposed investigative commission.
24 Frank, *Thunder and the Dawn,* pp. 382 ff. By permission of The Macmillan Company, publishers.

Government takes countervailing action through deficit expenditure programs, the result is to hoard or lose a portion of the current income paid
out, reducing the funds spent for productive purposes and thereby restricting employment and the amount of income produced. The distribution of income, and the habits of savings and investment, may be such as
to restrict national income in this way even in the absence of monopoly
profits. To the extent that such profits are realized, they increase such
tendencies. The extension of monopoly power and the resulting intensification of the maldistribution of income thus has a specific effect in
restricting the total national income.[25]

It is, thus, quite evident that the belief that economic concentration,
maldistribution, and monopolistic prices are responsible for maladjustments and dislocations of the economy was widely accepted. Economists, reformers, political leaders, and the public in general had
supported the thesis. It is significant that even before the recession
of 1937, when recovery seemed certain, the *Fortune* survey of public
opinion showed a marked sentiment against economic concentration.[26]
In response to the question "Do you think that a business monopoly
is beneficial, more beneficial than harmful, more harmful than beneficial, or harmful?" only 12 percent said "beneficial," 13 percent said
"more beneficial than harmful," 22 percent said "more harmful than
beneficial," and 45 percent, "harmful." In response to the query why
monopolies are harmful, those who thought that they are answered
as follows: oppression of small competitors, 36 percent; higher prices,
22 percent; concentration of wealth, 20 percent; restriction of buyers'
liberty, 9 percent; corruption of lawmakers, 8 percent; suppression
of new ideas, 6 percent.

THE RECESSION OF 1937

But in spite of all that has been said, in all probability there would
have been no TNEC had it not been for the setback which recovery
suffered early in 1937. The TNEC was, therefore, in part a product
of the historic past and in part the immediate result of the recession
of 1937. From 1933 to 1937 the economic and industrial outlook had
become increasingly more hopeful; Administration leaders felt that
they had found the way out and proudly boasted, "We planned it that
way." But the recession was so precipitate and so severe that leaders
in Washington soon felt that it was high time to make a searching
analysis of the American economy in the hope of discovering what
brought on the collapse in 1929 and wrecked the recovery program

25 U.S., National Resources Committee, *The Structure of the American Economy*, Part 2.
26 *Fortune*, XIV (October, 1936), 215.

in 1937. Less kindly critics have said, with some justification, no doubt, that the Administration set forth upon the so-called monopoly investigation as a face-saving procedure or with the intent of finding a whipping boy to divert the public mind from the failure of New Deal policies to bring about a sustained recovery. The president of a large life insurance company wrote that proposals for an investigation constituted a "tirade of speeches setting up the alibi that all the trouble was due to business concentration and monopoly." [27]

The critics of the Administration immediately labeled the proposed investigation as an attack upon business. This viewpoint was presented in the *New York Times* as follows: "one Administrative official after another drenched all hope of a conciliatory attitude toward 'big business' in a downpour of invective. . . . The Administration had satisfied itself that prices for certain key industrial products had been artificially maintained to the detriment of its recovery program." [28] Some saw political demagoguery as a motive using monopoly as a sure-fire political expletive.[29] Others said that the Administration had set about with a New Deal version of "Who Killed Cock Robin?"—a search for a villain, a role which was destined to be played by "tycoons" and "big business."

WARNINGS OF ADMINISTRATION ECONOMISTS

It will be somewhat difficult, nevertheless profitable, to trace the immediate steps leading up to the President's request for a "monopoly investigation." Somewhere an idea was born. Just when and where the decision was made may never be known. The idea had existed in embryo fashion, shapeless, in the public mind for years. Nevertheless, certain events and discussions gave it form and precision, until finally it emerged in a Presidential message. In a sense, the Administration was definitely pledged to take some form of action with respect to monopoly. Both the 1932 and the 1936 party platforms had advocated strengthening and impartial enforcement of antitrust laws to prevent monopoly and unfair trade practices in order to protect labor and the small business man. In 1936 the party platform contained the following pledge:

Monopolies and the concentration of economic power, the creation of Republican rule and privilege, continue to be the master of the producer,

27 Parkinson, "A Call to Action," *Printers' Ink*, CLXXXV (October 13, 1938), 11.
28 Belair, "New Deal Opens Fight on Big-Business Front," *The New York Times*, January 2, 1938.
29 *Time*, December 12, 1938, pp. 11–13.

the exploiter of the consumer, and the enemy of the independent opera-
tor. This is a problem challenging the unceasing effort of untrammeled
public officials in every branch of the Government. We pledge vigorously
and fearlessly to enforce the criminal and civil provisions of the existing
antitrust laws and to the extent that their effectiveness has been weakened
by new corporate devices or judicial construction, we propose by law to
restore their efficacy in stamping out monopolistic practices and the concentration of economic power.[30]

How the above pledge would have been carried out had it not
been for the recession of 1937 is a question best left to the imagina-
tion. But even before the economic relapse there were some within
the Administration who professed to see the handwriting on the
wall. Two of these were Leon Henderson, at that time Consulting
Economist for the Works Progress Administration, and Mordecai Ezekiel, Economic Adviser to the Department of Agriculture. Henderson,
in a speech before the Peoples' Lobby on April 24, 1937, decried the
trend of rising prices then current, especially since wages did not keep
pace. He said that if wages could not be made to keep up with prices,
there was no possibility of winning the race against inflation. Many of
the alarming price rises, he said, were the results of monopolies and
monopolistic manipulation. He noted that copper producers throughout the world had deliberately "ganged up" and restricted the production of copper. Then he cited a very impressive list of commodities
whose prices had been similarly subject to control.[31] On the same day
Dr. Ezekiel expressed similar apprehension and was quoted as saying
that if industry does not adopt a more reasonable policy, "but continues to jack up prices at the rates noted recently," the Government
might find it necessary to step in with "a drastic change in fiscal
policy." [32] This sounds more ominous even than a monopoly hearing.

The next significant event leading up to the message of April 29
was the now-famous prediction of Leon Henderson. Much of Mr.
Henderson's later rise to prominence dates back to the combination
of his fortune and insight when making this forecast. In May, 1937,
in a memorandum entitled "Booms and Busts," he predicted a major
business recession within six months.[33] He argued that prices were
rising so rapidly that purchasing power was failing to keep pace. Too

[30] *Congressional Record,* Vol. LXXX, Part 10, p. 10410.
[31] *Congressional Record,* Vol. LXXXI, Part 10, p. 1499.
[32] *The New York Times,* April 25, 1937, p. 19.
[33] See Lubell, "The Daring Young Man on the Flying Pri-cees," *The Saturday Evening
Post,* September 13, 1941, p. 84. An account is also found in *Time,* December 12, 1938,
p. 13.

much was going into profits and savings, which, in turn, as a result of the consequent curtailed purchasing power, failed to find profitable investment. The events which followed were a fulfillment of the prophecy, and Mr. Henderson was hailed as "the only economist in the Administration who saw what was coming." Though, perhaps, at the moment, a voice crying in the wilderness, Henderson lost no opportunity to express these convictions. In a speech before the National Association of Purchasing Agents, on May 24, 1937, he warned that concentrated control of business is increasing and that this fact is reflected in inordinate price rises.

THE NEED FOR BASIC ECONOMIC RESEARCH

In October, 1937, the recession which Mr. Henderson predicted got under way. By November and December the Administration had ample cause for worry; the elusive nature of the prosperity or recovery of the previous three years had become apparent. The ills which tormented the economic system were more deep-seated and inherent than some had assumed. The palliatives and stimuli which had been administered and which had succeeded in ameliorating conditions thus far were seen to be insufficient to supply the necessary correctives. The economic system had experienced great changes and suffered severe dislocations. There had been a slowing down of population growth, a restriction of investment opportunities, a rise of inflexible price structures, a concentration of industrial control behind new manipulations of the corporate device, a basic change in the nature of foreign trade, and a probable increase of the inequalities of income distribution. This seemed to call for a thoroughgoing analysis of economic institutions and behavior.

Nevertheless, the actual suggestion for such a study had to await further evolution of administrative policy. In the meantime, late in 1937 several additional embers were added to the fire. On November 29 Attorney General Cummings of the President's Cabinet appeared before the Association of Grocery Manufacturers of America and indicated that others close to the Administration had moved to the Means-Henderson-Ezekiel point of view. He declared that the trend toward undue concentration of wealth and economic control "is unmistakable." [34]

Shortly thereafter both Assistant Attorney General Jackson and Secretary of Interior Ickes revealed the leaning of administrative think-

[34] *Congressional Record*, Vol. LXXX, Part 1, p. 23.

ing and lent their leadership to a program of policing monopoly. Late in December, 1937, Robert Jackson made a radio address in which he assailed monopolists and big business, blaming their policies for many of the economic ills of the country.[35] He asserted that "the monopolist and those so near monopoly as to control their prices . . . by profiteering have simply priced themselves . . . into a slump." He said that monopoly had followed a policy of skimming "all the cream off recovery for itself." "Monopoly prices and monopoly profits jumped beyond all reason and away above the price level that small business could get." Hence, "monopoly and big business has thrown us off balance." Before the month was over Mr. Jackson voiced these opinions again.[36]

Almost immediately, as though co-operating in a common program to create a public opinion, Secretary Ickes took to the radio.[37] In a powerful speech he spoke of a proposed antitrust fight which was to be a battle to the finish between plutocracy, which he characterized as "America's 60 Families," and democracy, which he represented as being the nation's 120,000,000 people. After speaking of the dangers of socially uncontrolled corporate concentration, he proclaimed that "the new America must be a land of free business, not of ruthless big business—a land of free men, not of economic slaves." Thus, Mr. Ickes justified further policing of big business:

Practically all of our greatest historical figures are famous because of their persistent and courageous fight to prevent and control the over-concentration of wealth and power in a few hands. Thomas Jefferson, our first great leader in this fight, knew what it was to be cursed as a Jacobin and a destroyer of the Constitution by the wealthy tycoons of his time.

Andrew Jackson in his determination to curb the power of the Bank of the United States, felt the fury of the Wall Street of his day. He, too, was denounced as a dictator, as a wrecker of our institutions, in language even more vitriolic than the condemnations which are now being hurled by some of our financial earls at Franklin D. Roosevelt.[38]

The rapid sequence of these pronouncements by men high in the Administration could scarcely be characterized as mere coincidence. Here, seemingly, was a studied program toward a more or less definitely formulated objective. It was not surprising, therefore, to find Mr. Henderson on New Year's Day, 1938, saying that the break-

---

[35] *The New York Times,* December 27, 1937, p. 1.
[36] *Ibid.,* December 30, 1937, p. 1.
[37] *Ibid.,* December 31, 1937, p. 6.
[38] *Congressional Record,* Vol. LXXXIII, Part 1, p. 205.

down of recovery was plainly the result of the fact that there was not
enough purchasing power in the hands of the people to purchase the
full output of the farms and factories and that this disparity between
purchasing power and production was due to the fact that prices had
risen faster and longer than wages. Henderson's analysis of the collapse of 1937 was as follows:

Were monopolies responsible for this price rise which crippled workable
relationships in the American economy by reducing the general public's
capacity to consume? My answer is emphatically "Yes." I believe the "un-
balance" in prices was touched off by monopoly prices. Not all prices began their rise in August 1936. Far from it. In the main, the price increases
occurred in those commodities for which some group, public or private,
or both, is deliberately manipulating output and prices. Inadequate purchasing power is the central reason for the slump, and the causes of the
decline in purchasing power are to be sought in price manipulations, and
the concentration of ownership which makes monopoly possible over wide
and strategic areas. The blunt truth is that a large part of the American
economy is no longer competitive, though not all the rigidity, by all
means, is due to private controls.[39]

Still another step in the preparation of the public and the Congress
for a more concrete program was the annual report of Attorney
General Cummings, calling for a revision of the antitrust laws, which
he described as "inadequate." [40] The largest section of the Attorney
General's report was turned over to Robert Jackson, who supplied
detailed support for these recommendations. Mr. Jackson, as has
been shown, had more than once held that monopolies were responsible for the recession.

It is clear that by this time there was quite general agreement
within the Administration that something should be done about
monopoly. However, neither Mr. Jackson nor Mr. Cummings suggested any specific program. It was still nearly four months before
the April 29 speech, and apparently no precise plan had been evolved.
When President Roosevelt was challenged by an apprehensive re-
porter in the press conference of January 1, he indicated that the
antimonopoly campaign was not to be directed against business in general or big business as such; the attack was to be aimed at the recalcitrant and offending minority—the counterpart of those whom Theodore Roosevelt labeled the "malefactors of great wealth."

Two days later the President's annual message to Congress con-

[39] McKee, "Monopoly Investigators," *The Commonweal*, XXIX (November 4, 1938), 37.
Also see *The New York Times*, January 2, 1938.
[40] *The New York Times*, January 4, 1938, p. 1.

tained no suggestion of an investigation such as the TNEC; he made definite reference to, but did not place major emphasis upon, the question of concentration of economic control. Nevertheless, whatever plan he may have had in mind did not as yet appear to have crystallized. He spoke of the abuses of business, but was careful to note that business as a whole was not guilty of them. He insisted that an attack on these abuses did not constitute an attack upon business. He then proceeded to the question of concentration:

Another group of problems affecting business, which cannot be termed specific abuses, gives us food for grave thought about the future. Generally such problems arise out of the concentration of economic control to the detriment of the body politic—control of other people's money, other people's labor, other people's lives.

In many instances such concentration cannot be justified on the ground of operation efficiency. . . .

The work undertaken by Andrew Jackson and Woodrow Wilson is not finished yet . . . I do not propose to let the people down.[41]

In his press conference on the following day the President seemed to favor a scheme of planned production resembling European cartel systems.[42] He spoke of some sort of arrangement whereby business and industrial leaders would gather about a common table with the representatives of government to determine production policies (not completely unlike the NRA codes) without fear of prosecution under the antitrust laws. He indicated that the antimonopoly campaign would be directed against relatively few big corporations at the top and against a minority of business and industrial "chiselers" at the bottom of the economic pile.

At the beginning of 1938, therefore, the idea of a searching inquiry such as that of the TNEC seems to have been as amorphous as ever. The complex of elements were all there—the antimonopoly heritage of the Middle Ages, the doctrines of the common law, the American antitrust tradition, the maldistribution theories of depressions, and the collapse of the recovery program—but as yet, no specific program of action.

DETAILED PLANS FOR AN INVESTIGATION

Then came a meeting at Warm Springs, Georgia, when the elements were woven into a pattern and the idea of a TNEC began to crystallize.[43] Among those who attended the meeting were Robert

41 *Congressional Record,* Vol. LXIII, Part 1, pp. 8–11.
42 *The New York Times,* January 5, 1938, p. 5.
43 "Competition or Control," *Business Week,* October 8, 1938, p. 18.

Jackson and Harry Hopkins. The results of the discussions soon emerged in the form of a statement to a special Senate committee investigating unemployment and relief.[44] On this occasion Mr. Hopkins set forth in a clear manner the Administration viewpoint that the recession had been caused primarily by unwarranted price increases and by the failure of consumer purchasing power to keep pace with production. On this point he said:

I want to discuss briefly a general condition which leads to unemployment. . . . The general situation can best be stated in the following words: Consumer's purchasing power is not large enough to buy the goods that industry could produce. The low incomes of a large part of our population make it impossible for them to buy enough. The large incomes are only partially spent, the rest is kept out of buying channels. Some of this saved income is used for investing in new plant and equipment. But the deficiency of demand retards this investment and funds lie idle. . . . Industry will produce goods if there is demand for them.[45]

To support this thesis Mr. Hopkins offered data compiled by the Bureau of Labor Statistics to show that fourteen groups of commodities, representing 23 percent of the value of all commodities, actually increased in price between April, 1937, and February, 1938 (a period of falling prices), while a second group, representing 28 percent of the value of all commodities, declined in price less than half as much as the all-commodity price level. He maintained that in order for the price system to work effectively, it is imperative that prices be flexible and that they adjust themselves to demand. Thus, Mr. Hopkins advocated the return to a competitive economy:

I conceive two large principles which should be at work in our national policy—one is that of Government contribution to purchasing power when it is needed and the other is competition. I believe that competition on a scale that we have not known for many years is an absolute requirement without which the dynamics and benefits of the Government's efforts are likely to be sapped away. National intervention to stimulate competition is the democratic method since purchasing power in the hands of the people must then be won by competition. The form of the industrial pattern, therefore, is determined not by the judgment or caprice of a few monopolists but by the whole community.[46]

Mr. Hopkins's appearance before the Senate committee preceded the President's message of April 29 by scarcely more than three weeks. During the intervening days the plan took definite shape, so that the President was prepared to ask for a special committee to analyze

[44] *Congressional Record*, Vol. LXXXIII, Part 10, p. 1430.
[45] *Ibid.*   [46] *Ibid.*, p. 1435.

the problems of the American economy and to make appropriate recommendations.

THE PRESIDENT'S MONOPOLY MESSAGE

The message of the President was divided into six sections, together with an introduction and a conclusion.[47] In his introductory remarks he described the dangers to a democracy of an increasing growth of private power and of the failure of industry to provide employment and the essentials of an acceptable standard of living. In the first section, addressed to "The Growing Concentration of Economic Power," he presented statistical data to show that one-tenth of 1 percent of the corporations of the country owned 52 percent of the corporate assets, that "less than 5 percent of them owned 87 percent of all the assets," and that "one-tenth of 1 percent of them earned 50 percent of the net income of all of them." This and other evidence led the President to conclude that "we believe in a way of living in which political democracy and free private enterprise for profit should serve and protect each other—to insure a maximum of human liberty not for a few but for all."

In Section II, devoted to "Financial Control over Industry," the President decried the declining vigor of free private enterprise under "the heavy hand of integrated financial and management control." He found that private enterprise is ceasing to be free enterprise, and he spoke of an era of industrial empire-building under banker control. President Roosevelt devoted Section III to "The Decline of Competition and Its Effects on Employment." At this point he elaborated the now-familiar thesis that unemployment is a product of an inflexible (maintained) price system. "Competition Does Not Mean Exploitation" was the subject of Section IV; here the Chief Executive indicated that a return to competition does not mean an abandonment of child labor laws, fair labor standards, or necessarily a return to the excesses and abuses of a competitive system. In Section V, "The Choice before Us," the President concluded that the trend toward big business collectivism in industry has impelled ultimate collectivism in government. He asserted that the power now concentrating in the hands of the management of modern corporacy must be transferred directly to the public or delegated to its democratically responsible government.

In the final section the President presented "A Program." First, he

<hr />

[47] S. Doc. 173, 75th Cong., 3d sess.; see also Exhibit No. 1, *Hearings before the Temporary National Economic Committee*, Part 1, p. 185.

called for the enforcement of the antitrust laws; secondly, for an improvement of these laws themselves, which he found to be inadequate. In addition there was a request for an appropriation to study the many problems of American economic life. The President said, "To meet the situation I have described, there should be a thorough study of the concentration of economic power in American industry and the effect of that concentration upon the decline of competition. . . . The study should not be confined to the traditional antitrust field." Then he enumerated specific studies to be made: (1) improvement of antitrust procedure; (2) mergers and interlocking relationships; (3) financial controls; (4) investment trusts; (5) bank holding companies; (6) trade associations; (7) patent laws; (8) tax correctives; and (9) a Bureau of Industrial Economics. Finally, the President emphasized the social intent and purpose which motivated his recommendation to the Congress. This was not a blind trust-busting expedition. It was a search for economic results; it was "a program to preserve private enterprise" and to check the progress of collectivism in business. This was a temperate approach to a tremendous problem of far-reaching importance. The President felt assured that no man of good faith would misinterpret these proposals, "for idle factories and idle workers profit no man."

LEGISLATIVE HISTORY OF THE BILL CREATING THE TNEC

The President's address of April 29 called for a study of concentration of economic power; he requested that this inquiry be comprehensive and well financed. Nothing concrete was set forth, however, suggesting the organization of the proposed committee. Specific plans had to await conferences and agreements between members of the executive and the legislative branches. The final form of the TNEC was, as has been the case with most important legislation, a compromise. Hence, the eventual make-up of the Committee failed to conform with the ideas of either the Administration or the various congressional proposals, including the one which was ultimately written into law.

Even before the President's message several projects for a monopoly investigation had been presented to Congress. That such proposals were made is not at all surprising, considering the antimonopoly tradition; particularly would one expect them early in 1938 as a consequence of the teamwork and the oratory of Messrs. Henderson,

Jackson, Cummings, Hopkins, and Ickes. In December, 1937, Representative Shanley of Connecticut proposed the creation of a joint committee to hold hearings, to study antitrust problems, and to make recommendations to the Congress.[48] A month and a half later Representative Maverick of Texas presented a similar bill;[49] like its forerunner it failed to survive committee action. During the months of January and February Representative Dies of Texas made two attempts to capitalize on the increasing concern over industrial concentration and monopoly. His first resolution called for a committee from the House of Representatives to investigate monopolies.[50] This was followed a month later by a proposal for a joint committee of the House and Senate to undertake substantially the same responsibilities. The Dies resolutions quite obviously were inspired by the speeches of Messrs. Jackson and Ickes. As might be expected, however, they carried implications which were directly hostile to the Administration; Representative Dies proposed to give Mr. Ickes and Mr. Jackson "an opportunity to vindicate themselves," to learn if "monopolists have insidiously and covertly acquired control of the antitrust division," to discover if the NRA had "contributed to the growth and intrenchment of monopoly," and to discover what portion of New Deal expenditures "has gone into the pockets of the monopolists." Shortly after the second Dies proposal Senator Austin of Vermont, speaking on the floor of the Senate, called for a non-political, nonpartisan commission to study existing monopoly laws and, above all, to define what monopoly is and to analyze its relation to the general welfare. This was a month and a half before the President's message.[51]

THE LEADERSHIP OF SENATOR O'MAHONEY

Prior to April 29 three proposals had received public attention with respect to the problems of industrial concentration. The first was for the revival of the NRA or a modernized successor patterned after it. In his press conference of January 3 the President seemed to indicate that he was leaning toward that approach; even after the inauguration of the TNEC the President was suspected of such intentions. The second was for vigorous enforcement of the antitrust laws, a policy arduously championed by the Attorney General. A third approach

48 *Congressional Record*, Vol. LXXXIII, Part 1, p. 1128; also Part 6, p. 6087.
49 *Ibid.*, Part 1, p. 1323, and Part 12, p. 523.
50 *Ibid.*, Part 1, p. 75; also the Appendix, p. 529.
51 *Ibid.*, Part 3, p. 2757, and Part 8, p. 8506.

had been suggested by Senators Borah and O'Mahoney, and its principles had been incorporated in the Borah-O'Mahoney bill. Under its provisions, corporations of an interstate character would be required to procure licenses from an authorized Federal agency such as the Federal Trade Commission. Such licenses or charters would be granted only to corporations which met certain social standards required by the Congress and could be revoked if a corporation were found guilty by the courts of violating the antitrust laws. At one time the President was thought to have endorsed this plan.[52] The Borah-O'Mahoney Federal incorporation bill was about to come to the floor of the Senate when the President's monopoly message was delivered. One of the motives attributed to the President at that time was to head off the Borah-O'Mahoney bill by substituting an inquiry which would give him time and opportunity to develop his own plan for a unified New Deal policy toward big business and industrial concentration.[53]

One unschooled in the strategy to which legislators are forced by the exigencies of politics would be surprised, therefore, to discover that it was Senator O'Mahoney who became the first and the successful champion of the investigation requested by President Roosevelt. Shortly after the April message several bills were introduced in the House of Representatives calling for a committee to investigate monopoly or for the creation of a temporary national economic committee. Representative Nicholas introduced such a bill on May 5,[54] and Representative Cellar another exactly one week later.[55] The speed and the generalship of Senator O'Mahoney, however, placed his bill ahead of the rest. Less than a week intervened before he was ready with a proposal.[56]

Senator O'Mahoney appears to have been impelled by a combination of motives. He must, first of all, be credited with a conviction that there existed an opportunity for public service in analyzing industrial concentration. Then, too, he is said to have shared with his constituents in the West their traditional mistrust of the "money power" of the East. No doubt he saw in this move an opportunity for educating both the public and the Congress to the need for his

[52] *The New York Times,* January 1, 1938.
[53] "The So-Called Monopoly Committee," *Fortune,* XVIII (November, 1938), 72–73; "Monopoly Inquiry Holds Out Far-Reaching Possibilities," *News Week,* XII (July 18, 1938), 32.
[54] *Congressional Record,* Vol. LXXXIII, Part 6, p. 6397.
[55] *Ibid.,* p. 6843.   [56] *Ibid.,* p. 6261, and Part 12, p. 448.

own particular program of Federal licenses for interstate corporations. Furthermore, there was personal and political prestige to be gained by managing the investigation. Perhaps even of greater significance is the fact that Senator O'Mahoney was astute enough to recognize that the President's need for his leadership was almost as great as his own need to be back in the good graces of the Administration.[57] It was generally conceded at the time that his aggressive action following the monopoly message was a definite bid by the Senator for White House approval. It must not be thought, however, that his leadership was entirely in harmony with the plans of the Administration. His strategy was to wrest control, in whole or in part, from the Administration and vest the legislative branch with it. Certainly the net effect of his generalship was to preserve for Congress a vital interest in the investigation.

LEGISLATIVE VERSUS EXECUTIVE CONTROL

Senator O'Mahoney's first bill to create a temporary national economic committee failed to harmonize either with that finally adopted or with Administration plans. His original resolution called for a committee composed of two members from the Senate, two members from the House, and, in addition, the Attorney General and the chairman of both the Federal Trade Commission and the Securities and Exchange Commission. This would have created a committee of seven with the legislative members in control.[58] It was generally understood that the Administration wished Congress to authorize a purely executive investigation. In the April message President Roosevelt spoke of a "comprehensive study by the Federal Trade Commission, the Department of Justice, the Securities and Exchange Commission, and such other agencies of government as have special experience in various phases of the inquiry." There was no suggestion of legislative participation, in spite of the fact that weeks previously it had been suggested on the floors of both Houses.

It is quite clear that the Congress and the Executive were somewhat at odds as to who should control the investigation. Should it be the President? Should it be a congressional, a senatorial, or joint study by both Houses? Should it be an investigation participated in by both the executive and the legislative? If so, which branch should hold the balance of power? These were questions which demanded immediate

[57] Senator O'Mahoney, once considered a New Dealer, had vigorously opposed the President's court plan.
[58] *Congressional Record*, Vol. LXXXIII, Part 8, p. 8498; see also S. J. Resolution 291.

answer, and the result was, as usual, a compromise. A series of conferences were held behind the scenes shortly after the introduction of Senator O'Mahoney's bill. These conferences were attended by Senator O'Mahoney, Representative Sumners, chairman of the Committee on Judiciary in the House, and persons chosen by the President from various executive agencies.[59]

THE DEBATE ON THE BILL AND ITS PASSAGE IN THE SENATE

As a result of this collaboration and compromise between the interested parties, a new bill was written which was presented to the Senate in the form of a Joint Resolution—S. J. Resolution 300—to create a Temporary National Economic Committee.[60] Since this bill had the endorsement of both Senator O'Mahoney and Representative Sumners and was acceptable to the President and his advisers, it was hurriedly enacted into law. S. J. Resolution 300 was introduced in the Senate on May 23; it had been considered and reported favorably by the Senate Committee on Judiciary by June 7; it had been debated, amended, and passed by the Senate by June 9. In the House it received even more immediate approval. The bill, passed by the Senate on June 9 (Friday), was referred to the House on June 13 (Monday) and was passed on June 14. The completed bill was sent to, and signed by, the President on June 16, 1938, three weeks after its introduction by Senator O'Mahoney.[61]

There was very little debate in the Senate over the passage of the bill. This was an Administration measure adequately supported by the party in power. It appears that but one lone Senator raised his voice in opposition to it.[62] What little debate there was, centered about the provisions of the bill, not its ultimate passage. S. J. Resolution 300 originally provided for a committee of eleven, with the legislative members in the majority. By a series of adroit parliamentary moves the Administration forces neutralized this control. The original bill provided for six legislative members and five representatives of the executive as follows: Department of Justice, the Department of the Treasury, the Department of Labor, the Securities and Exchange Commission, and the Federal Trade Commission. To

[59] See explanation by Senator O'Mahoney in the *Congressional Record,* Vol. LXXXIII, Part 8, p. 8501, and by Representative Sumners, *ibid.,* pp. 9337, 9340.
[60] See Senator O'Mahoney's discussion of the history of S. J. Resolution 300, *ibid.,* Part 8, p. 8501.
[61] *Congressional Record,* Vol. LXXXIII, Part 12, p. 449.
[62] Senator Austin said, "In no way, however, do I intend to vote for the joint resolution," *ibid.,* Part 8, p. 8595.

secure a favorable report out of the Judiciary Committee, however, Mr. O'Mahoney apparently agreed to sponsor an amendment to strike out the Department of Labor and substitute the Department of Commerce for the avowed purpose of convincing the business world that the investigation was not designed as a punitive expedition.[63] The friends of labor, including Senators LaFollette and Norris, immediately challenged this amendment. Senator Norris, a champion of the Administration, said, "I cannot understand why anyone should desire to strike out the Department of Labor. . . . It seems to me proper to include both departments." [64] The effect, of course, would be to constitute a twelve-man committee, and Senator Norris said that he could see no harm in that. Senator O'Mahoney demonstrated his opposition to such a move, and his obvious but unstated reason was that it would destroy congressional control. Enough had happened to supply Administration leader Senator Barkley with his cue. He supported the inclusion of the Department of Labor and stated, "I do not see any fundamental objection to twelve members as compared with eleven." Senator O'Mahoney's response was to the effect that better results could be had through a smaller committee. Thus, under the organized leadership of the Administration (Senator Barkley) the amendment to substitute Commerce for Labor was defeated.[65] Apparently blocked in his purpose to keep the Committee under legislative control and being committed to obtain a place for Commerce, Senator O'Mahoney displayed his genius for compromise by moving to add the Department of Commerce. The amendment was agreed to.

During the debate considerable objection had been raised to the organization of the Committee itself. Although the question was not submitted to a vote, various Senators voiced opposition to an investigation by a joint committee. Senator Wheeler called it a very foolish precedent; he felt that it should be either a legislative or an executive committee, but by no means a hybrid. Senator King made a powerful plea against weakening the power of the legislative branch. Even the friendly Senator Norris argued "that not much good would be accomplished by a three-headed investigation.[66]

The chief contention was over the control of the funds to be expended in connection with the Committee's work. As it was finally passed, the Act provided for an immediate fund of $500,000, $100,000 of which was available for expenditure by the Committee itself, and

[63] Senator O'Mahoney, *ibid.*, p. 8593.   [64] *Ibid.*, p. 8590.
[65] *Ibid.*, p. 8594.   [66] *Ibid.*, p. 8500.

the remaining $400,000 was allocated to the President to be allotted as he directed among the executive departments in the performance of their work for the TNEC. Obviously, control of the purse strings meant control of the Committee and its work. At first Senator O'Mahoney had insisted upon Committee control of the funds, but later he compromised on this point, and when S. J. Resolution 300 shaped up, he came to the Senate prepared to support the Administration viewpoint. This matter had been fought out in the Senate Judiciary Committee Hearings and under Administrative pressure Presidential control had been agreed upon.[67] Nevertheless, when the bill reached the floor of the Senate, Senator Austin, its foe, introduced an amendment which would have provided allocation of the $400,000 to the Executive by specific committee action, but not for allocation by the Executive.[68] The President would not have been permitted to allocate "one thin dime" to any department except upon application to the Committee.[69] Senator Burke fought hard for this amendment, both in the Judiciary Committee and on the floor of the Senate.[70] Once more, however, the Administration forces swung into action. O'Mahoney's leadership was evident, even if not insistent.[71] Senator Norris made an eloquent plea for Presidential control, stating, "If I were president of the United States, I should not take five minutes to veto the joint resolution if it came to me in that form"; that is, requiring the President to come begging for funds.[72] Finally, Administration leader Barkley swung his organization into line by requesting that the amendment be rejected in order to give the President a free hand. "It seems unreasonable," he said, "to expect the President to take a tin cup and go around like a blind man begging for a little change, in order that he may authorize the executive department to do what he and we desire to have done, namely, to gather information, and make investigations and research.[73] The amendment was defeated shortly thereafter by a vote of almost two to one.[74] The victory in the Senate was a victory for Senator O'Mahoney and for the Administration; Senator O'Mahoney had preserved his prestige and leadership, and the Administration was in control of the Committee. With startling lack of ceremony, the resolution was passed in the Senate on June 9, 1938.[75]

[67] Ibid., p. 8339.
[69] Ibid., p. 8503.
[71] Ibid., p. 8338.
[73] Ibid., p. 8503.
[75] Ibid., p. 8595.

[68] Ibid., p. 8340.
[70] Ibid.
[72] Ibid., p. 8500.
[74] Ibid., p. 8591.

PROMPT ACTION IN THE HOUSE

On the same day that Senator O'Mahoney submitted his second bill to the Senate, Representative Sumners, who was working in close co-operation with him, submitted a companion bill to the House (H. J. Resolution 697).[76] The day following the Senate passage of the bill, the House version was reported upon favorably by the Judiciary Committee. Scarcely any hearings were held; none until that day. Senator O'Mahoney was the only witness appearing in behalf of the resolution.[77] Shortly thereafter the Senate version of the bill came to the House; it was referred to the Committee on the Judiciary [78] and almost immediately substituted for Representative Sumners's bill.[79] Thus, it required only the period over the weekend for the Senate version to be reported for action in the House.[80] The Administration forces were strong enough to put the bill through with very limited debate. It was nearly midnight when the resolution was taken up. The time allotted for the defense of the measure was granted to Representative Sumners; Representative Michener was leader of the forces of the opposition. But twenty minutes were granted to each side for debate. From the start it was recognized that "there was going to be an investigation" and that opposition was futile; such criticisms as were raised were made for the record, not with any expectation of altering the final outcome. Since time was limited, those who spoke against the bill were few, principally Representatives Michener (Michigan), Snell (New York), and Hancock (New York).

The chief attack was directed against the idea of an investigation itself. The inquiry was pictured as another New Deal instrumentality to torment and harass business. Congressman Michener said, "I do not believe that it is for the best interest of our country to pass any legislation at this time that might be used to harass, annoy, or intimidate any industry be it large or small." [81] He declared that we had had too much punitive legislation and punitive talk from the Administration. After setting forth the broad powers of the proposed Committee, he complained, "No committee or commission ever created by Congress has had such vast inquisitorial powers." [82] A few days previously Representative Lewis had made the same accusation. "I warn you," he said, "that by virtue of this reign of terror that is inspired

76 *Ibid.*, Part 12, p. 527.   77 Representative Michener, *ibid.*, Part 8, p. 9338.
78 *Ibid.*, p. 9129.   79 *Ibid.*, Part 12, p. 532.
80 *Ibid.*, Part 8, p. 9336.   81 *Ibid.*, p. 9341.
82 *Ibid.*

by such political inquisitions . . . this country is confronted with national distress of the most critical character." [83] Finally, Representative Rich foretold the dire results to be expected if the Committee were permitted to proceed. "Does not the gentleman think he better let the business of the country go ahead and try to get the country back on its feet instead of investigating everything? The first thing the gentleman knows his party will wreck the nation. It is time to stop a lot of this foolishness." [84]

The second major objection was that the resolution did not provide for a congressional investigation. It was complained that President Roosevelt had got what he wanted, namely, that "the representatives of the departments and agencies will do the investigating." [85] The Senate was accused of abdicating its powers and responsibilities to the Chief Executive "and his departmental satellites." [86] In this connection it would be expected that the Republican minority would object to Executive control over the major funds of the Committee. Representative Michener proposed to "trust the Committee" and give it complete control over the entire appropriation,[87] while Representative Hancock administered a severe tongue lashing to his colleagues as follows: "the most humiliating proposition that has ever been put up to the House of Representatives since I have been here . . . I think this is the most debasing resolution that has ever been presented to the Congress of the United States." [88]

Perhaps the most spectacular accusation was that the bill was being forced through the House after the application of the gag rule. To expedite proceedings Congressman Sumners had asked that the rules be suspended and the resolution passed.[89] This was the basis of the opposition's complaint. In the light of the limited time permitted for debate (which is by no means unusual in the House) and the suspension of rule, Mr. Michener said, "This suspension rule is the standing 'gag' rule in the House. . . . I ask you, Mr. Majority leader, whether this is a deliberate and considered action on the part of the House or is it the steam-roller method to force through a resolution that cannot stand the test of debate?" [90] This accusation was better oratory than it was a correct characterization, since the Congressman conceded that the Administration had ample power in the House to "pass this legislation or about any other legislation" it de-

83 *Ibid.*, p. 8891.
85 *Ibid.*, p. 9338.
87 *Ibid.*, Part 4, p. 4240.
89 *Ibid.*, p. 9336.

84 *Ibid.*, p. 9340.
86 *Ibid.*, p. 8891.
88 *Ibid.*, Part 8, p. 9337.
90 *Ibid.*, p. 9338.

sired. Soon the question was put to a vote as to whether the rules should be suspended and the resolution passed; the vote was ayes 237 and noes 33, which was substantially more than the two-thirds required.[91] Shortly before the vote was taken Congressman Michener said:

It is now after eleven o'clock. The midnight hour approaches. The House has been in session continuously and without recess since 12 o'clock noon. Many members are not on the floor. Many of those who are present are well-nigh exhausted and under these conditions the House is confronted with this far-reaching resolution.[92]

Thus, almost without debate, in a manner quite perfunctory, was passed legislation providing for the "greatest economic study in American history." In the following two days the bill was signed by the Speaker of the House,[93] the Vice President,[94] and the President,[95] and became law. This concludes the legislative history of the TNEC with the exception of minor amendments, one a year later granting an additional $600,000,[96] another authorizing additional copies of the hearings,[97] and a final amendment extending the life of the Committee to April 3, 1941, to permit it to make its report. No additional funds were authorized.[98]

[91] *Ibid.*, p. 9341.
[92] *Ibid.*, p. 9339.
[93] *Ibid.*, p. 9502.
[94] *Ibid.*, p. 9506.
[95] *Ibid.*, p. 9523.
[96] S. J. Resolution 90, 1939; see also *Congressional Record*, Vol. LXXXIV, Part 4, p. 4257.
[97] *Ibid.*, p. 3829.
[98] *Ibid.*, Vol. LXXXVI, Part 12, p. 13830.

CHAPTER III

COMMITTEE PERSONNEL
AND PROCEDURE

PUBLIC RESOLUTION 113 of the Seventy-fifth Congress, the act creating the TNEC, was signed by the Vice President and by the President on June 16, 1938. On the same day the legislative members of the Committee were chosen; thus, no time was lost in making the appointments.

THE SENATE MEMBERS

In accordance with custom the appointment of the three Senators to the Committee was given over to the Vice President. Vice President Garner was not a member of the New Deal circle or one with New Deal sentiments; hence, it would not be expected that his appointees would be men with decided liberal views. Nevertheless, he was known to share the Southern and Western distrust and fear of monopoly. He had been pleased with President Roosevelt's monopoly message and had gone to the White House to say so.[1] On June 16 the Senate clerk announced that "the Chair appoints the Senator from Wyoming" (Mr. O'Mahoney), "the Senator from Arizona" (Mr. Ashurst), and "the Senator from Idaho" (Mr. Borah).[2] Senator Ashurst, however, did not serve. The Vice President was obligated to offer him a place in respect for his position as chairman of the powerful Committee on the Judiciary. Senator Ashurst rose immediately in the Senate and declined the appointment. Then, in deference to senatorial etiquette, he suggested that Senator King, next in line and ranking majority member of the Judiciary Committee, be appointed in his stead.[3] In view of this request, Senator King was appointed;[4] thus, an anti-New Deal Democrat owed his place on the Committee to a New Deal colleague.

The membership of a great investigatory body such as the TNEC is of such importance that it will be well to present a brief account of the record and the point of view of each of these Senators. The first

[1] "The So-Called Monopoly Committee," *Fortune*, XVIII (November, 1938), 136.
[2] *Congressional Record*, Vol. LXXXIII, Part 8, pp. 9545–9546.
[3] *Ibid.*   [4] *Ibid.*

appointee was, of course, Senator O'Mahoney; by precedent he had won the chairmanship of the Committee. He had earned that appointment by preparing the bill which authorized the investigation and by managing its course through Congress. Senator O'Mahoney was born in Massachusetts; he was trained as a lawyer and was fifty-four years of age at the time of his appointment. As a young man he had gone West and had engaged in newspaper work in Colorado and Wyoming. Later, he came to Washington as secretary to Senator John B. Kendrick of Wyoming. Subsequently, he ran for the Senate and was defeated. In 1929 he was elected Democratic National Committeeman from Wyoming; in that capacity he attracted the attention of James A. Farley, chairman of the Democratic National Committee, who appointed him assistant postmaster general. When Senator Kendrick died, Mr. O'Mahoney was appointed to fill the vacancy; in 1934 he was elected to the Senate in his own right.

Senator O'Mahoney would be characterized as a liberal in politics. He was friendly to the New Deal and voted favorably on most of its measures. In fact, he was a welcome guest at the White House until the episode of the Supreme Court fight, when he broke with the Administration to become a leader of the opposition. For this he was numbered among those Senators who were slated for the Presidential "purge" in the coming elections. Thus, the first of the senatorial appointees was a liberal, but a man of aggressive and independent mind.

Senator O'Mahoney held definite convictions relative to the social economy, as well as to the role which the Committee should perform. He was no revolutionist, no radical reformer; to him, the purpose of the study was to preserve the profit system,[5] to maintain private enterprise, and to protect the democratic form of government.[6] The basic problem confronting the American people was the preservation of the advantages of mass production and the achievement of a stable prosperity; the latter could not be accomplished, he felt, until business was set free from all forms of arbitrary control.[7] The major obstacle was monopoly and monopolistic manipulation. "Make no mistake about it," he said, "these violations of business ethics and of the law . . . are the primary cause of our economic troubles." [8] To the

[5] *Hearings before the Temporary National Economic Committee*, p. 360.
[6] A radio address by Senator O'Mahoney quoted in the *Congressional Record*, Vol. LXXXIII, Part 8, p. 8596.
[7] O'Mahoney, "It's an Economic Study," *Printers' Ink*, CLXXXV (October 6, 1938), 21.
[8] Address by Senator O'Mahoney before the National Radio Forum, July, 1939, published in the *Congressional Record*, Vol. LXXXIV, Part 14, p. 3496.

Senator concentration of economic control was a matter of great importance; his concern had already expressed itself in the Borah-O'Mahoney bill previously discussed. It was his conviction that industrial giantism should be subservient to the public interest. But the chairman was concerned no less with concentration and centralization in government than he was with the growth and centralization of economic power. Concentration of power in the Government can be as dangerous as concentration in a large corporation.[9] Senator O'Mahoney expressed the opinion again and again that much of the expansion of political power in Washington has been a consequence of the growth and concentration of economic power.[10] The former has been forced by the latter; both are evils which may be checked by controlling economic giantism.[11] This choice facing the American people is reduced to a choice between free enterprise and government planning.[12] Yet government planning, undesirable as it was to Senator O'Mahoney, who feared and distrusted bureaucracy, was preferable to socially irresponsible planning by giant corporations and industrial combinations.[13] Economic planning, if we must have it at all, is preferably planning by public authority.[14] However, the Senator hoped for a better formula.

No one can read the testimony before the TNEC and the final report without realizing that to a large extent this was Senator O'Mahoney's committee and Senator O'Mahoney's show. One of the members whose attendance was most regular, he definitely left the imprint of his personality upon the hearings and the findings. To him goes much credit for the high plane upon which the hearings were kept. To him it was an objective study in search for facts, not a star chamber performance, not a publicity stunt, and not a muckraking expedition. Truly, he merited the praise of his colleagues, as expressed by Mr. Arnold in the final hearings:

May I further add something which I think every member of this Committee would like to have in the record—our indebtedness to the Chairman, Senator O'Mahoney. We have been busy with other things; we

---

[9] Address by Senator O'Mahoney before the New York Board of Trade, published in *Commercial and Financial Chronicle*, CXLVII (October 15, 1938), 2331.
[10] For one expression of this point of view see *Final Report and Recommendations of the Temporary National Economic Committee*, pp. 6, 64.
[11] O'Mahoney, "It's an Economic Study," *Printers' Ink*, CLXXXV (October 6, 1938), 21.
[12] Stone, "O'Mahoney Sums Up," *The Nation*, CLII (March 22, 1941), 315.
[13] Corey, "O'Mahoney Wants Facts, Not Scalps," *Nation's Business*, XXVI (September 28, 1938), 16.
[14] "Economic States," *Time*, XXXII (October 24, 1938), 59.

have attended the hearings when we could, but the great brunt of the work and the tremendous amount of organization has rested upon him, which he has discharged with great competence and, more than that, with brilliance.[15]

Senator King, too, was a lawyer, having practiced that profession before coming to Congress in 1897. He served as a Representative until 1917, at which time he was elected to the Senate; thus, he brought to the Committee forty years of experience in Federal office. Senator King was a life-long Democrat, but by no means a New Dealer. His anti-New Deal sentiments made his appointment to the Committee particularly pleasing to those who distrusted the Administration. A business journal spoke favorably of his punctilious respect for property and indicated that his presence reassured business.[16] He was by temperament and disposition a defender of the *status quo*. Except perhaps for advocating free trade and free silver, he had been "a verbose champion of things-as-they-are" [17] throughout his forty years in public life and was likely to suspect that suggestions for change had been instigated by communists.

If Senator King contributed anything of significance to the investigation, it would seem to be his constant defense of existing institutions and business practices. If testimony before the Committee indicated that abuses might be prevalent, he could sweep aside the evidence and imply his approval by "wages are higher and payroll is larger" [18] or "the prices of your commodity [have] been reduced." [19] If the social serviceability of the patent system was in question, it was sufficient for him to say, "the purpose . . . of the law itself is to give a monopoly to the patentee" [20] or "there is no legal obligation." [21] Here is a tacit assumption that legality is a sufficient test of the social worth of institutions and practices. On numerous occasions the Senator was quick to raise his voice when the investigation seemed to suggest that some act or policy did not contribute to the social good. Invariably a defense was implied in his questions or such questions served to coach the witness in favor of the indicated response. If the election machinery of life insurance companies was under question, it was enough for him that no policyholder had registered

15 *Final Report and Recommendations of the Temporary National Economic Committee*, p. 78.
16 "These Are the Monopoly Investigators," *Business Week*, July 2, 1938, p. 16.
17 "The So-Called Monopoly Committee," *Fortune*, XVIII (November, 1938), 136.
18 *Hearings before the Temporary National Economic Committee*, Part 2, p. 547.
19 *Ibid.*, pp. 533, 546; also see Part 5, p. 1728.
20 *Ibid.*, Part 2, p. 298.   21 *Ibid.*, p. 519.

a complaint [22] or that the directors had acted under the law.[23] If it appeared that the directors of great life insurance companies had used their positions so as to violate a trust, again it was sufficient that they, too, had acted within the law; he could find excuses for the manner in which they had distributed company deposits among fellow trustees.[24] Similar rationalizations of the world as it is can be found throughout the hearings.

In reading the hearings one cannot help but sense the unfriendly and antagonistic spirit in which Senator King approached the whole investigation. His position was foreshadowed by his outspoken criticism of the Borah-O'Mahoney bill,[25] which to him represented excessive government interference with business. Although avowedly in favor of the investigation itself, his action on the floor of the Senate might be interpreted as mild opposition to it.[26] Shortly after his appointment it was reported that he hoped that the work of the Committee would result in no change whatsoever.[27] It is probable that such would have been the case if fellow Committee members had been of the same disposition. His opposition was further demonstrated when he initiated a little investigation of his own shortly before the hearings were begun; his instructions to his aides were to disprove, if possible, any significant concentration of economic control. During the hearings he even went so far as to state to the executive of one of the country's greatest industrial combinations that "I would rather trust you than trust the Government." [28]

The hearings do not deal kindly with Senator King. In addition to his policy of obstructionism, there was evident a curious anxiety to lecture to those who attended and to those who by chance might later read the printed record and to impress them with his learning and erudition. Ofttimes he interrupted the continuity of the hearings with more or less irrelevant remarks which seem to have had little other purpose.[29] On numerous occasions the Senator gave evidence that he did not comprehend the general significance of the

22 *Ibid.*, Part 4, p. 1275.   23 *Ibid.*, p. 1378.   24 *Ibid.*, pp. 1455, 1460.
25 George, "The Personnel of Our National Economic Jury," *Duns Review,* XLVI (September, 1938), 11.
26 *Congressional Record,* Vol. LXXXIII, Part 7, p. 8338.
27 "Monopoly Inquiry Holds Out Far-Reaching Possibilities," *News Week,* XII (July 18, 1938), 34.
28 *Hearings before the Temporary National Economic Committee,* Part 9, p. 3624.
29 Nothing will be gained by belaboring the point, however, if the reader is interested, he is referred to a few illustrative cases: *ibid.,* Part 1, pp. 22, 48, 55, 59, 77, 79, 84, 94, 105; Part 2, p. 321; Part 4, p. 1204; Part 5, pp. 1730, 2015; Part 30, p. 17087.

testimony being presented or grasp its social implications.[30] Nevertheless, Senator King was regular in his attendance until he failed to be re-elected to his seat in the Senate. Senator James Mead took his place.

Senator Borah was the third member appointed by the Vice President. He was not only the third Senator but the third lawyer as well. Senator Borah came from Idaho; he was a Republican of very independent mind, so independent, in fact, and so powerful had been his influence that he was one time characterized as the "third house" of Congress. Though a liberal, he was no New Dealer. It is interesting to note that he, too, had been very influential in waging the fight to defeat the President's Supreme Court plan. The Senator earned his place on the Committee because of his Republican affiliations and his sponsorship of the Borah-O'Mahoney bill. For many years he had been knight-errant of the Senate in attacking monopolies. He held definite convictions that high prices due to monopolistic control were a cause of the economic woes of the nation. He placed his faith in free competition, which he held to be necessary to progress. He felt that wherever it can be shown that monopoly is natural and desirable the Government should own the industries concerned.[31]

In his prime Senator Borah might have made a strong member of the Committee and contributed much to its achievements. As it was, time was against Senator Borah and no doubt against the TNEC as well. His attendance at Committee hearings became less frequent, and his contributions less virile. His health and strength declined until he attended no more. His death occurred while the inquiry was in progress. There appears in the record for January 24, 1940, a fitting tribute to this colleague who used his "great power in advancing the cause of human freedom." [32] Senator White was appointed to fill the vacancy.

THE HOUSE MEMBERS

The privilege of appointing the House members fell to the Speaker of the House, Representative Bankhead. It might be expected that since the Speaker had New Deal leanings his appointees would support that view. Such, however, was not the case; only one of them

[30] Numerous instances may be cited: Part 1, pp. 18, 19, 35, 48, 54, 59, 62, 133, 139, 150; Part 9, p. 3844; Part 26, pp. 13593, 13621, 13622, 13629, 13638, 13660, 13661, 13705.

[31] Yarros, "Senator Borah and Monopolies," *The Christian Century*, LIII (February 12, 1936), 262.

[32] *Hearings before the Temporary National Economic Committee*, Part 26, p. 13648.

might be labeled a New Dealer. Representative Sumners had won a place for himself because of his position as Chairman of the Judiciary Committee and because of his sponsorship of the bill. Legislative courtesy demanded the appointment of a Republican; the lot fell to Representative Reece of Tennessee. The final appointment went to Representative Eicher, a Democrat from Iowa and a man of well-known New Deal sentiments.

Representative Hatton W. Sumners, a Democrat from Texas, became vice chairman of the TNEC. Prior to his service in Congress he had practiced law and served on the bench in his home state. He first came to Congress in 1913 and had served continuously since that time. Because of his position on the House Judiciary Committee and because of his service in guiding the legislation through the Committee and through the House, his appointment could scarcely have been avoided. Nevertheless, the Administration had reason to prefer him to most Judiciary Committee members, because he had more consistently supported New Deal legislation.[33] But Representative Sumners was certainly not a New Dealer; neither by predilection nor by practice. He is best described as one of the "old line" Democrats, one of the most influential of them, in fact. Moreover, he, too, had vigorously opposed the President's Supreme Court plan, and his speech against the bill was probably one of the ablest made in either House.[34] Representative Sumners was known to be reluctant to assume a position on the Committee, and it was only through the persuasion of his colleagues and the personal intervention of the President that this reluctance was overcome.[35]

The vice chairman seemed to find the hearings dull and tedious, and frequently he failed to attend. Apparently he had little use or sympathy for the painstaking factual and statistical approach by which many of the presentations were made. Now and then he would be heard to say, "charts bother me," [36] or when in response to one of his questions the witnesses volunteered that he "might be interested in some statistics we have here," his answer characteristically would be, "not many of them." [37]

[33] "The So-Called Monopoly Committee," *Fortune*, XVIII (November, 1938), 136.
[34] McKee, "Monopoly Investigators," *The Commonweal*, XXIX (November 4, 1938), 36.
[35] Corey, "O'Mahoney Wants Facts, Not Scalps," *Nation's Business*, XXVI (September 28, 1938), 72; "The So-Called Monopoly Committee," *Fortune*, XVIII (November, 1938), 136; George, "The Personnel of Our National Economic Jury," *Duns Review*, XLVI (September, 1938), 12.
[36] *Hearings before the Temporary National Economic Committee*, Part 15, p. 8328.
[37] *Ibid.*, Part 28, p. 15263; see also Part 29, p. 15820.

Representative Sumners came to the Committee with strong convictions as to the role which the Federal Government should play in economic life. He seemed to fear Federal concentration more than he did industrial concentration. When Federal intervention was suggested, he was constantly reminding his colleagues to remember "that we do really have some states." [38] To him, most of the nation's economic ills are best solved by the people, or at least along local or state lines. Congress must not take functions away from the states.[39] He seems to have had an abiding faith that somehow, if left to themselves, the people would solve their economic difficulties; "We must look to the people," he said. "I don't believe the people in America are quite ready yet to surrender the responsibility of government to a great Federal bureaucracy." [40] Consistent with his laissez faire, look-to-the-people attitude was a belief that natural law regulates economic affairs, adjusting all things and obviating the necessity or desirability of organized administrative supervision of economic institutions and practices. He spoke of a "plan of nature," and it was this approach which he brought to the problems considered by the TNEC.

. . . we seem to have forgotten that there is a living God whose laws control everywhere, guiding, directing, and compelling human beings to be governed by them in their economic and political government, as distinguished from being governed by the theories of men . . . whom we have followed while economic and governmental concentration have reached the development which threatens our democracy.[41]

Congressman Carroll Reece owed his appointment in part to the tradition that there should be at least one House Republican on the Committee. When his selection was announced, it was said that Speaker Bankhead had chosen the Administration's favorite Republican.[42] Representative Reece was from Tennessee. He brought to the Committee a rich academic background, having been educated in various colleges and universities, including New York University and the University of London. He had taught economics and served as Assistant Dean of the School of Commerce at New York University. Probably it would be inaccurate to label him either a conservative or a liberal; [43] his appointment, nevertheless, was greeted as reassuring to business.[44] A careful study of the TNEC hearings does not indicate

[38] *Final Report and Recommendations of the Temporary National Economic Committee,* p. 529; see also p. 666.
[39] *Ibid.,* p. 158.   [40] *Ibid.,* p. 601.   [41] *Ibid.,* p. 50.
[42] "The So-Called Monopoly Committee," *Fortune,* XVIII (November, 1938), 136.
[43] *Ibid.*
[44] "These Are the Monopoly Investigators," *Business Week,* July 2, 1938, p. 17.

that his attendance was particularly regular or that he contributed materially to their progress.

The third and last legislative member was Edward C. Eicher of Iowa. Representative Eicher was considered to be a 100 percent New Dealer and, of course, a Democrat. A lawyer by training and experience, he had been elected to Congress from a traditionally Republican district. In Congress he was a member of the Committee of Interstate and Foreign Commerce, a fact which contributed to his appointment to the TNEC. Shortly thereafter, however, owing to political developments and difficulties at home, he withdrew his candidacy for reelection to Congress. Although he took his duties on the Committee seriously, he served for only a few days, being replaced by Representative Williams of Missouri.

THE EXECUTIVE MEMBERS

During the latter part of June six of the Committee's members were appointed by the President from the executive departments specified in the Act creating the TNEC. It is perhaps significant that not the President, but Robert Jackson, his trust-busting Solicitor General, announced these appointments,[45] which were as follows: Thurman W. Arnold (Justice), William O. Douglas (SEC), Garland S. Ferguson (FTC), Isador Lubin (Labor), Herman Oliphant (Treasury), and Richard C. Patterson, Jr. (Commerce). They represented some of the ablest men in the Administration and constituted a group with strong liberal or New Deal tendencies. Among them there was little dissent from the general thesis that monopoly and monopolistic practices were a major cause of economic dislocations.

Thurman W. Arnold represented the Department of Justice. He had come to Washington from Wyoming, where he had practiced law and taken part in political life. Educated at Princeton and the Harvard Law School, he had taught at Yale and at West Virginia; he had served as mayor of Laramie and as a member of the Wyoming legislature and as a trial lawyer for the Securities and Exchange Commission. Prior to his appointment to the Committee he was well known for his books, *The Symbols of Government* and *The Folklore of Capitalism*. Mr. Arnold was a Democrat with pronounced liberal and New Deal predilections. Though viewed with misgivings by the average business man, the Assistant Attorney General was no foe of capitalism; he believed that the system should be preserved and made

[45] "Six and Six," *Time*, XXXII (July 4, 1938), 9.

to function more adequately.[46] According to Mr. Arnold the American people faced the choice between complete government control of business and effective regulation of the system of private competitive enterprise.[47] He was a strong champion of enforcement of the antitrust laws as the best way to keep the Government out of business. Left alone, monopoly sooner or later means government interference.[48] Free competitive enterprise, unrestrained by monopolistic manipulations, was the cornerstone of Mr. Arnold's solution for the ills of the economy. He was not, however, unconcerned about Representative Sumners's fears of bigness in government, which to him is often the fruit of bigness in business. The antidote to these evils is an effective antimonopoly program and a competitive enterprise. To this end he answered Representative Sumners:

I agree with Congressman Sumners' fear of increasing Federal regulation and taking away the power from the States. I differ a little bit as to his diagnosis as to how this camel got into the tent. I have always believed that the creation of a twilight zone under the guise of protecting States' rights, a zone where nobody could effectively act, has created a situation which suddenly required drastic Federal action. You do not increase State powers, nor do you increase popular confidence in State powers by telling the State governments: "Act and control this situation," when you know, as a practical matter, they can't control it at all. So it seems to me that the real problem here is whether the States can control this thing. If they can't, then the quickest way to move the camel into the tent and get all the other camels in is to ignore it, pretend they are exercising State powers, and wake up . . . and find that we have got to take legislation and actions far more drastic than would have been necessary otherwise.[49]

Another committeeman of unusual ability was William O. Douglas, who represented the Securities and Exchange Commission. Mr. Douglas had been educated at law, and like Mr. Arnold had taught law at Yale. He was considered to be one of the outstanding members of the New Deal circle. As chairman of the Securities and Exchange Commission he had gained first-hand insight into the problems of business and financial regulation. He brought to the Committee a

[46] In response to Senator O'Mahoney's question whether his writings could be construed as opposing capitalism, he answered: "Well, Senator, if you were a dentist and had devoted your life to the study of better methods of cleaning, caring for, and preserving the teeth, would that mean you were against teeth?" (George, "The Personnel of Our National Economic Jury," *Duns Review*, XLVI (September, 1938), 13.
[47] McKee, "Monopoly Investigators," *The Commonweal*, XXIX (November 4, 1938), 36.
[48] George, "The Personnel of Our National Economic Jury," *Duns Review*, XLVI (September, 1938), 8.
[49] *Final Report and Recommendations of the Temporary National Economic Committee*, pp. 589–590.

"brilliant mind, an aggressive spirit, a liberal philosophy, and a judicious temperament." [50] Unfortunately, his services were soon required elsewhere, and he was advanced to the Supreme Court after serving with the TNEC for six months. His place was filled successively by SEC Commissioners Jerome N. Frank and Sumner Pike.

Another appointment was the able Garland S. Ferguson, Jr., chairman of the Federal Trade Commission. Mr. Ferguson was a Democrat with reputedly conservative leanings. He was a lawyer who, since 1927, had served with the Federal Trade Commission. In his relation with the FTC he at one time or another had supervised almost every important branch of that agency. His rich insight into business practices and his experience with the regulation of business made him an exceedingly valuable member. He had, of course, a very wide knowledge of the less socially desirable aspects of business behavior. In particular, he was expected to reflect the Federal Trade Commission's opposition to resale price maintenance which had been legalized by the Miller-Tydings Act and many so-called fair trade laws.

Isador Lubin was another strong appointee to the Committee; he represents one of the four who contributed most to its progress. Few were more regular in attendance or contributed more positively to the development of the hearings. Mr. Lubin had entered public service from a background of academic life. He had been professor of economics at Michigan and Missouri universities and was later a member of the staff of the Brookings Institution. He had a wealth of experience in and had made fruitful contributions to previous governmental researches. His immediate position was that of Commissioner of Labor Statistics, at which assignment he had proven his stature. He was recognized as liberal, scholarly, and objective, but none the less as a capable and aggressive New Dealer.

The Treasury Department was represented by Mr. Herman Oliphant. Like a number of his colleagues he had a legal background and had served on university faculties. Since 1915 he had taught law at the universities of Chicago, Columbia, and Johns Hopkins. In 1933 he had come to Washington as general counsel to the Farm Credit Administration, and subsequently he had joined the Treasury Department; at the time of his appointment to the TNEC he was general counsel to that agency. He was known as a champion of small business and was generally credited with the authorship of the corporate sur-

[50] George, "The Personnel of Our National Economic Jury," *Duns Review*, XLVI (September, 1938), 14.

plus tax. The Committee was deprived of his full contribution by his
untimely death about a year after the hearings got under way; he was
replaced by J. J. O'Connell.

Richard Patterson, Jr., was the first of four men who in turn represented the Department of Commerce on the TNEC. He was the
only member with any significant experience as a business executive.
Trained as an engineer, he had served as assistant to the president of
the J. G. White Engineering Corporation, as engineer for the E. I.
du Pont de Nemours Company, and as executive vice president and
director of the National Broadcasting Company. He had also had
other important connections in the commercial and industrial world.
Mr. Patterson had served as a very useful and diplomatic go-between
for New Dealers and influential business men, thus promoting understanding among those who had grown to distrust one another. Before
the inauguration of the hearings he held a number of "shirt sleeve"
conferences between the investigators and those to be investigated.
Inasmuch as it proved to be the policy for the Commerce representative to champion and at times to exonerate business policy, Mr. Patterson was the logical choice for that post. He was succeeded by the
following, each in his turn: Clarence Avildson, Sumner Pike,[51] and
Wayne Taylor.

In addition to the duly appointed members, Public Resolution 113
provided that each of the executive members might designate an alternate to act for him in his absence. The alternates were appointed immediately after the selection of the original Committee. The list
which follows shows who originally served in that capacity: Wendell
Berge (Justice), Jerome N. Frank (SEC), Ewin L. Davis (FTC), A.
Ford Hinrichs (Labor), Christian Joy Peoples (Treasury), and M.
Joseph Meehan (Commerce). Changes occurred from time to time.

THE EXECUTIVE SECRETARY

Two personalities, Senator O'Mahoney and Leon Henderson, above
all others dominated the TNEC. Immediately after the organization
of the Committee Leon Henderson was named executive secretary.
Prior to serving in this capacity he had earned a rather brilliant reputation in administrative circles. Mr. Henderson was an economist,
educated at Swarthmore; he had taught at the University of Penn-

---

[51] Mr. Pike served the Committee in several capacities, first as alternate for the SEC,
later as representative for the Department of Commerce, and finally as the representative for the SEC.

sylvania. Later he was director of the Department of Remedial Loans for the Russell Sage Foundation, from which position he moved to various advisory assignments within the New Deal; he was successively adviser to General Johnson of the NRA, director of the Research and Planning Division of the NRA, economic adviser to the Senate Committee on Manufactures, adviser to the Democratic National Committee, and consulting economist to the Works Progress Administration.[52]

Mr. Henderson was very definitely a New Dealer; in fact, he was considered by critics as one of the "inner circle." Liberal in his views, ready and willing to defend them, he had played an important part in the creation of the TNEC itself. His views on monopoly and its relation to the Great Depression were well known to men in public life. He was, however, no pessimist, nor was he unfriendly to capitalism,[53] although business was said to have lost confidence in the soundness of his ideas. Leon Henderson, a man of unusual intellectual capacity and a dynamo of energy, played an important role in planning, organizing, and directing the researches which preceded the hearings. He gave full time to these duties; so energetic was his leadership and so fruitful were the results that astonished Committee members called him "the Paul Bunyan of Bureaucracy." [54]

It is unfortunate that Mr. Henderson was not permitted to remain at this post, for once again the personnel was disrupted by the loss of a member. A few months after the hearings began he was appointed to the Securities and Exchange Commission, at which time he took Commissioner Frank's place as alternate to the TNEC. Some months later the pressure of national defense required his services elsewhere, and the Committee was deprived of his active participation, although it retained his interest and loyalty. At this time a new title was conferred upon him—Economic Coordinator. These urgent duties demanded most of his attention; the new title was largely a matter of courtesy, although it did have the value of retaining his participation during the final weeks of the TNEC.

[52] *Hearings before the Temporary National Economic Committee,* pp. 157–158. For very interesting accounts of the life and activities of Leon Henderson, see also Davenport, "What Price Henderson," *Collier's,* CVIII (September 6, 1941), 18; and Lubell, "The Daring Young Man on the Flying Pri-cees," *The Saturday Evening Post,* CCXIV (September 13, 1941), 84.

[53] See *Hearings before the Temporary National Economic Committee,* pp. 163–165, and p. 12109.

[54] Lubell, "The Daring Young Man on the Flying Pri-cees," *The Saturday Evening Post,* CCXIV (September 13, 1941), 84.

THE COMMITTEE AS A WHOLE

This, then, was what American journalists were pleased to call "our blue ribbon economic jury." [55] As a whole the Committee was made up of men of varying philosophies and backgrounds. It is notable that they were essentially from the Middle West and the West. Nine of them were lawyers, two were economists, and one was an engineer who represented business; five had been university professors. Generally speaking, they were comparatively young men, men of middle age, but with considerable experience in politics and public service. Ten were Democrats of varying predilections and leanings, two were Republicans, at least three were conservatives, and four could properly be called New Dealers. Quite without exception they represented a middle-class philosophy; in fact, they were referred to as "tribunes of the middle class." [56] All favored the system of private profits and private enterprise; over and over again concern was expressed by almost every member over the future of existing political and economic institutions. They considered it the task of the Committee to discover a way to preserve the American social and economic pattern. In some respects, however, the real Committee consisted not of the appointed twelve but of the secretary and the staff of experts, analysts, statisticians, lawyers, and economists who did the basic research and prepared the data which eventually were presented for consideration by the members.

CHANGES IN PERSONNEL

Unfortunately, the Jury—if it could be so called—did not remain intact. Of the three original Senators, two were replaced because of death or failure to be re-elected. One of the three Representatives failed to remain with the Committee throughout the full period; the two who did were none too regular in their attendance. Only one-half of the original executive members were with the Committee when the hearings ended; the places of the three who departed were filled successively by six additional members. When Leon Henderson withdrew as executive secretary, this post was filled by James Brackett; he was replaced by Dewey Anderson, who was responsible for the secretary's final report.[57] Near the close of the hearings Theodore J.

---

[55] *Business Week*, May 20, 1939, pp. 34–36.
[56] MacDonald, "The Monopoly Committee: a Study in Frustration," *The American Scholar*, VIII (July, 1939), 308.
[57] *Final Report of the Executive Secretary to the Temporary National Economic Committee*, 1941.

Kreps joined the staff as economic adviser and made important contributions to the final proceedings.[58]

When Commissioner Douglas was appointed to the Supreme Court, his place was filled by SEC Commissioner Jerome Frank. Commissioner Frank was a Democrat and an original member of the New Deal "brain trust." He had been a corporation lawyer in Chicago and New York and later was a research associate at the Yale Law School. Between 1933 and 1935 he was general counsel to the Federal Surplus Relief Corporation and the Agricultural Adjustment Administration and special counsel to the Reconstruction Finance Corporation. In 1937 he was appointed to the Securities and Exchange Commission, of which he became chairman in 1939. In 1938 he published a book on monopoly,[59] in which he argued that mass production industries are not only efficient but also desirable and that we must have less rather than more competition. This interest made him an active member of the TNEC. He served from March, 1939, to April, 1940, when he was replaced by Sumner Pike.

Clarence Avildson was the second to represent the Department of Commerce on the Committee, succeeding Richard Patterson in November, 1939. He was a Republican and a representative of business, having served as an official of several tool manufacturing companies, including the United Drill and Tool Corporation, of which he was chairman and director. He was special adviser to the Secretary of Commerce with respect to problems of small business men, especially manufacturers.[60] Although his services with the TNEC were brief, he attended regularly and participated frequently, often championing current business practices; he was particularly active during the iron and steel hearings.

Mr. Avildson relinquished his place to Sumner Pike in January, 1940. The latter served but a short time, then reappeared in April of the same year to replace Jerome Frank, representing the Securities and Exchange Commission. Mr. Pike was a Republican, a "rugged individualist," and was on intimate terms with Wall Street.[61] His open-mindedness and independence impressed his colleagues. He came from the business world, having developed oil and mining enterprises in various parts of the world. He had served as financial adviser and secretary of the Continental Insurance Company, vice president

[58] See especially *Hearings before the Temporary National Economic Committee*, Part 30, pp. 16208 ff.
[59] Jerome Frank, *Save America First*, New York, Harpers, 1938.
[60] *The New York Times*, September 17, 1939, p. 20.   [61] *Ibid.*, May 23, 1940.

and director of the Case Pomeroy and Company, and business adviser to the Secretary of Commerce before he was appointed to the Securities and Exchange Commission.

After the death of Herman Oliphant, during the early months of the hearings, J. J. O'Connell, special assistant to the General Counsel of the Treasury Department, was appointed to the TNEC. His experience, aside from politics, had been with newspapers. Mr. O'Connell started his public life early, having been elected as a Democrat to the Montana House of Representatives at the age of twenty-one. He served as a Member of Congress from Montana between 1937 and 1939, and while there was one of the stanchest members of the progressive group; he was an ardent New Dealer. Due largely to the opposition of the copper mining interests in Montana he was defeated for re-election in 1938.

In December, 1938, Representative Clyde Williams, a Democrat from Missouri, was appointed to fill the vacancy left by Representative Eicher. He was a lawyer and a graduate of the University of Missouri. He was elected to Congress in 1927 and had held office since that time. His attendance at the hearings was quite regular, and his participation moderate. Three of the members who replaced former appointees served but short periods and played relatively minor roles. Senator White, a Republican from Maine, came to the Committee after the death of Senator Borah in January, 1940. He had been a member of Congress between 1917 and 1931 and was elected to the Senate in 1930 and 1936. His attendance at the hearings was irregular, and his participation slight. Senator Mead, a Democrat and a New Dealer from New York, was appointed to fill the vacancy left by Senator King. He had been a Member of Congress from New York between 1919 and 1939; in 1938 he was elected to replace the late Senator Copeland. He attended only the final sessions during February and March, 1941. Wayne Taylor, representing the Department of Commerce, took the place of Sumner Pike in February, 1941; he attended few of the remaining meetings. He was a Democrat and had served as vice president and trustee of the Export-Import Bank of Washington, as Assistant Secretary of the Treasury, and as Under Secretary of Commerce.

THE GENERAL OBJECTIVES OF THE INVESTIGATION

The purposes and objectives which led to the creation of the TNEC determined, of course, the organization of the researches undertaken,

the nature of the hearings held, and which segments of the national economy were placed under the microscope. To understand fully what the Committee set out to do, it would be helpful to discover what was in the minds of the President, the members of the Congress, and the Committee members themselves at the outset of the investigation.

THE PRESIDENT'S STATEMENT OF PURPOSES

The areas which the President proposed for Committee investigation have already been enumerated.[62] To the President the major function of the TNEC was to search for means to make the capitalistic economy function. He stated that ways must be found to revive and strengthen competition in order to preserve our traditional system of free enterprise. Full employment was the goal. In the initial message he had set forth the now famous phrase that "idle factories and idle workers profit no man"; a year later, in a letter to Senator O'Mahoney he added, "It might equally be said that idle dollars profit no man." [63] This, then, as conceived by the President, was not to be a mere monopolies investigation or another trust-busting campaign; it was to be a far-reaching analysis of the ills of the economy and a search for effective remedial measures.

THE ENUMERATED DUTIES OF THE TNEC

The second statement of objectives was, of course, the charter given to the Committee in the legislation providing for the TNEC.[64] It stated that it shall be the duty of the Committee to conduct a full investigation with respect to the matters enumerated by the President and to make a complete study of the nature of economic concentration and financial control over production with a view to determining (1) the causes of such concentration and control and their effects upon competition, (2) the effects of the existing price system and the price policies of industry upon the general level of trade, upon unemployment, upon long-term profits, and upon consumption, and (3) the effect of the existing tax, patent, and other government policies upon competition, price levels, unemployment, profits, and consumption.[65] This not only granted broad powers to the TNEC but also imposed upon it fundamental responsibilities.

[62] Chapter II; see also S. Doc. 173, 75th Cong., 3d sess.
[63] See *Hearings before the Temporary National Economic Committee*, Part 9, p. 4009.
[64] S. J. Resolution 300, to create a Temporary National Economic Committee.
[65] Public Resolution 113, 75th Cong.

THE PROBLEM STATED

Leon Henderson, executive secretary to the TNEC, was probably in a better position than anyone else to know and interpret its composite mind and its conception of objectives. At the outset of the hearings, but well after the Committee had formulated its plans, he set forth the basic problems confronting the TNEC. In doing so he said that the questions and issues listed flow "naturally from the ideas of the 12 members of the Committee and their alternates, as I have come to know them myself, as well as from the observations of the advisers and assistants who are counseling upon or directing the various studies under assignment from the Committee." [66] He proceeded, therefore, with a presentation of the issues before the Committee and by inference a statement of its purposes and objectives. The fundamental or over-all question, he said, was: "Why have we not had full employment and full utilization of our magnificent resources?" Then he outlined, one by one, the problems which demanded the attention of the TNEC, some of which follow:

1. What is the present status of competition?
2. Can this country in the future rely on competition as a mainspring of its economic system? If so, what changes are necessary?
3. To what degree and in what areas has competition been set aside?
4. To what extent is product competition a satisfactory substitute for price competition?
5. What are the wastes in the distributive system?
6. What devices have been used to defeat competition?
7. To what extent are the antitrust laws inadequate?
8. What part has concentration played in the decline of competition?
9. Does concentration affect adversely the distribution of income?
10. How flexible is the economy?
11. Why has new investment lagged?
12. Are our liberties endangered by the growth of private control?
13. Which segments of our economy have managed their prices and production? [67]

CHAIRMAN O'MAHONEY'S CONCEPTION OF THE TNEC

Senator O'Mahoney, as chairman of the TNEC, was qualified to speak with authority as to its objectives and purposes. While defending the Senate Resolution before the House Judiciary Committee, he had suggested that there was need of establishing "social control over

[66] *Hearings before the Temporary National Economic Committee*, Part 1, p. 180.
[67] At this point Mr. Henderson inserted in the record a comprehensive list of the main lines of study which he felt the resolution called for. See *ibid.*, p. 181.

the economic life of the nation." [68] There seems to be little doubt, moreover, that he looked upon the investigation as a vehicle for selling his bill for Federal licensing of corporations to the country. He was quoted to that effect in the public press.[69] But to Senator O'Mahoney the task of the TNEC was even more fundamental, comprehensive, and socially significant than this. The task, as the chairman saw it, was to examine the very structure and functioning of the economic system with a view to offering such remedial measures as might become apparent. "The end to be sought is a stable society in which the individual members have an opportunity to live with a certain degree of security and have the opportunity to pursue the activities which appeal to them," he said.[70] In other words, he declared that what was sought was a means by which the people would be able to increase production and distribute goods and services more equitably and more effectively than ever before.[71] To the chairman the basic problem before the Committee was unemployment; [72] this is illustrated by his remarks during the iron and steel hearings:

. . . there still remains the discovery of the formula by which the human resources of society may be conserved as the material resources are conserved. . . . That, I take it, is the fundamental work of this committee, to study how we may gear together all of these tremendous industries that mankind has developed so as to make it possible to provide security for all men, so as to provide a solution for the problem of unemployment—unemployment of men and unemployment of capital—which remains with us in spite of all these tremendous achievements of industry.[73]

During the petroleum hearings Senator O'Mahoney said, "The resolution by which the Committee was created, and the message of the President which was the cause for the creation of the committee, were both directed to the fundamental problem of how we can solve the question of unemployment, unemployment both of labor and of capital." [74] This would all seem to confirm the view held by Com-

[68] Quoted by Representative Michener, *Congressional Record*, Vol. LXXXIII, Part 8, p. 9339.
[69] For an account of his statement see "What to Expect from the Monopoly Investigation," *Commercial and Financial Chronicle*, CXLVII (July 23, 1938), 482.
[70] *Final Report and Recommendations of the Temporary National Economic Committee*, p. 437.
[71] *Ibid.*, p. 672.
[72] *Hearings before the Temporary National Economic Committee*, Part 14, p. 7098.
[73] *Ibid.*, Part 18, p. 10217.
[74] *Ibid.*, Part 15, p. 8165; see also *Final Report and Recommendations of the Temporary National Economic Committee*, p. 62.

missioner Lubin that the chief concern of the TNEC was to assure that "never again does a catastrophe occur like that which overwhelmed us in the early 1930's." [75] How far the Committee eventually deviated from these goal-sights will be revealed in a subsequent chapter.

THE MOBILIZATION OF PUBLIC OPINION

An unstated but somewhat apparent objective of the Administration is pertinent. The Administration was seeking a basis for a unified and consistent policy designed to reconstruct the economy and rescue it from the difficulties in which it had been floundering. There seems to be little doubt that a number of administrative leaders had partially formulated programs for the supervision and regulation of business and desired to use the TNEC as a sounding board with which to mobilize public opinion.[76] Apparently *The Magazine of Wall Street* sensed this objective when it said, "The general idea is to lay the foundation for legislation out of which will emerge a 'modernized capitalism.' " [77] Moreover, there was a sincere conviction that research itself was a necessary preparation for the formulation of policy. This viewpoint was aptly expressed by Representative Sumners in the House when defending the bill prior to its passage.[78]

THE PURPOSE CONSTRUCTIVE, NOT PUNITIVE

From the beginning members of the Committee were eager to establish in the public mind certain conclusions as to what the TNEC did not aim to do. There was little disposition on the part of members to use the investigation to indulge in sensational publicity stunts; nor did they intend to convert the witness stand into a pillory. The TNEC promised to be no "ghost dance," "fishing expedition," or "witch hunt," and it offered no "pyrotechniques." [79] Above all, the chairman insisted that the TNEC was not an "investigation"; [80] "Let us call it a study," he said. The Committee had organized a search

[75] *Final Report and Recommendations of the Temporary National Economic Committee,* p. 526.
[76] See Flynn, "Bigger and Better Monopolies," *The New Republic,* XCVI (October 26, 1938), 333; and Batchelor, "Business under the X-Ray," *The Atlantic Monthly,* CLXVII (January, 1941), 98.
[77] Stern, "Outline of a New Economic Order," *The Magazine of Wall Street,* LXII (September 24, 1938), 670.
[78] Representative Sumners, *Congressional Record,* Vol. LXXXIII, Part 8, p. 9340.
[79] "Off to a Good Start," *Business Week,* December 10, 1938, p. 48; see also *Final Report and Recommendations of the Temporary National Economic Committee,* p. 61; and "The So-Called Monopoly Committee," *Fortune,* XVIII (November, 1938), 72.
[80] *Hearings before the Temporary National Economic Committee,* Part 25, p. 13037.

for facts, not a criminal court or a grand jury seeking to ferret out malefactors and mete out punishment. Numerous statements by Committee members, usually by the chairman, served to demonstrate the serious purpose of those directing the studies of the TNEC.[81] This approach is neatly summarized in the following statement by the chairman:

From the very outset of our proceeding the chairman and the various members of the Committee have tried to make it plain that they are not attacking anybody or any industry, and that they are not investigating anybody with any punitive intent, but that the committee is engaged exclusively upon an effort to find out more about the economic machine than apparently is known either by the leaders of government or the leaders in industry.[82]

AN OBJECTIVE APPROACH

The more positive aspect of this purpose was expressed very early after the organization of the TNEC. The study was to be analytical, factual, and without preconception or bias. Secretary Henderson called it "factualization"; suspicions, instincts, preconceptions, predilections, half- and fully-informed theories were to be factualized and reduced from the realm of talk to statistics.[83] Repeatedly those in charge of the examinations indicated that "the endeavor of this presentation is to bring out the facts." [84] This was the spirit in which those responsible for the TNEC planned their activities; before the hearings began, the Committee had endorsed this viewpoint in a formal resolution as follows: "[it] is the unanimous sense of this committee that its function and purpose is to collect and analyze, through the medium of reports and public hearings, available facts pertaining to the items specified in Public Resolution 113 in an objective, unbiased, and dispassionate manner, and that it is the purpose of the committee to pursue its work solely from this point of view." [85]

THE BERLE MEMORANDUM

An interesting step taken in preparation for the Committee's work was the Berle memorandum. This "confidential" document created

---

[81] *Ibid.*, Part 15, p. 8206; see also Part 6, pp. 2420, 2446; Part 10, p. 4544; Part 17, pp. 9459, 9724; Part 23, p. 12075.
[82] *Ibid.*, Part 25, p. 13110; see also Part 18, p. 10381; Part 23, pp. 11859–11860.
[83] "Competition or Control," *Business Week*, October 8, 1938, p. 20.
[84] *Hearings before the Temporary National Economic Committee*, Part 22, p. 11479; see also W. O. Douglas, *ibid.*, Part 4, p. 1164; Gerhard A. Gesell, *ibid.*, Part 13, p. 6541; and Jerome N. Frank, *ibid.*, Part 10, pp. 4153–4154.
[85] Quoted by Senator O'Mahoney, *ibid.*, Vol. XII, Part 1, p. 2.

considerable consternation among Administration leaders and gained a great deal of notoriety in the press. Jerome Frank and Thurman Arnold, who held the Assistant Secretary of State, Adolf Berle, in high esteem, requested him to prepare a memorandum for the guidance of the Committee. This he did, and it seems to have been circulated among the members. This "Memorandum of Suggestions"—a twenty-three page document of more than 12,000 words—was to the point and spared no feelings. So spicy were its contents that it leaked out to the newspapers and thereby attracted a great deal of attention.[86] It was reported that Committee members were angry, and that the Administration was annoyed; it has been assumed by some that the situation was instrumental in Mr. Berle's resignation from his post with the State Department soon thereafter.

Mr. Berle's memorandum, though critical, was constructive in its intent; he attempted to guide the Committee in a positive direction. He argued that the TNEC was faced with something more fundamental than monopoly and urged that the study be turned into a searching inquiry of business organization and practices. He warned against the bias which had characterized similar investigations in the past and attacked "fallacious economic thinking," "pet panaceas," "public misconceptions," "preconceptions," and "unwarranted assumptions," which, it seems, he feared might addle the efforts of the TNEC. He contradicted some of these unwarranted assumptions as follows: (1) small business is not necessarily competitive; (2) small business is by no means necessarily humane; (3) large-scale enterprise is not always more efficient; (4) concentration of power has little to do with the private fortunes of individuals; (5) legislating competition simply does not work out; and (6) mere interruption of habits and social machinery means nothing unless an equivalent or better machinery is provided. He seemed to disparage the Borah-O'Mahoney bill and to doubt the efficacy of the Administration's labor legislation and profits tax program. He reminded the Committee not to place its hope in any single cure-all or to attempt to solve the nation's economic problems by a return to the good old days when all enterprise was small and independent and when mass production was

86 "Berle's Proposals," *News Week,* August 29, 1938, p. 35; "Berle's Monopoly Report in Full; 'Must' Reading for Advertisers," *Printers' Ink,* Vol. CLXXXIV (September 1, 1938); "The So-Called Monopoly Committee," *Fortune,* Vol. XVIII (November, 1938); "Berle's Confidential Memorandum," *Commercial and Financial Chronicle,* Vol. CXLVII (August 27, 1938); "Code for Investigators," *Business Week* (September 3, 1938). See also *Hearings before the Temporary National Economic Committee,* Part 5, p. 1919.

unheard of. The most stinging rebuke of all was embodied in the much-quoted statement which follows: "A fair criticism of the technique of the New Deal has been that it indulged in shot gun impositions of regulation without adequate definition of standard." [87]

But there was also a strong positive and constructive tone to Berle's memorandum. He said that any attempt to control monopoly should seek to "provide more goods, better grades and cheaper goods . . . provide more jobs, better paying and steadier jobs . . . provide continuous ready access to capital financing needed to create and maintain additional plants . . . provide for a continuous development of the arts." [88] In summarizing his observations Mr. Berle set forth what he conceived to be the objectives which should guide the TNEC:

First, the general scope of the investigation ought to be a search for an organization of business that actually works; second, the standard must be whether it supplies the existing and developing wants of the people as they appear; third, that this involves the provision of an adequate supply of goods; fourth, and a distribution system that takes these goods toward known wants to the maximum degree possible; fifth, that the system must provide a maximum number of people with means of satisfying those wants through a contribution to the system; sixth, that the system must provide the people engaged in the process with a manner of life, which at least tends to satisfy a fair proportion of their wants; seventh, the system must evolve a method of organization that does not interfere unduly, actually or potentially, with the liberty of the individual (that its controls must release more individuality than they suppress); and, eighth, that there is no need to assume that these tests will be met by any single system or any single standard of size or set of practices at any given point.[89]

In retrospect it would appear that the net effect of the Berle memorandum was wholesome; a study of the final recommendations of the Committee would result in the futile wish that these objectives had been adhered to more zealously.

PLANNING THE INVESTIGATIONS

The law creating the TNEC had been passed and Committee members had been chosen by the latter part of June, 1938. No hearings were held until nearly six months later. This interlude is explainable in part by the fact that congressional elections absorbed the attention of various members, but it was due primarily to the fact that much groundwork, research, and other preliminary details required

[87] "Berle's Confidential Memorandum," *Commercial and Financial Chronicle,* CXLVII (August 27, 1938), 1279.
[88] *Ibid.*   [89] *Ibid.,* p. 1278.

careful and extensive elaboration before anything worthwhile could be developed in the hearings. A staff had to be selected, an organization effected, assignments made, research undertaken, and a *modus operandi* laid out.

Even before the Committee met, it was generally understood what investigations each administrative agency would undertake.[90] The press had informed the public, quite accurately, that the first probe would relate to patents under the sponsorship of the Department of Justice. Several departments had a wealth of information in their files which awaited analysis and public exposition. The TNEC offered an excellent opportunity to exploit these possibilities, inasmuch as it provided the public authorization, the stimulus, the staff, and the financial support with which to undertake the assignment. The Securities and Exchange Commission had a fund of information relating to proxy abuses; the Department of Justice had made a good start toward an oil study. The Federal Trade Commission had available data which had been collected for years pertaining to manipulative practices in business. The Department of Commerce had a similar wealth of experience and recorded data, while the Department of Labor and the Bureau of Labor Statistics were primed with information about price rigidities, employment irregularities, and wage standards. Similarly, the Treasury Department, as the world's largest purchaser, had information in its files which when analyzed would reveal a great deal about identical bids and maintained prices.

After the first meetings of the Committee notice was given to the press revealing what phase of the study each of the six agencies would undertake: (1) the Department of Justice was to present data concerning industrial combination and price policies of industries; (2) the Securities and Exchange Commission, the investments of insurance companies, investment banking, and corporate finance; (3) the Federal Trade Commission, existing combinations in industry and problems of production and distribution; (4) the Department of Labor, the effect of industrial combination on labor, employment, and living conditions; (5) the Department of the Treasury, government contracts, especially in the rubber, steel, and cement industries, and also a broad study of antitrust laws in the United States and Great Britain; (6) the Department of Commerce, a general analysis of the

90 See "Patent System Probe First on Monopoly List," *News Week,* XII (December 5, 1938), 34; and McKee, "Monopoly Investigators," *The Commonweal,* XXIX (November 4, 1938), 35 ff.

size of various industrial combinations, based on records of the NRA, files of the Bureau of Foreign and Domestic Commerce, and the Census Bureau.

The record reveals that some of these projects were developed in the hearings and some in the monographs; others do not seem to have materialized at all. Altogether, fifteen separate hearings were held; each was carefully prepared in advance by one of the executive departments or by someone appointed by the TNEC. Subjects covered were as follows: (1) patents, conducted by the Department of Justice; (2) life insurance, by the Securities and Exchange Commission; (3) monopolistic practices, the Federal Trade Commission; (4) the liquor industry, the Federal Trade Commission; (5) milk and poultry industries, the Federal Trade Commission; (6) problems of the consumer, the Consumers' Counsel of the Department of Agriculture; (7) savings and investment, the Securities and Exchange Commission; (8) the construction industry, the TNEC and its staff; (9) the petroleum industry, the American Petroleum Institute; (10) iron and steel, the Department of Justice; (11) war and prices, the TNEC and its staff; (12) cartels, the TNEC and its staff; (13) interstate trade barriers, the Department of Commerce; (14) technology and the concentration of economic power, the TNEC and its staff. An analytic statement of the budget allocations to various executive departments to finance these studies may be found in the final report of the Committee.[91]

The resolution creating the TNEC directed the various departments to appear before the Committee to present such evidence by examination of witnesses or introduction of reports and documents as seemed pertinent to the study at hand. Each department was to present its case in its own way, permitting the Committee to sit in judgment before formulating conclusions. Thus, the proceedings assumed a judicial and dispassionate calm, quite academic in character. The general conduct of the inquiry was in the charge of an executive committee composed at first of the following: Senator O'Mahoney, Representative Sumners, Isador Lubin, Thurman Arnold, and Richard Patterson. Chairman Ferguson and Chairman Douglas later became members. Long before the Committee met to hear evidence, a great battery of technicians on the various departmental staffs and on the staff of the TNEC prepared the groundwork; econ-

[91] *Final Report and Recommendations of the Temporary National Economic Committee*, pp. 72–73, 694–695.

omists, accountants, statisticians, lawyers, and clerks worked busily for months to collect and prepare the data.

The TNEC itself assembled a staff of many members, ranging in number from a maximum of eighty-two in April, 1939, to thirty in December, 1940. Each department organized its own TNEC unit. There were probably 150 officials and clerks devoting most of their time to the investigation during the months immediately preceding and following the opening sessions of the Committee. Most impressive of the departmental units was the organization built up by the Securities and Exchange Commission, which received the largest allotment from the budget—$255,000. Its staff labored for months preceding the hearings, marshaling the necessary information; other agencies followed similar procedures.

METHODS OF INVESTIGATION

One of the methods employed by the investigators was the use of the questionnaire. The Securities and Exchange Commission submitted a searching questionnaire to the life insurance companies, from which eventually were compiled statistical tables [92] which insurance executives are reputed to have valued at $25,000.[93] Another illustration of the questionnaire technique is the one worked out jointly by the Department of Justice and the Federal Trade Commission and sent to fifty-four steel companies.

As has been indicated, departmental files were available as a reservoir of information to the research staffs; in addition, however, the TNEC was empowered to examine corporation records whenever it was deemed necessary for the success of the investigation.[94] Public Resolution 113 had vested the TNEC with the usual authority to summon witnesses and subpoena relevant documents and reports. Before many weeks had elapsed many business men and firms were confronted with a "subpoena duces tecum"—calling for books and records. As more or less reluctant and resentful tributes, various witnesses testified to the thoroughness of these "fine-tooth" investigations of corporate records. In the investment banking hearings Mr. Nehemkis of the Securities and Exchange Commission said that the firm

92 *Hearings before the Temporary National Economic Committee*, Part 10-A, *Life Insurance—Operating Results and Investments of the Twenty-six Largest Legal Reserve Life Insurance Companies Domiciled in the United States—1929–38.*
93 *Ibid.*, Part 28, pp. 14702, 14786, 14799.
94 *Final Report and Recommendations of the Temporary National Economic Committee*, p. 73.

Goldman, Sachs and Company had "very graciously given us full data and information of everything in . . . [their] files pertaining to . . . [what] we have been discussing today"; and again, "we lived there for many weeks." [95] Of the Morgan Stanley Company he said, "as Mr. Stanley knows, we have been living in his shop for months"; to which Mr. Stanley, with an air of resignation, replied, "yes, I know it." Not only were records examined on the spot, but also frequently they were ordered to appear at the hearings. For example, the Jones and Laughlin Steel Corporation was instructed to produce all records which might have any bearing on its public policies; this, in substance, required every memorandum, letter, or telegram which might indicate corporation policy or action relating to the antitrust laws.[96] One witness described as follows what others inferred to be a common practice: "I might say this, that everything that we have in our records has been sent down here. I was asked what to send and I looked at the subpoena and said, 'move the office down,' so that everything that we had is here." [97]

Often those in charge of the examinations were so much better informed than the witnesses as to corporate policy and behavior that the latter readily assented to or volunteered information which otherwise might not have been forthcoming. Said Mr. Levis, president of the Owen-Illinois Glass Company, in the patent hearings, "I wouldn't repudiate any suggestion, Mr. Cox. You have 8,000 pieces of my papers. . . . Show me the incident, and if I can refresh my memory I will tell you the truth." [98] A critic seemingly hostile to the TNEC wrote that the witnesses for business were generally no match for the agile and well-prepared minds of the Government's economic staff when it came to defending or rationalizing business policies.[99] An interesting illustration of this is noted in the liquor hearings; the president of the National Distillers Products Corporation, when queried about the financial operations of his own corporation, answered, "Mr. Buck (general counsel for the Federal Trade Commission) has all the details." [100]

[95] *Hearings before the Temporary National Economic Committee*, Part 24, pp. 12403–12404.
[96] Arthur Krock, *The New York Times* (August 11, 1939); "They Can't Do This to You, Can't They?" *The Saturday Evening Post*, CCXII (September 16, 1939), 22.
[97] Wilmer R. Shuh, *Hearings before the Temporary National Economic Committee*, Part 17, p. 9470.
[98] William E. Levis, *ibid.*, Part 2, p. 504; also pp. 483–500, 501.
[99] Batchelor, "Business under the X-Ray," *The Atlantic Monthly*, CLXVII (January, 1941), 99.
[100] *Hearings before the Temporary National Economic Committee*, Part 6, p. 2458.

BUSINESS STUDIES ITSELF

It would be erroneous, however, to assume that the representatives of corporate enterprises came to the inquiry unprepared and with no organization or program; quite the contrary. It is doubtful if they ever prepared for a public presentation quite as meticulously or as thoroughly as they did for the TNEC. The trade associations mustered every manner of data; it was said that hundreds of thousands of dollars were spent by large corporations such as General Motors, Standard Oil, United States Steel, and the Metropolitan Life Insurance Company. Their agents and lawyers prepared for months to be able to cope with the many questions concerning their operations and policies.[101] The life insurance interests, the American Petroleum Institute, and numerous others gave evidence of careful and painstaking planning for their day before the "peoples tribune." It was reported that executives of large corporations had made personal preparation for the examinations. Well-known economists were retained as coaches by some; others appealed for aid to the Harvard Graduate School of Business Administration and similar institutions. "In a few weeks they had sought to attain a specialized knowledge which it had taken their preceptors years to acquire." [102]

Some corporations went to elaborate lengths to prepare for the hearings. The House of Morgan organized a staff of seventeen people "working night and day" for many weeks.[103] The most pretentious organization was that set up by the United States Steel Corporation; according to the testimony of its president, U. S. Steel organized "a special TNEC group" consisting of thirty or more individuals.[104] It was said at the time that Steel was the only corporation prepared to meet the new committee techniques.[105] In order to match the Government's economists, the Steel Corporation had assembled a staff under the personal direction of Dr. Theodore O. Yntema, one of the country's leading authorities on statistics, from the School of Business of the University of Chicago. This staff was composed of employees of the corporation; some were economists, some graduate students employed for the purpose, and others were the corporation's lawyers

[101] Batchelor, "Business under the X-Ray," *The Atlantic Monthly*, CLXVII (January, 1941), 98.
[102] *Ibid.*, p. 100.
[103] *Hearings before the Temporary National Economic Committee*, Part 23, p. 12097.
[104] *Ibid.*, Part 26, pp. 13586–13587.
[105] Batchelor, "Business under the X-Ray," *The Altantic Monthly*, CLXVII (January, 1941), 99.

assigned to the project. The presentation was probably the most impressive, the most abstract, the most scientific, and the most statistical of all of the hearings. Seldom, if ever, was such a battery of scholars, statisticians, economists, and specialists arrayed against one another —those of Steel and those of the Government. The press reported it as the "Battle of the Ph.D.'s." The Steel Corporation took the hearings so seriously that it published a monumental three-volume summary of its case.[106] Despite the vigor with which the case was presented, analyzed, and rebutted, the representatives of both sides exchanged compliments as to the quality of the job done. One suspects that the members of the Committee, if in attendance, sat by amazed and confused, if not lost.[107]

STUART CHASE'S GLOSSARY OF WORDS

A memorandum which received considerable publicity in the press and in current periodicals was a contribution by Stuart Chase, a well-known and able writer, who has probably done more than any other American to popularize economic information and to stimulate economic thinking.[108] As a liberal, his sympathies were in harmony with the objectives of the New Deal. Mr. Chase had prepared a memorandum for the Securities and Exchange Commission, entitled "Preliminary Suggestions for Standardizing Terminology, or First Aid to the Layman." [109] This document, which apparently was intended as background for the investigators, probably would never have come to light had not Arthur Krock of *The New York Times* gained possession and made a public issue of it.[110] Mr. Chase had published a book on semantics,[111] and it was in this role as an authority on the proper use and effect of words that he set forth his suggestions to the

---

106 Exhibits Nos. 1409 to 1417, *Hearings before the Temporary National Economic Committee*, Part 26, pp. 13743–14083; Exhibit No. 1418, Part 27, p. 14619; these were published privately as well as inserted as exhibits in the record.

107 Note Senator King's lack of comprehension when faced with the terms significant to the analyses such as "elasticity of demand" (*Hearings*, Part 26, p. 13593) and "variable cost" (*Hearings*, Part 26, p. 13621). Senator King: "The cost of your ore for one year may be considerably different from the costs of ore for a preceding year, your labor costs vary. Those are variable, aren't they?"

108 Stuart Chase, *The Tragedy of Waste*, Macmillan, 1925; *Men and Machines*, Macmillan, 1929; *The New Deal*, Macmillan, 1932; *The Economy of Abundance*, Macmillan, 1934.

109 For a current discussion of this episode see "Propaganda Glossary," *Time*, XXXIII (June 19, 1939), 65; "Are We Saving Too Much," *Business Week* (May 20, 1939), 15; and "Business Heads Score Taxes As TNEC Enters Main Phase," *News Week*, XIII (May 29, 1939), 37.

110 Arthur Krock, *The New York Times* (June 7, 1939), 22.

111 Stuart Chase, *The Tyranny of Words*, Harcourt, 1938.

Committee. A fair statement would seem to be that he intended his paper as informal suggestions to aid the investigators to develop a standard terminology which would avoid confusion in the public mind and assist in the general understanding of what was taking place. Economic terminology at its best is apt to be confusing even to professionals and becomes exceedingly so when relayed to the public through press headlines and text. It would seem, moreover, that the suggestions were advanced to coach both those in charge of the hearings and witnesses in the proper choice of words to the end that New Deal objectives and policy would be portrayed in their most attractive light. It was this aspect which was played up by hostile critics.

The Chase memorandum was primarily a glossary of words suggesting "good" words for examiners and witnesses to use and "bad" words which should be avoided if possible. "Capitalism" is an emotional word, a fighting word, and should be avoided as far as possible; so also is the "profit system." It would be better judgment to use "our economy" or "our economic system." "Spending" is a bad word; it is better to talk about "government running expenses" and "government plant." Spending should be associated, as far as possible, with "wages," "purchasing power," and "business sales"—all good words. The term "consumption economy" should likewise be avoided; it is better to use "pay-as-you-go economy." There are other good words which might profitably be employed. The concept of government debt should be associated with investment wherever possible. However, "investment" is a loose and ambiguous term "physical investment" is something you can "kick with your foot," and "financial investment" is something which may "crumble in your hand." These are but a few on the list of word taboos and approvals in the Chase glossary.

As a consequence of the notoriety which the affair received, the SEC and members of the Committee disavowed any connection with it or any practical use of it.[112] None the less, some time preceding the Krock editorial we find this colloquy in the hearings:

MR. NEHEMKIS. Dr. Hansen, before you continue, so that the record may be clear, in connection with your discussion of the preceding chart, that is to say the chart which appeared on the easel at the right, you had occasion to use the phrase "capital stock." I take it you meant by capital stock physical plant, something you can kick with your feet?

[112] "Propaganda Glossary," Time, XXXIII (June 19, 1939), 68.

Dr. HANSEN. That is right.

Mr. NEHEMKIS. As distinguished from a piece of paper which you crumble in your hand, is that correct?

Dr. HANSEN. That is right.[113]

Three months after the press attack, we find the president of a large life insurance company twitting the Committee over the Chase memorandum. In response, the examiner for the SEC, too innocently, asked, "Who is Mr. Chase?" Thereupon, Mr. Henderson, then of the SEC, who seemed to have been ruffled by the exchange, took the occasion to disclaim official sanction of the memorandum:

I get what you mean. I think you have been badly misinformed. If you are referring to a memorandum which Mr. Chase prepared, no member of this committee saw that memorandum in advance of its publication in the press. . . . Mr. Chase wrote a book and has long been interested in what he calls semantics. . . . And he undertook, in connection with some work he was doing, to write a suggestion on semantics, but it has nothing at all to do with questioning by this committee, or any terminology which we use. . . . That was never a matter of record in these proceedings.[114]

The work of the TNEC, nevertheless, presents an interesting study to the student of semantics. From the outset there was the problem of confusion of terms. Monopoly, capitalism, democracy, regulation, co-operation, and concentration are household words which in the minds of many people have affixed to them numerous emotions and sentiments. They are ambiguous omnibus words which rarely mean the same thing to two people. Committee members and witnesses found themselves pronouncing and hearing the same terms, but speaking to each other in different tongues and ofttimes suffering the delusion that they had understood the thought processes of one another.[115] A refreshing but only half-serious suggestion was made by one Committee member that words strongly filled with emotional content be abandoned for a new vocabulary such as "ugwug," "agwag," and "wiffwaff." On at least one occasion an attempt was made to give precise meaning to the vocabulary used; in the technology hearings a carefully prepared document was presented describing and defining terms.[116]

Another interesting aspect of the semantic problem was the fre-

[113] *Hearings before the Temporary National Economic Committee,* Part 9, p. 3511.
[114] *Ibid.,* Part 13, pp. 6554–6555.
[115] One witness called this to the attention of the Committee in *Hearings before the Temporary National Economic Committee,* Part 2, p. 358.
[116] *Hearings before the Temporary National Economic Committee,* Part 30, p. 16516.

quent fencing between witnesses and examiners over the meaning of words. Witnesses, when caught in a tight corner because the language they had used was lucid and frank, resorted to the semantic defense. Over and over again the defense was made that words do not mean what they say. Steel people whose correspondence gave proof of collusion sought refuge by saying, "I was not as choice in my language as I might have been," [117] or that such words as "permitted," used in connection with quoted prices, and "incriminating," in connection with intercompany price conferences, were "an unfortunate choice of language." [118] In the investment banking hearings, when documents using the words "legacy," [119] "inherit," [120] and "proprietary interest" [121] clearly indicated combinations and understandings among the bankers, the words were deftly brushed aside as "misnomers" and of "no value." [122] The semantic escape was often the convenient, even if not convincing, reinterpretation of words which by themselves were rich in meaning and social significance.

SETTING AND ATMOSPHERE OF THE INVESTIGATION

Men recognized as representing the voice of business were fearful of the TNEC; they were in sympathy neither with the New Deal program nor with the stated objectives of the Committee. They objected to and were suspicious of the TNEC, especially because it might be subject to Executive domination.[123] No one could have been more energetic or sincere than the chairman, Senator O'Mahoney, in attempting to dispel these apprehensions. Early in June, before the Committee was organized, he made a statement to the press indicating that all members earnestly desired to offer constructive service.[124] In a few days Senator King followed with similar assurances.[125] Prob-

---

117 *Ibid.*, Part 18, p. 10347.
118 *Ibid.*, Part 20, pp. 10839–10841.
119 *Ibid.*, Part 22, p. 11494.
120 *Ibid.*, p. 11493.
121 *Ibid.*, p. 11602.
122 Many entertaining examples of the art of repudiating the obvious meaning of words may be found in the following citations: *ibid.*, Part 22, pp. 11554, 11563–11564, 11968; Part 19, p. 10347; Part 27, p. 14282; Part 20, pp. 10748, 10784.
123 For a few representative illustrations of business opinion at the time, see "What to Expect from the Monopoly Investigation," *Commercial and Financial Chronicle,* Vol. CXLVII (July 23, 1938); "Patent System Probe First on Monopoly List," *News Week,* XII (December 5, 1938), 34; Parkinson, "A Call to Action," *Printers' Ink,* CLXXXV (October 13, 1938), 12; "Anti Trust Inquiry," *News Week,* XII (July 4, 1938), 8; "Now Is the Time," *Printers' Ink,* CLXXXV (August 25, 1938), 86; MacDonald, "The Monopoly Committee; a Study in Frustration," *The American Scholar,* VIII (July, 1939), 297.
124 "What to Expect from the Monopoly Investigation," *Commercial and Financial Chronicle,* CXLVII (July 23, 1938), 482.
125 *Ibid.*

ably most reassuring of all was a statement from the administrative branch voicing the same sentiment. This came in the words of Chairman Douglas of the Securities and Exchange Commission; he promised that the Committee was bent on "a substantial piece of work" and that there would be no trace of witch-burning.[126] Pages could be filled with subsequent comments by Senator O'Mahoney designed to win the confidence of the business world.[127]

Closely related to these verbal overtures was the liaison work by Richard C. Patterson, representing the Department of Commerce. In an effort to create a better understanding between the Administration and industrial leaders and desiring to get the TNEC off to a constructive start, he inaugurated a series of "shirt sleeve" dinners, where he gathered the new investigators and key industrial executives.[128] Men who had grown suspicious of one another met face to face and in a friendly fashion, became better acquainted, and gained a clearer understanding of the task which confronted the TNEC. These efforts appear to have convinced business men that it would be to their advantage to co-operate. Shortly thereafter those in responsible positions spoke of the TNEC as a "God-given opportunity" for the business world to contribute constructively.[129] The New York Chamber of Commerce called upon industrial leaders and business men to give the Committee the benefit of their practical experience. The general disposition of business was, at least reluctantly and defensively, co-operative. It might fairly be said that the Committee was well launched.

As might be expected, deference was paid occasionally to the press, but the hearings were by no means a publicity stunt for the aggrandizement of any person or group. There was apparent no studied attempt to stage-manage the hearings or to employ public relations counsels to exploit the daily proceedings before the public. A magazine representing business paid tribute by saying that "rodeo methods" were not evident, that "smoke signals on the front page" were not sent up, and that there were no attempts "to barbecue the leaders of business." [130] Another journal complimented the Committee for the

---

126 *Ibid.*
127 See, for example, "Monopoly and the U. S. System," *The Commonweal*, XXIX (December 16, 1938), 215.
128 "These Are the Monopoly Investigators," *Business Week*, July 2, 1938, p. 15.
129 Parkinson, "Now Is the Time," *Printers' Ink*, CLXXXV (August 25, 1938), 86.
130 Corey, "O'Mahoney Wants Facts, Not Scalps," *Nation's Business*, XXVI (September 28, 1938), 15.

absence of "bally-hoo and press agency." [131] The academic calm of a research project characterized the TNEC procedure.

It was decided to subpoena every witness who appeared. This was not necessary in all cases, of course, but was done to avoid discrimination. Witnesses were entitled to receive pay, but in many instances those appearing for industry were reluctant to put in claims for compensation. Quite without exception witnesses were sworn in and testified under oath. They were not permitted to indulge in lengthy lectures of their own, but were held strictly to the subject at hand and were required to respond only to the questions posed. A departure from procedure in previous hearings was the policy of denying witnesses the privilege of reading prepared statements and handing such statements simultaneously to the press. Although most witnesses, other than those representing the Government, brought along their counsel, the latter were not permitted the privilege of cross-examination. Neither could attorneys object or protest, as is so frequently done in ordinary court procedure. Prepared statements were permitted to go into the record, however, as exhibits in the appendix; these documents often paralleled closely the oral testimony. This was permitted only with the consent (apparently always given) of the department in charge, which usually insisted upon the opportunity of examining the statement in advance of the oral testimony or before its admission as an exhibit. At times witnesses attempted, for a purpose, to read into the record extraneous material of a controversial character, whereupon the Committee felt compelled to evoke the rule in the interest of orderly procedure.[132] Not always did the TNEC members observe the spirit of their own rule, even though the letter was adhered to. Senator King violated it in the glass hearings by offering to receive evidence which the Committee had rejected,[133] and even the chairman was the author of a technical circumvention in the investment banking hearings.[134] Apparently this rule applied only to outside witnesses; greater latitude was allowed staff members. The presentations by Messrs. Lubin,[135] Henderson,[136] Thorp,[137] Hansen,[138] Altman,[139] Davenport,[140] and Fetter [141] were thoroughly pre-

[131] "Berle Monopoly Report in Full; 'Must' Reading for Advertisers," *Printers' Ink*, CLXXXIV (September 1, 1938), 15.

[132] See, for example, the glass hearings, *Hearings before the Temporary National Economic Committee*, Part 2, pp. 44, 601–602.

[133] *Ibid.*, pp. 601–602.   [134] *Ibid.*, Part 23, p. 11993.

[135] *Ibid.*, Part 1, p. 3.   [136] *Ibid.*, p. 157.   [137] *Ibid.*, p. 81.

[138] *Ibid.*, Part 9, p. 3495.   [139] *Ibid.*, p. 3669.

[140] *Ibid.*, Part 10, p. 4282.   [141] *Ibid.*, Part 5, p. 1657.

pared and resembled carefully organized lectures; they proceeded uninterrupted by questions from counsel.

The Committee had determined to follow an informal procedure; rules of evidence were to be respected, but liberally construed. Technicalities of the law would not be permitted to interfere with a conscientious search for facts. This policy was quite successfully followed throughout. Absent was the belabored, slow-moving courtroom process. This is illustrated by an instance in which the chairman read into the record valuable information which the legal-minded Senator King would have excluded. In that instance Senator O'Mahoney declared: "May I say that the utmost latitude is allowed in hearings of this kind. We have not pretended at any time to enforce the rules of evidence. . . . This committee is sitting, not as a jury would sit, to pass upon a strict legal question, but in an effort to learn the fundamental facts about our economic system." [142] Whereupon, he read the disputed evidence into the record. On this occasion his decision favored the Government examiner; on another, he favored the witness over the protest of the examiner.[143]

The hearings were conducted on a high plane, and the attitude of both Committee members and examiners toward witnesses was commendable. To paraphrase the chairman, the Committee was not out to lay traps for people; [144] on the contrary, witnesses were guided and coached to protect them from making statements which might either embarrass or incriminate them. This protection was extended to great industrial leaders as well as to ordinary men; [145] facts were more important than guilt or guile. A congenial spirit pervaded, much to the credit of everyone concerned. Witnesses frequently were thanked and commended by Committee members, and on occasion the latter were themselves recipients of similar acclamation.

In any such undertaking it is to be expected that there would appear recalcitrant and obdurate witnesses; particularly was this the case in the insurance hearings. Insurance executives were often cagey, reluctant, and evasive.[146] So obstinate and unco-operative were they that Mr. Henderson on one occasion offered to "buy a drink" for the first direct answer of "yes" or "no." [147] Another apparently studied policy was the practice of out-talking the counsel as a "nonresponsive"

[142] *Ibid.*, Part 23, pp. 12082–12083.   [143] *Ibid.*, Part 12, p. 5833.
[144] *Ibid.*, Part 7, p. 2912.
[145] *Ibid.*, Part 4, p. 1328; Part 13, p. 6565; Part 30, pp. 16471, 16658.
[146] *Ibid.*, Part 28, pp. 14787, 15190–15191, 15197; Part 10, pp. 4429, 4521, 4531, 4543, 4611.
[147] *Ibid.*, Part 10, p. 4599.

method of replying to questions.[148] The president of the country's largest life insurance company assumed an attitude aptly described as patronizing condescension or amusement.[149] A similar pose was taken by the president of the Steel Corporation, whose testimony has been characterized as a masterpiece of "evasion, equivocation, and quibble." [150] In spite of these displays of nonco-operation and reluctance, instances are rare in which either the examiner or a Committee member took the witness to task as did Chairman O'Mahoney in the beryllium study.[151] Occasionally witnesses were victims of what Commissioner Henderson called "fallen arches of the medulla oblongata"; [152] at critical places in the testimony relating to steel, beryllium, investment banking, and life insurance, memories usually acute suffered interesting and obliging lapses.[153]

MAGNITUDE OF THE STUDY

Because of the sheer magnitude of the undertaking the TNEC investigation will rank as one of the greatest inquiries of American history. Never was so exhaustive an attempt made to compile significant data concerning the national economy. The inquiry extended over a period of two years, nine months, and two days. The Committee began its hearings December 1, 1938; there followed eighteen months of intermittent meetings. The last public session was on March 11, 1941 [154] During the 193 days of hearings, 552 witnesses testified [155] and 95 industries were represented. This testimony fills 37 volumes of printed material, containing more than 17,000 pages. The published record includes 3,300 exhibits, some of which, such as the steel exhibits, are extensive documents in themselves. In addition to the printed record, 43 monographs were prepared by the TNEC staff on specific economic problems. Altogether Congress appropriated $1,070,000 to the TNEC; of this sum $220,000 was used to finance the TNEC staff, and $850,000 was allocated to the co-operating executive departments.[156]

---

148 *Ibid.*, Part 28, pp. 15170, 15173, 15181.   149 See *ibid.*, Part 4, p. 1280.
150 For numerous evidences see *ibid.*, Part 27, pp. 14159–14274.
151 *Ibid.*, Part 5, p. 2112.   152 *Ibid.*, Part 20, p. 10873.
153 *Ibid.*, pp. 10785, 10873; Part 27, p. 14322; Part 5, pp. 2032, 2036, 2040; Part 23, p. 11966; Part 13, pp. 6379, 6380, 6475.
154 *Final Report and Recommendations of the Temporary National Economic Committee*, p. 696.   155 *Ibid.*, p. 67.
156 Financial statement of the TNEC, *Final Report and Recommendations of the Temporary National Economic Committee*, p. 730. For a description of the allocations made to the different departments see pp. 72, 86.

CHAPTER IV

AN OUTLINE OF
THE HEARINGS

A^{N ENDEAVOR} will be made to present in this chapter a concise outline and summary of the hearings of the Temporary National Economic Committee. To present a thoroughgoing summary would require a volume in itself. Although this entire study relates solely to the hearings, the approach follows neither a time sequence nor an industry basis; its over-all purpose is to analyze the many pages of testimony and the exhibits to discover what light they throw upon the structure and behavior of the economic system. The analysis, therefore, will be functional and structural; the discovery of practices and principles will be the chief concern. This being the case, it would seem appropriate to devote an early section to a condensed outline presenting the salient features of the hearings.[1]

Economic prologue.—In the preliminary hearings testimony was offered by Isador Lubin (Commissioner of Labor Statistics), Willard Thorp (adviser on economic studies for the Department of Commerce), and Leon Henderson (executive secretary to the TNEC) to supply an economic background for the studies to be undertaken and a frame of reference for future deliberations. These men considered it the task of the TNEC to find a formula to "make capitalism work" (Part 1).

A. They defined capitalism as a basic philosophy, a set of legal and political institutions, and a cluster of operating policies predicated upon several basic assumptions (Part 1, pp. 157–183).
   1. The worth and dignity of the individual
   2. Private property
   3. Freedom of contract

[1] This outline may be supplemented to advantage by the table of contents found in each volume of the hearings. These topical reference guides have been assembled in summary fashion on pp. 695–708 in the *Final Report and Recommendations of the Temporary National Economic Committee* and have been published separately in the pamphlet, *Description of Hearings and Monographs of the Temporary National Economic Committee*. Other summaries relating to the hearings may be found on pp. 5–13 of the *Preliminary Report* of the TNEC (S. Doc. 95, 76th Cong., 1st sess.) and pp. 80–84 of the *Final Report*.

4. Approximate equality of bargaining power
5. Minimum of interference by law
6. Relatively free trade among nations
7. Market prices as the prime regulator of productive resources and distribution
8. Mobility of labor and capital

B. These basic assumptions have felt the impact of change and require re-examination.
  1. Individualism and free choice have been struck a tremendous blow by the disappearance of free land and the passing of the frontier.
  2. The rise of heavy industry, new types of merchandising, and the extensive use of the corporate device have resulted in a decline of competition.
  3. With the appearance of an excess of savings over new investment the capital market no longer is absorbing the nation's savings.
  4. Consumer debt, which has risen to nearly $9,000,000,000, tends to intensify business fluctuations.
  5. Instead of adhering strictly to a program of laissez faire, the Government has intervened in industry by creating public utilities, by granting subsidies, by providing tariff protection, and by engaging in business for itself.

C. Inordinate waste of economic resources resulted from the breakdown of the capitalistic system between 1929 and 1939 (Part 1, pp. 12–70).
  1. During this interval 43,000,000 man-years were lost, representing a wastage of man power nearly 35 percent greater than that utilized in 1929.
  2. Losses of wages and salaries between 1929 and 1939 cost American workers $120,000,000,000.
  3. Profits lost by the owners of industry amounted to $20,000,000,000.
  4. Farmers lost $38,000,000,000, or more than 900 percent of their income in 1929.
  5. During this 10 year interval the national income fell $133,000,000,000 short of the 1929 level.
  6. The Federal Government found it necessary to spend between $2,000,000,000 and $6,000,000,000 annually to alleviate hunger and want.

D. Capitalism is dependent upon mass distribution (Part 1, pp. 74–80).
  1. Individual incomes are insufficient to provide a market for the many goods the economy is capable of producing.
     a) Less than 3 percent of American families receive incomes of $5,000 or more.
     b) Less than 13 percent receive incomes of $2,500 or more.
     c) Fifty-four percent of the families receive incomes of $1,250 or less, most of this group receiving materially less.
        i. If incomes of all this portion of the population were raised to $1,250, their expanded purchases would require an actual increase in the productive capacity of the country.

E. Industrial concentration has become characteristic of the economy (Part 1, pp. 81–156).
   1. It has become hazardous for a new enterpriser to enter business; the average life of a new business concern is short.
   2. The obstacles to starting in business are great.
      a) Necessary resources may be controlled by existing enterprises.
      b) Patent rights may stand as a bar to new enterprise.
      c) Market outlets may be controlled.
      d) Heavy initial advertising costs are often an impediment.
      e) Large capital requirements essential to modern industrialism constitute a barrier.
   3. The door of opportunity is only theoretically open.

Patents.—An investigation of the patent system was conducted by the Departments of Justice and Commerce (Parts 2 and 3).

A. The Department of Justice held hearings on 3 industries—automobiles, glass-container, and beryllium—revealing the manner in which patents are employed to bring about concentration of control and disclosing other weaknesses of the patent system.
   1. The automobile industry has usually employed the monopoly privileges conferred by the patent laws in a manner benefiting the whole industry.
      a) Since 1915 members of the Automobile Manufacturers Association have followed a practice of relatively free exchange of patents; generally improved techniques have been available to all members without fee, thus contributing to the progress of the industry and to the welfare of the consuming public.
      b) The Ford Motor Company ordinarily has granted royalty-free use of its patents to all who ask for them (Part 2, pp. 257–258); it also encourages the inventor to exploit his invention and to sell the product to the Company (Part 2, pp. 259, 261, 264, 271, 274).
      c) General Motors has granted licenses to use its patents to anyone who applies (Part 2, pp. 335–337, 369).
   2. In contrast to the social use of patents by the automobile industry, the glass-container industry presents a picture of the major abuses possible.
      a) By controlling patents, two companies, Hartford-Empire and the Owens-Illinois Glass Company, have dominated the industry.
      b) The Hartford-Empire Company has restricted output by refusing to grant new licenses for the production of bottles (Part 2, p. 620).
      c) A main purpose of their policy has been "to block the development of machines which might be constructed by others" (Part 2, pp. 386, 776).
      d) Patents held by potential competitors have been "fenced in,"

and this has forced them to license improvements, to sell out at the monopolist's price, or to use his machines (Part 2, pp. 381–386, 472, 558, 560).

e) Hartford-Empire Company has employed the patent interference procedure to delay applications for patents by the inventors of competitive processes (Parts 2, pp. 455–456).

f) They have threatened or harassed by litigation new inventions in the glass-container industry (Part 2, pp. 437, 524–525).
  i. With money and the best-informed patent attorneys against them, defendants have been relatively helpless.
  ii. Independents thus have been forced to come to terms with the Hartford-Empire (Part 2, pp. 536–540).

g) By court delay, by interference suits, and by other methods of litigation the monopolists have held up patent applications (Part 2, pp. 439–441).

B. The Department of Commerce defended the essentials of the patent system and proposed a number of amendments and modifications (Part 3).

Life insurance.—A study of the life insurance industry was undertaken by the Securities and Exchange Commission (Parts 4, 10, 10-A, 12, 13, 28).

A. The management of life insurance company funds has come to play a dominant role in the financial history of the country.
  1. Whereas population has doubled in 50 years, life insurance assets have increased 2,500 percent.
  2. In 1937 the total assets of 308 legal reserve life insurance companies amounted to $28,000,000,000, exceeding by almost $10,000,000,000 the combined assets of savings banks and building and loan associations in this country.
  3. Industry and government find themselves increasingly dependent upon life insurance companies for essential financing.

B. The hearings revealed a number of weaknesses and shortcomings of life insurance operations.
  1. Supervision by state authorities appears to be inadequate (*Final Report*, pp. 561, 567).
    a) Tenure of office for supervisory authorities has been insecure and irregular.
    b) Extraneous responsibilities have interfered with their duties.
    c) Low pay and inadequate staff have been common.
  2. Most of the large life insurance companies have been mutualized; policyholders, however, actually exercise little control (Part 4, pp. 1296–1300, 1371–1378, 1389–1391, 1400–1407).
    a) Under the New York Law (which controls many of the principal companies) it is practically impossible for policyholders to elect directors who have not been selected by those already in office.

   b) Life insurance companies do little to inform policyholders of elections; fewer than $\frac{5}{100}$ of 1 percent ordinarily vote.

   c) There is apparently a need for reappraisal of election machinery to assure its functioning as originally intended.

3. Directors of mutual companies are selected to represent the interests of policyholders, but too often this responsibility has been disregarded (Part 4, pp. 1270–1279, 1412–1472; Part 13, pp. 6654–6657).

   a) In some of the largest companies directors have sought and exploited their posts for personal gain.

   b) The evidence revealed a need for measures to ensure that the interests of policyholders be adequately served.

4. Bigness of the insurance companies seems to be the goal and standard of successful management, and inadequate attention is given to the resultant problems (Part 4, pp. 1197, 1249, 1422, 1424; Part 13, pp. 6561, 6593; Part 28, pp. 14780–14782).

5. Selling practices have often been wasteful and harmful (Part 13, pp. 6513–6562).

   a) High-pressure and forced sales have sold many policies.

   b) The lapse ratio of insurance policies presents an alarming picture.

Monopolistic practices.—The Federal Trade Commission reviewed its experience with monopolies in the United States (Parts 5 and 5-A).

A. The Commission expressed its faith in the system of free enterprise and called for open and fair competition and for rigorous enforcement of the antitrust laws.

B. Its presentation was drawn from recent cases involving 59 cease and desist orders against monopolistic practices and restraints of trade (Part 5-A).

1. In spite of more than 50 years of the Sherman Act and its amendments, in the era from 1930 to 1938 monopoly was quite unabated.

2. Present-day monopoly devices include: tying contracts, uniform price agreements, conspiracies to control bids, price discrimination, base price systems, zoning systems, restriction of output, the blacklist, resale price maintenance, and threats of boycott (Part 5, p. 1724).

The liquor industry.—The FTC continued its study of monopolistic practices by investigating the liquor industry, revealing a striking example of oligopolistic control (Part 6).

A. In 1938 four large whiskey distilleries—Schenley Distillers Corporation, National Distillers Products Corporation, Joseph E. Seagram and Sons, Inc., and Hiram Walker and Sons, Inc.—operated 20 of the 97

distilleries in the United States and produced 60,000,000 gallons of the total of 94,990,000 (Part 6, p. 2436).

B. Whiskey producers maintained monopoly prices, charging what the traffic would bear (Part 6, pp. 2473–2479).

C. The industry made frequent use of exclusive contracts and resale price maintenance (Part 6, pp. 2551–2568).

The milk and poultry industries.—The FTC concluded its presentation of monopoly practices with a study of the milk and poultry industries (Part 7).

A. The rise of monopoly in milk distribution has been recent, resulting, in part, from the demand for improved hygienic standards (Part 7, pp. 2754–2763).

1. Most large cities passed ordinances requiring pasteurization plants.

2. Independent distributors found it inconvenient to meet the requirements of the law and today flourish only in smaller communities where pasteurization is not compulsory.

3. In 1923 the National Dairy Products Corporation was organized. It initiated a program of acquiring or building pasteurization plants throughout the country; it had acquired 360 dairy companies by 1938.

4. The Borden Company followed a similar program of acquiring control of the "gateways" through which commerce in milk must flow.

5. These two companies imposed monopoly prices wherever their control permitted.

   a) Delivered milk prices to consumers were relatively inflexible, even during the depression.

   b) Retail prices dropped but 20 percent during this period, but the prices paid to farmers dropped 50 percent (Part 7, p. 2800).

   c) The milk monopolies tightened their grip on both buying and selling prices (Part 7, pp. 2778–2779, 2797, 2855–2856, 2888–2889).

      i. When the National Dairy Products Corporation was organized in 1923, the dairy farmer received 52 percent of the consumer's milk dollar and the distributor, 48 percent (Part 7, p. 2800).

      ii. In 1933 the farmer received 35 percent and the distributor, 65 percent.

B. The poultry industry received scant attention by the Committee; these hearings constituted a study of racketeering quite as much as of monopoly (Part 7, pp. 2866–2881).

1. Testimony related to the New York poultry market, the country's largest market for live poultry.

2. About 30 commission merchants dominated the market.

3. Violence and organized sabotage were common methods of convincing others to co-operate.

Problems of the consumer.—The Department of Agriculture was allotted $8,000 for a study of consumer problems (Part 8).

A. Testimony was developed from various sources: a manufacturer, a purchasing agent, the director of a consumers' adviser agency, an executive of a mail order house, and four housewives.
B. Subjects considered included grade labeling, consumer standards, advertising, resale price maintenance, and consumer organizations.
C. A main theme of the hearings was that the consumer is insufficiently informed.
   1. He is no longer able to make wise choices on the basis of his senses.
   2. Packaging, descriptive terms, and prices are deceptive (Part 8, pp. 3293, 3298, 3315–3320, 3327).
D. A plea was made for standard grading and labeling.
   1. The consumer needs assurance of a fair return for the allocation of his limited income.
   2. Honest, accurate, and meaningful grade labels can be developed with great advantage to the consumer (Part 8, p. 3352).
E. The recent development of an organized consumer movement has brought with it those who would exploit the consumer.
   1. Pseudo consumer organizations have operated with disguised purposes (Part 8, pp. 3376–3396).
   2. Frequently testing and approval organizations, instead of serving the consumer, have been clandestine schemes to promote particular products.
F. The Consumers' Counsel made the following recommendations (Part 8, p. 3454):
   1. Standards for consumer goods should be made available wherever practicable.
   2. Sizes of packages and containers should be standardized to eliminate deception and confusion.
   3. Resale price maintenance laws should be studied to determine their effects upon consumers.
   4. A study should be made of organizations purporting to be commodity rating agencies and of related problems.
   5. A central agency should be established in the Federal Government to foster and protect consumer interests.

Savings and investment.—The SEC conducted a study of savings and investment with relation to the problem of full employment (Part 9).

A. One of the most important phases of these hearings was devoted to an analysis of the causes and events of the Great Depression.
   1. Industrial capitalism has developed a high savings economy.

2. Savings either find profitable investment or they are hoarded.
3. If hoarded, they disappear from the economic stream and result in underemployment of men, resources, and machines.

B. The dynamics of capitalism requires continuous investment.
   1. Capitalism is distinguished from earlier types of economic organization by the volume of savings and investment which takes place.
   2. These vast savings ordinarily are concentrated among relatively few persons.
      a) The top 10 percent of America's families save 86 percent of the savings, whereas the poorest 80 percent account for only 2 percent of the savings.
      b) Institutional savings increasingly have become characteristic of the economy.
   3. Income which is neither spent nor invested creates unemployment.
      a) If spent for consumers' goods, it finds its way back into the economic stream and stimulates commercial and industrial activity.
      b) If invested, it is spent for capital goods and likewise reverts to the industrial stream.
      c) If hoarded, it is diverted and withheld from the economic stream, resulting in underemployment of men, resources, and machines.
   4. The two streams, savings and investment, are the keys to the economic dislocations of the day (Dr. Alvin Hansen, Part 9, pp. 3495–3520, 3538–3559, 3837–3859).
      a) That portion of the national income which is saved should be returned to the stream by the means of investment.
      b) The health of the economic system depends directly upon the continuous placing of large capital expenditures.
   5. The depression of 1929 was a unique phenomenon.
      a) It cannot be explained in terms of traditional business cycle analysis.
         i. The old forces which brought an end to previous depressions have disappeared with the new structural framework.
         ii. The formative period of capitalism has passed; the rapid expansion and opening of new territories have approached an end.

C. Procedures were recommended by Dr. Hansen to mitigate the impact of depressions (Part 8, pp. 3837–3859).
   1. There are 3 possible roads to full employment:
      a) Private capital outlays—expansion of plant and equipment in commercial manufacturing, mining, railroad, public utility, and residential construction.
      b) Public investment—self-liquidative or other public projects directly or indirectly productive.
      c) Community consumption—increasing the standard of living of the masses by means of social services, public health, public recreation, low-cost housing, etc.

    2. Whenever private investment fails to absorb the stream of savings, public investment should be employed to fill the breach.

D. Industry no longer is dependent upon private reservoirs of savings.

    1. Until recently American industry has gone to the financial markets and has depended upon the savings accumulated by individuals.

    2. Industry has begun to supply its own capital needs from new methods of internal finance.

        a) Between 1921 and 1937 Class I railroads expended about $10,000,000,000 on capital outlays for expansion, replacements, etc., 72 percent of which came from railroad income (Part 9, pp. 3565–3575).

        b) Under normal conditions, the United States Steel Corporation, with all its subsidiaries, is financially self-sufficient (Part 9, pp. 3576–3595).

        c) The electrical manufacturing industry not only has financed itself but also has retired millions of its preferred stocks and bonds (Part 9, pp. 3598–3631).

        d) The dynamic aircraft industry has been financed by interested corporations without the aid of public savings (Part 9, p. 3637).

        e) The automotive industries revealed that they have no need of the public market for their financing (Part 9, pp. 3657–3658).

    3. When industry no longer absorbs public savings, there results a great accumulation of idle funds which breeds idle men and idle machines.

The petroleum industry.—The American Petroleum Institute presented the industry's economic problem "from the point of view of business and industry itself" (Parts 14, 14-A, 15, 15-A, 16, 17, 17-A).

A. The petroleum industry presents a striking example of concentration of economic resources and power.

    1. In 1938 the 20 great integrated companies owned more than 66 percent of the nation's petroleum-producing assets.

    2. They dominated 72 percent of the crude oil pipe-line mileage.

    3. They controlled 96 percent of the refinable crude oil and 83 percent of the production of gasoline (Part 14, pp. 7103, 7171).

B. Independent dealers have been subjected to "squeeze" tactics by the integrated companies who have endeavored to keep crude oil prices up and those of refined oil down (Part 14, pp. 7228, 7266–7269, 7292, 7305–7306, 7336, 7367–7369; Part 15, pp. 8152, 8232; Part 16, p. 8848).

    1. Independent retail dealers are gradually being eliminated.

        a) Integrated companies, in effect, have subsidized the retail sale of products at their own outlets.

        b) Independents have been forced to operate on narrow margins.

        c) Independents have been required to sell but one line of product, that of a major company.

   d) If they fail to fall in line, various devices have been used to
   coerce them.
C. Price leadership is a monopoly device commonly resorted to in the
   petroleum industry (Part 14, pp. 7224, 7281, 7369, 7417–7419; Part 15,
   pp. 8431–8433, 8437; Part 16, pp. 8880, 8888, 8949, 8952, 8961, 8965,
   8972–8974, 9040, 9045–9047, 9055; Part 17, p. 9400).
   1. In each producing field the company which has the largest interest
      in the purchase of crude oil usually sets prices and acts as price
      leader.
   2. A similar situation obtains in the gasoline retailing industry.
      a) Usually the largest seller in a given region is the leader.
      b) The majors work without written agreement, merely using a
      common set of policies and procedures.
D. The oil monopolist has been aided by arrangements with the railroads
   and state conservation authorities (Part 14, pp. 7116, 7127, 7135–7136,
   7139–7141, 7191, 7283, 7343, 7362–7366; Part 15, pp. 8184–8185, 8188,
   8208, 8211, 8226, 8230–8232, 8315, 8364).
   1. Major refiners have arrived at understandings with railroads pro-
      viding for reciprocal destruction of each other's competitors—truck-
      ers and independent refiners.
   2. State programs of oil conservation have been converted into agencies
      of price and supply control; wells have been shut down in response
      to price changes and marketing pressures.
E. Pipe lines play a significant role in the petroleum industry.
   1. There is marked concentration of ownership and control.
      a) Ninety-six percent of the gasoline pipe lines are in the hands of
      16 major producers.
      b) Fifty-seven percent of the crude oil gathering pipe-line mileage
      and 89 percent of the crude oil trunk line mileage are controlled
      by the 20 majors.
   2. Pipe lines almost exclusively serve the major integrated companies;
      several factors tend to prevent independents from using them (Part
      14, p. 7251; Part 17, p. 9381).
      a) Absence of pipe-line facilities near independent refineries.
      b) Loading of existing facilities to capacity by their owners.
      c) High minimum tender requirements (Part 15, p. 8300; Part 17,
      p. 9758).
   3. Pipe-line earnings are remarkably high (Part 14, pp. 7106, 7237–
      7238, 7257, 7262–7263, 7376; Part 14-A, p. 7725; Part 15, pp. 8247,
      8303, 8306; Part 16, pp. 8841–8842, 8849; Part 17, pp. 9715–9717,
      9755, 9759–9760).
      a) In 1938 major pipe-line companies earned 28 percent on the de-
      preciated value of their investment.
      b) Frequently these earnings were at the expense of the inde-
      pendents.
      i. Transportation rates were in excess of cost, and out of line
      with those ordinarily allowed to regulated common carriers.

c) Pipe-line profits, in effect, were used to subsidize other operations of the majors.

The iron and steel industry.—The most extensive hearings conducted by the TNEC related to the iron and steel industry (Parts 8, 19, 20, 26, 27).

A. Ten large corporations dominate the production of iron ore and steel in the United States.
  1. These 10 corporations own 88 percent of the total assets of the steel industry.
  2. Forty percent of these assets are owned by one company, the United States Steel Corporation, and 15 percent are owned by the second largest, the Bethlehem Steel Corporation.
  3. These 10 companies co-operate to restrict output and to fix prices; they maintain a common front before consumer, laborer, and Government officials.
B. The industry has maintained unusually rigid prices; price leadership has been common (Part 18, p. 10439).
  1. By general consent the Lake Erie base price for iron ore has been accepted by all producers, the first substantial sale of iron ore each year constituting the price for the season (Part 18, pp. 10305–10311).
  2. The basing-point system is the most prominent method of price control in the steel industry (Part 18, pp. 10611–10620).
    a) It is the practice whereby all producers charge identical delivered prices at the various destinations to which steel is sold and shipped.
    b) These prices are computed from the agreed price at a designated basing-point plus freight charges from the basing-point to the point of delivery.
    c) Overt evidence of conspiracy is thereby avoided though there is a meeting of minds to control the market.
  3. Following the Pittsburgh plus decision, in 1924, the steel industry adopted the multiple basing-point system.
    a) Several basing-points are established, each serving a particular territory instead of one for the whole area.
    b) The FTC contends that this system is a violation of the Pittsburgh plus order and that the basing-point system should be abolished.
  4. The Steel Corporation defended the basing-point system before the TNEC (Part 19, pp. 10509–10512). It asserted that:
    a) The base prices are not consistently collected.
    b) There is a material difference between nominal or base prices and realized prices.
    c) Though base prices are held rigid, competition exists in the form of price concessions and departures from the base.

C. The United States Steel Corporation retained Dr. Theodore Yntema, economist from the University of Chicago, and his staff to present steel's case to the TNEC (Part 26, pp. 13586–13617).
   1. He contended that the demand for steel is inelastic and that the quantity of steel that can be sold is relatively unresponsive to changes in the level of steel prices.
   2. He argued that much of the total unit cost of steel is variable or out-of-pocket cost which does not decline materially as total production increases.
   3. Price reductions for steel, therefore, would be of little avail.
      a) Demand or employment would not be stimulated.
      b) Gross income to the steel people would not increase.
      c) Steel costs would rise as production increases.
      d) Steel profits would be reduced, or deficits would increase.
   4. Government economists criticized the defense by Dr. Yntema (Part 26, pp. 13618–13622, 13630, 13694–13709, 13773–13789).
      a) The analysis was arrived at *post hoc* to rationalize a monopoly price policy of years standing.
      b) Many untested assumptions enter into the Steel Corporation's analysis.
         i. The computations of fixed and variable costs are by necessity estimates or statistical guesses.
         ii. Dr. Yntema's calculations are derived from cost data neither intended for nor suitable to the type of analysis attempted.

War and prices.—After the outbreak of the war, in September, 1939, President Roosevelt requested the TNEC to watch prices of basic materials (Part 21).

A. A careful study was made of the effect of war on prices.
   1. An analysis of wartime trends and the consequent economic dislocations of the first World War was presented.
   2. Witnesses from representative industries agreed that price increases, as in the previous war, should be avoided if possible.
B. After the organization of the new Defense Council the Committee was relieved of its responsibilities (*Final Report,* p. 82).

Investment banking.—The study of investment banking was conducted by the SEC (Parts 22–24).

A. The purpose of the inquiry was threefold:
   1. To study the manner in which investment banking processes have been adjusted to conform with the provisions of the Banking Act of 1933.
   2. To determine the extent to which concentration exists in investment banking.

3. To discover the manner in which business is conducted in the under-writing field.

B. A study was made of the degree of compliance with the Banking Act of 1933 requiring separation of security affiliates (Part 22, p. 11402; Part 24, p. 12444).

1. Brown Brothers Harriman and Company continued its securities activities under a new name (Part 22, pp. 11385–11400).

   a) Before 1933 it was a partnership engaged in both commercial and investment banking.

   b) After 1933 it organized a new corporation to deal with securities under the name of Brown Harriman and Company, which continued to do business at the old address.

   c) It is questionable whether the spirit, intent, and purpose of the Banking Act had been observed.

2. Another case is that of the First National Bank of Boston (Part 22, pp. 11512–11524).

   a) This bank underwent a similar token reorganization.

   b) A new security corporation was organized under the name of the First Boston Corporation.

   c) The personnel and location remained unchanged, continuing operation as before.

3. A third case involved the Bankers Trust Company of New York (Part 24, pp. 12417–12453).

   a) Before 1933 it had engaged in the underwriting business; after that it retained an interest in security sales through an ingenious agency device.

   b) This enabled the bank to organize underwriting syndicates, to participate in underwriting profits, and to build up reciprocal obligations among underwriters.

4. Another case concerned J. P. Morgan and Company (Part 22, pp. 11550–11554, 11577–11581, 11583–11584, 11777; Part 23, pp. 11928–11978, 12008–12010, 12020–12046).

   a) After 1933 the Morgan Company elected to discontinue its security business; a new firm, the Morgan Stanley and Company, was incorporated to handle these operations.

   b) Three Morgan partners controlled more than 60 percent of the common stock in the new firm, which in essence was a closed corporation.

   c) This new firm took over the bulk of the business done by J. P. Morgan and Company, the same individuals carrying on.

   d) The old Company, however, continued to play a significant role in the underwriting field, advising and guiding funding and re-funding operations.

   e) Evidence seemed to indicate that J. P. Morgan and Company continued to exercise a powerful influence over the underwriting business of the nation.

C. A special analysis was made of concentration in the underwriting and sale of registered securities (Part 24, pp. 12689–12710).

   1. Between 1934 and 1937 about $10,000,000,000 worth of securities were registered with the SEC.

   2. Ninety-six percent of these were sold to the public through the channels of investment banking syndicates.

      a) The great majority of the 730 members of the Investment Bankers Association shared only a small portion of this market.

         i. Six firms, or 1 percent, managed 57 percent of the total registered issues handled by investment bankers; 14 additional firms managed 21 percent of the total.

         ii. Five percent, or 38 firms, managed 91 percent of registered securities; 692 of the 730 underwriters managed but 9 percent of the issues.

      b) Even greater concentration exists in the management of better-quality securities.

         i. The Morgan Stanley and Company managed 27 percent of all grades of bonds, but 65 percent of the best grades.

         ii. The 18 leading New York firms managed 85 percent of the first-grade bond issues, but only 65 percent of all grades.

D. Monopoly trends in finance banking are far-reaching.

   1. Evidence demonstrates the dominant position of Morgan. When investment bankers sought privileges, they appealed to the "corner"; when the "corner" ordered, the others complied (Part 22, pp.11583–11584, 11586, 11589, 11593–11594; Part 23, p. 11872).

   2. Competition is not tolerated, and banks are not permitted to poach on each other's reserves (Part 24, p. 12484).

      a) Once an underwriter secures the business of a client, that business is considered his property.

      b) Firms attempting to change underwriters ordinarily meet with discouragement.

      c) Shopping around by clients to obtain competitive offers is looked upon with disfavor (Part 24, pp. 12504–12508).

      d) It is "unethical and bad business to compete" (Part 24, pp. 12482, 12487).

   3. Syndicates formed to market securities for a firm acquired what in effect became a vested right to the same proportionate distribution of all future business of that firm.

      a) Once a syndicate for a firm, always a syndicate; once a member of the syndicate, always a member (Part 22, p. 11507).

      b) Once a proportionate share of the syndicate distribution, always the same proportionate share (Part 22, pp. 11569, 11592–11603; Part 23, pp. 11865, 11973, 12214–12215; Part 24, p. 12343).

         i. Prior to 1920 six underwriters dominated the marketing of A. T. & T. securities, each handling about the same proportionate share (Part 23, pp. 11861, 11893).

         ii. Following a meeting in 1920, dominated by Morgan, subse-

quent issues of A. T. & T. were handled in a quite identical
manner (Part 23, pp. 11892, 11911, 12214, 12219, 12234).

   iii. A similar group shared almost as rigidly in the issues of the
Chicago Union Station Company (Part 22, pp. 11438, 11461,
11641).

  c) Members in syndicates appointed their own successors in subsequent underwritings (Part 22, pp. 11454, 11462–11470).

4. Investment banking houses kept records (cuff books) of participation awarded them and made allocation on a *quid pro quo* basis of
issues which they themselves managed.

Cartels.—The TNEC staff conducted the study of cartels (Part 25).

A. Several types of cartels have come to be recognized (Part 25, pp. 13040–
13045):
1. Term-fixing or trade-practice cartels regulate the methods of conducting business among the members and the terms of sale, such as
terms of payment, discounts, penalties for arrears, terms of credit,
conditions of guaranty, delivery of free goods, servicing and service
charges, packing, and allowance on returns.
2. Price fixing or price cartels are alliances which regulate sales prices;
a variety of methods are used, such as: the open price system, uniform cost accounting systems, and the "bid depository."
3. The customer dividing or the territorial cartel, sometimes called
the zone cartel, has been used in the cement, brick, sand, and gravel
industries.
4. Production or production control cartels are combinations among
producers to limit production in accordance with some agreed plan.
5. The syndicate or the centralized sales cartel is illustrated by the
basing-point system, known in the steel industry as the Pittsburgh
plus system.
6. The profit cartel is in reality a pool.
7. International cartels are supercartels functioning in the world
market.

B. Conditions favorable to cartel organization (Part 25, pp. 13038, 13087,
13350).
1. The market must show some degree of inelasticity of demand.
2. The product ordinarily needs to be standardized and easily defina-
ble as to its character, quality, and content, such as copper, pig iron,
nitrate, and light bulbs.
3. Industries in which there are heavy overhead or fixed costs are most
likely to be cartelized.
4. Prospective members must show a certain receptiveness to concerted
and collective action.

C. Benefits sought and often realized from cartels were summarized as
follows (Part 25, pp. 13081–13082):
1. Production costs are lower because of product standardization, pro-

duction controls, reduction of competitive overexpansion, reduction of risk, research, patent pools, and managerial co-operation.

2. Marketing costs are lower because of advertising economies, uniformity of terms of sale, allocation of markets, and intercartel agreements.

3. Cyclical fluctuations are smoothed out by adjusting productive capacity to consumption, by stabilizing employment, and by control of prices.

D. The cartel type of industrial organization is not new in the United States. The term "cartel" has lacked definiteness and clarity in use, however; cartels have been common in everything but in name (Part 25, pp. 13310–13347).

1. There is little but terminology to distinguish pools from cartels.

   a) Formal agreements have resulted in uniform prices, restriction of output, allocation of markets, and division of territory.

   b) Such industrial alliances have been found in the following industries: iron and steel, meat, nails, glass bottles, petroleum, sugar, tobacco, whiskey, and gun powder.

2. Trade associations have functioned as price cartels.

   a) In 1938 there were about 2,000 national trade associations in the United States.

   b) The associations collect for their members a wide variety of statistics which are sometimes used to harness the industry for monopolistic ends.

   c) Association members often agree on uniform terms of sale, covering such matters as credit terms, cash discounts, customer classifications, quantity discounts, trade-in values, sales contracts, allowances, and guarantees.

   d) Between 1930 and 1940, 65 industries were found by the FTC to have employed trade associations to restrain trade (Part 25, pp. 13315–13318).

3. The NRA codes constituted compulsory cartelization (Part 25, pp. 13319–13335).

   a) Trade associations were dominant in drafting and organizing the codes; in 600 out of 850 codes the code secretary and the association's chief executive were one.

   b) New associations were born, and small associations were integrated into larger with increased power and prestige.

   c) Price and market control was often a first objective of these oligopolies.

      i. All the 850 codes studied effected some regulation over terms of sale.

      ii. Five hundred and sixty carried provisions designed to govern prices.

      iii. More than 400 required the usual "period of intimidation" before listed prices could be changed.

4. The Webb-Pomerene Act exempted from the antitrust laws associa-

tions of producers engaging solely in export trade (Part 20, p. 10923).

   a) Such associations have included the Copper Exporters, Inc.; the Steel Export Corporation; the Sugar Export Corporation; the Cement Export Company, Inc.; the Rubber Export Association; and the Plate Glass Export Corporation.

   b) These associations, combining as they did the principal domestic producers, worked in close harmony in the home market as well (Part 25, pp. 13131–13132, 13157).

     i. Members of the Copper Export Association acted in concert with respect to production policy.

     ii. The Steel Exporters Association entered into an agreement to exclude foreign producers from the United States market (Part 20, pp. 10947–10953).

       a) This cartel sought in conjunction with the international cartel to extend its control over the domestic market by forcing reluctant producers into the combine or by liquidating them (Part 20, p. 10958).

Interstate trade barriers.—The Department of Commerce was requested to investigate and present testimony concerning the character, extent, and effects of interstate trade barriers (Part 29).

A. An interstate trade barrier has been defined as a statute, regulation, or practice which operates or tends to operate to the disadvantage of persons, products, or commodities coming from sister states to the advantage of local residents or industries (Part 29, p. 15736).

  1. Usually the purpose of such barriers is to grant some special group within the state a preferred position to the disadvantage of others beyond the state boundary.

  2. They ordinarily result in disadvantage to domestic consumers, who are thereby restricted to a narrower market.

B. Trade barriers fall into 4 principal categories (Part 29, p. 15780):

  1. Statutes which obviously are discriminatory or retaliatory and are openly directed against out-of-state trade.

  2. Statutes which apparently are not discriminatory on paper, but are definitely so in operation.

    a) They often impose some special marketing regulation, as in the case of dairy products and margarine.

    b) Their ostensible purpose is the protection of public welfare.

  3. Statutes which apply equally to residents and nonresidents but which burden out-of-state business because of their diversity in the several states.

  4. Statutes not discriminatory in purpose or effect, but which may be made so through discriminatory administration.

C. The principal motive for the erection of trade barriers is to protect the domestic market for the benefit of a particular economic group.

D. There are several outstanding examples of trade barriers.

1. A rather pitiful example, because of the burden it lays upon the poor, is the taxation of oleomargarine.
   a) Many states have imposed taxes.
   b) The Federal Government has levied a tax of 10 cents per pound on colored margarine.
   c) Twenty-three states have adopted excise taxes varying from 5 cents on uncolored margarine to 15 cents on all margarines (Part 29, pp. 15851, 16138).
   d) Licenses of from $1.00 to $1,000 a year have been imposed; 9 states require a license by the manufacturer; 16 states, by the wholesaler; 13, by the retailer; 6 require licenses by restaurants and boarding houses; 1, Wisconsin, requires a license of consumers who purchase margarine.
   e) The motive and the effect is to suppress commerce in this product by taxing it out of existence (Part 29, pp. 15832–15834, 15853–15855, 15861, 16136–16139).
2. Barriers to interstate motor transport result from the multiplicity of diverse taxes, licenses, and regulatory laws (Part 29, pp. 15790–15792, 15803–15810, 16127–16131).
3. Several states have established ports of entry and highway checking stations (Part 29, p. 15812).
4. The power of inspection at times has constituted a trade barrier and has even been used as an embargo (Part 29, pp. 15794–15795).
5. Another type of barrier is created by laws granting preferential treatment to local products and merchants (Part 29, p. 15813).
6. Other barriers are regulations and taxes on various forms of advertising, quarantine and inspection regulations, definitions and standards, state of origin and similar legislation, and direct selling regulations and prohibitions.

E. Trade barriers appear to be on the increase (Part 29, pp. 15740 15748, 15767, 15797).

F. The economic effects of trade barriers are serious.
   1. Mass production, standardization, low-cost production and marketing, and general efficiency owe a great deal to the wide markets made possible by the Federal free-trade system; barriers tend to choke and strangle this system (Part 29, pp. 15743–15773).
   2. Many instances of retaliation and economic warfare have characterized this struggle between the states (Part 29, pp. 15745–15770, 15774, 15892, 16083, 16092).

G. Several important suggestions were offered for the removal of trade barriers (Part 29, pp. 15751, 15987, 15990–15992, 16091; *see also* the *Final Report,* pp. 342–351).
   1. Greater co-operation among states to secure uniform standards of weight, quality, and public safety.
   2. Reciprocity among states with respect to licensing, inspection, taxing, etc., to reduce the cumulative burden of local requirements.

3. The organization of a joint committee to study the general problem and make recommendations.

Technology and concentration of economic power.—The TNEC staff conducted hearings on technology and its social consequences (Part 30).

A. The "steady improvement in technology has been the distinguishing mark of our time. No generation in history has seen anything to compare with the advance of science and invention accomplished during this generation" (Part 30, p. 16207); nevertheless, "we still have not learned how to apply the wonders of technology to the abundance of nature" (Part 30, p. 16208).

B. Thanks to modern technology the manpower productivity of Western countries has increased steadily for nearly 200 years, and today this improvement seems as dynamic as ever (Part 30, pp. 16229, 16883, 16904).

C. Man, however, has often been a victim of the machine process.
   1. The long-run social advantage of technology is great, but the problem of the displaced worker is vital.
   2. The TNEC confirmed the conclusion of the Industrial Commission of 1898 that industrialization destroyed labor skills (Part 30, pp. 16221–16222, 16341).
      a) In the automobile industry the tendency is increasingly toward lower skilled occupations (Part 30, p. 16386); Edsel Ford testified that only about 10 percent of the workers engaged in producing automobiles need to be skilled (Part 30, p. 16341).
      b) This trend has unfortunate social consequences:
         i. The laborer receives less satisfaction from his job.
         ii. He receives less purchasing power.
         iii. The concentration of economic power is intensified as control over production passes from worker to capitalist.
   3. Displaced workers fail to find jobs.
      a) The testimony of Michael Russell, "an exhibit of human wreckage," demonstrates that a man who has worked years to acquire a skill finds it difficult, if not impossible, to secure employment when displaced (Part 30, p. 16460).
      b) If the net productivity of mechanical innovation fails to be passed on the public, machines and invention create unemployment (Part 30, pp. 16252–16253).
      c) Between 1923 and 1929 only 91 new men were employed in industries for every 100 displaced (Part 30, pp. 16246–16247).
   4. The burden of technological unemployment should be borne, not by the individual, but by society at large, according to Dr. Lubin (Part 30, pp. 17252, 17260).
      a) A manufacturer, an economist, and a labor leader urged that the

dismissal wage be employed to alleviate the distress of technological unemployment (Part 30, pp. 16448–16454, 16748–16755, 17136, 17263).

b) Dr. Lubin would make dismissal compensation compulsory, comparing it to workmen's compensation and accident insurance.

c) Fifteen countries have already adopted such measures.

d) Spokesmen for various American firms endorsed the principle of the dismissal wage and described its use in their industries.

CHAPTER V

THE ECONOMIC
SETTING

SHORTLY BEFORE the death of ex-President Coolidge he made a most provocative statement. His apparent bewilderment characterized a people and an age unable to achieve orientation in the swift current of change induced by the technological revolution. His statement revealed the temper of a people rushing from an epoch of unstable prosperity into a period of depression, with consequent disorganization and despair. The former President said, "We are in a new era to which I do not belong. When I read of the new-fangled things that are popular now, I realize that my time in public affairs is past. I wouldn't know how to handle them if I were called upon to do so." We are in a new age. We are called upon to cope with the problems of that age. Great technological changes have been effected, requiring momentous social and institutional adjustments.

Cultural anthropologists speak of a problem—the social lag—which arises when the institutional and functional aspects of the social pattern get out of kilter with regard to the mechanical and the technical. Modern techniques of production are calling forth new schemes of social organization. It would seem, nevertheless, that the patterns of thought which guided statesmen of the nineteenth century have become more deeply entrenched in the thinking of the twentieth. Leon Henderson described the more salient of these habit patterns as the basic assumptions underlying the organization of our economic society: [1] (1) reliance in the ability of individuals, in free association, to design affirmatively the main forms and directions of life; (2) faith in the efficacy of private property and freedom of contract; (3) the assumption of equality of bargaining power; (4) belief that the pursuit of self-interest will serve the community interest; (5) belief in holding the rules of the game to a minimum; and (6) faith in the function of price and the market place to bring about the best combination and allocation of productive resources.

However much these assumptions may or may not have been satis-

[1] *Hearings before the Temporary National Economic Committee,* Part 1, pp. 157–183.

factorily adapted to their day, there is no gainsaying the fact that technologically the twentieth century has departed radically from that of the nineteenth. In the place of the handicraft system has come mass-method machine production; in the place of the individualistic entrepreneur of the Adam Smith type has come the joint stock company, thence the giant corporation and the ultra-complex holding company. In the place of a predominantly agrarian economy has come a highly industrialized society. In the place of relatively simple mechanical devices, such as spinning jennies, power looms, and cotton gins, have appeared giant rotary presses, flying fortresses, giant power projects, and blast furnaces. Everywhere the setting, from which was born the economic ideology and methodology of the nineteenth century, has undergone far-reaching and fundamental changes. Despite these great industrial changes, the habits of mind, the thought patterns, of the past century project themselves into the modern age. The illusion of the nineteenth century perpetuates itself.

The illusion takes several forms. First, it is sometimes assumed that there was a period in the past when a freely competitive, laissez-faire system existed which functioned quite satisfactorily in the allocation of resources. Secondly, it is assumed that a set of rules or principles adapted to one epoch of social and industrial evolution is satisfactorily adjusted to a later and more advanced stage. Third, the facile and escapist legerdemain is sometimes adopted of interpreting the complex pattern of social institutions of the day in terms of the simple economy of yesterday. Writers and men in public office often assume the existence of an automatic self-adjusting economy and in so doing assume the nonexistence of important problems.

This flight from the reality of a complex modern economy finds a counterpart in a fetish relating to economic organization. The fetish is competition. It is a sort of emotional, cultlike, uncritical acceptance and repetition of the notion that competition is characteristic, feasible, and desirable. Even the monopolists who appeared before the TNEC seriously spoke and thought in terms of a competitive pattern, apparently unable to grasp the reality and the extent of monopoly control in the modern scheme of organization. Then, there is the unchallenged premise, so often expressed, that competition is feasible—feasible in a world of the heavy industry and mass production techniques so characteristic of the twentieth century. There is the belief that competition is not only feasible but also desirable. Throughout the TNEC inquiry no one appeared to subject these basic questions

to searching analysis. Hearings and testimony proceeded with established preconceptions as to the role competition should play. The illusion of the nineteenth century was a point of departure for the problem-solvers of the twentieth.

Certain portions of the TNEC hearings serve to emphasize how different the modern economy is from the simple, automatic, self-correcting, laissez-faire concept which still grips the minds of many economists, statesmen, and business men. In the place of an individualistic economy we find an age of corporacy characterized by great masses of property intricately organized around a legal fiction —the corporation. In the place of free association among men we find great combinations of trade associations conspiring together in ways undreamed of by Adam Smith. In the place of a simple, relatively stable economy of shopkeepers and craftsmen we find a dynamic technology swept along by a swiftly moving stream of inventions, innovations, and discoveries guided by a small army of technicians who are giving us a new "planned economy," at least on the mechanical side. Instead of a world of relatively free competition we find one which pays lip service to that ideal, but readily embraces anticompetitive practices.

AN AGE OF CORPORACY

Little can be done in this section except to emphasize what the reader already knows. Corporations are so familiar that we take them for granted, and having done so we proceed to think of them in terms of natural individuals and neglect the social implications of these great creatures of the law. The age of individualism, if one ever existed, has given way to an age of corporacy. As individualism was submerged in the tribal commune, in the labor gangs who built the pyramids, on the medieval manor, and in socialistic experiments such as Sunnybrook Farm and Soviet Russia, so it is set aside in this day of corporacy. Men work in great co-operative enterprises, not as free competitive producers, but as wage earners, frequently of a great combination created under a charter granted by the state.

The corporation is characteristic of the modern economy. The old individualistic producer remains, however, as a remnant of the Smithite economy; in fact, the individual is numerically more in evidence than the corporation. There are about 6,000,000 farmers in America —mostly individual enterprisers. In mining, manufacturing, wholesale trade, retail trade, and the service industries there are about

2,000,000 firms; [2] most of them are individuals or partnerships in business. Corporations number about 500,000. But even numerically, the corporation is becoming more characteristic. Whereas the number of firms, including corporations, increased only 45 percent between 1910 and 1930, the number of corporations increased by 90 percent. When one considers the difference in the volume of production and the economic power of the corporation, the comparison becomes even more one-sided.

Numerically small though the corporation may be, it is by no means insignificant. In many of our most important industries the corporation dominates the field; it accounts for 90 percent or more of production in the electric power, communication, mining, manufacturing, and transportation industries. In finance it accounts for 84 percent of the business, and in trade, 58 percent. An estimate of

TABLE 1. IMPORTANCE OF CORPORATE ACTIVITY
(*In designated industries, 1937*)

Industry	Percentage of Business Done by Corporations in Each Industry
Electric light and power and manufactured gas	100
Communication	100
Mining	96
Manufacturing	92
Transportation	89
Finance	84
Government	58
Trade	58
Contract construction	36
Service	30
Miscellaneous	33
Agriculture	7

Source: *Hearings before the Temporary National Economic Committee,* Part 1, p. 96.

the total volume of business for the entire country indicates that corporations account for nearly 65 percent. On the basis of production we are indeed in an age of corporacy.

Likewise, from the standpoint of those who employ workers, this is an age of corporacy. Twenty-five percent of those who employ wage earners employ but one worker; corporations account for virtually none of this group. At the other extreme, 195 employers, or about one one-hundredth of 1 percent of the total, employ more than 10,000

[2] *Ibid.,* Part 1, pp. 83–100.

employees each and account for more than 12 percent of all employees; corporations account for substantially all of this group. In other words, 25 per cent of the employers employ 1 percent of the employees, 50 percent employ 4 percent of the employees, and 76 percent of the employers employ 11 percent. Still another contrast: 50 percent of the employers (the smallest) employ only 4 percent of the workers, whereas nine-tenths of 1 percent of the employers (the largest) employ 50 percent of the workers. The age of corporate employment is here and with it a materially different world from that envisioned by the physiocrats.

The corporation is an artificial creature of the state, created to perform an essential social function. It has no power other than that granted to it. Created as a fictitious person, clothed with some of the privileges of natural persons, by court action and lenient legislation it has gradually gathered more and more privileges. The assets of some corporations are greater than the total wealth of the states in which they are privileged to do business. Many have grants of power which no state would have sanctioned fifty years ago. Some have entered into "treaties," cartels, and other arrangements with foreign countries and foreign corporations which constitute acts beyond the legal power even of the states which awarded them their charters.

THE IMPORTANCE OF THE TRADE ASSOCIATION

Obviously to speak of this as an age of corporacy is to give an incomplete characterization. Long ago corporations grouped themselves together in combinations for co-operative, monopolistic, or predatory purposes—ofttimes for the latter. Pools, trusts, holding companies, and other types of combination have had their day, but quietly and quite unobtrusively there has risen a new type of association, less obvious in its control and less ruthless in its elimination of competition, whose influence and mastery of industry remains unrecognized. The trade association functions in an atmosphere of co-operation and congeniality and renders a number of useful services, with the result that its less desirable activities often pass unnoticed.

A trade association has been defined as a voluntary, nonprofit organization of enterprises engaged in a particular type of business. Such enterprises may be individuals, partnerships, or corporations, and in nearly all associations are competitors.[3] Trade associations may or may not be incorporated. Since they are composed of competing

[3] Temporary National Economic Committee Monograph No. 18, p. 1.

or erstwhile competing enterprisers, the associations, themselves, produce and sell no goods and make no profits; trade associations are service organizations operated for the benefit of their members. Ordinarily they are financed by dues paid by the members, usually in proportion to sales, output, capital, payroll, or some similar standard. They are administered by governing boards chosen by the members and usually employ staffs of varying size.

Probably the most significant development toward cartels in America during the present century has been the rise of trade associations. They developed during the latter part of the nineteenth century, but at that time tended principally to be social gatherings or clandestine arrangements. The enunciation of the "rule of reason" by the Supreme Court in 1911 and the publication of the book *The New Competition*,[4] recommending the development of price reporting organizations, gave momentum to the trade association movement. It is estimated that in 1938 there were about 7,800 trade associations in the United States;[5] nearly 6,000 of these were local organizations, whereas about 2,000 were national in scope.

In its ascent to power the trade association is indebted to government sponsorship and aid. During the administrations of Presidents Coolidge and Hoover trade associations were encouraged; the latter, first as Secretary of Commerce and later as Executive, championed the associations and put the services of his department at their disposal. This was the period which one historian called that of "government alliance with the great trade associations," or, as Mr. Hoover characterized it, "passing from a period of extreme individualistic action into a period of associated activities." The second period of government sponsorship occurred during the days of the NRA, when the associations took the initiative in drafting and presenting the codes. Old associations took on new life, and new ones rose to power and affluence. Most of the codes were administered by the associations, and often the code authority was an association executive.[6] Eventually the NRA was struck down by the Supreme Court, but many of the cartels thus created continued to operate.

The functions of trade associations might be grouped in two categories: the ostensible, or obvious, and the collusive, or clandestine. In other words, trade association activities might be classed as those making social contributions and those of a monopolistic and preda-

---

[4] *Hearings before the Temporary National Economic Committee,* Part 25, p. 13312.
[5] *Ibid.,* Part 1, p. 139.   [6] *Ibid.,* Part 25, pp. 13319–13321.

tory nature. The former functions are often publicized, whereas the latter are less tangible and are seldom admitted. The purpose of this section is to set forth the constructive and co-operative role of trade associations, but at the same time to emphasize that organizations capable of achieving these objectives are fraught with the potentialities of social abuses. These co-operative activities have included simplification and standardization of procedures and products, industrial research, interchange of patent rights, joint advertising, trade promotion, traffic information, codes of business ethics, settlement of disputes, co-operative insurance, joint representation before government bodies, labor relations activities, interchange of credit information, and collection and distribution of statistical information.

The TNEC hearings bear witness to the far-reaching influence and the broad ramifications of trade association activities. This is illustrated by their role before the Federal Trade Commission and their presentations to the TNEC. The Federal Trade Commission is charged by the Congress with the enforcement of the rules of fair competition. During the decade ended in 1938 the trade association was the frequent, if not the most common, instrument employed by those with monopolistic intent to "deprive individual sellers of their freedom to determine their output or prices at which they might sell, or to exclude others from the industry." The chairman of the FTC testified that most of the unlawful restraint cases which came to the Commission involved trade associations in one way or another.[7] A list of the industries wherein the associations were thus involved reads like a catalogue of the major industries of America.[8]

Likewise, the TNEC hearings themselves bear testimony to the influence of the trade associations. Each hearing and each volume appears to involve these organizations, and their role is more often dominant than secondary. In the patent hearings an important witness was a representative of the Automotive Parts and Equipment Manufacturers Association, which spoke for 375 member firms.[9]

Two trade associations represented the life insurance companies in the hearings relating to that industry: the Group Association and the Association of Life Insurance Presidents. The stated objective of the first was to "promote sound underwriting practices and to pre-

---

[7] *Final Report and Recommendations of the Temporary National Economic Committee*, p. 305.
[8] *Hearings before the Temporary National Economic Committee*, Part 25, p. 13318; see also Exhibit 2173 for a list of trade associations involved, p. 13560.
[9] *Ibid.*, Part 3, p. 1046.

vent abuses cropping up in business." The "abuses" it feared appear
to be almost any type of competition; the testimony indicates that this
organization endeavored quite successfully to establish uniform rates,
uniform contracts, and simultaneous rate increases.[10] The other organization was the Association of Life Insurance Presidents. This
powerful association, representing some of the greatest financial institutions in the world, succeeded in combining them for co-operative
projects. With an annual budget of nearly half a million dollars it
carried on a number of activities of questionable social serviceability.[11]
It lobbied successfully against savings bank insurance laws in Missouri, Pennsylvania, Rhode Island, New York, and elsewhere. It
compiled a "card index" of the members of the Florida legislature
while undertaking to defeat certain tax measures in that state, and
its ultimate control of the Georgia legislature by entertainment, campaign contributions, efforts to get elected men who "owe us something
instead of our owing them," and "seeing that their wives and daughters were looked after properly" is reminiscent of the days of
Credit Mobilier and the tactics of the railroads following the epoch
of the Granger laws.

Trade associations were very active in the hearings relating to the
liquor industry. The Distilled Spirits Institute [12] was organized under the aegis of the NRA; when the latter was overthrown by the
Court, it was survived by the trade association. The institute's annual
income approximated a quarter of a million dollars. It engaged in
extensive publicity and lobby activities and contributed to the system
of maintained prices characteristic of the whiskey industry.

The hearings devoted to the construction industry revealed the
operations of several such organizations. Here we even find a trade
association of trade associations: the National Small Homes Demon-
stration Committee, backed by the powerful United States Lumber
Manufacturers Association and the National Lumber Retailers Association. In one instance a locally organized association of retailers
of building materials [13] imposed uniform prices, required licenses
of all retailers (as though it were a public regulatory body), and generally controlled the trade. It appears that trade association activity
had about reached its zenith in the construction industry.[14] There
were three such organizations for general contractors, with about

10 *Ibid.*, Part 10, pp. 4153–4279.   11 *Ibid.*, pp. 4345–4447.
12 *Ibid.*, Part 6, pp. 2629–2654.   13 *Ibid.*, Part 11, pp. 5007–5012.
14 *Ibid.*, pp. 5227–5228.

2,500 members; there were eleven associations for subcontractors, with 15,000 members, and thirty-eight associations of distributors, with 45,000 members; in the building materials industry there were 133 associations.

Nowhere did the role of the trade associations show up more prominently than it did in the petroleum hearings which were initiated at the behest of one of them. As the chairman said, "The facts and opinions now presented have been selected not by the Committee or any of the agencies represented on the Committee, but by spokesmen of the oil industry . . . the American Petroleum Institute." [15] Here, as so often when business wishes to speak or act, it chose to function through a trade association. The Petroleum Institute described itself as the largest and most inclusive trade association of the petroleum industry; independent operators, however, described it as "dominated and controlled by major oil companies." [16] But this trade association was not the only one to be heard. When the independent petroleum dealers presented the problems they faced in a commercial world dominated by the majors, it was a trade association which spoke for them, the National Oil Marketers Association,[17] representing 250 independent concerns. Their story was strengthened by the testimony of 350 independent wholesale merchants (serving 2,200 retail outlets), who were represented by their organization, the Motor Equipment Wholesalers' Association,[18] and of similar groups, such as the Maryland Association of Petroleum Retailers [19] and the Petroleum Retailers Association.[20]

How the economy is intricately woven into a network of trade associations is illustrated by the testimony of Wilmer R. Schuh, a retail oil dealer. "I am a member of the Retail Gasoline Dealers Association of Milwaukee, which is a member of the Retail Gasoline Dealers Association of Wisconsin. This association is, in turn, a member of the National Association of Petroleum Retailers." [21] The latter association claimed to represent 10,000 dealers. How this particular association became a tool of the major oil companies, how it controlled price competition among its members and resorted to ruthless methods to fix prices, is one of the high lights of the findings of the TNEC.[22]

We are even confronted by a trade association in the powerful and highly concentrated steel industry, where a few great corporations

15 *Ibid.*, Part 14, p. 7097.   16 *Ibid.*, p. 7272.   17 *Ibid.*, Part 16, p. 8837.
18 *Ibid.*, p. 8921.   19 *Ibid.*, p. 8934.   20 *Ibid.*, p. 9023.
21 *Ibid.*, Part 17, p. 9430.   22 *Ibid.*, pp. 9435–9466.

dominate the field. A common method by which the steel companies maintain prices is the basing-point system. This system was implemented and administered by the Iron and Steel Institute. During the days of the NRA the code authority and the board of directors of the Steel Institute were one and the same. As part of its code of fair competition the steel industry endorsed and enforced the basing-point system. Long after the demise of the NRA the trade association continued to be the focus around which these price-fixing activities were continued.

It was aptly demonstrated in the cartel hearings that the trade association is the American counterpart of the German cartel. Although trade associations cropped up frequently in the other hearings as representatives of organized business, in the cartel hearings they themselves were the subject of study. Under the NRA these organizations reached their heydey and succeeded in the compulsory cartelization of industry, with the associations as the legally constituted agencies of control.[23] The legal basis for this control disappeared when the NRA was declared unconstitutional, but the cartels remained with little loss of vitality.

Even the investment bankers had their trade association. Its president testified, "I am president of the Investment Bankers Association of America, a voluntary association composed of 723 dealers in securities, having 1,410 offices located in 210 cities and in 40 States."[24] This highly organized group effected a harmony so complete that the underwriting field was divided among them by arrangements which stood unchallenged for years. They arrived at an unformulated code whereby competition was eliminated and "proprietary" interests became "frozen."

Nowhere, it seems, could the story of the American economy be told without involving trade associations. In the studies of interstate trade barriers it was the National Cottonseed Products Association[25] and the National Association of Margarine Manufacturers[26] who told of discriminations against oleomargarine. It was the National Association of Direct Selling Companies, with 225 members, who described the barriers against house-to-house distribution.[27] The American Trucking Association,[28] a federation of fifty-one different trade associations, the National Council of Private Motor Truck Owners, Inc.,[29] and the National Association of Motor Bus Operators, rep-

23 *Ibid.*, Part 25, pp. 13311–13325.   24 *Ibid.*, Part 23, p. 11887.
25 *Ibid.*, Part 29, p. 15824.   26 *Ibid.*, p. 15842.   27 *Ibid.*, p. 15965.
28 *Ibid.*, p. 16031.   29 *Ibid.*, pp. 16059, 16065.

resenting 600 member firms and numerous state associations, all joined forces to present an illuminating description of the numerous barriers erected against motor transport.[30] While trade associations were thus making public complaints against barriers which have damaged their economic interests, other associations were quietly working and lobbying to perpetuate these barriers and to erect others to assure themselves of the benefits such impediments create.

The trade association has performed a multiple role in the national economy; it is a research organization, a lobby, a statistical agency, a trade promotion unit, and a device of monopoly. But whatever role or roles it may choose to play, it is an element of tremendous influence in American economic life. It represents a scheme of collective bargaining, uniting corporations great and small; it creates an economic superstructure far removed from the system of craftsmen, shopkeepers, and individual enterprisers so essential to the thinking of the Manchester School.

A DYNAMIC ECONOMY

A third important characteristic of the American economy is its dynamic pace. Even the rapid changes one usually associates with the industrial revolution of the nineteenth century scarcely compare with the far-reaching innovations of the twentieth. Those of the nineteenth were noticeable because they were disruptive and catastrophic, whereas those of the present age come into a world accustomed to change. Throughout the reading of the TNEC hearings one is impressed again and again by this fact. Invention is the key to our times. When inventions were novel and unusual, they were disruptive and noteworthy; today they are commonplace and expected. The most significant innovation of the nineteenth century, according to Dr. Alfred North Whitehead,[31] was the "invention of the art of invention." Hitherto such contributions had ordinarily come from chance discoveries or from the brilliant observations of "cranks" and those who "tinkered." More recently there has evolved a new type of invention—that by analysis, research, and experimentation—a cold-blooded, calculated process guided by fixed rules and procedures. "It is this technique of scientific blue printing by means of involved chemical and mathematical formulas which has made the industrial research laboratory the creator of new processes and new products." [32]

Since the nineteenth century inventions have appeared with in-

30 *Ibid.*, p. 16065.   31 *Ibid.*, Part 30, p. 16212.   32 *Ibid.*, p. 16213.

creasing crescendo.[33] Lewis Mumford characterizes the century between 1830 and 1930 as a period of change from an eotechnic to a neotechnic age, with a paleotechnic age between.[34] In the eotechnic age, 1830–1840, power was derived principally from wind and water, and wood was the basic material of construction. The world and distances were large, measured by a land and sea travel speed of about ten miles per hour. Then came the use of coal, iron, limestone, and mechanical devices, and with them, the paleotechnic era. The world shrank because of a new and terrific land speed of sixty-five miles per hour and an ocean speed of thirty-five miles. But electric power, radio, biochemistry, and chemical interaction created a new order. With it came a more rapid pace, and the world again shrank in size because of the new travel distances on land and regular air speeds of two hundred miles per hour.

A few examples will illustrate how almost every aspect of the economy is undergoing constant change as a result of new techniques and new processes. Some of our most prominent industries are entirely engaged in the production of articles recently unknown. In its annual report for 1937 the Du Pont Company showed that 40 percent of its products were unheard of eight years earlier; these included Duco finisher, enamels, synthetic camphor, ponsol dyes, synthetic methanol, urea, viscose rayon, and cellophane.[35] The revolutionary nylon had not yet appeared, of course. The representative of a great business-machine manufacturer described a new automatic typewriter, capable of turning out twenty copies at a time. Textile producers told of new weaving processes enabling twelve workers to tend the same number of machines which had required forty-six attendants ten years previously, thereby increasing the output per worker by nearly three times in a decade.[36] Electric light utilities described how they had reduced coal consumption 40 percent per kilowatt-hour generated.[37]

Modern technology and invention have revolutionized labor productivity. A study by Carl Snyder shows that the productivity per worker in manufacturing was more than doubled between 1870 and 1930.[38] Another study, by Dr. Spurgeon Bell, indicates that in the twenty years preceding 1938 the productivity of labor increased more than 44 percent in manufacturing, 44 percent in railroads, 99 percent

---

[33] See the list of the most significant inventions since the tenth century, *ibid.*, pp. 16212, 17269 ff.
[34] *Ibid.*, pp. 16259–16260.   [35] *Ibid.*, p. 16241.   [36] *Ibid.*, p. 16882.
[37] *Ibid.*, p. 17188.   [38] *Ibid.*, p. 16223.

in mineral industries, 116 percent in electric light and power, 40 percent in the automobile industry, 51 percent in the steel industry, 55 percent in paper manufacturing, 38 percent in cotton textiles, and 153 percent in the tobacco industry.[39] Another investigation by the National Conference Board reveals that between 1923 and 1938 the man-hours required per ton of steel had declined 36 percent.[40] In the railroad industry more traffic is moving constantly with less labor. In the short period between 1933 and 1937 freight ton-miles and passenger miles increased about 50 percent, but the number of employees increased only 25 percent. These figures are hardly representative, because of the peculiar phase of the business cycle to which they apply; the trend, however, is illustrated by the fact that freight and passenger traffic declined 25 percent between the boom year 1929 and 1930, whereas employment dropped more than 40 percent.

A similar pattern with respect to labor productivity was revealed by the National Research Project of the WPA: "In terms of traffic units, the average output per work-hour increased from 109 in 1923 (on a 1920 basis) to 128 in 1929, to 140 in 1933, and to 175 in 1936." [41] These conclusions are borne out by the studies of the Bureau of Labor Statistics referred to below. Representatives of labor in the electrical manufacturing industry asserted that in 1939, as compared with ten years previously, the same work could be done with 24 percent fewer workers in producing electrical machinery and 50 percent fewer workers in making radios.[42] Dr Frederick C. Mills, of the National Bureau of Economic Research, found that between 1899 and 1929 man-hour productivity had increased 125 percent in manufacturing, an average increase of about 24 percent each decade; in the decade

TABLE 2. OUTPUT PER MAN-HOUR
(*1923–25 average = 100*)

Year	Manufacturing	Bituminous Coal Mining	Anthracite Mining	Steam Railroads
1909	62	67	85	
1914	72	75	90	75
1923	94	99	104	96
1929	120	107	100	114
1932	125	110	119	112
1936	140	119	149	140
1937	137	122	158	143

Source: *Hearings before the Temporary National Economic Committee*, Part 1, p. 223.

[39] *Ibid.*, p. 16220. [40] *Ibid.*, p. 16483. [41] *Ibid.*, p. 16904. [42] *Ibid.*, p. 16730.

ended in 1929, however, the rate had increased to 46 percent.[43] Still another study was that by the United States Bureau of Labor Statistics; Dr. Witt Bowden of that agency said, "Productivity in terms of average output per man-hour worked in 1936 was 32.8 percent greater than in 1926, and 80.9 percent greater than in 1916." [44] According to the Bureau, the output per man-hour in manufacturing increased from an index of 60 in 1909 to 140 in 1936, an increase of 130 percent in 27 years. In the coal industry output increased from an index of 69 to 122, and in railroads from 75 to 143 in a shorter period of 23 years.[45]

These are tremendous changes. No one would claim, however, that the economic system had made full utilization of existing plant and technology. Despite this underemployment of knowledge and constructed capacity these great advances have been achieved. Perhaps it is confusing the issue to speak of it as an increase in labor productivity, since in another sense it represents an increase of capital productivity. But inasmuch as the economy is run by men and presumably for men, it is realistic to talk of it as an increase of labor productivity. This suggests a new and basic problem which confronts this generation as it has confronted no age before it—what is to be done about the increased manpower productivity? It suggests that the number one problem of this age is that of devising ways to increase consumption by the average man commensurate with the increased productivity.

INDUSTRIAL RESEARCH

Since 1920 a good deal has been said about the desirability of a planned economy. In a technological sense we are rapidly approaching such an economy. Our institutional economy—by which is meant the manner in which we organize the material forces of production— is still primarily a process of trial and error, the heritage of political and social evolution. But rapidly on the technological side the economy has become the product of thoroughgoing planning, study, and research.

As human labor in its crudest form was the principal force shaping production among our more primitive ancestors, the efforts of the research laboratory dictate the processes of this generation. Dr. Davis, Director of Science Service, described science and research as follows: "The investigators engaged in scientific research are the re-

[43] *Ibid.*, p. 17129.   [44] *Ibid.*, p. 16904.
[45] *Ibid.*, Part 1, pp. 58–59.

makers of civilization and the true molders of history. They may be called the catalysts of civilization. . . . They are in our universities, in our Government laboratories, and in our industrial research laboratories." [46] Research, which essentially is the discovery of new knowledge by means of systematic examination, may be classified under three categories: [47] pure basic research, applied research, and research for control of a product. Much of the pure basic research is carried on in the universities and other academic institutions, but the contributions of industry to this field are by no means insignificant. The other two types are largely the product of organized industry.

Scientific research is a salient characteristic of our age. It is estimated that an army of 100,000 individuals is thus engaged in the United States; probably an equal number could be found similarly employed throughout the rest of the world. It is estimated that the annual budget to finance industrial research projects in the United States totals more than $200,000,000.[48] In addition to 2,000 major corporations sponsoring such investigations, more than 200 colleges and universities, 40 trade associations, and 250 commercial laboratories are also thus engaged. To this may be added the work of the Federal Government with its great staff and numerous laboratories; the annual Federal budget for research is said to be $35,000,000. It is significant, nevertheless, that the great majority of industrial enterprises maintain no research departments,[49] a fact which indicates that research and the cost of financing research laboratories is another important factor leading to industrial concentration in the United States. Few but the mighty maintain great research laboratories, and these projects help the mighty to become mightier.

It will be helpful at this point to describe the research facilities of a few great industrial concerns; this will serve to characterize modern productive methods. The first industrial laboratory in the United States was organized in 1901 by the General Electric Company; it was started by Dr. Whitney of the Massachusetts Institute of Technology, together with Elihu Thompson and Dr. Steinmetz. Today this laboratory has developed into what has been called the General Electric House of Magic.[50] It has an annual budget of more than $1,000,-000 a year and employs 300 workers. This by no means represents the total research work of this great corporation, which maintains at least fifteen other important laboratories. These are engaged in the

---

[46] *Ibid.*, Part 30, p. 16270.
[48] *Ibid.*, Part 30, p. 16271.
[50] *Ibid.*, Part 3, pp. 911–918.

[47] *Ibid.*, Part 3, pp. 872–873.
[49] *Ibid.*, p. 17227.

more practical work of developing and testing materials, whereas the main laboratory is devoted principally to fundamental research work.

The largest, and possibly the greatest, research laboratory in the world is the Bell Telephone Laboratory. The telephone industry had outgrown its ability to develop adequately by depending upon random unplanned invention. Moreover, it had outgrown a "second stage in which inventive ability and genius was teamed up with engineering skills, skills of the trained engineer, and had reached a stage in which it was clear that some other kind of attack on many problems had to be made." [51] So a great research laboratory was born; it grew from four employees in 1903 to an establishment with many thousands in 1939. From its ceaseless investigations have flowed many benefits to the corporation and to the world. The General Motors Corporation spends annually nearly $2,000,000 for pure research devoted principally to the development of new products and new devices. Additional sums are spent for engineering research involving the more immediate problems of production; between 1925 and 1938 the corporation spent more than $170,000,000 in these lines.[52]

The plastic industry represents an interesting contribution of industrial research. Here a completely new line of products has emerged from the research laboratory and threatens to revolutionize many industrial processes. In 1938 the Bakelite Corporation alone was supplying thirty-five different industries with its product for more than 15,000 different articles ranging from radio tube bases to safety razor handles. This corporation maintains its own research laboratory, which employs 250 men; its annual research budget usually exceeds one-half million dollars.[53]

This list of illustrations could be multiplied again and again, but they are sufficient to indicate the trend. More and more productive skill is being transferred from the individual worker to the research laboratory; more and more frequently the products of industry come from planned co-operative scientific investigations; more and more often new processes are born in the laboratory rather than from the inspiration, insight, and intuition of an independent genius.

Obviously these great scientific efforts are not sterile; neither are they designed solely to ascertain academic knowledge or to search for fundamental principles. Industry has a realistic and practical bent; laboratory expenditures must pay for themselves on the balance sheet.

[51] *Ibid.*, p. 951. [52] *Ibid.*, Part 9, pp. 3655–3656.
[53] *Ibid.*, Part 3, pp. 1077–1091.

They must more than pay for themselves. This purpose is aptly described in the following words of a corporation executive:

Oh, yes; we supply them with the equipment, we pay them to do the work, we direct what work they are to do. We can't permit our research men to work on their own. They might go into very interesting fields which would be of no use to us, not commercial. We do not run an academic laboratory. We are in business, and although we do some molecule chasing and let a few men have their heads in work along lines in which they might feel inclined to do something, a greater part of our research work is directly applied to the needs of the business, and much of the research work is dictated by our customers or by prospective customers.[54]

Comment already has been made relative to the 15,000 products of the Bakelite laboratories and to the fact that in 1937 40 percent of the products of the Du Pont Corporation were unknown in 1929. Ours is an economy in which product revolution and innovation is so commonplace that it passes quite unnoticed. Yet they merit emphasis—these fruits of the "laboratory revolution." A few illustrations should suffice. From the General Electric "House of Magic" have come many improvements; probably chief among these has been the improvement of the electric light bulb. "The United States public paid about $90,000,000 for the lamps it bought in 1938. If it had to buy the carbon lamps of 1900 to produce the same amount of light, its lamp bill would have been increased by $600,000,000 for that one year, $2,000,000 per working day." [55] This, however, was not the only saving; the same amount of light has required less current, so much so that had the lamps of 1900 been used it would have cost $3,000,000,000 additional for power, or $10,000,000 per working day. Moreover, the increased consumption of power made possible by these lowered costs has itself contributed to a reduction of power rates.

From the Bell Telephone Laboratory has come another product, a vacuum tube—used principally in the telephone service, but adaptable to radio—which has produced an unseen revolution. Its life is about fifty times that of the tube it replaced, and its power consumption is materially less. In reduced power consumption and replacement cost, it has saved the telephone industry $10,000,000 annually.[56] So it goes; the television industry has developed a tube which will record the light of a candle ten miles distant,[57] and the glass industry reports many improvements and savings coming from its laboratories.

[54] *Ibid.*, p. 1089.
[55] *Ibid.*, p. 917.
[56] *Ibid.*, pp. 953–960.
[57] *Ibid.*, p. 986.

But nothing will be gained by multiplying these illustrations. The point has been made: the fruits of modern research are enormous, and this bids well to becoming the age of the "laboratory revolution." Probably we are on the threshold of this revolution rather than in the midst of it. Those best qualified to form a judgment have testified that research laboratories will continue to increase in number and to increase their contributions. Furthermore, there are great unexplored fields still waiting scientific investigation.[58]

The research laboratory is an example of the highly co-operative character of modern economic life. Much as we may talk of the role of the rugged individualist or of the importance of private enterprise, there is no evading the fact that modern research is essentially an associative activity wherein many technicians work jointly on a common project. The laboratory, not the individual, develops the process or creates the device. Frequently the individual receives only nominal title or recognition for the invention, if, indeed, it is traceable to any individual. The laboratory, the organization, the facilities, the project, and the motive are largely provided by the corporation. The efficiency of the individual flows from them; it is a co-operative enterprise. The whole complex creates an economy quite different from the individualistic enterprise system of which textbooks still speak; it is becoming a planned economy—at least on the technical side.

THE ECLIPSE OF COMPETITION

A later chapter will be devoted to monopolistic practices within the economy. This brief section will emphasize the fact that there is a broad breach between the degree of competition which by many is presumed to exist in American industrial life and the degree which actually does exist. We talk of competition, we rationalize the economy in terms of competition, we have formed a habit of interpreting it in these terms, and, of course, those who have a vested interest or a concealed purpose for doing so emphasize the competitive aspects of their industry in preference to collusive and noncompetitive behavior.

"Competition" is a term which men have learned to employ with quite the same animistic and emotional content as certain mystical catch phrases used by the benighted sign worshipers of less civilized ages. The concept of competition has become a fetish, and the word a shibboleth. Competition would seem to be something inherently

[58] *Ibid.*, Part 30, pp. 16273–16291.

or mystically good and desirable in or of itself. Both its desirability and its very existence often pass quite unchallenged, as were the gnomes and the elfs of former centuries. Its *anting-anting* and *tabu* are ostentatiously and overtly observed, though often quite ritualistically circumvented. The belief in free and unrestricted competition has become part of the folklore of the twentieth century, a heritage of the nineteenth. Scarcely anyone who testified before the TNEC cared to challenge the assumption that competition is the proper basis of economic behavior. Members of the Committee, especially the chairman and vice chairman, appeared to have faith that in some way a return to free competition would supply the ultimate solution to the problems of modern times. This "old oaken bucket" complex seemed to represent a desire to escape to the simple life which obtained before the problems of modern corporacy, mass production, and modern industrialism appeared.

The great industrialists who appeared before the Committee proclaimed their loyalty to and belief in the competitive system. Apparently sincere and oblivious of the fact that the industry they represent constitutes a striking example of monopoly control, representatives of the steel industry constantly asserted, "competition is very keen in the steel industry," [59] "you have to be competitive and you meet that competition," [60] "in our processes there is that of meeting the competitive situation," [61] "our general policy as to prices is to be competitive," [62] "I still believe, Mr. O'Connell, in the fundamental law of competition in business, yes, I thoroughly believe in that," [63] and "well, it is pretty hard for me to visualize in the steel industry how there could be more competition on price without ruining the industry." [64]

The last citation is an unintentional but eloquent affirmation of the statement by Walter Lippmann that "competition is something of which producers have only as much as they cannot eliminate," [65] which is pretty close to the basic theory of many in industry—that unrestricted competition should be required of everyone except "us," that monopolies should be rigorously checked in every industry except this particular one, in which "we" are merely "eliminating the abuses of competition," and that the fostering arm of the law should never be extended except in this peculiar case, in which

59 *Ibid.*, Part 19, p. 10525; see also pp. 10553, 10555, 10561.
60 *Ibid.*, p. 10563.   61 *Ibid.*, p. 10587.   62 *Ibid.*, p. 10601.
63 *Ibid.*, p. 10608; see also p. 10625.   64 *Ibid.*, p. 10662; see also p. 10751.
65 *Ibid.*, Part 25, p. 13085.

"we" happen to be the beneficiaries. Note the sincerity of this attitude in the following remark to the Committee: "Senator, in theory, I do not believe in participation of the Government in private business. In this particular type of problem I don't know any other answer." [66]

Nothing in the above discussion is intended either as approval or disapproval of the belief in the efficacy of a freely competitive system. What is intended is to show the strength with which the doctrine is held, the uncritical attitude with which the problem is usually approached, and the prevalence of the idea that free competition is characteristic of the economy.

[66] *Ibid.*, Part 9, p. 3959.

CHAPTER VI

INDEXES OF ECONOMIC CONCENTRATION

T HE JOINT RESOLUTION authorizing the TNEC called for an investigation of monopoly and the concentration of economic power.[1] Each of the eighty-four publications released by the Committee carried the title "Investigation of Concentration of Economic Power." It can scarcely be said, however, that this was the major function of the TNEC; nevertheless, valuable material was assembled showing the extent to which the ownership, management, and control of industry has become centralized.

The final report of the TNEC stated that the principal instrument of concentration of economic power and wealth has been the corporate charter.[2] This, of course, is quite obvious, but merits emphasis. The state, through its statutes, has made the corporation possible; the power to grant charters carries with it the right to limit the terms of such franchises. In spite of the competitive liberality with which corporate charters have been broadcast, it is always within the power of the state, or for that matter of the nation, to amend the "rules of the game" and to subject its own creatures to its will. If it is decided that concentration of economic power, in and of itself, is an evil or that great combinations have abused their trust, there always remains a remedy—to circumscribe the conditions set forth in the corporate charter.

As it is, many of the forty-eight states have legalized creatures more powerful than themselves, and by reciprocity these creatures have been permitted to operate beyond the boundaries of the creating agency. There are in the United States thirty corporations with assets of more than $1,000,000,000 each.[3] The largest of these is the Metropolitan Life Insurance Company, followed by the American Telephone and Telegraph Company; the smallest of this group of giants is the Banker's Trust Company. By contrast, only ten states—New

1 Public Resolution No. 113, 75th Cong.
2 *Final Report and Recommendations of the Temporary National Economic Committee,* p. 28.
3 *Ibid.,* pp. 675–677.

TABLE 3. TOTAL ASSESSED VALUATION OF STATES (1937)
COMPARED WITH TOTAL ASSETS OF THIRTY "BILLION-
DOLLAR" CORPORATIONS (1935)

State and Corporation		Billion Dollars
New York		25.70
Pennsylvania		12.40
Ohio		8.80
California		7.80
Massachusetts		6.30
Michigan		6.20
New Jersey		6.20
Illinois		5.20
Indiana		5.10
Wisconsin		4.80
Metropolitan Life Insurance	4.23	
American Telephone and Telegraph Co.	3.99	
Missouri		3.80
Texas		3.20
Iowa		3.20
Prudential Insurance Co.	3.12	
Connecticut		2.90
Pennsylvania Railroad Co.	2.86	
Kansas		2.70
Maryland		2.60
Kentucky		2.40
New York Central Railroad Co.	2.35	
Chase National Bank	2.33	
New York Life Insurance Co.	2.22	
North Carolina		2.20
Nebraska		2.10
Minnesota		2.00
Standard Oil Co.	1.89	
National City Bank of New York	1.88	
Guaranty Trust Co.	1.84	
Equitable Life Assurance Co.	1.82	
United States Steel Corporation	1.82	
District of Columbia		1.78
West Virginia		1.74
Allegheny Corporation	1.73	
Southern Pacific Railroad Co.	1.67	
General Motors Corp.	1.49	
Tennessee		1.47
Consolidated Edison Co. of N. Y.	1.38	
Rhode Island		1.36
Louisiana		1.34

State and Corporation	Billion Dollars	
Bank of America	1.27	
Mutual Life Insurance Co. of N. Y.	1.24	
Oklahoma		1.22
Commonwealth and Southern Corp.	1.17	
Great Northern Railway Co.	1.15	
Continental Illinois Nat'l Bank and Trust	1.14	
Northern Pacific Railroad Co.	1.13	
Associated Gas and Electric Co.	1.12	
Baltimore and Ohio Railroad Co.	1.11	
City Service Co.	1.11	
Colorado		1.10
Atchison, Topeka and Santa Fe R. R. Co.	1.09	
Washington		1.08
Northwestern Mutual Life Insurance Co.	1.07	
Union Pacific Railroad Co.	1.07	
Georgia		1.06
North American Co.	1.04	
South Dakota		1.03
Banker's Trust Co.	1.03	
Alabama		.92
Oregon		.89
Maine		.66
Florida		.60
New Hampshire		.58
Utah		.52
North Dakota		.49
Mississippi		.44
Arkansas		.43
Idaho		.38
Arizona		.36
South Carolina		.36
Montana		.33
Vermont		.32
Delaware		.31
New Mexico		.29
Wyoming		.28
Nevada		.18

Source: *Final Report and Recommendations of the Temporary National Economic Committee*, pp. 676–677.

York, Pennsylvania, Ohio, California, Massachusetts, Michigan, New Jersey, Illinois, Indiana, and Wisconsin—have within their borders property and wealth valued at more than the assets of the largest of these great corporations. On the other hand, the two corporations first named are richer than any of the remaining thirty-eight states. Rank-

ing below the "poorest" of these billion-dollar corporations (the Banker's Trust Company, with assets of $1,030,000,000) were eighteen states, each with total taxable property of less than $1,000,000,000.

INDUSTRIAL CONCENTRATION AS MANIFESTED BY EMPLOYMENT DATA AND BY CORPORATE ASSETS

Reference was made in an earlier section to the dominant role of corporations in the economic system; it was found that they controlled 100 percent of the communications industry, 100 percent of gas and electric power, 96 percent of mining, 92 percent of manufacturing, and so forth. Further concentration has occurred, however, within these industries resulting in a narrower circle of control. Two measures of such concentration are found in the employment data and in the assets of corporations. On the basis of employment, most corporations are small; they employ few workers and play a relatively unimportant role in the market place. Thus, the majority of the corporations are of less economic significance than are a small minority, the giant corporations. Twenty-five percent of all the employers of the country employ but 1 worker; 50 percent employ 3 workers or less; 75 percent, 9 or less; and 90 percent, 30 or less. Yet the latter group, including 90 percent of the employers, employ less than 20 percent of the employees. At the other extreme we find one one-hundredth of 1 percent of the employers, the large ones (each employing 10,000 workers or more), account for more than 12 percent of the workers; 1 percent account for 48 percent of the workers; and 5 percent account for 70 percent.[4]

Industrial concentration is even more marked when the ownership of corporate assets is taken as an index. Based on the reports of 400,000 corporations which filed balance sheets with the Bureau of Internal Revenue in 1935, 55 percent of the corporations held only 1.4 percent of the total recorded assets. At the other extreme, however, a small handful, 780 corporations in all, each owned assets of $50,000,000 or more, but constituted only two-tenths of 1 percent of all the corporations; nevertheless, they possessed 52 percent of the assets.

The above figures would be more significant, however, if they referred only to nonfinancial corporations. The assets of financial enterprises are highly concentrated. Excluding the data for these corporations the result is still one of high concentration: 61 percent of

---

[4] Data for the above discussion are taken from the *Hearings before the Temporary National Economic Committee,* Part 1, pp. 96–103, 229.

the corporations own only 2 percent of the assets; 92 percent own 12 percent; and 99 percent own less than 30. From the standpoint of the large corporations, one-tenth of 1 percent of the corporations own nearly 50 percent of the assets, 1 percent own more than 70 percent, and 10 percent own approximately 90 percent of the assets.[5]

THE GIANT CORPORATIONS

Any attempt to define a large corporation must start with some arbitrary figure as a criterion. Dr. Willard Thorp [6] defined a large corporation as one with assets of more than $5,000,000.[7] Relatively few corporations attain that status, yet the names of those which do become household words. The great corporations are small in number, but loom large in power and influence. Concentration is most marked in the field of transportation and public utilities; here less

TABLE 4. ASSETS OF LARGE CORPORATIONS OF $5,000,000
AND MORE: PERCENTAGE OF INDUSTRY TOTAL, 1935

Branch of Activity	Percentage of Total Corporate Assets	Percentage of Total Number of Corporations
Transportation and public utilities	93	4.6
Finance	78	2.6
Manufacturing	66	1.5
Mining and quarrying	65	2.5
Trade	35	.0.3
Service	31	.6
Agriculture	28	.7
Construction	25	.2

Source: *Hearings before the Temporary National Economic Committee*, Part 1, p. 230.

than 5 percent of the corporations own nearly 95 percent of the assets of the industry. In finance, 2.6 percent own 78 percent of the assets; in manufacturing, 1.5 percent own 66 percent; in mining and quarrying, 2.5 percent own 65 percent; and in trade, 0.3 percent own 35 percent.[8]

Corporations quite completely dominate the field of manufacturing, being responsible for 92 percent of total output. In the previous section it was seen that the great manufacturing corporations, with assets of more than $5,000,000 each, owned 66 percent of the prop-

[5] *Ibid.*, pp. 104–106, 230.
[6] Adviser on economic studies, Department of Commerce.
[7] *Hearings before the Temporary National Economic Committee*, Part 1, pp. 106–109.
[8] *Ibid.*, p. 107.

erty although they constituted less than 2 percent of the corporations engaged in manufacturing. That, of course, is an average, but when individual industries are examined (see Table 5), it is found that 6 percent of the tobacco corporations own 92 percent of the

TABLE 5. ASSETS OF LARGE MANUFACTURING CORPORATIONS OF
$5,000,000 AND MORE
PERCENTAGE OF INDUSTRY TOTAL, 1935

Industry	Percentage of Total Corporate Assets	Percentage of Total Number of Corporations
Tobacco products	92	5.9
Chemicals and allied products	86	2.7
Rubber products	80	4.3
Metal and metal products	74	2.0
Paper and pulp products	62	3.5
Food and kindred products	60	1.2
Stone, clay, and glass products	56	1.8
Printing, publishing, and allied industries	43	.7
Textiles and their products	39	1.0
Forest products	38	1.0
Liquor and beverages	29	1.0

Source: *Hearings before the Temporary National Economic Committee*, Part 1, p. 231.

assets; 3 percent of the chemicals own 86 percent; 4 percent of the rubber concerns own 80 percent, and so forth; even in the liquor industry, where concentration is less marked, 1 percent of the firms own 29 percent of the assets.

CONCENTRATION IN CLUSTERS [9]

Where conditions of the market and of production are suited to the rise of one great corporation, it is not surprising that often the same forces create additional giants in the same industry. The field, then, becomes dominated by giants; for example, in the tobacco industry, 6 percent of the firms own 92 percent of the assets, and in the cigarette industry, where three companies produce 80 percent of the output. Such competition as does exist becomes competition of the giants, monopolistic competition,[10] with a shadow side show of competition among small firms which operate with little net influence on the total market. Giantism, therefore, seems to come in clusters. There is little of it in the women's clothing industry, but a great deal in the glass bottle industry.

[9] See *ibid.*, pp. 115, 137.   [10] The more precise term—"oligopoly."

You may examine the 89 . . . largest manufacturing and mining enterprises in the country. There is a decided tendency for them to appear in groups or in clusters. Twenty out of the eighty-nine are petroleum companies, 11 are iron and steel, 4 automobiles, 4 tires, 4 coal, 3 copper, 3 meat packing, 3 paper, and then there are 12 cases of pairs, companies that one would put together, like General Electric and Westinghouse, for example. The remaining 21 have no rival, you might say, on the list, but most of them can hardly be thought of as being dominant in their industry.[11]

Dr. Thorp illustrated this tendency toward industrial oligopoly with data relating to centralization in particular industries. In this instance the measure employed is the percentage of total output produced by a few firms. Thus, in 1936 four companies produced 100 percent of the cornbinders manufactured in the country, and three companies produced 80 percent of the cigarettes. Similar concentration characterized the market with respect to other products as indicated in Table 6.[12]

TABLE 6. PERCENTAGES OF TOTAL OUTPUT PRODUCED BY A
FEW DOMINANT FIRMS IN THE PRODUCTION OF
SELECTED COMMODITIES

Product	Number of Companies	Percentage of Output	Date
Virgin aluminum	1	100	1937
Automobiles	3	86	1937
Beef products	2	47	1935
Bakery products	3	20	1934
Cans	3	90	1935
Cement industry	5	40	1931
Cigarettes	3	80	1934
Coal (bituminous)	4	10	1932
Copper	4	78	1935
Corn binders	4	100	1936
Corn planters	6	91	1936
Flour	3	29	1935
Plate glass	2	95	1935
Safety glass	2	90	1935
Iron ore	4	64	1935
Oil wells	4	20	1935
Steel	3	61	1935
Whiskey	4	58	1938
Women's clothing	4	2	1935
Wood pulp	4	35	1935
Zinc	4	43	1935

11 *Hearings before the Temporary National Economic Committee,* Part 1, p. 115.
12 *Ibid.,* p. 137.

CONCENTRATION AMONG LIFE INSURANCE COMPANIES

Life insurance companies furnish an impressive study of concentration of economic power.[13] Approximately 365 insurance companies are doing business in the United States. A few giants predominate, however, doing the bulk of the business and owning most of the

TABLE 7. ASSETS OF LIFE INSURANCE COMPANIES: ADMITTED ASSETS OF THE SIXTEEN LARGEST LIFE INSURANCE COMPANIES IN COMPARISON WITH THE ADMITTED ASSETS OF ALL 308 COMPANIES REPORTING AS OF DECEMBER 31, 1937

Company	In Millions of Dollars	As a Percentage of the Total of 308 Companies Reporting	As a Cumulative Percentage of the Total 308 Companies Reporting
1. Metropolitan Life	4,720	18.0	18.0
2. Prudential	3,584	13.7	31.7
3. New York Life	2,520	9.6	41.3
4. Equitable Life Assurance	2,106	8.0	49.3
5. Mutual Life	1,349	5.1	54.4
Subtotal	14,279	54.4	
6. Northwestern Mutual	1,178	4.5	58.9
7. Travelers	914	3.5	62.4
8. John Hancock Mutual Life	855	3.3	65.7
9. Penn Mutual Life	668	2.5	68.2
10. Mutual Benefit Life	646	2.5	70.7
11. Massachusetts Mutual	610	2.3	73.0
12. Aetna Life	577	2.2	75.2
13. New England Mutual	402	1.5	76.7
14. Union Central	359	1.4	78.1
15. Provident Mutual	331	1.3	79.4
16. Connecticut Mutual	312	1.2	80.6
Subtotal	6,852	26.2	
Total of 16 largest companies	21,131	80.6	80.6
All other companies (292 companies)	5,118	19.4	19.4
Grand total (308 companies)	26,249	100.0	100.0

Source: *Hearings before the Temporary National Economic Committee*, Part 4, p. 1514.

[13] For testimony relative to the material which follows, see *ibid.*, Part 4, pp. 1189–1196; see also Part 9, pp. 3749–3753, Part 28, pp. 14701–14705, and the *Final Report and Recommendations of the Temporary National Economic Committee*, pp. 580–581.

assets. The largest is the Metropolitan Life Insurance Company; not only is it the largest life insurance company, but it is the nation's largest business concern as well. In 1937 it accounted for nearly $5,000,000,000, or 18 percent, of the total assets ($26,000,000,000) of all companies. The resources of the Metropolitan are about the equivalent of those of the 290 smallest companies in the business. The Prudential Insurance Company ranks second with assets of more than $3,000,000,000, accounting for 14 percent of all life insurance assets; then follow the New York Life, with 10 percent, the Equitable Life Assurance Society, with 8 percent, and the Mutual Life Insurance Company of New York, accounting for 5 percent. These five companies are also among the eighteen largest concerns of the United States. Together, they control more than one-half (54.4 percent) of the total resources of the life insurance industry. The next eleven companies, themselves giants, having an average of nearly one-half billion dollars each, control an additional 26 percent. Thus, the first sixteen companies control 81 percent of the assets of the industry.[14] In other words, one-half of 1 percent of all the corporations account for more than 80 percent of the assets.[15] This creates the illusion that the remaining 292 corporations, which account for only 19 percent of the assets, are small and insignificant firms. Such is hardly the case; twenty of them have assets of more than $100,000,000 each, and forty of them are large enough to be listed among the 200 largest corporations of the country.

Not only are life insurance assets clustered under the control of a few corporations, but there is another type of clustering even more marked—concentration by territories. Six of the largest companies are located in the New York area—four in New York, and two in New Jersey. These six own 57 percent of all life insurance assets. Ten of the twenty-five largest companies have their home offices in New England and account for 17 percent. The twenty-five largest companies account for 87 percent of the total assets of life insurance companies. In addition to those already named, one of these is found in California, one in Wisconsin, two in Iowa, two in Pennsylvania, two in Ohio, and one in Indiana.[16] Most of the states are thus unaccounted for among the great companies.

14 In 1938 the twenty-six largest companies controlled 87 percent.
15 Based on a study of 308 insurance companies that returned questionnaires to the SEC.
16 *Hearings before the Temporary National Economic Committee*, Part 4, p. 1193.

THE METROPOLITAN LIFE INSURANCE COMPANY

The apex of this cluster of concentration in the life insurance business is represented by the Metropolitan Life Insurance Company. Through its policies, its investments, and other activities it is directly influential in the lives of more people than any other business corporation. It is the largest life insurance corporation in the world, and, on the basis of 1937 data, the largest business corporation in the United States, with assets greater than those of the United States Steel Corporation and the General Motors Corporation combined. Attention has already been called to the fact that it is financially as powerful as the 290 smallest firms in the field. An indication of Metropolitan's great size is the fact that nearly 29,000,000 individuals are insured by this corporation alone.[17] These represent not policies, but policyholders. Metropolitan is the chief insurer of newborn babies; during the first year of their lives it insures one-fifth of all those born in the United States; in some states the ratio is as high as one-third. The younger generation is probably more widely covered by insurance than the older; nevertheless, Metropolitan insures every fifth man in the country. In many cities, such as St. Louis, the ratio is as high as one out of every three.[18]

Metropolitan's financial operations are staggering. Its corporate assets are approaching $5,000,000,000, and the paid-for life insurance issued in 1938 was nearly $2,000,000,000. Each year this company is called upon to invest or reinvest $700,000,000, or more than $2,000,000 each working day. The magnitude of these operations is illustrated by three separate investments described before the TNEC. In 1929 the company placed a mortgage for more than $27,000,000 on the Empire State Building,[19] and its president testified that an investment of this size is of no greater significance to Metropolitan than is a $10,000 loan to many companies. Another sizable "egg" in the enormous Metropolitan "basket" is a large-scale housing project built for its account on Long Island.[20] This great enterprise represents an investment of $7,500,000; it includes a unified complex of more than fifty apartment houses, together with stores, theaters, garages, and other business enterprises. More than 12,000 dwelling units including 42,000 rooms are provided. Another loan, amounting to $43,000,-

[17] The majority by industrial policies.
[18] *Hearings before the Temporary National Economic Committee*, Part 4, p. 1238; Part 12, p. 5955.
[19] *Ibid.*, Part 28, pp. 15170–15171.   [20] *Ibid.*, Part 11, pp. 5130–5142.

ooo, was made when Rockefeller Center was developed.[21] Although these illustrations are exceptional, they reveal the scale of operations the Metropolitan is capable of undertaking.

CONCENTRATION AMONG INDUSTRIAL INSURANCE COMPANIES

Standard rating agencies list sixty-six companies as writing industrial insurance. Here, as in the case of those writing standard life policies, the bulk of the business is done by a few firms. Three companies dominate this business; [22] the largest, the Prudential Life Insurance Company of America, had $7,574,000,000 of industrial insurance in force in 1937 and accounted for 37 percent of the business. The Metropolitan had almost as much. These two companies,

TABLE 8. RELATIVE IMPORTANCE OF THE TEN LARGEST INDUS-
TRIAL LIFE INSURANCE COMPANIES AS MEASURED BY THE
AMOUNTS OF INDUSTRIAL INSURANCE IN FORCE
DECEMBER 31, 1937

Company	Industrial Insurance in Force (Millions)	Percentage	Cumulative Percentage
Prudential	7,574	36.8	36.8
Metropolitan Life	7,512	36.5	73.3
John Hancock Mutual Life	1,684	8.2	81.5
Western and Southern Life	577	2.8	84.3
American National	461	2.2	86.5
National Life and Accident	393	1.9	88.4
Life Insurance Company of Virginia	302	1.5	89.9
Monumental Life	200	1.0	90.9
Life and Casualty Insurance Co.	164	.8	91.7
Industrial Life and Health Insurance Co.	85	.4	92.1
Total of above 10 companies	$18,952	92.1	92.1
Total of 56 other companies	1,639	7.9	100.0
Grand total of 66 companies	$20,591	100.0	100.0

Source: *Hearings before the Temporary National Economic Committee*, Part 12, p. 6166.

therefore, were responsible for nearly three-fourths of the business; in other words, 3 percent of the companies accounted for 75 percent of the insurance. Ranking third was the John Hancock Company, which wrote more than 8 percent of the policies. The ten leading

21 *Ibid.*, Part 28, p. 15323; see also p. 15180.
22 *Ibid.*, Part 4, p. 1167; see also Part 12, p. 5603.

concerns, including only 15 percent of the companies, accounted for more than 90 percent of the industrial policies in force.

THE GROWING FINANCIAL POWER OF INSURANCE COMPANIES

Concentration of economic power within the life insurance companies is by no means new; as early as in 1906 the Armstrong report [23] stated:

No tendency in modern financial conditions has created more widespread apprehension than the tendency to vast combinations of capital and assets. But while in the case of railroads and industrials these vast amounts are mostly fixed in particular productive activities, the larger part of the huge accumulations of life insurance companies consists of assets readily convertible into money and susceptible of application to varied uses. It is this fact which has placed the officers and members of finance committees of life insurance companies in positions of conspicuous financial power.[24]

Apparently these comments are even more applicable today than they were forty years ago, since the size of the life insurance industry has increased as well as concentration within the industry.

Insurance companies gather together vast sums from thousands of policyholders. In 1938 approximately 65,000,000 individuals in the United States were insured, or substantially one-half the total population. Life insurance companies have become the semi-official savings institutions of the nation. In 1935 the Metropolitan Life Insurance Company collected premiums in New York State alone amounting to nearly $150,000,000, or the equivalent of about one-half the total tax revenues of the state that year. The total premium collection from all sources by Metropolitan in 1935 was nearly $1,000,-000,000, or substantially three times the entire tax collections of New York—the state which regulates its activities. In Wisconsin, the Northwestern Mutual is the largest company; in 1936 it collected in total premiums nearly twice the amount of the tax collections of the state.

The assets of life insurance companies have increased markedly. The increase since 1910 has been substantially 500 percent, which is materially greater than that experienced by savings banks, savings deposits in commercial banks, or building and loan associations. By 1935 life insurance assets had become twice as large as those of the Federal Reserve Banks and nearly 70 percent of the total value of all farm property of the United States. Likewise, life insurance com-

23 State of New York, Assembly Doc. No. 41, Vol. X, p. 389.
24 *Hearings before the Temporary National Economic Committee,* Part 28, p. 14698.

pany income has shown great gains. Although the national income increased about 800 percent between 1880 and 1940, life insurance income increased by more than 6,000 percent.

The percentage ratio of life insurance income to total national income rose from one-tenth of 1 percent in 1880, 1.6 percent in 1890, 2.2 percent in 1900, 2.5 percent in 1910, 2.8 percent in 1915, 2.6 percent in 1920, 4.1 percent in 1925, 6.7 percent in 1930, 9 percent in 1931, 11.6 percent in 1932.[25]

Life insurance has thus become the nation's most dynamic savings institution. Between 1929 and 1938 the total assets of savings institutions in the United States (including life insurance companies, building and loan associations, commercial bank savings accounts, savings banks, postal savings, and baby bonds) increased from $58,-000,000,000 to $70,000,000,000.[26] It is particularly significant that 95 percent of this increase was accounted for by life insurance companies, and 85 percent of it by the twenty-six largest companies. Life insurance companies have become the great national reservoir of savings. Each year these financial institutions come to the market seeking to place investments of nearly $4,000,000,000; this represents an average daily flow of more than $10,000,000.[27] These companies exercise a dominant influence in the investment markets. More than 50 percent of life insurance portfolios are in the form of cash or marketable securities;[28] this being the case, they exert a greater influence in financial circles than an industrial concern of a similar size. Because of their vital role in this respect Dr. Donald H. Davenport, special economic consultant of the SEC, commented as follows: ". . . a very unusual degree of public interest attaches to the management of the life insurance companies. Not only is insurance a business of great size, but it directly affects the stability of our society." [29]

In 1939 an editorial in the *Magazine of Wall Street* stated, "It would be hardly an exaggeration to say that the assets of the life-insurance companies as a whole represent roughly a first mortgage on the country's business and industry." [30] In support of this statement the magazine presented data similar to those which previously had been presented to the TNEC.[31] Indeed, it would appear that insur-

25 *Ibid.*, Part 4, p. 1182.   26 *Ibid.*, Part 28, p. 14725.
27 *Ibid.*, p. 14698.   28 *Ibid.*, Part 4, p. 1196.
29 *Ibid.*
30 December 28, 1939; see also *Hearings before the Temporary National Economic Committee*, Part 28, pp. 14698, 14724.
31 *Hearings before the Temporary National Economic Committee*, Part 4, pp. 1201–1210.

ance companies do hold a first mortgage on America. Forty-nine leading life insurance companies which have been in continuous operation since 1906, representing 98 percent of life insurance assets in 1906 and 92 percent in 1938, own 11 percent of the Federal debt, 10 percent of the state debt, 23 percent of all railway bonds, 22 percent of the total public utility debt outstanding, and 15 percent of the industrial debt. They own 11 percent of all farm mortgages and 15 percent of urban mortgages. Thus, these reservoirs of the people's savings have far-reaching claims against the wealth of the nation.

CONCENTRATION OF SAVINGS AND INDUSTRIAL CONCENTRATION

The facts that life insurance companies gather the savings of thousands of policyholders and that most of these great reservoirs are concentrated under the control of a few large institutions lead in a very subtle and unplanned fashion to greater concentration in the industrial world. Both large and small firms seek to tap the savings reservoirs of the country. Earlier hearings spent a great deal of time analyzing the difficulties of small industrial establishments in securing capital and credit.[32] It appears that our financial institutions do not adequately serve the needs of small business, that the insurance reservoirs are not readily accessible to such firms, and that as a consequence the administration of life insurance resources has encouraged industrial concentration.

Insurance companies seek the securities of well-known firms, and for administrative purposes they seek sizable blocks. Funds are thus gathered from many small sources and placed in large sums. When questioned by the chairman, the president of Metropolitan agreed that small business is handicapped in obtaining access to insurance funds.

THE CHAIRMAN. A large proportion of the income of the insurance companies is therefore derived from persons of small means, but upon the other hand the businessman who wants a small loan, for reasons over which perhaps the insurance companies have no control, is unable to find a reservoir of capital with the insurance companies. Isn't that the fact?

MR. ECKER. That is true as far as small loans are concerned of the type you are speaking of. May I elaborate a little bit on that point?

THE CHAIRMAN. I was going to ask you just one other question, and that is, how many loans do you suppose you have under, let us say $1,000,000?

MR. ECKER. My impression is about six or seven that were under that at the time made.[33]

32 *Ibid.*, Part 9.　　　　　　33 *Ibid.*, Part 28, p. 15320.

So the very organization of the life insurance industry makes it inexpedient to extend credit except in a manner which fosters industrial concentration. According to the same witness it is not good business to make small loans.

I think our better field in this economic structure, as far as making capital available to small industries is concerned, is not in the very small loans but in the loans, say, from one million and two million up to five million, some place in there, where we can save the expense of bond issues and public distribution, and even in that group the expenses involved relatively are high. I think that is a better field for us under all the circumstances than in the loans of, say, $200,000 on down.[34]

CONCENTRATION IN THE STEEL INDUSTRY

The United States Steel Corporation is the second largest industrial concern in America.[35] Close to the Steel Corporation, both in size and harmony of policy, are the other major steel-producing firms. Historically, steel offers, perhaps, the best illustration in the United States of a continuous record of monopoly over a long period of years, achieved through informal co-operation and collusion. Here concentration finds almost its perfect illustration. Ten great corporations dominate the steel industry. The Iron and Steel Institute lists 164 companies producing steel in 1938.[36] Not all of them produced a full line, of course; 125 produced hot rolled products; 34 had a capacity for pig iron and alloy products; and a few subsidiary firms raised the total to 164. Actually the number is larger, since there are others equipped for limited production in given fields.

Concentration of steel assets is marked. In 1938 the ten largest companies accounted for 88 percent of the assets of the steel industry. One company, the United States Steel Corporation, constituting less than 1 percent of the total number of firms, owned 40 percent of the assets, or more than two and one-half times those of its nearest rival and more than three times those of the 124 smallest presumed competitors. Two companies, representing less than 1.5 percent of all the firms, owned 55 percent of the assets. The Bethlehem Steel Corporation ranked second and was substantially twice as large as its nearest rival—the Republic Steel Corporation. These three companies accounted for nearly two-thirds of the total assets of the industry. The

---

[34] *Ibid.*, p. 15321.
[35] Financial, public utility, and railroad corporations excluded.
[36] *Hearings before the Temporary National Economic Committee,* Part 18, pp. 10407–10408.

TABLE 9. INVESTED CAPITAL OF THE TEN LARGEST STEEL COMPANIES, 1937

	Invested Capital in Millions of Dollars	Percentage	Cumulative Percentage
Total invested capital for the industry	4,281	100	100
1. United States Steel Corp.	1,718	40	40
2. Bethlehem Steel Corp.	657	15	55
3. Republic Steel Corp.	329	8	63
4. Jones & Laughlin Steel Corp.	198	5	68
5. Youngstown Sheet and Tube Co.	199	5	73
6. National Steel Corp.	180	4	77
7. Inland Steel Co.	143	3	80
8. American Rolling Mills Co.	132	3	83
9. Wheeling Steel Corp.	110	3	86
10. Crucible Steel Co. of America	103	2	88
Totals for the ten companies	3,771	88	
All others	510	12	

Source: *Hearings before the Temporary National Economic Committee,* Part 18, p. 10408.

ten largest firms, representing only about 6 percent of the total, had title to 88 percent of the assets, leaving only 12 percent for the remaining 148 concerns.

Another measure of concentration, perhaps a more significant one, is productive capacity. Since there are many items of steel, the degree of concentration of productive capacity perhaps can best be measured in terms of selected products such as pig iron, steel ingots, and hot rolled steel. It is found that the United States Steel Corporation dominates almost every field of production; it has 40 percent of the total capacity for pig iron, 35 percent for steel ingots, 31 percent for hot rolled steel, 36 percent for plates, 37 percent for wire rods, 53 percent for heavy shapes, and 58 percent for heavy rails.[37] In general, the ten largest companies, as measured by investment, are also the ten largest in terms of productive capacity. Very significantly, the five largest owned 73 percent of the total assets and accounted for from 43 to 94 percent of the productive capacity for most products.

It scarcely could be said that this completes the story of concentration in the steel industry. Were the five or ten large steel producers merged into one giant monopoly, that would represent concentration indeed. Since there is ample evidence of concerted action, uniform

[37] *Ibid.,* p. 10409.

policy, and collusive co-operation among steel producers, it is clear that concentration in fact is much more comprehensive than that which is overt.

CONCENTRATION IN INVESTMENT BANKING

Probably no sector of the American economy has typified the concentration of economic power to the average citizen as has the field of investment banking. For decades, since the days of Fisk, Gould, Cooke, and the elder Morgan, "Wall Street" has symbolized financial power and the monopoly of money. The position of Wall Street has not been an illusion; numerous evidences have testified to the power of the investment bankers. Their influence is extensive and ofttimes subtle. The National Resources Committee found that in 1935 there was a Morgan First National group of forty-one large corporations closely knit together by interlocking directorships and other associations centering around the "House of Morgan." [38] This group included thirteen industrial corporations, headed by United States Steel Corporation, twelve utility corporations, headed by the American Telephone and Telegraph Company, thirty-seven electric generating companies, eleven of the nation's major railroads, and several important financial institutions. There were similar groups centered around other financial houses.

It is obvious that the control exercised by the great underwriting houses cannot be measured either by the size of their balance sheets or by the volume of business done. Their unusual position in the business of underwriting securities gives them a strategic influence over virtually every corporate agency they serve. They have access to confidential financial information unavailable to others, they advise on financial matters, they interlock on the boards of numerous corporations, and they officiate at the birth, death, and rebirth of corporate entities.

It is possible, however, to compare the relative strength and influence of investment banks within the group itself. This has been made possible by an analysis of information supplied to the SEC.[39] In 1938 the Investment Bankers Association reported a total membership of 730; thirty-eight of them, however, tended to dominate the field. In the period between 1934 and 1939 securities valued at

[38] National Resources Committee, *The Structure of the American Economy*, 1939, Part 1, pp. 160–163.
[39] *Hearings before the Temporary National Economic Committee*, Part 24, pp. 12688–12710.

$9,600,000,000 were registered with the SEC; $9,200,000,000 of these were sold to the public through the medium of investment bankers. Of the latter amount, 91 percent was managed by the thirty-eight leading investment firms. In other words, 5 percent of the investment

TABLE 10. PERCENTAGE OF REGISTERED BOND, PREFERRED STOCK, AND COMMON STOCK ISSUES MANAGED BY SELECTED INVESTMENT BANKING FIRMS, 1934–1939

Banking Firms	Bonds	Preferred Stock	Common Stock	All Issues
Morgan Stanley & Co., Inc.	25.9	9.2	8.0	23.2
The First Boston Corp.	12.0	5.1		10.7
Kuhn, Loeb & Co.	7.7	0.2	4.3	6.7
Dillon Read & Co.	7.4	10.3	1.7	7.4
Smith, Barney & Co.	4.5	9.8	5.0	5.1
Blyth & Company, Corp.	4.3	4.0	2.7	4.2
Total 6 New York City firms	61.8	38.6	21.7	57.3
14 other New York firms	20.0	29.1	27.7	21.3
Total 20 New York City firms	81.8	67.7	49.4	78.6
18 firms outside New York City	12.8	5.3	13.1	12.1
Total 38 firms	94.6	73.0	62.5	90.7
All other firms	5.4	27.0	37.5	9.3
All firms	100.0	100.0	100.0	100.0

Source: *Hearings before the Temporary National Economic Committee*, Part 24, p. 12991.

houses dominated 91 percent of the business. The six leading firms (Morgan Stanley and Company; The First Boston Corporation; Dillon Read and Company; Kuhn, Loeb and Company; Smith, Barney and Company; and Blyth and Company), constituting less than 1 percent of the total, managed 57 percent of the business, and the leading house, less than one-half of 1 percent of the total, managed more than 23 percent. The House of Morgan managed more than twice as many securities as the smallest 692 firms and more than twice that of any of its immediate competitors.

An interesting aspect of this concentration appears when certain types of securities are classified as to quality. Based upon the findings of standard rating agencies, bonds were classified according to four grades, from best to poorest.[40] The six leading investment banking firms mentioned above had a near monopoly of all the first-grade

[40] *Ibid.*, Part 24, pp. 12692–12704.

bonds.[41] The Morgan firm managed 65 percent of the first-grade bonds—more than half—leaving only 35 percent to be divided among the other 37 firms. When the bonds are broken down according to industries, Morgan managed 69 percent of the best grade manufacturing bonds, 52 percent of those in utilities, 100 percent of the railroad, and 74 percent of all the rest. The six leading firms, of course, con-

TABLE 11. QUALITY OF BOND ISSUES MANAGED BY 38 INVESTMENT BANKING FIRMS, ALL INDUSTRIES, JANUARY, 1934—JUNE, 1939

(In percentage)

Banking Firms	First Grade	Second Grade	Third Grade	Fourth Grade	Below Fourth Grade	All Grades
Morgan Stanley & Co.	65.0	31.4	11.3	10.9	14.6	27.3
The First Boston Corp.	16.1	16.3	11.8	7.9	0.5	12.7
Kuhn, Loeb & Co.			15.2	18.4	9.2	8.1
Dillon Read & Co.	4.2	13.8	7.3	3.2	3.0	7.8
Smith, Barney & Co.	0.7	2.7	8.4	5.0	15.8	4.8
Blyth & Company, Corp.		9.0	0.7	6.0	6.6	4.6
Total 6 New York City firms	86.0	73.2	54.7	51.4	49.7	65.3
14 other New York City firms	14.0	13.5	26.5	30.6	28.6	21.1
Total 20 New York City firms	100.0	86.7	81.2	82.0	78.3	86.4
18 firms outside New York City	0.0	13.3	18.8	18.0	21.7	13.6
Total	100.0	100.0	100.0	100.0	100.0	100.0

Source: *Hearings before the Temporary National Economic Committee,* Part 24, p. 12993.

centrated under their control a much larger percentage of the business; they managed 86 percent of the first grade bonds in all industries, 69 percent of those in manufacturing, 85 percent of the utility, 100 percent of the railroad, and 87 percent of the remainder. It is quite clear that the Morgan firm and the five other large houses had the choice of all issues. Moreover, when all five grades of bonds are considered, the same six continued to dominate the field; they managed 65 percent of all bonds, 60 percent of the utilities, 76 percent of all railroads, and 74 percent of the remainder. Thus, the management of the nation's most important security issues is pretty well dom-

[41] Based on the bonds registered with the SEC between 1934 and 1939 and which were managed by the thirty-eight leading investment bankers.

inated by a few firms. No better summary could be given for this section of the hearings than that presented by Dr. Oscar L. Altman.

First, from the period September 16, 1935, that is to say the day it began business operations, until June 30, 1939, Morgan Stanley & Co., Inc., managed 32% of all the registered bond issues managed by thirty-eight leading firms. It managed all of the first-grade registered bond issues of manufacturing companies; 71% of all the first-grade registered bond issues of electric light and power, gas, and water companies; all of the first-grade registered bond issues of transportation and communication companies, principally telephone issues; and 74% of all the first-grade registered bond issues of all other issuers. During this period, Morgan Stanley & Co., Inc. managed four-fifths of all the first-grade registered bond issues managed by thirty-eight leading firms in the United States.

Second, none of the investment banking firms located outside of New York City managed any of the first-grade registered bond issues referred to during the period from January, 1934, through June, 1939. The lower the grade of the security, the larger the relative originating importance of the firms outside of New York City.

Third, during the period from September 16, 1935, through June 30, 1939, Morgan Stanley & Co., Inc., managed $2,000,000,000 of registered bond issues, of which 43% fell within the first grade and 79% within the first two grades. During the same period, The First Boston Corporation, Kuhn, Loeb & Co., Dillon Read & Co., Smith, Barney & Co., and Blyth & Co., Inc. also managed $2,000,000,000 of registered bond issues, of which 4% fell within the first grade and 42% within the first two grades. Fourteen other New York City firms managed $1,300,000,000 of registered bond issues during this period, of which 9% fell in the first grade and 24% in the first two grades. Finally, during the same period, eighteen leading firms outside of New York City managed $900,000,000 of the registered bond issues, of which none fell within the first grade, and 31% within the second grade.

Fourth, eight leading firms in the United States, Morgan Stanley & Co., Inc., Kuhn, Loeb & Co., The First Boston Corporation, Blyth & Co., Inc., Dillon Read & Co., Mellon Securities Corporation, Harriman Ripley & Co., Inc., and Smith, Barney & Co., managed $7,400,000,000 of securities from June 14, 1934, to June 30, 1939. On the average these eight firms reserved more than one-half of the total of the issues managed by them as their underwriting participations; the remainder was divided among all the other investment bankers in the United States.

Fifth, these eight firms had underwriting participations of $4,300,000,-000. On the average, 86% of this total represented participations in issues managed by these firms and the remaining 14% represented participations in issues managed by all other investment bankers.[42]

42 *Hearings before the Temporary National Economic Committee*, Part 24, pp. 12710–12711.

Probably outweighing the imposing statistics which have been presented are the many verbal tributes offered to the Morgan domination in the field of investment banking. Apparently the House of Morgan called the tune, and other firms, great and small, danced with alacrity.[43] The "corner," as the Morgan firm was known, assumed the characteristics of a shrine where the faithful and fearful burnt their offerings.[44] Representatives of leading investment houses, nominally competitors, paid tribute to the Morgan "constructive leadership" [45] and calmly acknowledged that their firms had been willing bedfellows at the "corner": "Our main job is to get under the covers and as close to them as is possible." [46] They openly avowed that "it is desirable to have the good will of the House of Morgan" [47] in order to prosper in the business and sought by devious ways to court that favor, one effective way being to maintain substantial deposits at "the corner." [48] That the "House" was cognizant of its power and fearful that a social accounting might be called for seems evident from correspondence among the bankers with respect to their appearance before the TNEC; an example follows.

In talking with Harold Stanley today, I found that their questionnaire on underwritings and participations, concerning which I wrote you early this week, was prompted solely by the thought that they may be called in one day to answer a charge of monopoly, and that they are getting together as much information as they can to answer promptly any questions which may be asked.[49]

CONCENTRATION IN THE PETROLEUM INDUSTRY

No history of monopoly in the United States would be complete without extensive attention being given to the petroleum industry and to the Standard Oil Company. Although the prosecution of the Standard Oil Company under the Sherman Act did weaken its grip on the industry, it was no more successful in establishing competition for the oil industry than were the monopoly statutes in general able to keep the industrial pattern free from monopolistic domination.

Petroleum is the nation's fourth largest industry; its assets are nearly $15,000,000,000, or double what they were twenty years ago. The oil industry in reality is several industries integrally related,

43 *Ibid.*, Part 23, p. 11872; Part 22, pp. 11583, 11586, 11593.
44 *Ibid.*, Part 23, pp. 12013–12014, 12017, 12020, 12036; Part 22, pp. 11578, 11584, 11587.
45 *Ibid.*, Part 22, p. 11552.   46 *Ibid.*, p. 11554.
47 *Ibid.*, p. 11578.   48 *Ibid.*, pp. 11578–11580.
49 *Ibid.*, p. 11594.

including the production of crude oil, transportation, refining, and marketing. Most of the oil business is conducted by great integrated companies. Organized in a vertical manner, they operate all stages of the productive process from the oil derrick in the field to the service station at the roadside.[50] There are, of course, numerous independent producers of crude oil, independent refiners, and independent retailers, but they are dwarfed by the magnitude of the integrated corporations. The process of integration has fostered the growth of large business units, much larger than is found in most fields of American industry. The ultimate effect has been monopolistic or, more precisely, what recent writers characterize as monopolistic competition.

TABLE 12. THE TWENTY MAJOR OIL COMPANIES, LISTED IN
ORDER OF THEIR TOTAL ASSETS, DECEMBER 31, 1938

Name of Company	State of Incorporation	Date of Incorporation
1. Standard Oil Co.	New Jersey	1882
2. Socony-Vacuum Oil Co.	New York	1882
3. Standard Oil Co.	Indiana	1889
4. The Texas Corp.	Delaware	1926
5. Standard Oil Co. of California	Delaware	1926
6. Gulf Oil Corp.	Pennsylvania	1922
7. Cities Service Co.	Delaware	1910
8. Shell Union Oil Corp.	Delaware	1922
9. Consolidated Oil Corp.	New York	1919
10. Phillips Petroleum Co.	Delaware	1917
11. Tide Water Associated Oil Co.	Delaware	1926
12. The Atlantic Refining Co.	Pennsylvania	1870
13. The Pure Oil Co.	Ohio	1914
14. Union Oil Co. of California	California	1890
15. Sun Oil Co.	New Jersey	1901
16. The Ohio Oil Co.	Ohio	1887
17. Continental Oil Co.	Delaware	1920
18. The Standard Oil Co.	Ohio	1870
19. Mid-Continent Petroleum Corp.	Delaware	1917
20. Skelly Oil Co.	Delaware	1919

Source: *Hearings before the Temporary National Economic Committee,* Part 14-A, p. 7708.

The petroleum industry is dominated by twenty integrated corporations. Nearly two-thirds of the assets of the petroleum business are owned by these giants, which dwarf all the rest in each of the four fields of oil production: extraction, refining, transportation, and

50 *Ibid.,* Part 14, pp. 7100–7113.

marketing. The twenty major companies own 67 percent of the total assets of the oil industry, they produce 53 percent of the crude oil, own 57 percent of the gathering pipe-line mileage, operate 89 percent of the trunk pipe-line mileage,[51] receive 86 percent of the pipe-line operating income, own 87 percent of the tonnage of tankers, hold title to 96 percent of the stocks of refined petroleum, control 76

TABLE 13. THE DOMINANCE OF THE TWENTY LARGE INTEGRATED COMPANIES IN THE PETROLEUM INDUSTRY

Branch of Industry	Number of Companies	Percentage
Total investment	20	67
Domestic producing oil wells	20	24
Production of crude oil	20	53
Crude oil gathering pipe-line mileage	20	57
Crude oil trunk pipe-line mileage	14	89
Total crude oil pipe-line mileage	20	72
Investment in pipe lines	15	77
Pipe line operating income	15	86
Deadweight tonnage of tankers	15	87
Stocks of refinable crude oil	20	97
Daily crude oil capacity	20	76
Daily cracking capacity	20	85
Crude oil runs to stills	20	83
Production of gasoline	20	84
Stocks of finished gasoline	20	90
Stocks of lubricants	20	93
Six selected stock figures	20	94
Gasoline pipe-line mileage	16	96
Domestic sales of gasoline	18	80

Source: *Hearings before the Temporary National Economic Committee,* Part 14, p. 7103.

percent of daily crude oil capacity, and 85 percent of the daily cracking capacity, hold 90 and 93 percent of the finished stocks of gasoline and lubricants, respectively, own 96 percent of gasoline pipe-line mileage, and handle 80 percent of domestic gasoline sales. Moreover, ten of these companies own half of the gross proved oil reserves of the nation.[52]

This centralization of assets and control is more extensive than apparent. These concerns co-operate with one another and ofttimes conduct their business more as one entity than as rigorous com-

[51] In some instances the concentration is in fewer hands than the twenty; in this case fourteen corporations are dominant.

[52] *Hearings before the Temporary National Economic Committee,* Part 14, p. 7392.

petitors. They co-operate in the common use of pipe lines, they are interrelated through stock holdings in patent companies, they are joined through common stock ownership and joint ownership of operating affiliates. Moreover, the fact that officers of these giants ordinarily manage the companies subject to little or no check by the stockholders permits them to rule almost as dictators and to enter into common understandings with each other.[53] Another significant fact about this concentration is that it is growing; in the decade prior to 1938 the control of the twenty companies over crude production rose from 46 to 53 percent, over principal finished products from 76 to 94 percent, over refining capacity from 66 to 76 percent, and over gasoline production from 71 to 84 percent. Concentration apparently feeds on itself.[54]

But the account of centralization of ownership and control in the petroleum industry is only partially complete if it is left at this point. The twenty integrated companies are not all of the same size. The five largest, representing 30 percent of the firms, owned 60 percent of the assets in 1938, and the largest owned 25 percent. This is concentration of concentration and giantism among giants. In fact, the largest, the Standard Oil Company of New Jersey, owned assets equal to more than those possessed by the twelve least powerful of the twenty. Fifty percent of the companies accounted for only 17 percent of the assets, and 75 percent of the companies owned but 40 percent.[55] The distribution of ownership among the powerful companies presents but another aspect of the uneven distribution in the industry as a whole.

CONCENTRATION IN OTHER INDUSTRIES

No attempt was made by the TNEC to make an over-all analysis of concentration in the United States, industry by industry. The material which has been presented here has been pieced together from various and scattered sections of the hearings. Information is available with respect to several other industries as well, including the copper, whiskey, tobacco, milk, and the building industries.

In the copper industry three large corporations dominated the field in 1937, producing 78 percent of the output.[56] The largest pro-

[53] In the annual meetings of seventeen of the integrated companies their officers voted 99 percent of the common stocks voted.
[54] *Hearings before the Temporary National Economic Committee,* Part 14, p. 7105.
[55] *Ibid.,* Part 17, p. 9863, Exhibit No. 1318.
[56] *Ibid.,* Part 25, pp. 13100–13103, 13390.

ducer, Kennecott, expanded from 1 percent of the nation's total production in 1915 to 36 percent in 1937. The second largest, Anaconda, expanded from 18 to 23 percent during the same period, and Phelps Dodge, the third in rank, expanded from 8 to 19 percent of the total.

TABLE 14. CONCENTRATION OF MINE PRODUCTION OF COPPER
IN THE UNITED STATES FOR SELECTED YEARS, 1915–1937
(Percentage of production)

Company	1915	1929	1935	1937
Total United States companies	100.0	100.0	100.0	100.0
Sixteen largest companies (1915)	82.2	81.4	83.4	87.5
Anaconda	17.7	19.0	21.0	22.9
Utah Copper (Kennecott, 1924)	10.4			
Calumet & Hecla and subsidiaries	10.0	6.6	7.4	4.4
Phelps Dodge	8.2	8.6	23.3	18.8
Chino (Ray, 1924)	4.6			
Calumet & Arizona (Phelps Dodge, 1931)	4.4	6.2		
Nevada Consolidated (Kennecott, 1932)	4.4	13.0		
Ray Consolidated (Nevada Consolidated, 1926)	4.2			
Copper Range	3.8	1.2	2.2	1.0
United Verde (Phelps Dodge, 1935)	3.1	6.9		
Miami	2.9	2.9	3.9	4.2
Arizona Copper (Phelps Dodge, 1921)	2.6			
Old Dominion	1.9	.9		
Quincy	1.6	.2		.3
North Butte	1.4	.2		
Kennecott	1.0	15.8	25.6	35.9
All others	17.8	18.6	16.6	12.5

Source: *Hearings before the Temporary National Economic Committee*, Part 25, p. 13390.

These figures demonstrate two salient facts: first, the high degree of concentration in the industry and, second, the prominence of a trend toward further centralization. The sixteen largest producers in 1915, though some of them had disappeared, likewise expanded their control from 82 percent to 87 percent of the total.

Four firms dominate the whiskey industry in the United States: Schenley Distillers Corporation, National Distillers Products Corporation, Joseph E. Seagram and Sons, Inc., and Hiram Walker and Sons, Inc.[57] In 1938 these four corporations owned twenty of the ninety-seven whiskey distilleries in the country. Concentration was greater than these figures indicate, however, since, in terms of production, these twenty distilleries produced nearly two-thirds of the

[57] *Ibid.*, Part 6, pp. 2435–2439, 2678–2684.

total output. During successive years between 1934 and 1938 these four companies produced 60, 46, 45, 47, and 64 percent, respectively, of the total product. During this period the same companies held title to 60, 55, 48, 52, and 54 percent of total stocks of bonded whiskey held in warehouses throughout the United States. Even greater concentration was evident with respect to the ownership of stocks of aged whiskey, the percentages for the same years being 72, 79, 78, 91, and 78. As in the case of other industries described in this chapter, the liquor industry offers an excellent example of concentration, collaboration, maintained prices, and uniform policy—in a word, oligopoly.

The tobacco industry is familiar to anyone acquainted with the history of monopoly in the United States. In spite of the successful prosecution of the "tobacco trust" after the turn of the century, monopolistic remnants carried over. Uniform pricing during the past decade is, perhaps, best illustrated by the behavior of the major cigarette brands. Testimony before the TNEC indicated that little evidence of monopoly practice was found in the production, processing, warehousing, distribution, or marketing of leaf tobacco. Even here, however, considerable concentration of control exists; [58] five buyers of leaf tobacco ordinarily purchase 75 percent of the total domestic production.

Centralization is more pronounced in the manufacturing branch of the industry; in 1934 thirteen manufacturers sold more than 97 percent of the cigarettes, more than 90 percent of the smoking tobacco, 75 percent of the chewing tobacco, and more than 98 percent of the snuff sold in the United States. Even these figures fail to reveal the degree of concentration which exists, since three companies dominate the cigarette industry (80 percent), and three sell most of the snuff (97 percent). That absence of price-fixing agreements and evidence of outright collusion does not preclude the possibility of unified action has been well illustrated by their pricing policies.

The distribution of fluid milk would scarcely seem to adapt itself to combination; one usually thinks of concentration in connection with steel, tobacco, oil, glass, and aluminum. Nevertheless, since the requirement of compulsory pasteurization, two great milk combinations have risen to power in eastern cities. As in the case of the oil monopoly of old which rose to power through control of the refineries,

[58] *Ibid.*, Part 5, pp. 1817–1821.

the two milk combinations built their control around the legally required pasteurization plants.

The companies referred to are the National Dairy Products Corporation and the Borden Company. Between 1923 and 1938 they absorbed more than 500 dairy firms operating primarily in eastern cities.[59] By 1932 these two companies, with their operating subsidiaries, had assets of nearly $500,000,000 and annual gross sales of more than $550,000,000. They controlled the product of more than 3,000,000 dairy farms and possessed a near monopoly of the fluid milk distribution in numerous cities. In describing these two companies Dr. Frederic C. Howe [60] presented the following data concerning the extent of their control in nineteen cities:

1. New York City: Sheffield Farms Co., a subsidiary of National Dairy Products Corp. and the Borden Co., controls slightly in excess of 50 percent of the milk distribution. When Dairymen's League is added the figure is increased to about 70 percent.

2. Philadelphia: Four companies control approximately 85 percent of the distribution; this includes the subsidiaries of the National Dairy Products Corporation, the Supplee-Wills-Jones Milk Co. which distributes about 34 percent of the total.

3. Baltimore: Subsidiaries of the National Dairy Products Corp. control approximately 85 percent of the distribution.

4. Washington, D.C.: Subsidiaries of the National Dairy Products Corp. control about 55 percent of the distribution.

5. Pittsburgh: Two companies control about 57 percent of the distribution, divided as follows: Rieck-McJunkin Co., a subsidiary of National Dairy Products Corp., 38 percent and Meadow Gold Dairies, a subsidiary of the Beatrice Creamery, 19 percent. The next largest company is the Otto Milk Co., an independent, which controls 8 percent.

6. Detroit: 27 percent of the distribution is controlled by the Detroit Creamery Co. and the Ebling Co., which are subsidiaries of National Dairy Products Corp., and 25 percent by the Borden Co., making a total of 52 percent. The Kennedy Dairy Co., which is a subsidiary of the United States Dairy Products Co., handles about 6 percent of the total distribution. In all there are about 129 distributors in the Detroit sales area as defined in the old agreement, although only about 30 are within the city of Detroit proper.

7. Boston: Two large companies, Whiting Co. and H. P. Hood & Sons, control 14 percent and 27 percent respectively of the total distribution, or a total of 41 percent. About 10 percent of the total distribution is made through the First National Stores. In addition there are about 475 small dealers in the Boston sales area.

8. St. Louis: The St. Louis Dairy Co., a subsidiary of the National Dairy

59 *Ibid.*, Part 7, pp. 2763–2993.
60 Former Consumers' Counsel of the Agricultural Adjustment Administration.

Products Corp., controls about 40 percent of the fluid milk distribution in that city.

9. Louisville, Ky.: The largest distributor among the 23 distributors is a subsidiary of the National Dairy Products Corp. and controls about 34 percent of the total distribution.

10. Los Angeles: The National Dairy Products Corp. occupies a strong position; a public hearing is being held in Los Angeles at the present time.

11. Bridgeport, Conn.: The Borden Co. controls about 50 percent of the distribution (Department of Justice estimate as of 1930).

12. Wilmington, Del.: National Dairy Products Corp. controls about 45 percent (Department of Justice estimate).

13. Richmond, Va.: United States Dairy Products Co. controls about 59 percent of the distribution (Department of Justice estimate).

14. Akron, Ohio: 53 percent of the fluid milk distribution is controlled by the National Dairy Products Corp. and 39 percent by the Borden Co., making a total of 92 percent (Department of Justice estimate).

15. Columbus, Ohio: The Borden Co. controls 48 percent of the milk distribution (Department of Justice estimate).

16. Milwaukee, Wis.: 33 percent of the total fluid-milk distribution is controlled by National Dairy Products Corp. and 51 percent by the Borden Co., or a total of 84 percent (Department of Justice estimate as of 1930).

17. Denver, Col.: The Beatrice Creamery Co. controls about 30 percent (Department of Justice estimate as of 1930).

18. Salt Lake City and Ogden, Utah: The Pet Milk Co. controls about 36 percent.[61]

Two segments of the construction industry will illustrate the degree of economic centralization which has developed within the field: first, the construction contract industry and, second, the materials manufacturing industry. In the contracting industry the majority of employers, 53 percent, employ three or fewer employees, accounting, however, for only 11 percent of the employees. Those employing less than ten workers account for 83 percent of the employers but for less than a third of the employees. Thus, one-fiftieth of 1 percent of the employers give employment to nearly 4 percent of the workers, and 5 percent of the employers account for substantially one-half of the workers. One finds half the employees in enterprises which employ fewer than twenty-eight workers (accounting for 95 percent of the employers) and half in enterprises which employ more than twenty-seven workers.

The other segment of the construction industry is the manufactured materials division from which source comes most of the materials which the contractor uses. Dr. Willard Thorp presented data

61 *Hearings before the Temporary National Economic Committee*, Part 7, pp. 2763–2764.

Table 15. Selected Industries Producing Construction Materials, 1937

Product	Value of Product in Thousands of Dollars 1937	1935	Percentage of Total Value of Product Contributed by Four Leading Companies, 1935
Steel:			
Structural and ornamental	292,756	160,762	24
Steel works and rolling mill products:			
Structural shapes	148,630	67,308	49
Sheet metal	159,096	109,333	49
Rails and joints	78,722	39,112	49
Heating, cooling, and cooking apparatus:			
Heating and cooking equipment:			
Other than electric	182,153	122,836	38
Electric	270,431	174,393	38
Air conditioning	60,548		46
Fans	2,770		46
Paints and varnishes	538,461	417,000	32
Plumbing:			
Plumbers' supplies	113,920	75,631	34
Wrought pipe	113,769	73,849	47
Cast iron pipe	61,118	37,870	38
Cement, tile, and brick:			
Cement	183,201	120,417	29
Clay	163,261	111,197	19
Lime	35,022	23,322	22
Sand lime brick	1,618	654	63
Electrical equipment:			
Lighting equipment	35,678		23
Electric wire cable	131,627		44
Plaster, wallboard, etc.:			
Gypsum	42,616	26,300	75
Wallboard	41,049	23,848	54
Building paper	32,630	19,450	14
Roofing	102,562	16,172	43
Glass, flat	100,938	68,266	45
Asbestos	63,794	62,421	63
Builders' hardware	53,067	28,848	36
Metal doors and shutters	49,914	22,740	30
Window shades	23,574	20,324	24
Window screens	14,748	8,668	23
Asphalted felt base floor covering and linoleum	33,548	52,398	82
Elevators	21,235	9,110	44

Source: *Hearings before the Temporary National Economic Committee*, Part 11, p. 5511.

to the Committee showing the degree to which the four leading firms in 1937 dominated the production of specified construction materials; [62] this is revealed by the material presented in Table 15, derived

TABLE 16. PRODUCTS BY KIND, QUANTITY, AND/OR VALUE FOR ALL COMPANIES AND FOR FOUR LEADING COMPANIES IN THE PLUMBING INDUSTRY, 1937

Product	Production of Four Leading Companies: Percentage of Total Value for All Companies	Total Number of Companies
Enameled iron sanitary ware		
Bathtubs	73	13
Lavatories	69	15
Laundry tubs	81	13
Sink and laundry tray combinations	80	10
Sinks	64	13
Flush tanks	91	8
Drinking fountains	91	7
Tanks and shells for water heaters	56	7
Range boilers		
Galvanized iron	42	12
Copper and nonferrous alloy	58	14
Vitreous china plumbing fixtures		
Bathroom and toilet fixtures		
Closet bowls		
Siphon jets	81	17
Washdowns	83	19
Reverse traps	80	14
Flush tanks		
Lowdown	61	19
Lavatories	88	17
Stalls	87	10
Other bathroom and toilet fixtures	71	21
Other vitreous china fixtures	81	11
Semi-vitreous or porcelain plumbing fixtures	83	8
Faucets and spigots	31	41
Other plumbers' brass goods	35	123
Toilet seats		
Wood	46	21
Concrete laundry trays	38	32

Source: *Hearings before the Temporary National Economic Committee*, Part 11, pp. 5542–5543.

[62] Adapted from *ibid.*, Part 11, pp. 5203–5212, 5511.

from statistics compiled by the Bureau of the Census. Similar trends are shown by figures assembled by the Bureau of Mines relating to the production of construction materials in industries whose products are mined. Where the same products are mentioned, concentration appears to be greater. In 1937, according to this study, the four leading firms in the respective industries were responsible for 80 percent of the production of gypsum, 33 percent of sandstone, 84 percent of marble, and 63 percent of asphalt.[63]

When a specific product is considered, instead of all products within an industry (for example, bathtubs and flush tanks), concentration is shown to be even more marked. For all products in the plumbing industry the production figure for the four leading firms was between 35 and 40 percent. There were, however, 208 companies active in this field, but not all produced each specific product. Table 16 reveals the extent to which concentration exists among producers of specified plumbing facilities as measured by the percentage of production by the four leading firms.[64] It is thus evident that four companies account for 75 percent or more of the total United States production of the following products: enameled iron laundry tubs, enameled iron sink and laundry-tray combinations, enameled iron flush tanks, enameled iron drinking fountains, vitreous china siphon-jet closet bowls, vitreous china reverse-trap closet bowls, vitreous china lavatories, vitreous china stalls, and other vitreous china bathroom and toilet fixtures.

Even here the story is only partially complete. The construction materials industry has very few producers to begin with; it is what writers have in mind when they use the term oligopoly. Here is an industry which supplies thousands of building contractors, who in turn represent millions of consumers; yet the number of suppliers is limited: there are only 13 firms in the whole country which produce bathtubs, 8 who manufacture enameled sanitary flush tanks, 30 who produce asphalt smooth-roll roofing, 11 who manufacture waterproof roofing, and 4 who produce linoleum.[65]

Table 17, based upon a study of 264 products, presents another illuminating analysis of the degree of concentration in the construction materials industry. The importance of the leading firm for each product is shown. It is significant that for 36 commodities (4 percent of the total), the leading company accounted for more than one-half

63 *Ibid.*, pp. 5207, 5512.   64 *Ibid.*, adapted from Part 11, pp. 5542–5543.
65 *Ibid.*, Part 11, p. 5212.

TABLE 17. IMPORTANCE OF THE LEADING FIRM IN RELATION TO
TOTAL PRODUCTION OF 264 BUILDING MATERIAL PRODUCTS,
1937

Percentage of U. S. Total Production Accounted for by Leading Company	PRODUCTS		VALUE OF PRODUCTS	
	Number	Percentage of Total	In Millions	Percentage of Total
Under 10	19	7	$185	9
10.0–19.9	67	26	792	37
20.0–29.9	48	18	230	11
30.0–39.9	51	19	322	15
40.0–49.9	43	16	314	15
50.0–59.9	23	9	249	12
60 and over	13	5	17	1
Total	264	100	2,109	100

Source: *Hearings before the Temporary National Economic Committee,* Part 11, p. 5548.

of the total production; for 43 additional products (16 percent of the total), the leading company produced more than 40 percent; and for 51 products, more than 30 percent.

This concludes the study of concentration in United States industry. It cannot be asserted that the analysis is complete or that the most representative industries have been discussed. It does go far, nevertheless, to show how extensive oligopoly, monopolistic competition, uniform industrial policies, and maintained prices have become in modern economic life. The trust, the pool, the combination, and other techniques of the past, and even the powerful trade association of the present are rendered quite unnecessary in these industries, where the number of producers is so limited that a gentleman's world of "live and let live" can be effectuated without formality, without overt evidence of collusion, and without fear of prosecution.

CHAPTER VII

EXPLOITING THE ARM
OF THE LAW

THERE IS a philosophy which seems to pervade the thinking of many enterprisers of the country—a point of view which regards the state as a potential ally, whose authority is to be exploited to aid the business ventures of those sufficiently ingenious to gain its collaboration. The arm of the law often has been employed to destroy competitors when enterprisers have found themselves unable to compete in a fair and free market. Frequently the police power has been invoked to assist ambitious managers in imposing conditions of monopoly upon an unwary public, and this action has been rationalized by euphonious slogans such as "fair trade," "stabilizing industry," and "eliminating the abuses of competition."

In the guise of public interest, measures have been sought through the application of safety codes, patent laws, and consumer protection, to outlaw the method by which the other fellow operates his business, and the taxing power has been employed to impose burdens which drive him from the field. At times legal devices have been invented to deny the consumer freedom of choice and to coerce him, through the inherent power of the state, to purchase the wares of those who, through stronger political bargaining power or craftiness, have obtained legislation in which vested interests are concealed. Deceptive and sugar-coated in name, such laws are defended by advocates, who rarely reveal the intended beneficiaries, but extol the advantages allegedly accruing to the public. Measures of this type usually have one thing in common: whatever benefits do exist or are presumed to exist are concrete and immediate, and the recipient or the imagined recipient can easily visualize his gain, whereas the victims of such devices, the great majority upon whom the burdens must fall, find the analysis of their positions difficult, inasmuch as the disadvantages are indirect, diffused, and difficult of measurement.

These practices go deep into the very theory of government. The dichotomy is clear between an autocratic monarchy, on the one hand, which looks upon the people as pawns of its authority and pleasure,

and a representative democracy, on the other, which genuinely re-flects the interest of the population, granting neither privilege nor favor to any class or group. But rarely if ever can such governments be found; absolute monarchies seldom are completely callous of or oblivious to the welfare of the underlying population, and parliamen-tary governments often are forced to yield to classes which place their own interests paramount to those of society.

Probably the best that can be said of pressure-group politics is that the stratagems of designing interest groups frequently conflict and neutralize one another. Often, however, they are unopposed and are antagonistic only to the welfare of the unorganized, inarticulate pub-lic, which at times may even be duped by ingenious propaganda. Seldom are the proponents of such programs of privilege so naïve as to attempt to promote their cause by revealing the ultimate incidence of their schemes or the real recipients of favor. But the disturbing factor is that the special interest groups may be so well organized and their access to the instruments of publicity so convenient that the very character of representative government and of free economy is undergoing a basic and far-reaching transformation. There may be in process the establishment of a tradition which looks unchalleng-ingly upon the use of the Government as a handmaiden to serve minority economic interests.

No effort was made by the TNEC to appraise this trend or to as-semble facts as to its existence, but no economic study as broad as that conducted by the Committee could fail to reveal, here and there, numerous examples of this characteristic of our age. Examples they are, and only examples, but a few will be considered in the present chapter.

FAIR TRADE LAWS

One of the most aggressive movements in recent years, representing a triumphant coup by an economic minority, is styled in the statutes generally, but none the less inaccurately, as "fair trade" laws. Pro-fessor Fetter has aptly described this movement as follows: "We have been witnessing the latest attempt of monopoly under the deceptive slogan of fair competition to restrict economic freedom and to further narrow the remaining frontier of industrial opportunity." [1] The pro-ponents and beneficiaries of these statutes espouse their schemes by assigning to them pleasant-sounding and question-begging appella-

[1] *Hearings before the Temporary National Economic Committee,* Part 5, p. 1676.

tions; the programs are sold, not on their merits, but by their names.

By 1939 forty-three state legislatures had enacted "fair trade" laws, the only exceptions being Texas, Missouri, Vermont, Alabama, Delaware, and the District of Columbia. These statutes are, in fact, resale price maintenance laws giving the manufacturer the right to determine the price of the article to the consumer even after he has relinquished ownership to the jobber, wholesaler, and retailer. The statutes provide that when a manufacturer and a retailer sign a resale price contract, all other retailers who have notice of the contract must refrain from selling below that price. This permits the manufacturer, with the aid of a retailer, to coerce all merchants to observe what in effect is a monopoly price and to deny the right of free competition among the retail merchants of the product.

That a special interest group, by the well-known device of mobilizing political pressure, succeeded in imposing "fair trade" control upon the American people seems evident from the testimony before the TNEC. The project of promoting this type of price maintenance was undertaken almost exclusively by the drug trade of the country; no considerable amount of support came from any other source.[2] The whole undertaking demonstrates how legislators will yield to pressure when no counterbalancing influence is at hand to assist the lawmaker to maintain his equilibrium or to hold his ground. Numerous illustrations of the strategy used by the drug trade to obtain the adoption of "fair trade" laws were submitted for the record; they are rather aptly summarized in the following editorial of a prominent organ of business.

Most importantly, it set up the National Association of Retail Druggists as a power which in three short years was to roll up a record of accomplishment unmatched by any other pressure group in the country's history. . . . Having won the resale price maintenance fight in the face of the most overwhelming obstacles, the National Association of Retail Druggists is entitled to take rank as the Nation's most powerful trade association today.[3]

Thus, there is placed in the hands of the manufacturer the power to impose a price maintenance contract upon all retailers. This, in effect, legalizes what had been held to be illegal under the monopoly laws and by the restraint-of-trade doctrine. Retailers heretofore had

[2] *Ibid.*, Part 8, pp. 3366–3375, 3460–3465.
[3] Quoted from *Business Week*, August 28, 1937, in the *Hearings before the Temporary National Economic Committee*, Part 8, p. 3467.

been forbidden to enter into conspiracies or agreements to restrain competition among themselves, but what they had been forbidden to do horizontally, they are now given legislative warrant to do vertically; through the medium of the manufacturer all retailers may be coerced to maintain a fixed price. That the retail drug trade has operated in this manner and has employed methods to whip reluctant manufacturers into line is indicated by the following excerpts from leading trade journals.

In the drug and cosmetic fields many manufacturers are being compelled to operate under these laws against their wishes and better judgment. Pressure is being brought to bear through the retailers' associations and their fair-trade committees. Manufacturers who do not file minimum prices are having their troubles with independent outlets in some States. . . . The Committees are not permitted, supposedly, by law to dictate what the minimum prices shall be but they are doing just that by refusing to approve contracts containing prices which do not give the retailer what they consider to be a fair profit margin. In most cases the committees are insisting on a mark-up of at least 20 percent and usually 33⅓ percent.[4]

Following a mid-January mass meeting, druggists of the New York metropolitan area seemed likely to clear their shelves of items manufactured by five leading manufacturers. . . . To inject action into the meeting in place of talk, the younger element among the druggists "tossed out" the "old guard" and replaced them with younger leaders. . . . Simultaneously with the suggested removal of products of the five banned manufacturers from their shelves, the retailers launched an attack on two New York newspapers, the *Times* and the *World-Telegram*.

A boycott of the products of manufacturers who do not use and enforce fair-trade contracts, and exposé of manufacturers who are "secretly allied" with R. H. Macy & Co., and a concerted effort to fight private brands, were threatened by druggists at the militant fair-trade victory meeting held in conjunction with the convention of the New York Pharmaceutical Council at Hotel Pennsylvania, New York City, recently.[5]

A successful technique of interest group legislation is to propel the desired statute through the legislature in order to achieve a *fait accompli* before the public is aware of the proposal and before organized resistance can develop and to establish it as a legal institution before it can be challenged. The "fair trade" laws seem to have been maneuvered through state legislatures in this manner; a witness described the process as follows:

[4] *Printers' Ink*, August 26, 1937, p. 6, quoted by the *Hearings before the Temporary National Economic Committee*, Part 8, p. 3373.
[5] *Drug Trade News*, April 26, 1937, p. 1, quoted by the *Hearings before the Temporary National Economic Committee*, Part 8, p. 3372.

The bill was given the ambiguous and appealing name of "fair trade" law. A systematic effort was made to prevent public hearings and to secure the enactment of the bill without public debate. This effort was successful. There was a public hearing on the bill in only three states out of the first thirty-two in which it was passed, and in one of these the hearing followed the passage. Indeed, there was so little consideration of any kind that, although the original draft of the bill contained a stenographic error which made utter nonsense out of one of the most important provisions, this error appeared without change in the statutes of eleven states before it was caught and corrected. Another stenographic error, not quite so serious, was included in the laws of seventeen states. Some members of state legislatures subsequently told consumers' organizations that they did not know what they were voting on.[6]

The manner in which Federal legislation was obtained to reinforce state "fair trade" laws illustrates once more how it might have been impossible to secure the passage of such statutes had they been presented and debated on their merits. The Miller-Tydings Act was passed by the Congress in 1937, as a rider to the District of Columbia appropriation bill. Possibly it might have been favorably received by the Congress at a later date, but it is doubtful that it could have become a law, since the President indicated that he would have vetoed it had he been given the opportunity to consider it as a separate bill.[7] At the same time the Federal Trade Commission strongly opposed the measure.[8]

The Miller-Tydings Act repealed an important provision of the Sherman Act. Until the passage of state "fair trade" laws and of the Miller-Tydings Act, price-fixing agreements were held to be illegal.[9] But in 1937, Section 1 of the Sherman Act was amended to exempt from prosecution retailers and manufacturers who enter into price maintenance contracts under the authority of state "fair trade" statutes. Thus, an important segment of the Sherman Act was abrogated, and a hitherto illegal practice was made legal. In the Beech-Nut case, in 1922, the practice now employed under "fair trade" laws was held by the Supreme Court to violate the Sherman Act in that it tended to suppress and prevent freedom of competition.[10] It also was held

6 *Final Report and Recommendations of the Temporary National Economic Committee*, pp. 232–233.
7 *Ibid.*, p. 122; *Hearings before the Temporary National Economic Committee*, Part 5, p. 1762.
8 *Hearings before the Temporary National Economic Committee*, Part 5, pp. 1761–1763.
9 *Ibid.*, p. 1760.
10 The Beech-Nut Case, 257 U.S. 441 (1922); see *Hearings before the Temporary National Economic Committee*, Part 5, p. 1760.

to violate the Federal Trade Commission Act and to constitute an unfair method of competition. After the passage of state "fair trade" laws, however, the Court held that an Illinois statute was not unconstitutional and that a state could sanction contracts which fix prices for designated products. The power of price maintenance was made complete by the passage of the Miller-Tydings Act, which, according to the Assistant Attorney General, has become "a cloak for many conspiracies in restraint of trade."

According to the conclusions drawn after a thorough study by the Federal Trade Commission, the net social effect of retail price maintenance is bad and contrary to the interests of consumers.[11] No evidence was presented to the TNEC as to the actual effect of "fair trade" laws upon prices themselves, but the attention of the Committee was called to the fact that four independent nongovernmental studies had been made, and in each it was found that their general effect is to increase prices.[12] From the standpoint of the retailer, price maintenance is looked upon as a device to eliminate the rigors of competition and to "keep everybody in the business." A proponent of "fair trade" stated it as follows.

There are 4,000,000 people engaged in retail distribution. They distribute $33,000,000,000 of your products of the farm and the factory and the field. If you are interested in maintaining the American system, which is the profit system, you are going to have to do something to try to make it possible for those 4,000,000 people to be happy and content with a margin of profit and a fair return on their efforts.[13]

The spokesman just quoted has, in effect, denounced the belief in a system of free competition and individual enterprise. He himself aptly described the designs of retailers seeking this type of price umbrella.

Let's put it this way. The laborer is worthy of his hire, and a sale without a profit is a sale without honor, and an indictment of the American people. Nobody has any right to be asked to distribute your products or to manufacture or to sell without an adequate return unless you don't believe in the profit system.[14]

Such a program of "keeping everyone in the business" would, of course, resolve itself into a scheme of subsidizing inefficiency or of

[11] Ibid., pp. 2170–2172.
[12] Final Report and Recommendations of the Temporary National Economic Committee, pp. 149–153.
[13] Hearings before the Temporary National Economic Committee, Part 6, p. 2557.
[14] Ibid., Part 6, p. 2558.

extending monopoly profits to all those producing above the margin. This, however, does not seem to disturb the advocates of price maintenance,[15] as is illustrated by the following colloquy during the hearings.

MR. BERGE. Do you think that conditions could be frozen so that the unintelligent could be kept in business regardless of his efficiency?
MR. WACHTEL. He renders a service, he is a fellow neighbor.[16]

The illusion has been created that the "fair trade" laws were sponsored primarily by and for the protection of retail merchants. That this illusion persists is a tribute to the adroit manner in which the manufacturers were able to hold themselves in the background. The two organs of the drug trade chiefly responsible for the effectiveness of the "fair trade" campaign ostensibly were the organs of retailers. Actually the principal beneficiaries of "fair trade" laws have been the manufacturers, who were thus able to extend their control of price beyond the area of ownership. This fact was recognized by the Supreme Court in the Dearborn case, in which it was held that such statutes were intended primarily to protect the manufacturers. The program, of course, would have been impossible without the co-operation of the retailers; consequently, some semblance had to be made of sharing with them the larger price margins thus made possible. However, little choice is available to the retailer; under the laws the manufacturer alone has the power to take the initiative and to elect whether or not his product should be "fair-traded." Nor do retailers ordinarily determine the mark-up margins—they are fixed by the manufacturer.

Thus, a system of commercial paternalism has been established by law. The power of monopoly has been granted to manufacturers, who by contract with a single retailer may impose price control upon retailers, who thereafter exist by the largess of the manufacturer. That this paternalism is an important feature of the "fair trade" system is neatly epitomized in the following exchange between a TNEC member and a witness.

MR. O'CONNELL. And I understood you also to say that the theory of that is that where you have, as you put it, an intelligent group of retailers, they need the protection which your company, and apparently only your company, is in a position to give them; is that right?
MR. WACHTEL. I hope no retailer will hold it against me, but it is true.
MR. O'CONNELL. I take it that is the position of your company, that in

15 *Ibid.*, p. 2563. 16 *Ibid.*, p. 2567.

the absence of this paternalistic interest your company takes over the retail field, the unintelligent retailers, at least, would go broke.

MR. WACHTEL. And he thanks us for it.

MR. O'CONNELL. The unintelligent thanks you for it?

MR. WACHTEL. Yes, sir.[17]

"Fair trade" laws abandon the concept of the desirability of competitive prices; they operate under the assumption that retail prices should be subject to control by authority. They assume, however, that that regulation should be imposed, not by a responsible government, not by any agency representing the consumer, not by the retailers whose prices are controlled, but by the manufacturers, who, in this age of product differentiation and mass production, have come to look upon competition as something good for all phases of the economy but their own; to paraphrase one writer, competition is something of which producers have only as much as they cannot eliminate.[18]

THE NRA

The depression which began in 1929 brought with it a period during which the Government was induced to enter into a partnership with the trade associations. Trade associations are special interest groups—they do not represent the public, independent research foundations, or consumers, but are interested primarily in the welfare of the owners of business. Apparently their organizers easily persuaded themselves that they should be sponsored under the aegis of government. This point of view won out in 1933, when the NRA was organized; compulsory cartelization of American industry proceeded to take place under the banner of the Blue Eagle.

Two points of view commonly are held concerning the relationship of business to government. One is that competition should pervade the economy, and, if necessary, be enforced by the Government; the other, that business should be regulated. The NRA represented the adoption of the latter point of view; the antitrust laws were set aside, and industry was organized under codes. Those who endorse the policy of regulated business likewise are divided into two camps. One would have the Government police business, establish the rules of the game, and assure that the interests of capital, labor, and the public are fairly protected. The other view holds that business should police itself. The NRA represented a triumph of the latter policy.

17 *Ibid.*, pp. 2566–2567.   18 *Ibid.*, Part 25, p. 13085.

"Codes of fair competition" were drawn up to govern industry; they were exempt from the prohibitions of the antitrust laws, and, most startling of all, their mandates became mandates of the Government itself. "Self-rule" in industry became a long-cherished realization. The "American way," as it was called, represented business regulation by government sanction, but not by government. As one witness characterized it, the large manufacturers of steel were called in and told: "Gentlemen, now write your own ticket." [19]

Generally the codes of fair competition were written by the trade associations, as well as administered and policed by them.[20] More than 800 codes were drawn up, each with its own rules and regulations as to what constitutes "fair competition." That business ethics could be subject to so many interpretations did not seem to surprise the framers of the codes; yet one is impressed by the following reaction of Professor Fetter.

The notion that you would have a separate ethical code for each one of five or six hundred industries is an absurdity. The ethical code is a code of common, decent practice, fair practice, and I think if that were laid down in simple terms, then the problem of administration under a body like the Federal Trade Commission would be fairly simple.[21]

Commerce is a two-sided operation, involving the consuming public as well as the representatives of business. It is striking that to one side alone should be delegated full authority to determine the rules of the game governing this important relationship. It is as though the Government had decided that business should be regulated and then abdicated its authority in this regard. It would be difficult to conceive of a game of football for which the rules were determined by the players of one team only, who declared the penalties, imposed the sanctions, and selected the officials. Yet such a situation is analogous to the NRA codes establishing self-rule for business.

The NRA approved 874 codes; many regulations were set forth establishing uniform practices for industry, controlling many relationships wherein competition might otherwise obtain.[22] Thus, monopoly conditions were imposed for many segments of the economy;

[19] *Ibid.*, Part 5, pp. 1704–1705.
[20] *Ibid.*, Part 25, pp. 13319–13320. It is interesting to note once more the use of the euphonious and question-begging label "code of fair competition," instead of a more objective and descriptive term such as "compulsory cartel," "legalized pool," or "industrial self-regulation."
[21] *Ibid.*, Part 5, p. 1981.
[22] *Ibid.*, Part 25, pp. 13319–13327; see also Temporary National Economic Committee Monograph No. 21, *Competition and Monopoly in American Industry*, pp. 260–267.

the more important monopolistic devices, designedly promoted by the NRA, include the following:

Uniform terms of sale.—Eight hundred and fifty codes established regulations governing terms of sale. A long list of specific prohibitions usually were elaborated restricting special concessions to consumers, including such matters as quotation and invoice forms, bidding and awarding procedures, customer classifications, discounts, bill datings, credit practices, installment sales, deferred payments, interest charges, guarantees of quality, long-term contracts, options, time and form of payments, return of merchandise, sales on consignment, sales on trial or approval, cancellation of contracts, trade-in allowances, advertising allowances, supplementary services, combination sales, rebates, premiums, free deals, containers, coupons, samples, prizes, absorption of freight, delivery of better qualities or larger quantities than those specified, sale of used and discounted goods, payment of fees and commissions, and the maintenance of resale prices.

Limitation of output.—Many codes provided either for direct limitation of output or for the restriction of productive capacity. Four codes set limits for the size of inventories and compelled manufacturers to confine their operations to the volume of current sales. Fifty-three codes established limits for the construction, relocation, or conversion of productive capacity. Twenty-four went so far as to forbid producers to add new productive capacity without permission. Sixty codes limited the working hours per day and week during which plants could be operated. Somewhat the same purposes were served by establishing production or sales quotas —assigned by five codes.

Allocation of markets.—Another method designed to restrain competition was that of awarding zones and markets to specific producers. Various devices were employed to create quasi-tariff walls around designated areas. Some codes forbade freight allowances, others prohibited "dumping"—or the act of a firm selling outside its "normal market" at prices lower than "customary charges." Still other codes created zones and forbade producers outside such areas to sell below the prices charged by producers within.

Price fixing.—The mind of the monopolist frequently turns first to price. It is not surprising, therefore, to find that 560 of the first 677 codes made some provision to fix prices. A wide variety of devices were employed to achieve this end. *a*) Minimum prices. Twelve codes granted the code authority power to fix minimum prices without any reference to cost of production. *b*) Emergency prices. About 200 codes provided for the establishment of minimum prices in the event of an "emergency." What constituted an emergency was left, of course, to the discretion of the code authority. The evidence indicated that industry after industry had declared a state of emergency; representatives of the solid fuel trade said, "We have always had an emergency in retail solid fuel." *c*) Open price systems. One of the most effective methods of assuring uniform prices was the price reporting system required by 422 codes. Earlier decisions of the Supreme Court had held similar schemes to be illegal, but under the NRA they

flourished. The usual procedure required producers to file price schedules and to adhere to them. More often than not a waiting period was required before prices became effective; this period became known as the "period of intimidation," during which duress could be used upon members of the industry who were considered to be "out of line." *d*) Standard cost systems. One way to assure uniform prices is for the code authority (the trade association) to require all producers to use a common formula by which to calculate costs. Three hundred and sixty-one codes required the use of arbitrary standard costing systems which automatically led to common pricing. *e*) Sales below cost forbidden. Four hundred and three codes prohibited sales below cost. This provision varied from preventing a thoughtless competitor from failing to realize his true costs to the use of an arbitrary cost concept as a basis of pricing. Three hundred and fifty-two codes forbade members to sell below their individual costs. Fifty-one forbade them to sell below the average for the whole industry. A few codes permitted the code authority to itemize the presumed costs of the industry and to hold all members in violation of the code who sold below the total thus derived. In some codes not only uniform costs were required but uniform margins as well before arriving at selling prices.

Specific selling practices prohibited.—Another way by which the codes eliminated competition was to outlaw designated selling practices. It is unnecessary to mention all that might properly be considered under this heading; examples would include the prescription of maximum credit terms and trade-in allowances, the regulation of deferred payment practices, prohibition of sales on consignment, and the regulation of service and guaranties.

With the Schechter decision [23] in 1935 the structure of the NRA crumbled, but the reasoning by which the Supreme Court arrived at its opinion bore little relation to these monopolistic effects of the codes. The unconstitutionality of the NRA, however, was not sufficient to eliminate the new instruments of collaboration to which business had become accustomed and for which it had worked so arduously. The many new trade associations born of the NRA, temporarily championed and made obligatory by the Government, continued to function quite as before; old associations had become more virile and the principles written into the codes had become guiding policies. In fact, a frequent defense which antitrust violators subsequently advanced in Federal Trade Commission cases was that the particular practice with which they were charged had been either required or sanctioned by the NRA.[24]

The movement for "self-government" in industry, thus given a

[23] 295 U.S. 495.
[24] *Hearings before the Temporary National Economic Committee,* Part 5, pp. 1732, 1964.

strong impetus by the NRA, persisted after 1935. A few cases will illustrate. The Distilled Spirits Institute, which was organized in 1933 and whose officers became those of the code authority, continued to function as a trade association, fostering practices to "stabilize" the industry.[25] Similarly, the Valve and Fittings Institute, whose officers and those of the code authority for the industry interlocked, later was found to have been guilty of monopolistic practices, including price fixing and division of territory.[26] When the Iron and Steel Institute was organized under the NRA, the code provided that officers of the trade association should become the code authority. Immediately they outlawed twelve practices as unfair and agreed that any practice which the board of directors by a three-fourths vote declared to be unfair would be subject to penalty. This trade association regulated the terms of sale, determined the pricing system, succeeded in putting the basing-point system into the code, provided for production quotas, restricted output, and fostered other practices [27] which Adam Smith probably would have called "a conspiracy against the public." After the NRA was invalidated by the Court, it appears that the Iron and Steel Institute voted to maintain its code of "fair competition" and to continue its collaborative practices.[28] Likewise, maintained prices were more characteristic of the copper industry after the demise of the NRA than before its birth.[29]

SOCIAL CONTROL WITHOUT SOCIAL RESPONSIBILITY

Thus, it is evident that a substantial number of business men desire that the state grant to industrial groups the right to establish the rules which govern the relationships between themselves and the public. This they call by various names: "self-rule in business," "fair competition," or the "American way." It is more pleasant to repeat the euphonious term "fair competition" than to use the more realistic designation "monopoly"; it sounds better to speak of eliminating the "abuses of competition" than to suggest "conspiracy" or "restraint of trade." Neither pleasant words nor self-delusion, however, can conceal the basic motive for most of these schemes. One witness before the TNEC, himself guilty of some of the most flagrant types of restraint disclosed by the hearings, naïvely revealed what many less frank have in mind by fair competition: "I am opposed to price fixing," he said,

25 *Ibid.*, Part 6, pp. 2628–2631.   26 *Ibid.*, Part 5, p. 1738.
27 *Ibid.*, Part 25, pp. 13344–13345.   28 *Ibid.*, Part 27, pp. 14180–14181.
29 *Ibid.*, Part 25, pp. 13249–13253.

"and I am 100 percent in favor of fair competition." [30] Then, quite in the same breath, as it were, he explained what he had in mind by proposing a scheme well adapted to eliminate substantially all price competition: "I believe that one of the most important [device that I would recommend to curb a lot of these abuses] is an open price posting rule to bring it right out into the light of day where everybody can look at it." [31] In other words, fair competition is the absence of almost all competition; this appears to be the basic generalization deductible from the following colloquy.

MR. O'CONNELL. When does he become unfair? When does it become unfair for him to compete on a price basis? You say so long as he doesn't take too much of the business.

MR. SCHUH. Let's get practical. The Clarke Oil Co. in Milwaukee since 1931 has come from nowhere, one little station, to third position by cutting price. He is the third largest distributor in the city of Milwaukee. He will push Standard and Socony-Vacuum off that pedestal if they don't look out. I think, obviously, the fellow is foolish, because he is just trying to get too much business.

DR. LUBIN. Apparently he is making money by the deal; he is building stations.

MR. SCHUH. Yes; he is making money.

DR. LUBIN. What is unfair about it?

MR. SCHUH. Sooner or later some place he is going to trip and fall.

DR. LUBIN. That is going to be his hard luck; but in terms of fair competition, what is unfair about it?

MR. SCHUH. In every instance he built a station kitty-corner to two or three established stations, and he cut the price until some of those fellows have gone bankrupt. When you cause that, I think that isn't clean competition.

DR. LUBIN. In other words, you think that nobody should charge less than enough to keep everybody in business.

MR. SCHUH. No.

DR. LUBIN. Where do we draw the line?

MR. SCHUH. A fair price.

DR. LUBIN. Apparently his price is fair; he is making good profits.

MR. SCHUH. No; it is only fair because he has been able to grab the volume by adopting the methods that I describe.

DR. LUBIN. What is the function of business, of the businessman? It is to increase his output and increase his volume, isn't it, and if you can do it cheaper than the other fellow and still do it at a profit so that you are not taking unfair advantage of the other fellow in the sense that you make it impossible for him to make a profit because you are willing to forego a profit, what is unfair about it? Isn't that the essential of a modern business

[30] *Ibid.*, Part 17, p. 9467.　　　　[31] *Ibid.*, p. 9492.

scheme? Isn't that the essential of a competitive system and private enterprise? Are you advocating we change our whole competitive system and eliminate it?

Mr. Schuh. No.

Dr. Lubin. What would you substitute for it?

Mr. Schuh. I wouldn't substitute anything for it, but in this particular instance, if the companies had given us a competitive price, that is, had given us a price that we could pay, this man wouldn't have made the progress that he has made.

Dr. Lubin. Couldn't you have gone out and done the same thing he did?

Mr. Schuh. Yes.

Dr. Lubin. What is unfair about this?

Mr. Schuh. Because I don't think, in my opinion, that it is fair.

Dr. Lubin. What is unfair? What is your criterion of unfairness? What is your test?

Mr. Schuh. My criterion of fairness is to be reasonable and not to take advantage of your fellow businessmen.

Dr. Lubin. In other words, you are unreasonable if you want to make a profit.

Mr. Schuh. No. I think you are entitled to a profit.

Dr. Lubin. You are unreasonable if you are unwilling to make the maximum profit.

Mr. Schuh. No.

Dr. Lubin. Then what is your test of reasonableness?

Mr. Schuh. Your test of reasonableness is being fair about the prices that you establish.

Dr. Lubin. What is the test of fairness?

Mr. Schuh. Well, in many cases they stay a cent below us.

Dr. Lubin. But what is unfair about staying a cent below you if he can sell the product a cent cheaper than you can and still make money in the process?

· · ·

Mr. O'Connell. Obviously the whole problem is far from being solved, but you have suggested, or at least you have taken a position, and it is to my mind a little bit difficult to be very realistic and take the sort of position you have taken. I mean, what is reasonable and what is a fair price? That has very little to do with the competitive system.[82]

Soon after the demise of the NRA spokesmen of business asked the state legislatures and the Congress to enact legislation legalizing once more the "self-rule in industry" features of the NRA. In 1936 the United States Chamber of Commerce went on record as follows.

The anti-trust law shall be modified so as to make clear that the laws permit agreements increasing the possibilities of keeping production re-

[82] *Ibid.*, pp. 9503–9504.

lated to consumption. . . . Businesses desiring to combine should have opportunity to ascertain from a suitable Government authority whether or not the proposed combination will be in violation of the anti-trust laws. Each industry shall be permitted to formulate and to put into effect rules of fair competition which receive governmental approval. . . . Rules of fair competition formulated by a clearly preponderant part of an industry as suitable for the whole industry, with due consideration for small units and approved by the governmental agency, should be enforceable against all concerns in the industry.[33]

That business, or an influential portion of it, has maintained a sustaining interest in this type of "fair competition" is evidenced also by a United States Chamber of Commerce pronouncement in 1939.

There should be inquiry into need for legislation permitting industry rules of fair competition, allowing agreements increasing the possibilities of relating production to consumption. . . . There should be such modification of the antitrust laws as would make clear the legality of agreements increasing the possibilities of keeping production in proper relation to consumption, with protection of the public interest at all times through Government supervision of such agreements. There should likewise be opportunity for business concerns desiring to combine to ascertain from a suitable Government authority whether or not there will be violation of the antitrust laws.[34]

This, it would seem, raises the fundamental issue as to what type of economic society we are to have: shall it be unplanned and competitive, or shall it be planned and regulated? If planned and regulated, who shall be the planners and those responsible for the regulation? Those who ask for codes of fair competition have cast their vote for a planned and regulated economy and for a system in which the regulated shall be the regulators. As Mr. Schuh so eloquently phrased it, "I don't call it Government control; I call it Government help." [35] The arm of the law shall be used not as an instrument to protect the public, but to aid organized sellers to perfect a monopoly and to restrain "the dirty, lousy chiselers" [36] who undersell them and still make a profit.

This appears to be the philosophy of "self-rule," the philosophy which won out in the NRA. This is the renowned "crackdown" method of employing the sovereign power to belabor the so-called "chiseler" or anyone else who has the temerity to engage in rigorous competition. This is regulation of industry in the name of the state,

---

[33] *Ibid.*, Part 25, p. 13324.   [34] *Ibid.*, p. 13361.
[35] *Ibid.*, Part 17, p. 9491.
[36] See the interchange between Mr. Schuh and Senator King, *ibid.*, p. 9448.

but not in the interest of its citizens. This is social control without social responsibility and constitutes a use of the power of the state to abet the very practice against which Adam Smith so aptly warned.

People of the same trade seldom meet together, even for merriment and diversion, but the conversation ends in a conspiracy against the public, or in some contrivance to raise prices. It is impossible indeed to prevent such meetings, by any law which could either be executed, or would be consistent with liberty and justice. But though the law cannot hinder people of the same trade from sometimes assembling together, it ought to do nothing to facilitate such assemblies; much less to render them necessary.[37]

TRADE BARRIERS [38]

One section of the hearings emphasized the increasing importance of interstate trade barriers, many of which represent a perversion of the normal powers of the state and promote the advantage of special interest groups. The power to tax and to regulate industry in the public interest often has been employed as a mask by those who would destroy their competitors when unable to do so on a basis of price, service, or quality. The beneficiaries of trade barriers make numerous and conflicting claims with respect to the public good which is presumed to flow from their biased and piecemeal variety of economic planning. Perhaps in more instances than not they are deluded by their own forensics and are blameless of any hypocrisy.

The power to erect interstate trade barriers flows from the same fundamental source from which nearly all legal authority is derived. A sovereign state is vested with the power to protect the life, property, health, and morals of its citizens; in a democratically organized society, this is its chief purpose for existence. A second power is derived from the first—the right to levy taxes to support the foregoing powers. But the power to protect public health by reasonable inspection laws may be misapplied to deny producers access to given markets. The right to protect the highway from damage or destruction may be manipulated to grant a monopoly position to particular interest groups. The authority to impose quarantine restrictions against diseased fruits and vegetables may be twisted to assure particular producers a favored position in the home market.

The power to tax usually has been surrounded with the limitation that the revenues thus created shall be put to a public purpose. The

[37] Adam Smith, *The Wealth of Nations*, Random House, 1937, p. 128.
[38] *Hearings before the Temporary National Economic Committee*, Part 29; see also the section on "Interstate Trade Barriers," pp. 213-218.

characteristic thing about state barrier taxes, however, is that they are employed, not for revenue, but for regulation. Although the little revenue they create may be put to a public purpose, the effect of such taxes may be antisocial in the strict sense of the word. They are like chain-store taxes, which ordinarily have but one purpose—to drive one type of merchandising from the market in the interest of another whose operators do not feel able to compete unaided. Taxes often have been imposed for no other purpose than to burden or destroy some selected industry which the public seems to prefer and to divert consumer demand to the very producers who instigate the tax burden. The tax barrier fails of its purpose if it produces any substantial revenue; its purpose is to destroy. It places new administrative and financial burdens upon the state and diverts the productive resources of the community to less fruitful channels.

Such barriers do not represent a new use of the taxing power; taxes have been employed before for public regulation. But a sound administrative principle would appear to be that when taxes are employed for social regulation, the public at large should receive the major benefits, and the impost should result in as little impairment of economic efficiency as possible. To that end dangerous and poisonous yellow sulphurous matches have been taxed out of existence, and the issuance of paper money has been made subject to the regulation of the Federal Government. But taxes which serve as clubs, wielded by the state to beat down the competitors of a favored group of producers to the disadvantage of the consuming public would appear to be as bad social policy as the use of public revenues for individual benefit.

There appear to be three general types of interstate trade barriers which restrain competition and discriminate between competitors. One type seeks to discriminate between producers (of substantially the same product) on a territorial basis and to award the benefits of monopoly to those in the home market. Illustrative of this type are milk inspection laws which purport to be concerned only with public safety but which deliberately exclude, or discriminate against, more distant producers.[39] Another illustration is found in laws employed by Michigan and California against out-of-state liquor products.[40] A second type of interstate trade barrier is designed to favor producers of one product against those of a substitute. Oleomargarine tax laws illustrate this type of barrier. Other barriers are those which discrimi-

[39] *Ibid.*, pp. 15793–15795.   [40] *Ibid.*, pp. 15770–15892.

nate in favor of producers who offer one type of service in competition with another. For example, the so-called "Green River" ordinances [41] are designed to drive house-to-house salesmen and peddlers from the market for the benefit of local retailers, and many burdens which have been heaped upon truckers have been initiated by railroad interests.[42]

PUBLIC SAFETY CODES

There are many institutional and legal devices which, as a class, have originated and are justified because they establish rules and invoke sanctions to protect the public; these include health codes, safety codes, sanitary inspection, and the like. There can be little objection to such regulations so long as they are designed and administered as health, safety, and sanitation measures; frequently, however, economic interest groups obtain the passage of regulations which purport to offer public protection, but whose principal and covert purposes are to create a vested and often monopolistic position for a pressure group. To permit organized plumbers to make plumbing laws and organized electricians to establish the codes governing electrical installations, when the public, too, has a vital interest in these matters, also would be somewhat analogous to permitting one team at a football game to determine the rules and to select the referees despite the wishes of the opposing team or the spectators.

In the hearings relating to the construction industry, passing attention was given to the manifold building regulations and codes throughout the country which usually serve one of two basic purposes —the protection of the public and the creation of special monopoly privileges.[43] Often these codes are merely a local variety of the protective tariff. They usually require licenses before artisans are permitted to engage in repair or construction work, either for hire or for themselves. In many cities, for example, a scientifically trained electrical engineer would not be permitted to make even the most elementary installations about his own home, regardless of the quality of his work, nor would the building inspectors license him unless he could qualify as a member of the organized interest group. Most often the codes seem to favor contractors, though frequently they are designed to protect specific craft guilds. In one state licenses are required for anyone who undertakes "to construct, alter, repair, add to, sub-

---

[41] *Ibid.,* pp. 15967–15976.   [42] *Ibid.,* pp. 15767, 15789–15792, 15803–15823.
[43] *Ibid.,* Part 11, pp. 5150–5152.

tract from, improve, move, wreck, or demolish any building, highway, road, railroad, excavation, or other structure, project, development, or improvement, or to do any part thereof, including the erection of any scaffolding or other structure or works in connection therewith." [44] Thus, by this representative bias of the law, apparently anyone who drives a nail in his own house commits a crime against the contractors' fraternity. Such codes create legally established boycotts with respect to carpentry, plumbing, and electrical installations.

A somewhat related situation may arise when a safety code—not sought by a pressure group, but actually and wholly in the public interest—is turned subsequent to its enactment into a monopolistic device. An illustration of such a situation is described in the milk hearings.[45] In 1900, after a series of severe epidemics throughout the country, there developed an energetic campaign to purify milk. A standardized milk ordinance, recommended by the United States Public Health Service, was adopted by 900 cities.[46] These ordinances, quite properly it seems, required milk pasteurization. But a consequence not reckoned with was that the pasteurization plants became the foci around which great milk distributing combinations were created in the larger cities.[47] The pasteurization plants have been compared to the pipe lines and refineries which served as the foundation of the oil monopoly in the days of Standard Oil. They became "gateways of commerce" through which all trade must pass. They were too expensive for independents to maintain, and although public authority had required them, it had not seen fit to make them common carriers accessible to all producers. Hence, the combinations flourished under the aegis of the safety code.

More significant, perhaps, than the power which special economic groups wield through the formulation of codes is that which they often enjoy through their administration, whether such groups had a part in their formulation or not. Rules may be applied uniformly or with bias, rigorously or otherwise. If the pressure group can influence the choice of the safety inspectors, that in itself constitutes a powerful advantage. Often the inspector looks upon his job as a responsibility to his group rather than to the public. A striking example of this was revealed in the milk hearings, where an independent distributor, who sold milk at prices below those charged by the combination, found himself continually harassed by safety inspectors—sufficiently

44 *Ibid.*, p. 5150.   45 *Ibid.*, Part 7.
46 *Ibid.*, pp. 2760–2761.   47 *Ibid.*, pp. 2761–2762.

so as to discourage almost any producer who might dare to affront the combination.[48]

PATENTS

Some measures of government, by the very design of those who promote their adoption, represent the misuse of public power and of legal institutions for private benefit; others often become so as they develop, because they are shaped by the benefiting parties. The patent laws, as they frequently operate, fall into the latter category.[49]

The purpose of the patent laws is clearly set forth in the Constitution; Article 1, Section 8, empowers the Congress "to promote the progress of science and useful arts, by securing for limited times to authors and inventors the exclusive right to their respective writings and discoveries." Patents are, therefore, legal monopolies; they are intentionally so, and are awarded on the theory that the resultant public benefit will outweigh the rewards which accrue to inventors. Hence, the latter are given exclusive rights for a limited period to exploit their inventions.

Patents, however, promote two processes. One is creative, the other, restrictive; one encourages or rewards inventiveness, while the other fosters monopoly; one promotes production, the other fosters predation. There seems to have been little doubt in the minds of many who appeared before the TNEC that patents do encourage inventors and stimulate the inventive process. Even in an age when much of the invention is produced in the laboratory, the assurance of exclusive control of the product for a limited period of years encourages industrial concerns to undertake the expense of research and development. There seems also to have been agreement that the existing patent laws could be modified and modernized to suit twentieth-century economic conditions and better to serve their original purpose.

Likewise, there is ample evidence that the patent system as it has developed has fostered an unfortunate variety of practices antagonistic to the purpose which guided the framers of the Constitution. The system has not only encouraged the inventor but also sponsored the "exploiter," in the less desirable meaning of that term. A few of the practices employed are illustrated.

Patent fencing.—This process is aimed primarily at restraining the

[48] *Ibid.*, pp. 2832-2854.
[49] The section on "The Hartford-Empire Company," pp. 273-279, offers a striking illustration of the antisocial adaptation of the patent system.

inventors of competitive techniques from making effective use of their inventions, thus obstructing instead of promoting the progress of science and the useful arts. Patent fencing involves carefully studying the competing technique and surrounding it with numerous additional inventions, anticipating all mechanical principles by which improvements may be made, and rendering it impossible for the owner to exploit his invention without being subject to patent infringement suits.[50] One firm realistically stated its purpose as follows: "To secure patents on possible improvements of competing machines so as to 'fence in' those and prevent their reaching an improved stage." In other words, patents are used to strangle someone else's invention rather than as an inducement to technological progress. Instead of rewarding the entrepreneur, such a process subsidizes the undertaker.

Patent interference.—Patent interference procedures may be employed for either of two purposes. Its official use by the Patent Office is to determine which of two applicants for a given patent is justly entitled to it. Another and a less justifiable use involves nuisance applications for patents in order to harass and delay the development of a competitive process.[51]

Patent litigation.—The index of Parts 2 and 3 of the TNEC hearings points to many instances in which the litigation of patents has been employed to benefit a monopolistic combination rather than to promote the basic purposes of the patent system. Recourse to the courts in patent cases is permitted on the theory that the inventor may invoke the power of the state to protect his patent right. But often the court has been transformed from a haven of protection into an instrument by which the inventor may be harassed or browbeaten until he bows to the terms of his adversary. The rewards of invention thereby often go to the powerful rather than to those who create. It is not uncommon for an inventor to be forced to defend his rights in many court circuits simultaneously against powerful combinations which employ the ablest patent attorneys. Suits settled in his favor in the lower courts may be appealed, pyramiding expense upon expense, which few individuals are able to withstand. Harassed at every point, the inventor may find the unsatisfactory terms which are offered more acceptable than any practical alternative open to him.

These are but illustrative of the methods by which the arm of the

[50] For discussion of patent fencing see *Hearings before the Temporary National Economic Committee*, Part 2, pp. 381–384, 449–450, 460–461, 470–472, 558–560.
[51] Evidence of the abuse of the interference process may be found in *ibid.*, Part 2, pp. 452–460; and Part 3, pp. 854–862.

law, through the patent system, may be employed to reward the economic aggressor in the guise of serving the public good. Other complaints have been made; evidence was presented to the TNEC that patents have been used to suppress mechanical improvements rather than to exploit them in the interest of either the inventor or the public, that tying contracts have been employed to extend the control of a patent to unpatented processes and to "unborn" inventions, and that a system of restricted licenses often has been imposed to create privileges not anticipated by the founding fathers.

Patents are private property; they represent awards tendered by the state, not so much to reward the inventor, as to stimulate a social process—invention. The patent laws still do that, but they achieve many other results unintended and presumably unwanted. If this arm of the law is not to be employed for antisocial purposes, the patent system must be redesigned to "promote science and the useful arts." [52]

CONSERVATION AS A FAÇADE FOR PRICE FIXING

Informed citizens generally favor the conservation of natural resources, at least in principle. It is only when the members of an industry find it to their economic advantage to exploit natural resources in disregard of the social interest that they oppose conservation measures. But when an industry assumes the leadership and seeks conservation laws for itself, such a program is likely to receive a ready acceptance. At such a point, however, legislators interested in the public good might well recall the myth of the Trojan horse, or more realistically, Adam Smith's reminder that "people of the same trade seldom meet together . . . but the conversation ends in a conspiracy against the public, or some contrivance to raise prices." Such a contrivance seems to have been found in the program of proration in the petroleum industry.

Proration as it is administered in the oil-producing states represents either a program of conservation with incidental price fixing or a program of price fixing with incidental conservation. There appears to be little question, after reading the oil hearings,[53] that the price fixing aspect of the program is what commended it to the owners, but that it was offered to the public primarily as a conservation program.

Proration involves restricting the flow of crude oil to permit natural

[52] Many recommendations were offered to the TNEC; the Committee itself suggested modifications, some of which have been enacted into law. See Chapter XI.
[53] *Hearings before the Temporary National Economic Committee*, Parts 14–17.

forces to maintain the underground pressure of the well.[54] If oil wells are permitted to flow too rapidly, natural forces are inefficiently utilized, and the reservoir energy is exhausted before it brings to the surface all of the oil that it should. Scientific restriction of the rate of production results in the extraction of a larger proportion of the underground pool and lowers the cost of production in the field. There seems to be no question among experts that such practices promote conservation.

Proration was officially put into operation under the authority of state conservation laws. To render these laws more effective a number of oil-producing states (Texas, Oklahoma, Kansas, New Mexico, California, and Illinois) bound themselves together through the medium of the Interstate Oil Compact to initiate measures to prevent "the inefficient, excessive, or improper use of the reservoir energy" in their respective petroleum fields. Each state established its own regulatory body, and an Interstate Oil Compact Commission was created to recommend means of achieving co-ordinated action among the members. In order to facilitate the proration control program the advocates of the plan obtained the passage of a Federal statute, the Connally Act, which provides that petroleum produced in violation of state laws (hot oil) may not be moved in interstate or foreign commerce.

The Interstate Oil Compact avowedly avoided measures limiting production for the purpose of fixing prices, creating or perpetuating a monopoly,[55] or promoting regimentation. Despite these noble words one is impressed by the fact that the Compact is an instrumentality better adapted to price fixing than to the achievement of oil conservation. Conservation is essentially a local matter related to the control of production methods in particular fields. Conservation does not require uniform, concerted operation and neatly timed action among operators in the various producing fields; nevertheless, such concert seem to be the major contribution of the Interstate Compact.

Those who defended proration readily admitted that the principal motive behind the program was "economic." [56] They described the system as one which aimed to "balance production to consumption" or to "stabilize the industry." In fact, the practical administration of proration was achieved by keeping a watchful eye upon prices. On one occasion the Railroad Commission of Texas ordered a thirty-day

[54] *Ibid.*, Part 14, pp. 7112–7143.
[55] *Ibid.*, Part 15, p. 8235.
[56] *Ibid.*, Part 14, pp. 7115–7116, 7283; Part 15, pp. 8184, 8231, 8239.

shutdown of all oil wells in the state in order to force prices upward.[57] Five other states followed the leadership of Texas. An administrator of the proration program at the time frankly represented it as a price control measure:

On account of the drastic cut in the price of oil, which seems to be unwarranted as stocks of all oils are at a 12-year low and demand is at an all-time peak, we have called a special meeting of the Oil States Compact for 2 P. M. Tuesday at Oklahoma City in Governor Phillips' office. We hope you will come or send representatives to this important meeting to discuss the situation.[58]

In another state the chairman of the conservation commission issued a public statement that wells would be shut down if the price cut affected the production of that state. This pronouncement was made despite the testimony of the state engineer that there was no waste in that state. Thus, both before the courts and in public statements the experts asserted that proration was a conservation measure indifferent to prices, but a better characterization of the program would be that of a district judge in Texas who commented as follows: "They testify with such cocksureness and verisimilitude that it belied belief." He said that the Railroad Commission had "with an eye single, looked upon, with evil eye, the forbidden thing, namely, price," and that its orders, instead of being waste-prevention orders at that time, were in fact price-fixing orders.[59]

Conservation is essentially a scientific problem, an engineering matter; it has nothing to do with adjusting supply to demand, and it has no relationship to concerted shutdowns when the price of crude oil drops. Conservation would require the application of the best engineering practice to each well and to each field to promote the greatest possible production with the minimum of cost and, of course, with the least amount of unextracted oil remaining when the well ceases to produce.[60] But conservation of this type mixed with price fixing as a more or less dominating motive is proration in practice. It represents a misappropriation of the powers of the state for ulterior ends.

THE HOLDING COMPANY

For centuries, democratic societies, through their legislatures and courts, have established rules of the game defining the principles governing the economic interrelationships of men. Institutions have been

[57] *Ibid.*, p. 7366; Part 15, pp. 8226–8235.   [58] *Ibid.*, Part 15, p. 8234.
[59] *Ibid.*, p. 8208.
[60] *Ibid.*, Part 16, p. 8864; Part 14, pp. 7192, 7290, 7343–7344.

developed to implement these rules. But there are always men who fret under socially planned controls and seek to set them aside. Established institutions, however, do not readily yield, not even to the most powerful interest groups. Often a subtle and effective approach is that of harnessing and adapting institutions so that the desired objectives may be achieved by appearing to play by the old rules, while at the same time achieving ends which they forbid. Social inventions which serve such dual purposes often are eagerly sought and may become tremendously influential when discovered. Such an invention, apparently, is the holding company—a device through which men may do legally the things which legally they are forbidden to do.

Until 1888 holding companies could find no legal sanction in the United States. By the laws of the several states the right to hold the stocks of corporations was limited to natural persons. But as the pressure of antitrust legislation and litigation circumscribed the activities of men with monopolistic intent, the search for new devices to achieve forbidden ends became more intense. Such a device was legalized by the state of New Jersey in 1888; this legalization of the holding company created a revolution of corporate and industrial law.[61] The New Jersey statute provided that "any corporation may purchase, hold, sell, assign, transfer, mortgage, pledge, or otherwise dispose of the capital stock of . . . any other corporation . . . may exercise all the rights, powers or privileges of ownership, including the right to vote thereon." [62] The rapid growth of the holding company and its dominant position in industrial and financial organization is common knowledge. The significant points are that a creature of the law has arisen to nullify the historic purpose of corporate statutes and that the authority of the state again has been employed to promote the interests of self-seeking minorities.

Despite the several advantages ordinarily attributed to the holding company arrangement, instances are legion in which this legal device has been employed to obtain public sanction for acts which otherwise would be illegal. The holding company has been resorted to by individuals to escape the payment of the personal income tax to which other men under the same circumstances, but more scrupulous, or less crafty, have been subject by law. It has been the agent through which banks have continued to market securities or to engage in the equivalent of branch banking, although forbidden by the law or by their charters to do so. Probably it has been the major and the most

61 *Ibid.*, Part 5, p. 1667.   62 Sect. 51, General Corporation Law.

effective means by which monopolistic combinations have flourished despite the common law and the Sherman Act.[63] Utilities have found in the holding company a convenient means of controlling their competitors and of operating their businesses in contravention of the state laws under which they operate. It was found by the TNEC that life insurance companies were using this device to make loans to their officers in violation of the spirit, if not the letter, of the controlling statutes.[64]

It is irrelevant to discuss the many abuses of the holding company arrangement which have come to light during the past two decades. As almost any textbook on the subject will explain, it has been used to conceal profits, to defraud investors, and to drain subsidiaries of their earnings. The essential point here is that many of the uses of the holding company illustrate this frequent practice of shaping and adapting legal institutions to serve private ends antagonistic to public welfare.

PERVERSION OF THE PUBLIC UTILITY CONCEPT

The public utility concept evolved around the belief that certain industries possess economic characteristics and achieve a status which require that they be regulated for the common good. Basic to the public utility concept is the idea that both legal and economic institutions should serve group welfare and, if necessary, should be regulated to that end. Public utility regulation is usually imposed whenever an industry controls a basic necessity and, from the standpoint of operation and efficiency, is inherently monopolistic. In anouncing the decision of the Supreme Court in the famous Munn case,[65] Chief Justice Waite emphasized the point that the industry regulated was a "virtual monopoly," standing at the "very gateway of commerce" and taking a "toll from all who pass." In the same decision Justice Bradley said, "In other words, when it [an employment or business] becomes a practical monopoly, to which the citizen is compelled to resort . . . it is subject to regulation by the legislative power."

The assignment of public utility status to an industry, therefore, has been a protection for the citizen from monopoly. There has been strong pressure in recent years, however, to reverse this role and to use the public utility device as a means of perpetrating monopoly upon the public. With much talk of "stabilizing industry," of "con-

63 Hearings before the Temporary National Economic Committee, Part 7, p. 2776; Part 5, p. 1710.
64 Ibid., Part 13, pp. 6382–6456.   65 Munn v. Illinois, 94 U.S. 113 (1877).

servation," and of "eliminating the abuses and wastes of competition," producers in one field after another have endeavored to obtain public utility status for their industry quite as zealously as their forerunners opposed it. As the railroads fought it, the truckers have sought it. In 1935 the president of the American Trucking Association hailed the passage of the Motor Carrier Act in these words: "The benefits of the law should be enormous . . . we hope it will drive out the chiselers." [66] Much the same reasoning was attacked by Justice Sutherland, who spoke for the Court in the Oklahoma ice case.

Stated succinctly, a private corporation here seeks to prevent a competitor from entering the business of making and selling ice. . . . The control here asserted does not protect against monopoly, but tends to foster it. The aim is not to encourage competition, but to prevent it; not to regulate business, but to preclude persons from engaging in it. There is no difference in principle between this case and the attempt of the dairyman under state authority to prevent another from keeping cows and selling milk on the ground that there are enough dairymen in the business; or to prevent a shoemaker from making or selling shoes because shoemakers already in the occupation can make and sell all the shoes that are needed.[67]

The issue here is not the merits of the Court's decision in the Oklahoma ice case, but the trend which it observed in American economic life—a trend which would convert a device designed to provide public regulation of designated monopolistic industries into an instrument to project monopoly control into an otherwise competitive situation. The TNEC made no specific exploration of this trend, though such an investigation would have been fruitful. Nevertheless, a number of facts were revealed by the testimony. The activities concerning oil proration already described are relevant. The Guffey Coal Act, which organized coal production, likewise reveals this trend. It will suffice to refer to the activities of the milk producers, who have sought public utility status in many areas.[68] In analyzing this move it is well to remember that various motives may be operative at the same time, all contributing to the type of legislation which emerges. Producers may be seeking price control and restriction of competition at the same time that health officials seek restrictions to promote public safety. The drive often comes, however, from a vested-interest group, which likewise frequently influences the administration of the resultant statutes with respect to both their interpretation and their

[66] *The New York Times,* November 3, 1935.
[67] New State Ice Company v. Liebmann, 285 U.S. 262 (1932).
[68] *Hearings before the Temporary National Economic Committee,* Part 7, pp. 2832–2850.

application. The façades for the law often fail to reveal the basic motives, since the ostensible purpose is seldom the real purpose.

INNOCUOUS LAWS WHICH INSPIRE FALSE SECURITY

A negative means by which the arm of the law is sometimes employed to favor special-interest groups is the enactment of statutes which appear to establish controls sought by the public, but generally are ineffective. When it appears that a particular reform movement is sufficiently powerful to secure remedial legislation, it is not uncommon for the beneficiaries of the regime for which controls are sought to turn "reformers" themselves. Seeing that the demand for reform is sufficiently strong to obtain legislation despite their opposition, they elect to appear as champions of the cause and to write the new statutes. According to Walton Hamilton this is what happened to the Sherman Antitrust Act. Before its passage the opposition contrived "to deliver the child for nurture to the persons who have most interest in its death." [69] If the law can be emasculated before its passage, the demand for remedial legislation may be allayed, and the new law may serve to lull the public into a sense of false security. Critics have pointed to the pure food and drug laws as illustrations.

The case of the Monumental Life Insurance Company serves as a startling illustration of the operation of innocuous laws which purport to regulate, but actually are "fronts" for the absence of effective control.[70] In this case, when the evidence indicated that the management had profited at the expense of policyholders, the oft-repeated apologia of the managers was used, "We rooked them legally" or "We followed the letter of the law." It might be contended that statutes of this type offer less protection than the socially harmful activities which they cloak, since they fail to restrain the practices at which they ostensibly are aimed and block the adoption of effective legislative measures.

RULES OF THE GAME DESIGNED BY
ORGANIZED INTERESTS

A more positive approach involves taking the initiative in obtaining legislation regimenting either industry or the market for the benefit of a special-interest group. Illustrative of this were many of the provisions of the NRA codes, previously discussed. Likewise, in a later section it will be seen that a Delaware statute permitted corporate managers to pay dividends out of fictitious surplus accounts

[69] Temporary National Economic Committee Monograph No. 16, pp. 8–10.
[70] See pp. 281–284.

created by revaluing the capital stock of the corporation; by so doing, they were able to strengthen or perpetuate their control with no compensating advantage to the stockholders or to the public.[71] The TNEC made no special investigation of the extent to which legislation had been designed to serve the advantage of minority interests, but the Delaware law is one of numerous instances which came to light. The impression seems justified that many who talk of free enterprise or speak emotionally of the evils of government regulation desire restrictive measures in their own interest, but complete economic freedom elsewhere.[72]

THE MASQUERADE OF LAISSEZ FAIRE

The exploitation of the sovereign power for the advantage of minority economic groups may be negative as well as positive. Often the absence of ruling statutes may be as advantageous to particular interests as are the fruits which may be derived from class legislation. By its very nature social life is institutional and organizational, and the objectives of group welfare are often achieved only through the means of organized government and law. The successful blockage of such programs by vested-interest groups represents a negative exploitation of the arm of the law that is quite as real as the positive perversion of public institutions by the beneficiaries of the chain store taxes, "fair trade" laws, and price fixing statutes. The absence of the state as an active champion of the economic interests of its citizens is a telling characteristic of laissez faire. Often there exist groups who by one means or another have obtained a privileged position, unhindered by a do-nothing state; they develop a strong vested interest in negativism. Economic freedom, laissez faire, and noninterference become "natural rights," and to defend those "rights" they lobby as zealously as do those who benefit from tariffs, subsidies, and franchise privileges.

Many examples might be cited of cases in which strong pressure has been exerted to block the passage of remedial legislation which would destroy the privileged position of one minority or another. Two examples appear, at least incidentally, in the TNEC hearings. The first relates to the strong and successful organized opposition which consumers usually meet whenever they seek legislation to provide dependable standards and informative labels for consumer

[71] See pp. 284–286; see also *Hearings before the Temporary National Economic Committee,* Part 17, pp. 9617–9635.
[72] *Ibid.,* Part 30, p. 16258.

goods.[73] A second illustration of a successful defense of the let-alone policy (in this case more a defense of the *status quo* than a pure championing of an unrestricted market) relates to the effectively organized opposition by the life insurance executives to proposals in several states to permit citizens to purchase insurance policies from savings banks, as is now possible in Massachusetts.[74]

CONCLUSION

These manifold devices for perverting public authority and exploiting the arm of the law in order to enhance the economic position of a privileged few and to create or perpetuate vested interests are in complete disharmony with the spirit and the purpose of democratic institutions, which find their justification in promoting the common welfare. The exploitation of the state by special-interest groups is a throwback to epochs when monarchs used their sovereignty to bestow monopoly privileges upon the favorites of the crown, when medieval princes used baronial revenues for the pleasures of the court and the early bourgeoisie states evolved commercial policies to foster the interests of the trading classes. Perhaps the closest parallel in American economic history which approaches this disposition to exploit the power of the state for private purposes is the epoch following the Civil War; for a short period a code of business mores gave widespread approval to many practices of which the Credit Mobilier affair is a dramatic example.

Yet such practices seem to constitute or are in the process of becoming an established and honored *modus operandi* in the business world, one with serious social implications. No small amount of present-day economic ills is traceable to this tremendous misdirection of human effort. Altogether too much time, effort, planning, and inventive ingenuity have been diverted from production to predation and to schemes by which legal and governmental institutions may be harnessed to aid in gulling the unorganized. Many vested interests have arisen, each seeking the aid of the state to obtain a larger and larger share of the total social income and, in achieving individual success, shrinking and shrinking the very total it seeks to divide.

[73] A substantial portion of Part 8 of the hearings, "Problems of the Consumer," is devoted to the need for consumer goods standards and the successful opposition to them. A glance at the index of this volume is suggestive, and the comments on p. 3298 are illustrative.
[74] *Hearings before the Temporary National Economic Committee*, Part 10, pp. 4419–4503.

CHAPTER VIII

THE IMPLEMENTATION
OF MONOPOLY

WHEN READING the many thousand pages of testimony which constitute the TNEC hearings, one obtains the impression that little has been added to the extensive literature relating to monopolistic practices in the United States. For forty years or more treatises have described the numerous devices to which the monopolist has had recourse. Hence, one is neither surprised, nor does one gain new information of consequence with respect to the ways of monopoly. The testimony carefully elaborated the manner by which the basing-point system works—but this has long been common knowledge. It developed in detail the functioning of interstate trade barriers, but little was presented which was not available elsewhere. The same thing may be said concerning other instruments and methods of monopoly. The recurring impression which the reader receives is, "Why, this is not new; this is merely a labored and unnecessary catalogue of the obvious."

Such impressions are on the whole justified, but the very implications of these conclusions are of tremendous significance. Despite textbook analysis, public discussion, and demands for social reform, the fact that fifty years after the passage of the Sherman Act the machinery and methods of monopoly are so commonplace that they are accepted as a matter of course is the real import of the hearings. Their contribution is not the description of certain relationships and practices, but the analysis of the role which monopoly plays in the present-day economy. Many of the old instruments employed to control the market, such as the basing-point system and the holding company, are effective today, though modified and adapted to new conditions. Other methods have come to the fore and have achieved positions of prominence; they include fair trade laws, racketeering, and the trade association.

The ways of monopoly are protean; monopolists are less concerned with methods than with results. If one instrument is outlawed or for some practical purpose fails to produce the desired result, others are

employed. For the purpose of effective discussion it will be necessary to assign names and to identify the principal techniques. More realistically, however, sharp boundary lines do not exist. Different methods may be employed at the same time to achieve the same ends, and their operations may so overlap and intertwine as to make them indistinguishable—merely differing aspects of the same method. There are no clear-cut categories, and hence the discussions which follow may appear to be repetitious at points. Nevertheless, an attempt will be made to assemble and synthesize the materials brought to the attention of the TNEC which show the nature and extent of monopolistic practices in the United States.

"Monopoly," of course, is not a precise word; it is subject to many interpretations and may thus provoke many misunderstandings and much needless quibbling. There are degrees of monopoly, varying from no control to complete domination. Moreover, domination may be achieved by one producer or by a combination of producers. Combination may be overt and tangible, or it may represent subtle and intangible alliances and understandings unrecognized by the consuming public and unreached by the monopoly laws. "Monopoly" is used here in its broadest sense and is intended to embrace all arrangements by which producers effect varying degrees of market control and by which they succeed in obtaining for themselves some of the benefits of monopoly price. Variations from pure monopoly have been discussed in recent years under more precise terms, which include "monopolistic competition," "duopoly," "oligopoly," and "imperfect competition." [1]

PRICE LEADERSHIP

One of the most prominent types of monopolistic combination today is the loose, but effective, practice which has come to be known as "price leadership." Unlike the trust, the pool, the holding company, the merger, and other methods of combination prevalent at the turn of the century, price leadership is inconspicuous and offers little tangible evidence of collusion or conspiracy, however obvious its results may be. The practice is similar to the price pool, but there is no overt evidence of its existence, and it often represents nothing more than a tacit understanding among producers to "follow the leader" in price policy.

[1] See Chamberlain, *The Theory of Monopolistic Competition*, and Robinson, *The Economics of Imperfect Competition*.

Price leadership may become operative in a number of ways. Some-times it results from an unwritten agreement among producers, ar-rived at after deliberation and consultation. At times it occurs when one producing unit is so large and possesses such industrial strength that it dominates the field, with the result that lesser firms, guided by prudence and experience, indicate their willingness to follow the policies of the leader.[2] It may develop in an industry where there are a few giant firms of approximately equal strength, each with a healthy respect for the power of the others and each reluctant to engage them in all-out competition. The result, therefore, may be a "live-and-let-live," "follow-a-leader" truce. Other instances have occurred in which militant and aggressive producers in a given field have employed duress to whip competitors into a price leadership program.

Price leadership commends itself to those seeking to control the market not only because it is effective but also because it is beyond the reach of the law. When no agreement exists and when there is no formal organization, it is quite impossible to show collusion or con-spiracy. In fact, the defenders of price leadership have asserted that the very existence of the end product—uniform price—is in itself proof of effective competition, since in a regime of free competition all producers sell at one price—market price.

Prices determined under the price leadership regime probably con-stitute the most common form of controlled prices in the American market. Though relatively unknown a few decades ago, price leader-ship was described to the TNEC as one of the most dominant of prevalent types of monopoly. In recent years this method of control has been common in the following industries: crackers, newsprint, steel, anthracite, gasoline, flour, corn syrup, stoves, tin plate, cigarettes, and milk bottles.

It should not be concluded from these remarks that the price leader policy is clandestine or that its existence is denied by in-dustrialists with guilty consciences. On the contrary, the practice is openly referred to and discussed with frankness and candor. A few remarks by industrialists are illustrative. One corporation president said, "We generally make the prices"; [3] another told the TNEC, "I was very glad . . . of the opportunity to follow the Corporation's lead"; [4] others indicated that it was their practice never to initiate price changes but to meet them [5] and to follow a policy of "live-and-

[2] *Hearings before the Temporary National Economic Committee,* Part 5, p. 1771.
[3] *Ibid.,* Part 27, p. 14250.   [4] *Ibid.,* Part 19, p. 10592.   [5] *Ibid.,* p. 10659.

let-live." [6] One executive described the position of his firm thus: "We are too small to lead" [7] while another more supinely said, "We have to follow." [8] One industrialist testified that price leadership had been an established practice in his industry as far back as he could remember: "It is the custom of the industry. We have always done it." [9]

MARKETING GASOLINE

The instructions sent by its executive to the members of the National Association of Petroleum Retailers vividly describe the operation of price leadership.[10] After setting forth the intent of initiating a series of price increases for retail gasoline, the writer turned to the method by which uniform increased prices might be obtained. He proposed to emulate the example of the distributors.[11]

The answer has been before our eyes for many years. . . . In each territory there has been a supplier that was recognized as the market leader and other suppliers have merely met the competition set by the leader. . . . The dealers can do the same thing. . . . The leader must be a petroleum retailer and he must be followed by all other retailers in the territory.[12]

That such price control is a violation of the spirit and the purpose of the monopoly laws and constitutes a carefully implemented method of circumventing those statutes is emphasized by the care with which the trade association advised its members; concert, collusion, and "conspiracy against the public" was the aim and the purpose of the policy proposed, but all tangible evidence of such intrigue was to be avoided with meticulous care. The members of the trade association were told:

By this time you should be in a position to select your "market leader" who has the courage and those qualities of leadership that others recognize and will follow. After he is selected, give him your whole-hearted support. Remember to not agree upon a price, but each individual has the right to determine what he wants to do and to announce it, thus avoiding any conspiracy. Your "market leader" can set a price and the organization can send out a notice.[13]

Many independent retail gasoline dealers or their representatives testified that price leadership is a common practice at the filling sta-

[6] *Ibid.*, p. 10679.   [7] *Ibid.*, Part 27, p. 14282.
[8] *Ibid.*, Part 5, p. 2087.   [9] *Ibid.*, p. 2099.
[10] *Ibid.*, Part 16, pp. 9040–9045.
[11] For examples of price leadership in the crude oil industry see *ibid.*, Part 14, pp. 7224, 7417.
[12] *Hearings before the Temporary National Economic Committee*, Part 16, p. 9045.
[13] *Ibid.*, p. 9040.

tions. Usually the pace is set by one of the large integrated companies who, because of their oligopolistic positions, adopt the same policies and follow the same procedures. When one company posts a price cut, they all follow suit; when one posts a price raise, they fall in line.[14] Usually the market leader in a given area is the company which sells the largest gallonage in that area. Thus, the leader almost always is one of the great integrated companies and more often than not a member of the original Standard Oil group. Table 18 lists the market leaders for various areas in 1939.

TABLE 18. MARKET LEADERSHIP IN THE PETROLEUM INDUSTRY, 1939

Area	Price Leader
New York and New England	Socony-Vacuum Oil Corp.
Pennsylvania and Delaware	Atlantic Refining Co.
New Jersey, Maryland, District of Columbia, Virginia, North Carolina, and South Carolina	Standard Oil Co. of New Jersey
Ohio	Standard Oil Co. of Ohio
Kentucky, Mississippi, Alabama, Georgia, and Florida	Standard Oil Co. of Kentucky
Tennessee, Louisiana, and Arkansas	Standard Oil Co. of Louisiana
Michigan, Indiana, Wisconsin, Illinois, Iowa, Missouri, North Dakota, South Dakota, Nebraska, Kansas, and Minnesota	Standard Oil Co. of Indiana
Montana, Wyoming, Colorado, New Mexico, Idaho, and Utah	Continental Oil Co.
Washington, Oregon, California, Nevada, and Arizona	Standard Oil Co. of California
Oklahoma	Magnolia (subsidiary of Socony)
Texas	Magnolia or Texas Corp.

Source: *Hearings before the Temporary National Economic Committee,* Part 16, pp. 8880–8881.

An interesting illustration of the *modus operandi* employed to implement price leadership came to light in the Ohio area. The Pennzoil Company regularly required its retailers to market its product at prices established by the Standard Oil Company.[15] Frequently retailers of Pennzoil products knew as far as a day in advance the nature of price changes announced by Standard. Mimeographed price notices published by Standard Oil were distributed by the Pennzoil Company to its dealers. A formal pool or a trust arrangement could scarcely have been more effective.

[14] *Ibid.,* Part 14, p. 7369.   [15] *Ibid.,* Part 16, pp. 8952–8974.

THE STEEL INDUSTRY

In 1936 the president of the United States Steel Corporation testified before a Senate committee that price leadership was characteristic of the steel industry. The following testimony is pertinent:

MR. IRVIN. I would say we generally make the prices.

THE CHAIRMAN. You generally make the prices?

MR. IRVIN. Yes, sir; we generally make the prices, unless some of the other members of the industry think that that price may be too high and they make the price.

THE CHAIRMAN. You lead off, then, with a price charged, either up or down, at Gary, is that correct?

MR. IRVIN. Yes, sir.

. . .

We always notify the trade papers . . . and others interested as to what our prices are.

THE CHAIRMAN. Then the rest of them follow that?

MR. IRVIN. I think they do. That is, I say they generally do. They may quote the same price, but maybe they need some business and make a better price. We do not always know that until it is over.[16]

In the steel industry both the leader and those who were led freely acknowledged that this practice was customary. Mr. Eugene C. Grace, representing the Bethlehem Steel Corporation, preferred to designate it as "meeting a competitive situation" when his company adopted pricing policies in concert with the United States Steel Corporation.[17] Whatever the lead of the latter, whether the price change was up or down, the Bethlehem Steel Corporation followed. Mr. Grace appeared to be unable to cite any important instance in recent years when his company had taken the initiative or had been aggressive in quoting prices. He paid frequent tribute to the price leadership system and to the direction given it by the United States Steel Corporation. Some of his tributes were as follows: "It is a good guide for us"; [18] "We welcomed the opportunity"; "We needed it and we followed it"; [19] "I was very glad then of the opportunity to follow the Corporation's lead." [20]

Similarly, representatives of other steel companies indicated that they adhered to the policy fixed by the United States Steel Corporation. The president of the National Steel Corporation testified that his company never initiated a price and always met whatever price

16 *Ibid.*, Part 5, p. 1867, and Part 27, pp. 14250–14251.
17 *Ibid.*, Part 19, pp. 10586–10588, 10598–10603.
18 *Ibid.*, p. 10586.   19 *Ibid.*, p. 10587.   20 *Ibid.;* p. 10592.

was established. He preferred to call this "meeting competition" rather than to recognize it for what it was—monopoly price through price leadership.[21] Obviously, when no one cuts the base price established by the leader and all meet that price simultaneously, that is not competition. This concept of competition was more realistically acknowledged by some to be a policy of "live-and-let-live." [22]

OTHER INDUSTRIES

Despite the fact that the TNEC scrutinized the practices of only a few industries, it is significant that numerous instances of price leadership came to light. In addition to the steel and the gasoline industries, price leadership was found in the glass bottle, tag, group life insurance, and beryllium industries. The policies of glass bottle producers illustrate rather strikingly how price leadership becomes an important instrument of oligopoly. There are few manufacturers of any one particular type of glass bottle; eager for the profits afforded by monopoly, the managers of these firms have been quick to appreciate the advantages of following a price leader. The president of the Owens-Illinois Glass Company defined this policy as follows: "We can't ask any more than they ask as leaders in the line, and we are not going to take any less." [23] Thus, for milk bottles the leading producers announced identical prices over a substantial period of time; it was the same for other lines. There was nothing secret about it. In answer to a TNEC questionnaire one firm, the Hazel-Atlas Company, reported that it initiated the prices for wide-mouthed container ware, while it adopted the schedules of the Owens-Illinois Company on proprietary and prescription ware.[24] For each line throughout the industry there was a price leader to whom the rest deferred.

An ingenious application of the price leadership principle was employed under the NRA codes in the paper-tag industry. Members who did not choose to file prices were bound by the lowest prices and the most favorable terms of sale placed on file. But, interestingly enough, only one or two of the larger firms filed prices which were then circulated to the rest of the industry to regulate their charges. The most common practice in this industry was for a single seller to file, and thereupon everyone else in the industry was bound by that price.[25] The selection of the firm which should file its prices was mysteriously described as self-selection.

---

[21] *Ibid.*, p. 10659. [22] *Ibid.*, pp. 10678, 10679. [23] *Ibid.*, Part 2, p. 530.
[24] *Ibid.*, pp. 547–548. [25] *Ibid.*, Part 25, p. 13327.

There was a semblance of price leadership among the insurance companies. Some contracts written by group insurance companies are not subject to regulation by the state commissioners. It seems to have become the practice for the representatives of the companies to assemble in the Group Association meetings, at which times one company would announce that it was going to adopt a rate for a given type of contract, whereupon the rest followed its lead.[26] Likewise, a similar procedure was followed with respect to the rates charged to policyholders of nonparticipating life insurance. This type of policy is sold principally by stock companies [27] whose managers are more interested in the fruits of monopoly than would be expected in the case of mutual companies. Three companies located in Hartford ordinarily sell a preponderate proportion of nonparticipating insurance. Thus, the element of oligopoly is present, and with it both the motive and opportunity for price leadership. Consequently, smaller companies selling this type of insurance, scattered throughout the country, looked to the Hartford companies for leadership, and the latter in turn deferred to their largest company, the Travelers Insurance Company.

The beryllium industry offers another example of price leadership. A situation in which a few producers have relatively equal production and competitive strength is conducive to conspiracy; but when one producer is predominantly stronger than the rest, the elements which make for market leadership are present, and that firm often is able to lead the industry to a monopolistic basis without the necessity of clandestine agreement or collusion.[28] In the beryllium industry such a position was enjoyed by the American Brass Company. When it raised its prices, smaller firms raised theirs identically and simultaneously; when it lowered its prices, smaller firms did likewise.[29] The American Brass Company regularly sent a copy of all new price lists to competitors at the same time that the prices were announced to customers. Compliance evidently was immediately forthcoming and without exception. The president of the smallest competing firm—a one and one-half million dollar industry—testified that price leadership was a well-crystallized practice and that it "has been the custom of the industry for years on end." [30] An excerpt from the hearings at this point is revealing.

26 *Ibid.*, Part 10, p. 4199.   27 *Ibid.*, pp. 4224–4225.
28 *Ibid.*, Part 5, p. 1772.   29 *Ibid.*, p. 2125.
30 *Ibid.*, p. 2088.

MR. COX. And what company is the price leader?

MR. RANDALL. I would say The American Brass Co. holds that position.

MR. COX. And your company follows the prices which are announced by The American Brass?

MR. RANDALL. That is correct.

MR. COX. So that when they reduce the price you have to reduce it, too. Is that correct?

MR. RANDALL. Well, we don't have to, but we do.

MR. COX. And when they raise the price you raise the price.

MR. RANDALL. That is correct.

.   .   .

MR. COX. I will put this question to you, Mr. Randall. Why didn't you reduce the price of the fabricated product following that decrease in the price of the master alloy?

MR. RANDALL. Well, of course I would not make a reduction in the base price of beryllium copper unless The American Brass made a price reduction in beryllium copper.

.   .   .

MR ARNOLD. You exercise no individual judgment as to the price you charged for your product, then, in a situation?

MR. RANDALL. Well, I think that is about what it amounts to; yes, sir.

MR. ARNOLD. In other words, the situation is such that you can't pay any attention to the price of the raw material in fixing the prices.

MR. RANDALL. Of course, as Mr. Cox first stated, the industry is one of price leadership, and a small company like ours, making less than $1\frac{1}{2}$ percent of the total, we have to follow, and I think we have a statement of our price policy here which would perhaps clear that up a little.

MR. ARNOLD. When you say you have to follow, you don't mean anybody told you you had to follow?

MR. RANDALL. No, sir; I don't mean that at all.

MR. ARNOLD. But you have a feeling that something might happen if you didn't?

MR. RANDALL. I don't know what would happen.

MR. COX. You don't want to find out, do you?

THE CHAIRMAN. Well, as a matter of fact, Mr. Randall, if The American Brass Co. raised the price would the Brass Co. consult you about raising it?

MR. RANDALL. No, sir; not at all.

THE CHAIRMAN. You would, however, follow them without exercising any independent judgment as to whether or not it was desirable.

MR. RANDALL. That is correct.[31]

The statement describing his company's price policy to which the witness referred follows. "The price schedules issued by the River-

31 *Ibid.*, pp. 2086–2087.

side Metal Co. are contingent upon the prices published by the larger units of the industry. From time to time these larger units publish their scale of prices, and our company has no alternative except to meet such published prices in order to compete." [32] This statement is characteristic of many statements in the TNEC hearings in which industrialists speak glibly of meeting competition when describing situations in which competition has been solved by destroying it. At this stage of the hearings a Committee member aptly paraphrased the above statement as follows: "Our company has no alternative except to meet such published prices in order *not* to compete." [33]

THE BASING-POINT SYSTEM

A highly formalized, carefully elaborated kind of price leadership is found in the basing-point system. During the past twenty-five years, while the public mind was still occupied with thoughts about trusts, mergers, pools, and other ancient forms of combination, a newer type of restraint, more dynamic and better adapted to modern industrialism, has risen quite unobtrusively to a role of tremendous significance. According to the Federal Trade Commission a remarkably large number of industries have resorted to this type of price control, including those producing iron and steel, pig iron, cement, lime, lumber and lumber products, brick, asphalt shingles and roofing, window glass, white lead, metal lath, building tile, floor tile, gypsum plaster, bolts, nuts and rivets, cast-iron soil pipe, range boilers, valves and fittings, sewer pipes, paper and paper products, salt, sugar, corn derivatives, industrial alcohol, linseed oil, fertilizers, chemicals, transportation equipment, and power cable.[34] During the days of the NRA the principle of the basing-price system was written into the codes to establish price control for numerous industries.[35]

THE ESSENCE OF THE BASING-POINT SYSTEM

The essence of the basing-point system is price uniformity on a delivered price basis regardless of the point of delivery or the point of origin of the product; it involves a refusal to sell at f.o.b. prices.[36] The system works by an automatic formula. Each producer knows the price at the buyer's basing-point and, regardless of either his location

[32] *Ibid.*, p. 2089.   [33] *Ibid.*, p. 2090. Italics supplied.
[34] *Ibid.*, p. 1897, and the *Final Report and Recommendations of the Temporary National Economic Committee*, p. 33.
[35] *Hearings before the Temporary National Economic Committee*, Part 5, p. 1897.
[36] Several formal definitions of the basing-point system were presented to the TNEC; see *ibid.*, pp. 1861, 1866, 1934–1935.

or the location of the buyer, quotes a delivered price composed of the basing-price plus the specified freight tariff from the basing-point to the customer's location. In order, therefore, for all producers to quote identical prices it is not necessary to assemble secretly or to preview each other's bids. All that is necessary is for each firm to calculate its bids by the same formula. The United States Government has, in fact, received bids so identical that they were carried out to the fourth decimal place.[37] Thus, the fruits of collusion are had without overt forms of collusion.

An amusing case came to light in the steel industry during the days of the NRA when the steel code sanctioned the basing-point method. A major steel company complained to the code authority of the method by which one firm had obtained a Government contract involving a $60,000 purchase. Whereas other members had quoted a delivered price by carrying out decimals to two places, the low bidders were awarded the contract "because they carried the basing point price three places, resulting in their bid being 12 cents low." [38] When twelve cents worth of competition in a $60,000 deal becomes a matter of serious concern to the industry, that fact in itself pays eloquent tribute to the usual effectiveness of the method of control employed.

MONOPOLY IMPLEMENTED

The complexity of the method, however, should not be allowed to obscure the end and purpose of the basing-point system. Economic instruments seldom are elaborated as ends in themselves, though often they are defended as such. The basing-point system is an effective device in a new setting to restrain trade and to secure the benefits of oligopoly. Professor Fetter told the TNEC that "the basing-point practice is far and away the most successful single device that large American business . . . has hit upon in the last 75 years." [39] Under this system price competition is substantially obliterated, since all producers charge identical delivered prices regardless of the destination or the place of origin of the commodity. It is a system of reciprocity among oligopolists. The practice is to establish a price sufficiently high to enable all producers to ship over wide areas; each ordinarily refrains from making reductions in his own territory, thus permitting others to sell in that area. The system is very effective; in the steel industry price competition was successfully avoided between 1900 and 1920, even though the leading member of the oligopoly, the

[37] *Ibid.*, p. 1897.   [38] *Ibid.*, p. 1876.   [39] *Ibid.*, p. 1939.

United States Steel Corporation, shared a smaller portion of the business as time elapsed.[40]

The basing-point system not only is a potent method of price collusion but also becomes a powerful implement with which to impose sanctions upon producers who have the temerity or who are so indiscreet as to engage in price competition. Any producer who conducts his business according to the concepts of nineteenth-century economic liberalism and who attempts to obtain a larger share of the market by offering to undersell others is thereby denounced as a "chiseler" and a "price cutter." [41] To say that one is "trying to compete" is rather innocuous or may even suggest an honorable and desirable business practice, but to brand him for the same practice as a "chiseler" carries with it a stigma and an implication of moral turpitude which, because of the power of the label, often goes unanalyzed and unchallenged.[42]

Under the basing-point system there is an automatic penalty for anyone who indulges in old-fashioned competition. Should anyone cut below the established delivered price in any basing-point area, his reduced price becomes the new basing-point price for that area. Therefore, instead of obtaining a larger proportion of the business at the reduced price, he shares the market with the basing-price oligopoly, but at a lowered price; "then all delivered prices are identical again and the fellow hasn't gained anything by cutting his price except a headache." [43] The "chiseler" may even be penalized more positively. For example, if his production is predominantly one type of product (for example, tin sheets) and his sales ordinarily are made in his own local area, others may establish a low base price, for that product only, at his point of production without affecting prices in other areas and without disturbing the price structure for other products controlled by the oligopoly.

DEFENDED AS PERFECT COMPETITION

An apparently naïve but actually sophisticated rationalization of

[40] *Ibid.*, p. 1878.
[41] This use of the word "chiseler," like that of the expression "to stabilize prices," is but one of the many examples of the employment of "good" words to describe bad practices and "bad" words to describe good practices. So often is the word "chiseler" bandied about when referring to those who engage in old-fashioned and time-honored price competition that modern oligopolistic trade associationists and advocates of "fair trade" laws see nothing incongruous about using this term and at the same time extolling "free enterprise," "liberty," and "rugged individualism."
[42] *Hearings before the Temporary National Economic Committee*, Part 5, p. 1881.
[43] *Ibid.*, p. 1868.

the basing-point system has been advanced which maintains that it represents the quintessence of free competition. It is argued that, since in a free and perfect market all sellers receive the same prices, the basing-point system represents such a market nearly in its purest state. This defense of the system has been advanced more than once, and at times it appears to have convinced even high tribunals.[44] The executive secretary of the Iron and Steel Institute phrased this strange thesis as follows: "Competition is at its perfection of expression when all of the sellers are on the same price level." [45]

This claim rests either upon a lack of understanding of the economic processes and principles involved or develops from a deliberate desire to obfuscate the issue. Identity of market price and identity of delivered price stand at opposite poles with respect to either the relation of price to the buyer and seller or to the purity of competition and monopoly involved. One represents a single price in a single market determined by the interplay of many buyers and many sellers; the other represents a single bid price (an identical delivered price) with substantially different net realization prices, in other words a uniformity in the price quoted at places outside the market—predetermined by the use of a formula collusively derived.[46]

THE STEEL INDUSTRY

Since the turn of the century the story of the steel industry has been principally a story of the basing-point system, and any account of the basing-point system will deal primarily with the steel industry. In 1922 Colonel Bope, an executive of the Carnegie Steel Corporation, testified that before the formation of the United States Steel Corporation, Carnegie Brothers and Company had served as price leaders and that the method employed contained the essential elements of the basing system.[47] A "gentlemen's agreement," "an association to stabilize prices," was effective between 1880 and 1887. Between 1873 and 1903, however, price control in the industry was generally achieved through other devices, including pools, trade meetings, and later the Gary dinners.[48] Between 1903 and 1909, following the organization of the United States Steel Corporation, the Pittsburgh plus system provided the testing field for, and was the forerunner of, the many basing-point systems in operation today. Between 1901 and 1924 this method of pricing prevailed for many steel products; it

[44] *Ibid.*, p. 1911.   [45] *Ibid.*, p. 1882.
[46] *Ibid.*, pp. 1862–1863, 1873, 1882, 1911–1913.
[47] *Ibid.*, Part 27, p. 14263.   [48] *Ibid.*, p. 14261.

was employed in all parts of the country and by virtually all producers. The delivered price of steel quoted to any customer was the price at Pittsburgh, plus the freight from Pittsburgh, regardless of the location of the plant from which the product was shipped. In 1924 the Federal Trade Commission declared that the Pittsburgh plus practice was monopolistic and ordered its abandonment. The United States Steel Corporation issued a statement that it would comply, but denied that the practice was illegal. Almost immediately a multiple basing system was adopted, which later was even given legal sanction in the NRA codes.[49] The multiple basing-point system is the same in principle as the single basing-point system, a fact which was publicly recognized by the Iron and Steel Institute. It represses price competition and implements monopoly control.

THE MULTIPLE BASING-POINT SYSTEM

The elements of the multiple basing-price system in the steel industry are: uniform base prices, uniform charges for "extras," and uniform freight charges. Once the basing-point is established, be it Pittsburgh, Birmingham, or Chicago, the price leader, usually the United States Steel Corporation, publishes its base prices; other companies adhere to this tariff. These prices refer to the charges on products delivered at the point of production. The cost to a buyer in any other locality, however, is the price at the basing-point for his area plus the freight charges. All quotations represent delivered, not f.o.b., prices; basing-points do not necessarily have to be points of production.

The delivered price is thus composed of the base price plus the all-rail freight to the point of destination. The Iron and Steel Institute compiled a freight rate book to assure that each producer would include uniform freight costs in the final quoted price.[50] The determination of freight rates is a matter upon which even experts often differ, but with a standardized compilation of freight charges the chance of competition in this manner is obviated. In the steel industry no matter what means of transportation is used the all-rail freight cost is included.[51] Even if other methods of transportation are employed, the purchaser cannot avoid this charge. The United States Steel Corporation charges the all-rail freight rate, even though it retains for itself the right to ship by water or by truck whenever a saving can be

49 *Ibid.*, pp. 14313–14317.   50 *Ibid.*, p. 14321.
51 *Ibid.*, p. 14321; Part 5, p. 1892.

effected.[52] When asked whether a San Francisco purchaser could order steel at the Pittsburgh plant and haul it to his plant in his own trucks and thereby avoid the delivered price including the all-rail freight cost, a steel executive testified that he could not.[53] Under the NRA codes a somewhat more lenient policy was employed. If purchasers elected to haul the product in their own trucks, they were credited with 65 percent of the all-rail shipping costs.[54] Even with this relaxation of the delivered price rule, buyers were assessed 35 percent of a cost which was never incurred.

A striking illustration of this policy of requiring the buyer to pay the all-rail freight, regardless of his wishes or the means of transportation employed, came to light in the case of the Gulf Oil Corporation. This concern, which ordinarily makes very large purchases of steel tubing, purchased two large barges to operate on the Ohio River and proceeded to place orders with the Jones and Laughlin Steel Corporation.[55] When officials of the United States Steel Corporation heard of this deviation from policy, "the devil . . . broke loose," and they "raised cain and in some way or other stopped J. & L. from accepting this order. . . . The [subsidiary of United States Steel] . . . stood hard and fast by their policy that no pipe would be quoted other than f.o.b. destination." [56]

"Phantom freight" is a term which is applied when a customer is required to pay freight costs for services which have not been rendered.[57] This matter received extensive consideration by the TNEC; the chairman once referred to it as "fictitious freight" or "a freight charge which the railroads never get." [58] Phantom freight frequently is charged by plants that operate at places which have not been designated as basing-points; under the system they charge their customers the basing-point price plus the freight rates to the point of delivery even though they sell their product at home and no freight costs are incurred.[59] Phantom freight is inherent in the basing-point system; it arises whenever the imputed freight charges are greater than actual freight costs. As previously described, it also arises from the use of water or truck transportation.

If there is to be uniformity of the final delivered price, there must, of course, be uniformity of all elements which go into that price. Hence, another component which has figured prominently in steel

---

52 *Ibid.*, Part 5, p. 1892.　　53 *Ibid.*, Part 19, p. 10555.　　54 *Ibid.*, Part 27, p. 14182.
55 *Ibid.*, Part 20, p. 10836.　　56 *Ibid.*　　　　　　　　　　57 *Ibid.*, Part 5, p. 1884.
58 *Ibid.*　　　　　　　　　　　59 *Ibid.*, p. 1886; see also Part 27, p. 14324.

prices is what has come to be known as "extras." [60] Extras were described by the president of the United States Steel Corporation as additional charges (or deductions) to be made for some extra service rendered.[61] Ordinarily base prices are quoted according to some standard of size, width, gage, or grade of steel; customers, however, frequently desire to purchase quantities which vary from the quoted standard. The steel industry has elaborated the basing-price system to meet such contingencies and to assure uniform delivered prices. A "book of extras" was prepared for general use among steel firms to serve as a guide when quoting prices. Thus, if a customer requires steel sheets of a lighter gage or wider than those covered by the base price, it is only necessary to consult the "book of extras." Since all firms adhere to the base prices, consult the same freight schedules (prepared in advance), and rely upon the same book for extras, the system of identical delivered prices is perfected. Price leadership is, likewise, an essential feature of the "book of extras," inasmuch as one corporation (United States Steel) ordinarily calculates and publishes the extras, which the others adopt.[62]

When asked what factors determine the charges for extras, the president of the United States Steel Corporation said that they are based upon costs—"not only our cost, but a cross section of the costs of the industry." It was no secret that members of the industry frequently consulted with one another to arrive at these figures. "We talk costs of extras with our competitors." This mode of monopoly pricing, however, did not seem to lie in the territory covered by the Sherman or Clayton Acts; the TNEC was informed by a prominent executive, "I am advised by my general counsel that it is perfectly within our rights to do so." [63]

A PECULIAR DEFENSE OF THE BASING-POINT SYSTEM

The Federal Trade Commission contended that the basing-point system is monopolistic both in purpose and in effect. By way of defense the steel people admitted that this would be the case if the system functioned as it was supposed to. The vice president of the United States Steel Corporation had so testified.

To answer your question specifically, if that plan were universally followed, there would be no competition in so far as one element of competition is concerned, namely, price.[64]

[60] *Ibid.*, Part 27, p. 14322.
[62] *Ibid.*, pp. 10621, 10674.
[64] *Ibid.*, Part 27, pp. 14171, 14316.

[61] *Ibid.*, Part 19, pp. 10558–10564.
[63] *Ibid.*, p. 10560.

A similar admission was made by the president of the Steel Corporation.

We will concede, if that is the point that you are trying to make, that if base prices as announced were followed in every transaction, and that the nearest basing point to the consumer governed, and that the rail freight was added from that point, and the delivered price arrived at in that manner, there wouldn't be any competition in the steel industry. It would be a one-price industry, pure and simple.[65]

On what basis then did the steel people deny that the system was monopolistic? Their claim was that competition forced itself upon the industry, that the base prices were fictitious,[66] merely prices which "we want to get," [67] "prices that we feel are fair." [68] Thus, they defended the system by attempting to establish a distinction between "hoped for" prices and "realized prices," between basing-point controlled prices and actual selling prices. "We don't succeed in getting those prices," they said, "because competition won't permit it." [69] It was thereby inferred that the basing-point system merits social approval principally because it fails to work. It was argued that producers frequently cut below the base prices and that it was these departures which made competition severe.

The defenders of the basing-point system appear to be on very thin ice with respect to the assertion that their carefully articulated system of price control is honored in the breach. At no time during the testimony did the steel representatives offer factualized evidence of regular and persistent departures from basing-point prices. When requested to do so, they were evasive in their replies.[70] The absence of any indication of price wars among steel producers is rather convincing proof that whatever deviations there are from the basing-point system are minor and that the system as a whole has held up rather effectively. If any significant semblance of competition had actually appeared, a price war of unprecedented proportions would have been provoked, since the steel industry was organized with a few large producers generally producing at less than full capacity and these producers were faced with declining markets. Not only did the steel representatives fail to support their contention with facts, but they were actually inclined to resent the suggestion that they do not abide by the rules. This was revealed to a Senate committee in 1936 by the presidents of the two major companies.

[65] *Ibid.*, p. 14172. [66] *Ibid.*, Part 19, p. 10593.
[67] *Ibid.*, Part 27, p. 14172. [68] *Ibid.*, Part 19, p. 10511.
[69] *Ibid.*, p. 10512. [70] See, for example, *ibid.*, Part 27, pp. 14202, 14203.

THE CHAIRMAN. Now you were here yesterday when Mr. Grace was testifying.

MR. IRVIN. Yes.

THE CHAIRMAN. He stated there were occasions when you came into his territory and underbid his base price. Have you any specific examples of that?

MR. IRVIN. I think I stated this morning that I thought he made that in a rather facetious way. If I thought he intended it I would have resented it very much.[71]

There are times, however, when the most carefully tailored and finely labored apologies are belied by an inadvertent remark of a reluctant witness that reveals more in a moment than all the efforts to the contrary can camouflage. A spokesman for the United States Steel Corporation quite artlessly acknowledged that the industry had elected and had the power to elect to operate under a system of pricing and marketing of its own choosing. Obviously, if the system had been competitive, as they attempted to show, they would have enjoyed no such option to choose methods any more than any competitor can select the way by which his products and the products of thousands of others are to be priced. Nevertheless, the following remarkable statement was made to the TNEC.

The United States Steel Corporation does not take the position that there aren't any criticisms, justified criticisms, of the basing point system. Our position is that it is the best merchandising medium for our steel products that has been called to our attention, and also that if a better method is called to our attention we would be the first to adopt it.[72]

ECONOMIC WASTES OF THE BASING POINT SYSTEM

The Federal Trade Commission has taken the position that the basing-point system should be abolished.[73] This viewpoint is predicated not only on the conviction that it implements monopoly exploitation but also that it fosters a number of uneconomic practices, including cross-hauling, inefficient location of productive plants, and the construction of excessive plant capacity. These are economic wastes for which someone must pay, and, inasmuch as the system is ardently defended by those who employ it, it is apparent that they do not feel that the burden is theirs. It falls, of course, upon the ultimate consumers.[74]

Cross-hauling is a product of basing-point prices. The natural markets for particular plants tend to be eliminated by enabling virtually

71 *Ibid.*, p. 14289.   72 *Ibid.*, p. 14271.   73 *Ibid.*, p. 14329.
74 *Ibid.*, Part 5, p. 1894.

all producers to sell in substantially all areas. As the steel people themselves have stated, "the outstanding characteristic of the basing-point system is the fact that it puts rival producers on a footing of price equality with each other in all the consuming points over a wide area." [75] Steel mills thus find themselves selling a large portion of their output in distant territories, while distant mills ship identical products into their territories; these products pass each other en route.[76]

The basing-point system tends to destroy the advantages of favorable plant location. Sometimes it is employed deliberately to do so. In the classic case of the South Dakota state-owned cement plant,[77] a corporation several hundred miles distant put a basing-point at the location of the mill even though it owned no plant at that point. This was merely a punitive device to discipline a state which had dared to affront the existing combination. More often, however, uneconomic location is inherent in the basing-point system itself, which regularly inverts geographical relations for both producers and their customers. Under the umbrella of a controlled price system the test of profitable plant location ceases to be essentially a matter of cost of production and distribution; the emphasis shifts to the residual derived from controlled prices determined at arbitrarily selected regional bases.[78] Plants thereby may be established at uneconomic points in terms of production costs. That the steel people themselves have recognized this fact is illustrated by a statement filed with the TNEC.

However, it can be pointed out that in many respects the existence of the Pittsburgh plus method would have a natural tendency to encourage location of mills outside of rather than at Pittsburgh.[79]

This encouraged the location of mills at Chicago, Buffalo, Bethlehem, Sparrows Point, Cleveland, Birmingham, and so forth, and made possible the constant expansion of their facilities.[80]

Not only is there a tendency to foster uneconomic location of producing plants but also, once they have been established and the basing pattern more or less determined, it encourages the development of secondary processing plants using the finished material at locations which would not have been selected if costs had been determined competitively. Thus, the fruit of the controlled market is an artificial

[75] *Ibid.*, Part 27, p. 14174.
[76] For an interesting chart showing the extent of cross-haulage of steel in the northeastern states see *ibid.*, Part 5, pp. 1940, 2191.
[77] *Ibid.*, p. 1927.   [78] *Ibid.*, Part 27, pp. 14266–14276.
[79] *Ibid.*, p. 14266.   [80] *Ibid.*, p. 14268.

and uneconomic evolution of the industry. This fact is recognized by the advocates of the basing-price system, since they maintain that if the price umbrella were removed, the structural pattern of production thus fostered would totter like a precariously balanced house of cobs. The following statement is illustrative: "The above criticisms of the uniform f.o.b. mill price system have shown that it involves definite economic losses, it would destroy the investment in many plants, it would also act injuriously on many local communities whose welfare is dependent on the steel mills at that point." [81]

The Federal Trade Commission presented data to show, though the steel industry denied it, that the basing-point method creates another cost to the ultimate consumer—the cost of maintaining excess capacity within the industry. In the case of the steel industry, at all times since 1900 actual capacity (based upon data presented by the steel industry itself) has been in excess of the capacity, including reserve capacity, necessary to meet the requirements of peak years.[82] From 1901 to 1910 the ratio of production to capacity was 68 percent; from 1910 to 1920 it was 78 percent; from 1920 to 1930, 71 percent; and from 1930 to 1939, 45 percent.[83] A representative of the Federal Trade Commission paraphrased as follows the position taken by the steel industry with respect to the problem of excess capacity.

It [the United States Steel Corporation] argues in the first place that it [excess capacity] doesn't exist; in the second place that if it does exist there is no way of measuring it; third, that there is no feasible way of eliminating it; and fourth, that it has certain economic advantages which justify it.[84]

CONCERT AND COLLUSION

Legislation designed to control industrial activity often induces the regulated to assume the prerogatives of the regulator; there is a tendency for such legislation to drive underground the very practices for which controls are sought. Probably this is even more characteristic of the American economy (or legal system) because of the absorbing interest and willingness of the "gentlemen of the bar" to employ their talents to devise legal ways of doing what the law forbids and to invent ways of apparent conformity for those who refuse to conform. A significant achievement of many regulatory acts, therefore, is not the effective estoppage of practices which lawmakers have declared to be bad, but the refinement of those very activities to a fine art that

[81] *Ibid.*, p. 14273.
[82] *Ibid.*, pp. 14298–14300.
[83] *Ibid.*, p. 14327.
[84] *Ibid.*, p. 14327.

they may continue under new forms, with new cloaks, intangible, and quite beyond the pale of the law. With respect to monopoly laws, new devices often appear to replace those which have been outlawed. The result often is deference to antitrust legislation, but neither compliance nor obeisance; conformity by legalistic ritual, but observance neither in spirit nor in fact.

"Collusion" is quite as difficult to define as it is to detect. Unlike the pool, the trust, and the holding company, it relates, not to the machinery employed to restrain trade, but to the art by which such understandings are consummated. Collusive combinations may, and often do, employ a wide variety of devices with which to implement their purposes. The intent is to restrain trade; the end purpose is to obtain the fruits of monopoly; and the choice of instrumentalities is a matter of efficacy and expediency. There are two elements of collusion: secrecy and concerted purpose and action. As used here, it contains a third element—the intent to restrain trade, or, perhaps more accurately, the intent to violate the antitrust laws. The essence of collusion is combination and restraint without tangible evidence of agreement and without any proof of conspiracy, however obvious the fruits of combination may be in the market place. Thus, concerted action is secured, while at the same time all parties to the compact ostensibly continue to enjoy independence of action and maintain the appearance of competition. Collusion is difficult to define, intangible, impossible to measure, and immune to prosecution.

It is quite impossible to estimate the extent to which collusive practices are employed. Business conferences are legal, but agreements to restrain trade are not; a "consensus of opinion," however, may become more effective today than were the pools and trusts three decades ago. There are no precise boundary lines between what is referred to here as collusion and other types of restraint. For example, the trade association may exist, ostensibly at least, to perform only legal and socially useful functions, whereas its prime achievement may be the instrumentation of a "consensus of opinion" among its members.

The methods of collusion have become refined in response to the tremendous urge for monopoly profits, on the one hand, and the desire to circumvent the antitrust laws, on the other. Nevertheless, because of their widespread use many of these practices come to light or at least reveal strong circumstantial evidence of their existence. Despite the policy to hold only "informal meetings," to "keep no minutes," to "destroy all letters," and to "write no memos," tell-tale

evidence is frequently left behind, some of which eventually falls into the hands of investigators.[85] But the picture can seldom be made complete by piecing together the discoveries of investigators, the documents in evidence, and the testimony of reluctant witnesses; in order to discover the details of collusion you must probe men's minds— men who have strong motives for concealment, who have been well trained in the art of circumvention, and who are excellently advised as to the stratagems of the law.

THE IRON AND STEEL INDUSTRY

Those engaged in the production of steel frequently get together and arrive at understandings regarding production, price, terms of delivery, and conditions of sale. The steel industry lends itself readily to such arrangements, since mass-production methods are employed and the number of producing firms is relatively small.

Iron ore producers.—A dramatic moment occurred during the hearings when the executives of five of the nation's leading iron ore producing firms were placed on the witness stand.[86] These companies accounted for nearly one-half the country's iron ore production; together with the United States Steel Corporation they accounted for nearly 100 percent. Their importance, however, is even greater than these percentages imply. Inasmuch as the ore of the United States Steel Corporation is producer consumed, these five firms market most of the iron ore sold in crude form.

The simultaneous appearance of these six men (representing the five companies) was more or less symbolic of frequent though less-publicized associations of long standing. They had been, it appears, in constant touch with one another. One had written, "I am glad that the iron ore business is so largely in the hands of a small group of men who all work on a close and friendly basis." [87] When referring to their relationship, he spoke of the group as "our union." That they had acted in concert became evident from other correspondence. In matters pertaining to labor there had been an understanding for several years that they would not initiate any changes of working conditions or pay, without consultation with one another.[88] Each conducted his business with a feeling of assurance that no one would

[85] When one reflects on the element of chance and the improbability of these documents falling into the hands of the TNEC investigators, one is impressed by the extensity of the practice suggested by the evidence.

[86] *Hearings before the Temporary National Economic Committee*, Part 18, p. 10294; see also p. 10426.

[87] *Ibid.*, p. 10295.   [88] *Ibid.*, p. 10297.

adopt policies affecting these important matters without notification.[89] Such policies, said one official, "would be discussed among the big employers before any action was taken so that the industry might present a united front." [90]

An intriguing and mysterious reference to these frequent consultations is found in a telegram which spoke of a "very important meeting" involving the "same personnel previous meeting." Despite the obvious reference to the importance of this particular gathering of high officials and the implication that such consultations on policy and procedure were common, witnesses were unable to "remember" what had taken place. Thus, another "united front" prevailed with respect to poor memories when the Committee attempted to probe their minds to secure the facts.[91]

The Lake Erie base price.—A historic example of controlled price is what is known as the Lake Erie base price for iron ore. The Lake Erie price represents the price which ore producers charge their customers throughout a given year. It has been a very rigid price. Between 1924 and 1939 there were only three price changes; these were all upward. Only three changes during an epochal period when all nonadministered prices experienced wide fluctuations! [92] For four years during this fourteen-year interval the Lake Erie price held firmly at $4.25 per ton; for the seven years following 1929 it remained at $4.50; and during the next three years it did not vary from $4.95.

There appears to be a significant difference between the manner in which the Lake Erie price is supposed to be determined and that by which it actually is fixed. Although iron ore producers admit that it is their practice to adhere to the price, once it is fixed, they describe it as determined, at least in part, as are true competitive prices. Ostensibly the Lake Erie price is determined each year by the first substantial sale which takes place between buyer and seller. It is claimed that this sale reflects the "conditions of the market" and that thus a representative price is established.[93] This sale is thereupon recorded in the trade journals and becomes the fixed price for further spot transactions.

That a monopoly element is present, once the Lake Erie price is fixed, is more or less tacitly admitted by the companies which indicated that they rarely depart from it as far as spot sales are con-

[89] *Ibid.*, p. 10298.
[90] *Ibid.*, p. 10297.
[91] *Ibid.*, pp. 10300–10301.
[92] *Ibid.*, pp. 10311, 10439.
[93] *Ibid.*, pp. 10305–10310.

cerned.[94] But several additional monopolistic factors likewise are present, which the companies are somewhat reluctant to acknowledge. Chairman O'Mahoney spoke of a "permanent factor" [95] at work making for price rigidity not only within the year but also from year to year as well. How did it happen that year after year, when supposedly the first buyer and seller struck a bargain, by some coincidence, as it were, in their bargaining process they arrived at the identical price which ruled the year previously? This remarkable uniformity, this permanent factor, it seems quite apparent from the testimony, was the product of consultation and collusion among leading iron ore producers, who readied the stage each year before the first substantial sale and before its resulting price was recorded.

Two men, who because of their background qualify as expert witnesses, unintentionally supplied information regarding the method by which Lake Erie prices are determined. Both had written letters which came to the attention of the TNEC investigators. One was an "outsider," the executive of a Canadian steel firm, whose company was forced to purchase iron ore in what he considered to be a monopolized market.[96] He wrote to one of the American producing firms objecting to the fact that the price had been maintained at a level identical to that of the previous year. He spoke of it as a fictitious price, maintained in part because the integrated companies, such as the United States Steel Corporation, found it convenient to maintain an artificially high price (paid to themselves) for iron ore in order to justify high steel prices and to conceal profits. He argued that if any semblance of competition obtained in the iron ore market, the high Lake Erie price could not survive.

The other writer was an "insider," the executive of an iron ore producing firm which was in a position to benefit from monopoly controlled prices. Due to his relation to the business, to his father, and to his father's interest in the business, a series of letters unusually informal, frank, and illuminating found their way to the TNEC hearing room. In one letter he discussed the possibility of making a particularly large sale by resorting to competition and by by-passing the Lake Erie price; then he enumerated the possible repercussions which such price concessions would evoke.[97] Not willing to "incur the wrath of Jim" and "the old line companies," he advised in favor of adhering strictly to the established price. Then, quite artlessly, he

94 *Ibid.*, p. 10310.   95 *Ibid.*, p. 10320.   96 *Ibid.*, p. 10330.
97 *Ibid.*, pp. 10342–10343.

referred to recent relations among ore producers which lead him to conclude, "I believe the ore market can be more closely controlled." The approach to such control was described in the same letter: "I appreciate your anxiety to land this business but I believe it would be a dangerous thing to cut the price in any way whatsoever. We will, however, consult with the Big Four beforehand to assure ourselves that they will not try any such tricks." [98]

That these consultations and understandings were frequent occurrences seems clear. Another son-to-father letter revealed the following: "I saw Hoyt yesterday at which time he told me the ore magnates had decided to retain last year's market price. This price will be held regardless of what Ford does. We mailed our bid to Ford yesterday as did the others." [99] The author of this letter represented it as a sort of allegorical communication: "That is shorthand conversation from one person that knows how market price is arrived at, to another person that is familiar with how market price is arrived at." [100] Regardless of this disavowal of its clear implications, the correspondence indicates that leading ore producers did assemble to fix prices and that not even as powerful a buyer as the Ford Motor Company could break up the combination—at least in so far as it affected the general market. The following excerpt from the hearings is pertinent.

Mr. Feller. . . . What did you mean by the statement: "This price will be held regardless of what Ford does."

. . .

Mr. Patrick Butler. That to my mind means that regardless of what Ford does—what price Ford pays for his ore, the published market price would remain the same as it had in previous years.

Mr. Feller. Now I take it that the custom in the industry . . . is that the price at which the first substantial sale of the season is made becomes the Lake Erie base price. I take it from your testimony that if the Ford Motor Co., by virtue of its bargaining position, were to make the first substantial purchase of the season at a price less than the preceding year's market price, that the industry would not recognize that as the established Lake Erie base price.

Mr. Patrick Butler. I don't know that to be a fact—whether the industry would recognize it as the first substantial sale and set the market price, set the Lake Erie price.

Mr. Feller. What other meaning could your answer to my previous question have? Your answer was that the last year's market price would remain the market price regardless of what Ford did.

98 *Ibid.*, p. 10343. 99 *Ibid.*, p. 10321.
100 *Ibid.*, pp. 10326–10327.

Mr. Patrick Butler. The only deduction I can make is that there would be a sale prior to the Ford sale.

Mr. Feller. Supposing Ford were the first purchaser.

Mr. Patrick Butler. If Ford were the first purchaser and that price was published, that, I think, would establish the market price of the ore for that year.

Mr. Feller. Then the market price would not be held regardless of what Ford did?

Mr. Patrick Butler. It could be. If the iron ore people and their customers thought that the price that Ford paid did not reflect the economic conditions of the industry at that time, I would think they would be perfectly free to say that they would not recognize the Ford sale as binding upon them on their contracts for that year.

Mr. Feller. Then I take it that the custom is one that could be broken very easily if the price were not suitable to the producers of iron ore.

Mr. Patrick Butler. I wouldn't gather that.

Mr. Feller. Isn't that the implication from your statement? [101]

However strongly it might be maintained that market conditions at the first sale of the year determined iron ore prices, the fact remains that leading ore producers, when talking among themselves and not for the public ear, reasoned from different premises. Their language lent quiet support to the view that the price was arrived at in concert. One letter alluded to the fact that the price for the coming season had been determined in advance. Another memorandum presented in striking fashion how the Lake Erie price was fixed by informal agreements among a handful of men.

Mr. Hoyt called up today and after asking if Alex was in town, asked if I would come up to speak with him a minute. He told me of his talk with you last night and the agreement that he would see Mr. Girdler this morning. He said he had just been talking with him for an hour and a half, asking Mr. Girdler if he did not think it would be a good thing for the whole industry if the emergency freight charge be borne by the buyers of ore. He said that Mr. Girdler told him that if he would get Mr. Block and Mr. Weir to agree that adding the emergency freight to the ore price this year would be of psychological help in getting a better price for steel in the third quarter, that he would be in favor of it.

He said that of course Mr. Girdler and he both realized . . . that he, Hoyt, could not get any such assurance. Mr. Girdler felt that if this were not the case, the increase in freight rate should not be added to the price of ore. Mr. Hoyt then said he would go back and think it over and on parting said to Mr. Girdler: "Well, then if I announce in the papers that the price of ore is the same as last year, with the ore companies absorbing the increase in freight rate, I can consider that we have sold you a tonnage of ore at

101 *Ibid.*, p. 10333.

last year's price." Mr. Girdler's reply was: "Yes, we have made a deal."

Therefore, Mr. Hoyt said he wanted to announce in the papers this afternoon that the ore price has been set at $4.50 for this season, and asked if that would be alright for our company. I told him that I would have to call you on the telephone, and that it might be that you would prefer to have another talk with Mr. Girdler. . . . He suggested that if he did not hear from me by 4 o'clock they would go ahead and announce the price and asked what I thought you would think of that. I said that I felt that would not be the right thing—that you surely should be advised and reiterated that I did not think the delay of a day would make any difference.[102]

Producers of tubular products.—Similar understandings were consummated in the steel pipe industry. Three examples will illustrate. The first relates to the use of the basing-point system which quite obviously is the product of an unpublished treaty among producers. When a leading oil company attempted to purchase steel pipe at a producing plant and load it on its own barge to avoid the delivered price quotation, producers refused to sell. One producer was challenged as to the reason for both the price policy and the united front; he later described his answer as follows.

He wanted to know why he could not get pipe quoted f.o.b. barge siding, provided it was their own barge. We naturally said nothing of an incriminating nature and simply stated that we could take no part in this matter whatever, as we were not on the river and therefore totally disinterested. Our reply to his question as to why no pipe mill was permitted to quote on the basis above mentioned, was that we simply stated as long as we had been in this business, we had never known of any manufacturer quoting f.o.b. mill.[103]

The second illustration involves the use of informally but effectively organized pressures upon a producer of steel pipe who threatened to step out of line by competing on a price basis. He was subjected to duress by one producer after another, until one was able to report to the others in the following manner.

Since dictating the above, I have reached Mr. Strickland of Wheeling by telephone, who advised that he had already talked with you today. From Mr. Strickland's conversation, I learned that they had already been with Goble and that Wheeling is now going to revise their previously announced prices.[104]

The third illustration likewise came to light from correspondence which found its way into the hearings.[105] These letters, written in

102 *Ibid.*, pp. 10354–10355.   103 *Ibid.*, Part 20, p. 10837.   104 *Ibid.*, p. 10857.
105 It is, perhaps, significant that most of the correspondence of this character came from smaller firms rather than from those which ordinarily assume the position of price lead-

"strict confidence" because of the nature of the matter contained, spoke of a meeting of manufacturers seeking an agreement from the leading producer of seamless steel pipe not to reduce prices sufficiently to compete with pipe produced by the lap-weld method. To obtain this agreement it was indicated that "it was very necessary for these other mills to give up something in return." [106] Examination of the witness demonstrated how difficult it is to ascertain the facts or to prove the existence of such compacts. Though the witness wrote in "strict confidence," to which he evidently attached prime importance, and told of having "checked a second meeting," on the witness stand he knew of no meetings, remembered no bargains, and was aware of nothing which other mills had given up in return. Either because of a common understanding in the industry or because his firm was small and feared the consequences of frank testimony he was reluctant to reveal anything which would factualize the inferences of his letters. His "memory" was faulty, so much so that TNEC member Henderson protested.

I find it difficult to believe that concerning all this information, detailed here with great specificity, the memory process has so completely failed. I find it impossible to believe that American business could be carried on if there were so much evidence of fallen arches in the medulla oblongata.[107]

Producers of galvanized sheet.—There seems to have been a systematic exchange of opinions among producers of galvanized sheet before basing-point prices were fixed. This is the clear implication of a letter written by the executive of one of the smaller producing firms to a secretary of the trade association.

It was not definitely decided until late last evening to put into effect for fourth quarter a one-price policy allowing the galvanized sheet price to remain at $3.10 per 100 lb. for No. 24 gauge base f.o.b. Pittsburgh. A few of the larger interests such as Wierton and Inland were in favor of reducing the price to $3 base for No. 24 gauge f.o.b. Pittsburgh but this was finally defeated and it was agreed to allow all prices to remain the same as now in effect.

The announcement of no further jobber allowance after October 1 will be made by Continental on Tuesday of next week after which all mills can announce likewise. We, of course, in the meantime will notify our people which no doubt will be conducive of causing an influx of jobber business for shipment prior to October 1st.[108]

---

ership or which otherwise dominate the industry. Apparently the latter were sufficiently sophisticated with respect to the law so that they left no tell-tale milestones.
[106] *Hearings before the Temporary National Economic Committee*, Part 20, p. 10868.
[107] *Ibid.*, p. 10873.   [108] *Ibid.*, Part 27, p. 14281.

The author of this letter denied its meaning and content. Obviously a meeting of producers was held to discuss price policy; proposals and counter-proposals were made, some of which were "defeated." In view of the fact that the writer was reporting on what happened "last night," it belies his assertion that he was merely reporting street gossip. Evidently the producers, some of whom were identified, "decided" on a policy, "agreed" on a base price, and designated a price leader whom others should follow.[109] The adept manner in which the originator of the letter explained away its implications emphasizes the difficulty of proving the existence of collusion.

LIFE INSURANCE COMPANIES

Similar treaties and agreements were found to exist among life insurance companies, but they were reluctant to call them agreements, preferring rather to call them plans—plans, not to restrain trade, but to eliminate "ruinous" competition.

The Group Association.[110]—In 1926 the Group Association was organized "to promote sound underwriting practices and to prevent abuses cropping up in the business." [111] Through this agency and its forerunner competitive practices were brought under control or eliminated. As early as 1917 an informal combination was effected through frequent meetings of the officials and actuaries of companies selling group insurance. This organization proceeded to establish uniform rules, rates, and commissions among the major underwriters.[112]

Apparently there was considerable concern among the members of this group lest they should become involved with the antitrust laws. To prevent such a possibility overt agreements were carefully avoided, however real they became in fact. Procedure appears to have been meticulously planned to this purpose, as is indicated by the following description of their method of operation.

The recommendations of the informal committee of representatives can be adopted or rejected by each company, but as a general rule no recommendation is adopted by the committee unless the vote is unanimous. There is nothing binding upon any company to follow the underwriting rule, the recommended commission scale, or the rates which are recommended, but each company appreciates the advantages of cooperation to such an extent that it follows its own rules, which are generally based upon the recommendations of the committee.[113]

[109] *Ibid.*, pp. 14281–14286, 14321, 14506. [110] *Ibid.*, Part 10, pp. 4154–4222.
[111] *Ibid.*, p. 4183. [112] *Ibid.*, p. 4164. [113] *Ibid.*, p. 4166.

TNEC member Arnold, of the Antitrust Division, characterized this description of their *modus operandi* as follows.

It occurs to me from reading this that it is somewhat cagily drawn for the purpose of getting a complete understanding that competition will be eliminated and also for the purpose of making it appear that the law is not being violated. For example, you start out by saying that no recommendation is adopted by the committee unless the vote is unanimous. Then you say there is nothing binding on the company to follow these rules, and then you say, "Well, we are going to follow them anyhow." [114]

In 1926 the informal association was replaced, as has been indicated, by the Group Association. Its purpose, however, does not seem to have changed. In fact, members feared lest the more formal organization offer overt evidence of its achievements; this apprehension was expressed by one member in the following manner: "I am afraid the formal constitution of the proposed Group Life Association would be found only too satisfactory as evidence that the companies were combining to prevent such freedom of competition as would result in the maximum service being offered for the premiums collected." [115] This situation, however, was handled with finesse; the Association exercised unusual care in putting out its rules and minutes of meetings "to steer clear of any indication of combination in restraint of trade." [116] The aim of the organization was aptly epitomized in the following query and reply.

MR. ARNOLD. Am I correct in assuming that the phrase "to steer clear of any indication of combination in restraint of trade" means that you wanted the combination, but you wanted to steer clear of the indication of the combination?

MR. FLYNN. Yes; I think that is correct. [117]

Nonparticipating rates. [118]—Intercompany agreements were negotiated among the major stock companies selling nonparticipating life insurance. Three companies, located in Hartford, predominated in this field. Prior to 1933 they operated on a more or less competitive basis, having neither uniform rates nor uniform cash surrender values. After some discussion these companies decided to pool their knowledge and to pool their experience relative to rates. [119] They seemed to feel assured that if uniformity among the three leaders could be obtained, the other companies would "go along." [120]

114 *Ibid.*, p. 4167.
116 *Ibid.*, p. 4177.
118 *Ibid.*, pp. 4224–4280.
120 *Ibid.*, p. 4230.

115 *Ibid.*, pp. 4176–4177.
117 *Ibid.*
119 *Ibid.*, p. 4229.

The result of these negotiations was an agreement among the three largest nonparticipating companies to maintain uniform rates for ordinary insurance. They all agreed to increase rates, effective on the same date. Subsequently, they agreed on uniform surrender values. However much they acted in concert, "in deference . . . to antitrust" laws, the companies were careful that no notices of these intercompany agreements appeared in any of the trade publications.

Mr. Arnold. You thought it wise, in view of that split of opinion, then, in your group as to whether the antitrust laws applied, to conceal this machinery.

Mr. Beers. To avoid publicizing, absolutely. That is, our lawyers did not feel absolutely sure that they knew the answer; they thought the courts might have to decide something.[121]

The concept of fair competition which so frequently is indistinguishable from no competition seems to have guided company officials when striving for uniformity. The frank replies which one official made to questions posed by TNEC members indicates the extent to which their purpose was to eradicate competition.

Mr. Gesell. . . . were there not discussions held between the actuaries and representatives of your company and the other two companies with a view to reaching a uniform agreement which would no longer put the Aetna's modified life form out of line with the program which had generally been agreed to?

Mr. Beers. . . . We held several meetings and discussed what would be the answer to the question that had arisen. There was a difference of opinion and we thought that our premium rate was all right; they thought it should be higher. We reached a compromise.

Mr. Gesell. You raised yours somewhat, as a result?

Mr. Beers. Yes.

Mr. Gesell. Why was that done, if you thought the original rate was all right, Mr. Beers?

Mr. Beers. They thought it wasn't. When you are entering an agreement with other persons you must reach an agreement. You cannot insist on your own way with respect to one point.

. . .

Mr. Arnold. But in the word "fair" you mean that you want a rate which will not put any company at a competitive disadvantage. That is really what you meant by the word "fair."

Mr. Beers. As between these three companies I think that is right, although I used the word "fair," I believe, as meaning fair to the other companies by the terms of the agreement we were trying to reach.

121 *Ibid.*, p. 4257.

Mr. Arnold. You were all more comfortable in your minds when competition was eliminated.

Mr. Beers. Yes sir.[122]

Annuities.[123]—Life insurance companies frequently sell annuities. Over a period of twenty years leading insurance companies met regularly to discuss matters relating to such contracts. Gradually this business assumed greater importance as more and more sales were made. Soon, under the leadership of five companies, the urge to establish uniform rates and uniform commissions to agents began to assert itself. Eventually such uniformity was secured on a wide scale.[124] Some of the smaller companies appeared to be reluctant to "go along" until "missionary work" was done to obtain their adherence to the general program.

Athough voting at these intercompany meetings appears to have been a frequent method of arriving at agreements,[125] the procedure was skillfully designed to leave no tangible indication of concerted action. Meetings were entirely informal; no organization was created with established headquarters or officers, no minutes were kept, and no votes were recorded. Matters were discussed and lines of policy were laid out; actuaries who attended returned home to consult their companies, and, after so doing they reported concerning the extent to which compliance would be forthcoming. Through this clearing agency each company was kept informed as to what others were doing. The person who served as the clearing agent destroyed all records of the action taken. Agreement and uniformity were obtained, but the machinery of operation remained obscure.

Settlement options.[126]—There are various areas in which competition may develop among life insurance companies. One has to do with the types of settlement options offered to the insured or to the beneficiary. Competition at this point seems to have concerned insurance executives, hence they undertook to formulate rules of common policy. A call for a meeting in 1935 met with ready response, as is indicated by the reply of one who was invited: "I have felt for a long time that we, under the stress of competition, have become rather too liberal. . . . If some reasonable rules as to what may and may not be allowed can be adopted generally, we shall be glad to go along." [127]

122 *Ibid.*, pp. 4244–4245.
124 *Ibid.*, pp. 4512–4518, 4524.
126 *Ibid.*, pp. 4569–5619.

123 *Ibid.*, pp. 4505–4567.
125 *Ibid.*, pp. 4517–4520.
127 *Ibid.*, p. 4574.

There followed a series of meetings over a period of years which resulted in uniformity of practices affecting many aspects of settlement options.[128] At these meetings care was exercised not to take votes, but to obtain expressions of opinion or a statement of the policy which each company would follow; rather than arrive at an overt agreement, a "consensus of opinion" usually was secured outlining the practice to be followed.[129] In any event, the intent and the result were to restrain competition and to establish a combination. Seldom did the TNEC receive as frank an acknowledgment of this fact as it did in the following instance.

MR. GESELL. Am I correct in gathering from the last letter which I read that this question of settlement options did have some competitive importance? In other words, that companies with more liberal settlement-option provisions stood, perhaps, to gain in the sale of insurance as against companies which had stricter provisions?

DR. HUNTER. Yes.

MR. GESELL. If that is correct, I take it, it is also correct that one of the great interests of the companies attending these conferences was to bring about a uniformity of position on the part of the companies, so that that competitive advantage would not accrue to any particular company.

DR. HUNTER. To such an extent as it was possible.[130]

Similar intercompany agreements resulted from other conferences establishing uniform rules and eliminating competition with respect to surrender values, reinsurance, replacement, and related matters.[131] The desire for uniformity in many aspects of the life insurance business seemed to be strong, and methods of implementing this urge frequently were employed. Antitrust laws usually were ignored, except that meticulous care was exercised to shield from view the machinery of combination.

IN OTHER INDUSTRIES

Combination through quiet, unceremonious understandings among producers has been influential in many industries, including those producing steel alloys, glass, cement, and whiskey. It has been employed by security underwriters and by others to fortify patent monopolies. An interesting example of behind-the-scene price discussions and agreements involves the beryllium industry.[132] Leading producers of beryllium alloy kept each other currently informed with respect

[128] *Ibid.*, pp. 4589–4590, 4606, 4614–4618.   [129] *Ibid.*, p. 4592.
[130] *Ibid.*, p. 4584.   [131] *Ibid.*, pp. 4619–4686.
[132] *Ibid.*, Part 5, pp. 2099–2163.

to important merchandising policies including prices. Their correspondence indicated that they seldom introduced price changes without advance notification to one another. Mutual assurances were forthcoming from time to time to vitalize this understanding: "You will not neglect to notify us of any changes"; "Randall should be advised of this situation"; "we will have made up a tentative price schedule . . . our people feel strongly that no move should be made, and no publicity given to the new price, until the matter has been thoroughly discussed with Mr. Randall." Despite these and other proofs of concerted price policy, witnesses steadfastly denied the implications of their own written words quite as though they feared antitrust prosecution.

The fruit jar manufacturing industry offers another illustration of invisible restraints of trade.[133] When the Hartford-Empire Company succeeded in persuading Ball Brothers to take out a license to manufacture fruit jars and thereby avoid patent litigation, the Ball firm, because of its bargaining position, was able to insist upon restriction of production. This, of course, involved other producers, including the very important Hazel-Atlas Company. The latter indicated that it was willing "to go pretty far . . . to give Ball what he wants."[134] Consequently, the Hazel-Atlas Company agreed to restrict production. No agreement was signed; in lieu of a formal contract, oral commitments only were made. The testimony at this point depicts the procedure followed:

MR. LEVIS. As far as our company is concerned I have never signed an agreement to restrict, and I am informed by our counsel that there are no agreements in existence.

MR. COX. Quite apart from signing such agreements, you have reached no oral understandings with anyone with respect to the same thing?

MR. LEVIS. I can't answer that, Mr. Cox.

MR. COX. Why can't you answer that?

MR. LEVIS. I don't consider that would be an agreement. I may have talked about it, but I have no agreement of any kind.

MR. COX. What I am really trying to find out is whether you gave anyone an oral promise or assurance that you would not produce more than 100,000 gross in any given year.

MR. LEVIS. I don't recall it.

MR. COX. Would you say definitely that you never had done so?

MR. LEVIS. No; I probably may have. I have given a lot of people assurances on matters of that kind in a 25 years' business career.[135]

---

133 Ibid., Part 2, pp. 561–570.   134 Ibid., p. 561.
135 Ibid., p. 567.

Sometimes it is the lure of monopoly profits which impels producers to restrain trade; sometimes it is the fear of cutthroat competition. Sometimes collusion is achieved through appeal to common interest or by the use of moral suasion mixed, perhaps, with intimidation and threats of economic sanctions. Then there is a type of "moral suasion" which employs less subtle and less civilized arts of persuasion. The racketeer takes recourse to violence, intimidation, and terrorism to obtain his ends. Racketeering may be, and has been, of course, employed for other purposes than to perpetrate a monopoly. Rackets have been used to extract tribute from members of a trade or to enable the members of the trade to exact tribute from the public. The latter, of course, are the subject of this discussion. The border line between the duress and the sanctions employed by a great many monopolistic groups, on the one hand, and the techniques of the racketeer, on the other, is indistinct, and it would be idle to give it definition even for the sake of precision. But clearly when resort is had to the destruction of physical property, to the infliction of bodily harm, or to intimidation by threats to commit such acts that border line has been crossed.

Monopolistic arrangements have been enforced in some industries by damaging goods, interfering with their movement, breaking windows, throwing bombs, setting fires, and assaulting tradesmen. Restraint of trade by such methods has been imposed upon various industries, including glaziers, laundrymen, bakers, building contractors, operators of garages and filling stations, as well as dealers in ice, milk, beverages, fish, poultry, and artichokes.[136]

Monopolistic racketeering is found principally among small-scale producers. It may exist with or without the trade association. Where oligopoly is not so apparent and the opportunity to "get together" not as convenient as it is in the mass production industries—which by their very nature have few producing units—the racket may substitute for reason and suasion. The Wickersham Commission made the following comment regarding this subject.

In this possibility of forcible suppression of competition is to be found one important reason why rackets tend to make especially rapid headway in lines of business having numerous small and actively competing units, where it is difficult to avoid so-called "cut-throat competition" which keeps all but the most efficient units at the starvation point. Open price-fixing agreements are forbidden by law, and probably would not be lived up to

136 Temporary National Economic Committee Monograph No. 21, pp. 293–298.

if made; but the racket may provide an effectively policed method of bringing about noncompetitive conditions.[137]

Four examples of racketeering sanctions, imposed to coerce reluctant competitors to participate in collusive practices, were brought to the attention of the TNEC: two in the retail petroleum trade, one in the milk industry, and another in the poultry industry.

IN THE OIL INDUSTRY

Retailers of petroleum products have organized from time to time to suppress price competition. Sometimes the organizers have resorted to "strong-arm" tactics to obtain results. A retail trade association with headquarters in Milwaukee, after advising its members how to regiment the trade, proceeded to suggest ways of bulldozing recalcitrant tradesmen into compliance. One course was called the "blockade method," involving the deliberate placing of obstructions between the retailer and his market. The blockade method was described by its advocate.

If you have to use the blockade method, be sure that it is friendly and peaceful, so as to prevent injunctions for disturbing the peace or disorderly conduct or assault, conducting yourselves as customers who are making small purchases and utilizing the free services which the station offers to the public, and block the driveways for a short time only—but during the busiest part of the day.
If the blockade is used as a means of bringing the price-cutters to reason, withhold the blockade during any negotiations that follow and remember to be firm and fair in your demands.[138]

The author of the above memorandum was apparently not averse to using other types of intimidation.[139] This, however, did not represent an isolated instance of the use of the blockade. One dealer in Ohio who attempted to follow an independent pricing policy described how his hoses had been cut when he failed to adopt the prices suggested to him by the local gasoline retailers' association.[140] Moreover, members of the association drove into his station in large numbers, bought the minimum quantity of gasoline, demanded the maximum of service, remained inordinately long, and denied access to the station by the consuming public for a period of nearly two days. The following newspaper advertisement describes what happened to one

[137] National Commission on Law Observance and Enforcement, *Reports*, Vol. V, No. 12, *Report on the Cost of Crime*, 1931, p. 410.
[138] *Hearings before the Temporary National Economic Committee*, Part 16, p. 9309; see also pp. 9040–9041.
[139] *Ibid.*, Part 16, p. 9044.   [140] *Ibid.*, p. 8976.

retailer and represents an attempt to present his case to the court of public opinion.

One June 22nd and 23rd a large automobile caravan driven, fifty witnesses testify, by certain members of the Stark County Retail Gasoline Dealers Association and others, drove into the Red Head track-side gasoline station located at 522 Cherry Ave. NE., blocking the driveways with forty or fifty cars and trucks. Twenty-, fifty-, and hundred-dollar bills were flashed in payment of one-gallon purchases or less. Numerous services were requested, all with the obvious plan of tying up the station. When these "customers" ran out of service requests they still refused to move away from the pumps. Of course, this caused a general blockade of traffic, extending for several blocks, preventing the regular trade from getting gasoline. This un-American movement was the result of the Red Head being unwilling to enter into price collusion with its competitors to raise and peg gasoline prices in Stark County. A temporary injunction has been granted prohibiting this malicious mischief and other interference in the operation of the Red Head Station.[141]

IN THE MILK AND POULTRY INDUSTRIES

A few large distributors controlled the retail sale of milk in Detroit. In 1936 a new enterpriser inaugurated a system of distribution over the counter from milk depots. His prices to consumers were substantially lower than those charged from the wagon, and it appears that he paid more to the milk producer as well. The new distributor was not looked upon favorably by the milk combination, and he was soon subjected to various annoyances and interferences. Fighting brands were introduced, resulting in a substantial price war; state inspectors appeared on the scene to make an excessive number and an apparently capricious variety of inspections; the distributor's license was temporarily revoked, various legal interferences were instituted, bankruptcy proceedings were invoked, and threats of violence were made. In the same city another independent distributor had had his pasteurization plants bombed.[142]

The New York live poultry market offers a notorious example of racketeering; for a number of years it was dominated by a small group of commissionmen, twenty-seven to thirty in number. To consolidate their position they allied themselves with four labor unions. Other commissionmen were excluded from the market by being denied access to the supply of labor. The rights to haul chickens and to supply coops and feed were dispensed as exclusive monopolies and were exercised to extract monopoly prices. Slaughterhouse owners were

[141] *Ibid.*, pp. 8979–8980. [142] *Ibid.*, Part 7, pp. 2829–2862.

forced to purchase chickens from these commissionmen exclusively; those who attempted to do otherwise found their trucks overturned on the highways, discovered emery dust in their motors, or their chickens died from a diet of sand, gravel, and plaster of Paris, or were, perhaps, sprinkled with kerosene or poison.[143]

FAIR TRADE LAWS

The so-called fair trade statutes present an interesting paradox in American economic life when related to other measures representing the official position of the Government with respect to monopoly.[144] For the Government to champion monopoly by supporting resale price maintenance laws, euphoniously labeled "fair trade" laws, is a striking contrast to and contradiction of traditional policy. Though manufacturers long had favored resale price maintenance practices and at times had resorted to them, they had been rebuffed in accordance with the Sherman Act and its subsequent modifications. By 1922 resale price maintenance had been declared bad social policy, in conflict with the monopoly laws and therefore illegal.[145] It was held that this practice was destructive of competition, that it deprived the public of the benefits of a free market and low prices, and that it undermined business enterprise by putting the inefficient retailer on the same basis as the efficient. The Federal Trade Commission has never ceased to oppose this type of market restraint.

The first state to reverse the traditional American policy and to sanction this practice was California, which in 1931 enacted its Fair Trade Act. Later, under the NRA codes, by which the Sherman and Clayton Acts were generally relaxed, resale price maintenance was sanctioned by the Federal Government. After the NRA was invalidated by the courts in 1935, a number of states proceeded to enact "fair trade" laws. This subject has already been discussed at some length; it will suffice at this point to call attention to the fact that "fair trade" laws restrain competition.

SELF-GOVERNMENT IN INDUSTRY

An implement of monopoly which appears to be in high favor among business men has been called "self-rule in industry." Advocates

[143] *Ibid.*, pp. 2866–2880.
[144] For example, Sherman Act, Clayton Act, and Standard Oil Case, the Federal Trade Commission, etc.
[145] Dr. Miles Medical Company v. Park and Sons, 220 U.S. 373 (1911), United States v. Colgate and Company, 250 U.S. 300 (1919), Federal Trade Commission v. Beech-Nut Packing Company, 257 U.S. 441 (1922).

of this system believe that producers in each industry should be permitted to organize in associations and, as under the NRA, to design rules of the game (codes of "fair competition") to govern their relationship to each other, to the consumer, to the public, and to the market in general.

This viewpoint holds that all industry should be regulated, not as public utilities subject to government control in the common interest, but regulated by the members of the industry itself and in the interest of the industry. Accordingly, it is held that only representatives chosen from the ranks of the business are qualified to determine the behavior of the industry, that only they can be depended upon to make the right decisions, and that they are sufficiently socially minded not to put their own interest above that of the public.[146] Rules of the game are to be established, therefore, not by representatives of the consumer to protect his interests, not by the Government —the organized instrumentality of the public—not by the representatives of all business taken at large, but by the members of the individual industry itself.

Whenever such rules have been elaborated, they usually have exercised broad control over every aspect of the industry which might lead to competition. Codes of "fair competition" ordinarily provide for production control (limitation of output), price control (numerous devices have been employed to fix prices), uniform terms of sale, allocation of markets, outlawing of designated selling practices, and control of entry into the business.[147]

Whenever codes have been established, their designers have found it necessary to employ sanctions to ensure compliance. The concept that business men have a right to organize among themselves to control production, competition, and prices implies the right to police the industry to assure enforcement of the rules. Unable to employ the "arm of the law," as was possible under the NRA, to police the codes and in view of the questionable status of self-rule under the monopoly laws, the methods of the racketeer at times have been employed to enforce the rules of the game. In the bakery, butcher, restaurant, poultry, and laundry industries in large cities such as New York, Chicago, Philadelphia, and Boston, strong-arm and terroristic methods have been employed to penalize price cutting or to restrain new producers from entering the field.

---

[146] *Hearings before the Temporary National Economic Committee*, Part 2, p. 424; Part 10, pp. 4248–4250; Part 17, pp. 9503–9505; Part 25, pp. 13324, 13361.
[147] *Ibid.*, Part 25, pp. 13319–13327.

Materials taken from the TNEC hearings have been presented in an earlier chapter showing the character and the extent of the demands for self-rule in industry, as well as some of the results of such practices.

THE TRADE ASSOCIATION

The trade associations today appear to play a more dominant role in American economic life than did the trust during its prime. Through them industries may be combined to serve the public interest by increasing efficiency and reducing costs, or they may be brought together to conspire against the public and to achieve ends similar to those sought by pools, trusts, and other combinations.

Apparently trade associations have been more zealous in supporting activities which produce the fruits of monopoly than in promoting methods which reduce production costs, increase efficiency, and improve services rendered to the public. Rather than research and assistance to members, the impelling force behind the movement seems to be desire for industrial control. "The real core of the trade association movement has lain in its attack on free competition," says Whitney.[148] Trade association members and its literature seem most concerned with restraining price cutting, eliminating "chiselers," preventing the market from becoming "demoralized," and putting an end to the "abuses" and "excesses" of competition.

Many monopolistic methods have been implemented through trade associations, particularly the basing-point system and price leadership. Many activities of the associations have been directed in one form or another to restrain competition among the members and to control prices, limit production, or allocate markets. Among the numerous methods employed to this end are the organization of price reporting schemes, open price systems, the development of common cost accounting procedures, the collection and dissemination of statistics, standardization of accounts, the exchange of credit information, the agreement upon uniform terms of sale, and the adoption of other uniform policies with respect to quality, service, and prices.

According to the experience of the Federal Trade Commission, most of the cases of unlawful restraint brought to its attention have involved trade associations. In many cases they were the leaders, and the association secretaries were the prime movers in originating and implementing the plan.[149] Between 1928 and 1937 sixty-five important

[148] Whitney, *Trade Associations and Industrial Control*, p. 38.
[149] *Final Report and Recommendations of the Temporary National Economic Committee*, pp. 305–306.

industries were thus arraigned before the Federal Trade Commission.[150] A few cases will illustrate. The Water Valve and Hydrant Group of the Valve and Fittings Institute combined thirty-one corporations which employed a trade association to fix and maintain prices. They divided the United States into zones and established uniform delivered prices for their products.[151] Nineteen corporations combined under the Metal Window Institute, an unincorporated trade association. They established a central bureau to check estimates of bids for the sale of their products; they agreed to maintain uniform prices and uniform conditions of sale and discounts; they policed the activities of members to assure compliance; and they prevented nonmembers from becoming successful bidders on projects.[152]

The Window Glass Manufacturers' Association combined eight leading manufacturers of glass products. This association and the National Glass Distributors' Association conspired to enforce certain policies and sales methods upon the industry. Buyers were classified and different price schedules were established for each class. The Federal Trade Commission, after examining the extensive ramifications of the system, found that competition had been substantially lessened and that a monopoly in the sale and distribution of window glass had been effected.[153] In the case of the Material Dealers Alliance, a trade association composed of 150 dealers in building materials, including cement, brick, tile, sand, plaster, stone, gravel, lumber, roofing, and related products, so thoroughly dominated the area around Pittsburgh and Cleveland that it would require the most rigorous government regulation to equal it on a comparable scale. Retailers were classified and only "approved" dealers were permitted to operate. Veritable certificates of convenience and necessity were required by the monopolistic combination before a retailer was permitted to engage in the business. Prices were maintained, output restricted, boycotts threatened, and the industry rigidly controlled to eliminate almost all types of competition.

INTERSTATE TRADE BARRIERS

Competition is sometimes deliberately restrained by legislative mandate. The practice of the state of conferring special privileges and benefits upon favored subjects extends back at least to the period when monarchs gave monopoly privileges to favorites of the crown.

[150] *Hearings before the Temporary National Economic Committee,* Part 25, p. 13318; Exhibit 2173, p. 13560, lists trade associations involved.
[151] *Ibid.,* Part 5, pp. 1738–1739. [152] *Ibid.,* pp. 1741–1742. [153] *Ibid.,* pp. 1746–1747.

A classic example in recent years has been the use of the protective tariff to exclude competition by foreign enterprisers and to reserve the domestic market to home producers. Modern variants of the protective tariff, on a more local scale, are interstate trade barriers often introduced into law at the behest of organized pressure groups collaborating to obtain special privileges in the guise of the public good. Thus, although the Constitution provides that "no State shall, without consent of Congress, lay any imposts or duties on imports, or exports," the so-called "Balkanization" of the states has increased at a rapid rate. Much as trade between nations has been garroted and strangled by such devices as tariffs, quotas, licenses, exchange control, and monetary manipulation, trade between the states has likewise been impaired.

Emotional content has been read into so many economic terms that it is important that they be used only after precise definition, or abandoned altogether. Restrictions in the interest of social welfare may be stigmatized as trade barriers by special interest groups who would benefit by their removal. Actual trade barriers, on the other hand, may be lauded as beneficial by pressure groups who thereby enjoy a vested and predatory position. A trade barrier has been defined as a "statute, regulation or practice which operates or tends to operate to the disadvantage of persons, products, or services coming from sister States, to the advantage of local residents, products, and enterprises." [154] Its purpose is to grant some special group within the state a preferred position, resulting thereby in a disadvantage to others beyond the state boundary and usually in a disadvantage to domestic consumers, whose choice is thus restricted and who are forced to purchase in a limited market. By definition, therefore, restrictions designed to protect the public interest are not interstate trade barriers. Neither are laws requiring honest labeling and grading, since restriction is incidental to the social good. The same laws, however, may be perverted either by selective interpretation or by administration, with the result that the presumed social good is incidental only to the special benefits conferred.

Trade barriers seem to fall into four principal categories: [155] (1) Statutes which have obvious discriminatory and retaliatory purposes and are openly directed against out-of-state trade. Such barriers are limited in number, since the more usual method is to masquerade

---

[154] *Hearings before the Temporary National Economic Committee,* Part 29, p. 15736.
[155] *Ibid.,* p. 15780.

barriers under rationalized if not hypocritical banners. (2) Statutes which apparently are not discriminatory, but are definitely so in operation. These include laws which have for their avowed and ostensible purpose the protection of public welfare, but whose ill-concealed design is to lay a burden upon out-of-state products. They often impose some special marketing regulation, as has frequently been done for dairy products and margarines. (3) Statutes which on their face are equally applicable to residents and* nonresidents, but in practical operation burden out-of-state business. Typical of these are many regulations imposed for the public good which, because they vary in the several states, create trade impediments. A milk inspection law that is satisfactory for one area may not be recognized in another, which may have had an equally good inspection. (4) Statutes not discriminatory in purpose or effect may become so through discriminatory administration. Numerous administrative agencies exercise broad discretionary powers and frequently frame their regulations to the disadvantage of out-of-state products.

THE ATTACK ON OLEOMARGARINE

Examples of trade barriers are those which have been erected against oleomargarine. Poor people whose incomes do not permit the use of butter are discriminated against in order to bring the fruits of monopoly to producers of butter. Producers of the ingredients which go into the butter substitute are likewise at a disadvantage. Various barriers have been erected among the states. First are the taxes which have been imposed on margarines. Twenty-four states have adopted excise taxes; these usually run from five cents a pound on the uncolored product to fifteen cents on all margarines.[156] Southern states grant more favorable treatment to margarines produced from southern oil, such as cottonseed and peanut oil. The Federal Government has joined in this one-sided battle; in 1931 it imposed a tax of ten cents per pound on colored margarine, forcing, in effect, the exclusive sale of white margarine. Like a high protective tariff, this is a tax designed principally to destroy trade and is most effective when not collected.

In addition to taxes, licenses have been imposed ranging from $1.00 to $1,000 per year. The fee is highest in Wisconsin, Pennsylvania, and Montana. Nine states require a manufacturer's license, sixteen states place the burden on the wholesaler, thirteen impose it on the retailer,

---

[156] *Ibid.*, pp. 15852–15853, 16138.

and six even burden commercial users by requiring that restaurants and boarding houses shall be licensed. Wisconsin even requires a license of $1.00 (a consumer's license) for housewives who purchase margarine.[157] In fact, Wisconsin wars on three fronts, by requiring a license to sell (ranging up to $1,000), a license to buy, and a tax of fifteen cents on each pound. The need for butter and butter substitutes is amply illustrated by the persistent demand for margarine despite the burdens which have been heaped upon consumers. This is patently a harmful and perverted abuse of the taxing power.

The ostensible purpose of the tax and the license fees is the protection of the public. But despite the arguments and the rationalizations employed, their real purpose is quite obvious—the destruction of a business by taxing it out of existence. This is emphasized by the fact that the tax produces little revenue.[158] The objective of these measures, however, seems to have been adequately served. There has been a marked reduction of dealers and sales. In the fourteen states taxing cottonseed oil margarine only, sales declined by nearly 80,000,000 pounds a year.[159] In states taxing uncolored margarine (the tax varying from five to fifteen cents per pound), there was a tremendous dealer mortality after the imposition of the tax in 1931. A tax of five cents eliminated 99 percent of the dealers in Idaho, 46 percent in Iowa, and 61 percent in Utah. Other states imposed a tax of ten cents, which in North Dakota eliminated 100 percent of the dealers, in South Dakota 97 percent, in Tennessee 87 percent, and in Oklahoma 90 percent. The fifteen-cent tax was likewise effective; in Washington it caused 99.7 percent of the dealers to discontinue their sales of margarine and in Wisconsin, 99.9 percent. In the nine states taxing uncolored margarine, 81 percent of the dealers were eliminated. By 1939 margarine dealers were completely eliminated from Idaho, Washington, and Wisconsin, while only one remained in North Dakota.[160]

In addition to the burdens on oleomargarine thus far described, certain other barriers to the trade have been erected. Twenty states have prohibited the use of margarine in state institutions. In addition to the Federal Government, which imposes a tax of ten cents on each pound of colored margarine, thirty-one states specifically prohibit its sale altogether.[161] A large number and variety of packaging laws combine to create additional obstacles.

157 *Ibid.*, pp. 15785, 15860.   158 *Ibid.*, p. 16135; see also pp. 15831, 15854.
159 *Ibid.*, p. 16136.   160 *Ibid.*, pp. 15832–15834, 15853–15855, 15861, 16136–16139.
161 *Ibid.*, p. 15837.

There seems to be little popular demand for the laws thus described. No public welfare or social agency has ever sponsored them.[162] They represent the malfunctioning of the democratic process, whereby the law becomes an instrumentality of a special interest group. On nine occasions the public has had an opportunity to express itself on such measures; in each case statutes of this character have been rejected by the electorate.[163]

POWER OF INSPECTION A BARRIER

Another class of barrier, employed deliberately at times to exclude out-of-state products, originates with the police power of inspection to protect public morals and safety. This power has been used by some states to require labels which create the impression that "foreign" or "shipped" eggs are not fresh, thus establishing a preference for the home product.[164] Other burdens have been imposed in the case of milk.[165] Producers who ship beyond their own inspection area have been required to satisfy duplicate inspection regulations in the areas to which the milk is shipped, whereas a satisfactory system of reciprocity between areas would have sufficed. Similar embargoes on fruits, vegetables, nursery products, and livestock have been common.[166] Sometimes the inspection service has been used deliberately to exclude out-of-state products; "foreign" milk has been dyed red in Vermont.[167] At times the power of inspection has been exercised arbitrarily, as when West Virginia milk was barred from Pennsylvania. West Virginia threatened to retaliate, but inasmuch as Pennsylvania producers enjoyed a larger market in West Virginia than did its producers in Pennsylvania, the ban was quickly lifted.

PUBLIC PREFERENCE LAWS

Other examples of economic warfare between states are the laws extending preferences by a state to its own citizens and products. Such preferences are represented by regulations requiring the state to purchase products of local origin only, as in the case of coal or butter, stationery, flour, and products of its own "mines, forests and quarries." Other laws require that preference be given to local printers and contractors or to laborers from within the state.[168] Common as these statutes are, they differ little from the devices which Adam Smith

162 *Ibid.*, p. 15846.
164 *Ibid.*, p. 15805.
166 *Ibid.*, pp. 15798–15913.
168 *Ibid.*, p. 15813.

163 *Ibid.*, pp. 15846–15847.
165 *Ibid.*, pp. 15794–15795, 15871–15912.
167 *Ibid.*, pp. 15793–15794.

decried among nations which restrict the economy from achieving its fullest attainment.

THE ECONOMIC EFFECTS OF TRADE BARRIERS

It is, indeed, strange that Americans, witnessing, as they have, the disunity, the economic distress, and the dislocations of trade in Europe resulting from the erection of economic barriers and observing what chaos is developing between nations as a consequence of such economic warfare, should have recourse to the same devices between the states. The strength and the attainments of the American economy are due largely to a combination of three factors: the abundant natural resources, unparalleled anywhere else in the world, the advanced technological and industrial development of the country, and the fact that the absence of political boundaries and trade restrictions have given the nation the largest free-trade area in the world. Mass production, standardization, and low-cost production and marketing in America, together with regional specialization, are made possible by the wide markets afforded under the Federal free-trade system. State trade bariers undermine this economic foundation. One or two trade barriers would seem to have little effect, perhaps, except to create a vested and privileged class at the expense of the whole, but a thousand barriers operating simultaneously are clearly designed to choke and strangle the system itself. Already many instances of retaliation and economic warfare have characterized this struggle between the states.[169]

LARGE CAPITAL REQUIREMENTS

Regardless of the methods by which monopolies and combinations are created, a realistic approach would recognize that the large capital requirements essential to the organization of many modern productive enterprises constitute the foundation of monopoly. Modern technology makes necessary the employment of large capital units, and this fact creates a barrier to competition; it constitutes a motive for combination and furnishes a setting for collusion. It is a barrier to free entry, inasmuch as few are able to assemble the reserves necessary to organize a new industrial unit. It costs about $1,000,000 to establish a plant to produce glass bottles.[170] Similarly, it was estimated that it would take $25,000,000 to start to produce aluminum.[171] To under-

---

[169] *Ibid.*, pp. 15743–15774, 15892, 16092.   [170] *Ibid.*, Part 2, pp. 505–506.
[171] *Final Report and Recommendations of the Temporary National Economic Committee*, p. 492.

take the production of steel would be equally prohibitive, since a single blast furnace would cost $2,500,000, and a continuous mill for hot-rolled products would require $20,000,000. To enter the textile industry would be quite as difficult, since a new rayon plant costs $11,000,000, a nylon plant $8,000,000, and a new celanese plant, $10,000,000.[172] Because of the prohibitive cost, the opportunity to compete is thereby closed to all but a few. Furthermore, the sums are so large and the consequences of failure so heavy that many are reluctant to undertake the risk even when it is within their power.

Because of the large-scale operations of many industries and because they are adapted to mass production methods, unless the market functions more or less perfectly and each producing unit operates at full capacity—which it seldom does—they are usually decreasing-cost industries. As such they face recurring periods which result in ruinous price wars if competition characterizes the industry. Hence, the very nature of the business—the heavy capital investment and the importance of fixed costs of production—furnishes a strong motive to avert competition and to form combinations which restrain trade. To the motive of securing the fruits of monopoly is added, therefore, the desire to prevent competitive warfare and industrial fratricide.

Another fact is apparent from what has been set forth. The inherent characteristic of modern industry, which requires large capital investment and large-scale production in a number of fields, leaves room in the market for only a small number of producers. This forms a foundation for oligopoly and constitutes a favorable setting wherein a few find it within their power to come to terms. Such was the basis of the patent monopoly in the glass bottle industry,[173] the basing-point system for steel and cement,[174] the price leadership policy in the beryllium industry,[175] and the monopoly practices with respect to petroleum.[176]

TECHNOLOGY AND RESEARCH

Closely related to the part which heavy capital requirements play in the concentration of industrial control and the monopolization of the market is the similar role of modern technology and research. Less and less is production the simple result of the application of labor and tools or even the application of machinery and assembly lines. More and more, production has become the fruit of test tubes, the

172 *Hearings before the Temporary National Economic Committee,* Part 1, p. 90.
173 *Ibid.,* Part 2, pp. 505–506.   174 *Ibid.,* pp. 381–625.
175 *Ibid.,* Part 5, pp. 2011–2163.   176 *Ibid.,* Parts 14, 15.

microscope, and the crucible. Rayon, alloy steel, nylon, bakelite, vacuum tubes, television, high-octane gasoline, flying fortresses, and numerous other commercial products born in the scientific laboratory emphasize the importance of modern technology.

Research, however, is costly and, being so, often limits production and places its control in the hands of those who can afford to bear the initial cost of financing it. This point was succinctly set forth in a statement made by the president of the Ford Motor Company.

It is true that some technological changes in the line of improvements and new developments require much time and money and therefore, it is believed, can be done more readily by large industries. Many improvements probably would not be put to use except for the facilities of large industries, especially where their effectiveness depends upon large production. It is necessary at times to spend hundreds of dollars a day over a period of years before a new method or article can be put in production. The improved Ford crankshaft and method of making it is a good example of development of this type.[177]

Large financial outlays are necessary to organize and maintain a modern research laboratory. One laboratory alone among the sixteen currently maintained by the General Electric Company costs more than $1,000,000 a year to operate.[178] The annual budget for research and development by the Bell Telephone Laboratories is more than $20,000,000.[179] General Motors spends more than $10,000,000 a year for research purposes,[180] and the Bakelite firm, $500,000.[181] In order to survive, the dynamic character of our society virtually imposes upon a firm the necessity of doing continuous research; the costliness of the process tends to limit the field to big concerns, thus laying the basis for oligopoly and monopoly.

The best techniques are inherently monopolistic. Since such techniques will be born more and more in the laboratory and since, by the very nature of the process, they will be improvements principally of existing techniques, established laboratories and industries will be at a tremendous advantage. The tendency to centralized control is both vertical and horizontal—vertical in the sense that new processes to improve those already in use will be controlled chiefly by companies with laboratories already at work, and horizontal in the sense that these same laboratories in their researches will discover principles and develop methods which will find commercial employment to

---

177 *Ibid.*, Part 30, p. 16320.   178 *Ibid.*, Part 3, p. 915.
179 *Ibid.*, pp. 974–975.   180 *Ibid.*, Part 9, pp. 3655–3656.
181 *Ibid.*, Part 3, p. 1088.

dominate new fields of production and to project control into fields other than those in which the researches were originally conducted.

GATEWAYS AND BOTTLENECKS

From time to time monopolistic tendencies develop because of some gateway or bottleneck through which, perforce, commerce must flow. These conduits through which trade is channelized are, of course, owned in America almost always by private capital. Frequently they constitute indispensable means of transportation or equally essential processing plants. Such bottlenecks may be the result of technological or institutional causes. In the case of railroads and pipe lines they exist because modern technology causes some types of production to be more efficient than others, and these types are more or less inherently monopolistic.[182] This fact was recognized by Chief Justice Waite in the celebrated Munn case, who described the Chicago grain elevators as virtual monopolies, controlling the production of seven or eight great states, standing in the very gateway of commerce, and taking toll from all who pass.[183] In the case of franchises, patents, and pasteurization plants, however, such gateways represent centralized production and control, due, in large part, to the fact that the body politic has required production to be organized in a given manner.

Such foci of monopoly are not new; institutional controls were imposed when the guilds dominated medieval towns in the late Middle Ages. Moreover, it was due to the early existence of natural monopolies that the concept of public utilities evolved; at a very early time millers, hackmen, bakers, wharfingers, cotton gin operators, ferrymen, toll collectors, and inn keepers were subjected to public regulation.

Two striking examples of bottlenecks which enabled their owners to extend control from the immediate instrument at hand to broader aspects of the market were described before the TNEC: the ownership of oil pipe lines strengthened the influence of the great integrated petroleum companies in the refining and retailing fields, while the power of two great milk distributors was centered in the control of pasteurization plants.

PETROLEUM PIPE LINES

Control of the petroleum market by the major integrated companies reflects, to a very substantial extent, their control of the crude

[182] Decreasing cost industries.   [183] 94 U.S. 113 (1877).

oil and gasoline pipe lines. The presence or absence of competition within an industry may be determined largely by the ability of independents to move their product to the market. In the petroleum industry pipe-line transportation ordinarily is more efficient on a cost basis; most of the crude oil transported over inland routes moves through pipes. Fourteen large integrated oil companies, however, control 89 percent of the crude oil trunk line mileage, giving them an advantage over independent refiners and producers. The major integrated companies own 96 percent of the gasoline pipe lines and 57 percent of the crude oil gathering lines.[184]

Nominally, pipe lines are common carriers and subject to the control of the Interstate Commerce Commission. Such regulation, however, has neither been effective nor has it given independent producers free access to markets. In general, pipe-line rates are 100 percent of railroad rates. Thus, the integrated companies charge themselves high rates, imposing at the same time similar charges upon others who use the lines. Pipe-line profits are large and may be used by the integrated companies to subsidize their refining and retailing divisions. Independent retailers, refiners, and oil producers, however, have no such backlog upon which to depend, and the overcharges which they pay to the integrated companies for pipe-line services are, in effect, "drawbacks" used to their disadvantage.[185] The services of common carriers are available to all who desire them. Such is scarcely the case with the pipe lines. The gasoline lines are used almost exclusively by the majors.[186] Several factors contribute to the exclusion of independents from both the crude oil and the gasoline lines; these include the absence of pipe-line facilities near independent refineries, the fact that lines often are loaded to capacity by the products of their owners, and the existence of certain minimum tender requirements, which often are so high that independents cannot conveniently contract to use the pipe lines and are forced either to sell or to seek other facilities.[187] Many oil fields are served by only one trunk line, and the independent producer must either use the service of that concern or sell his oil in the field to it.

A sharp contrast exists between the railroads and the pipe lines as affected by interstate commerce laws. In 1906 railroads were forbidden by the commodities clause of the Hepburn Act to transport com-

184 *Hearings before the Temporary National Economic Committee,* Part 14, pp. 7103, 7171, 7172.
185 *Ibid.,* pp. 7233–7236.   186 *Ibid.,* p. 7251; see also Part 17, p. 9381.
187 *Ibid.,* Part 15, p. 8300; Part 17, p. 9758.

modities (e. g., coal) in the production of which they had an interest. This seemed necessary to assure the reality of the common carrier status of the railroads and to prevent their monopoly of fields of production to which they rendered service. No similar legal provision has required that the transportation of oil be divorced from production, refining, and retailing.

Pipe-line earnings are remarkably high, a fact which resulted from, as well as contributed to, the restriction of competitive opportunities in the industry. In 1938 the major pipe-line companies earned 28 percent on the depreciated value of their investment. Earnings ran as high as 51 percent for some companies.[188] The Great Lakes gasoline pipe line has been especially profitable; between 1935 and 1939 it paid its owners more than $4,000,000 a year, or more than 20 percent annually on the total investment. In five years it had paid for itself.[189] To a substantial degree these spectacular earnings were at the expense of the independents. Pipe-line transportation rates were in excess of cost and out of line with charges normally allowed to regulated common carriers. Hence, where lines were available to independents, the latter were forced to contribute to the profits of the integrated companies; they were, in effect, paying rebates to the major companies.[190] Independent refineries found themselves squeezed by the narrow margin allowed by the majors. The integrated companies charged high rates for transportation to and from the refineries; they made excessive profits on these operations. They could thus afford to take a loss on their refining and distribution operations; the independents, of course, could not. Pipe-line profits could be, and apparently were, used to subsidize the other operations of the majors, who thus enjoyed a position of dominance which could not be attributed to their efficiency.

MILK PASTEURIZATION PLANTS

The control of milk distribution in the hands of monopolistic combinations has occurred recently. It springs from a legal device instituted for laudable purposes. The drive for pure milk in urban centers required the erection of pasteurization plants. Small businesses and independents found it inconvenient to meet the requirements of the law, and big business entered more and more into the picture.[191]

188 *Ibid.*, Part 14, p. 7237; Part 14-A, p. 7725.
189 *Ibid.*, Part 15, p. 8303; see also Part 16, p. 8849.
190 For citations describing pipe-line profits see *ibid.*, Part 14, pp. 7106, 7237–7238, 7257, 7262–7263, 7376; Part 15, pp. 8247, 8303, 8306; Part 16, pp. 8841–8842, 8849; Part 17, pp. 9715–9717, 9755, 9759–9760.   191 *Ibid.*, Part 7, pp. 2754–2755, 2760–2763.

Soon more than 900 cities passed standardized ordinances requiring pasteurization plants. Only in the smaller cities, where pasteurization is not yet compulsory, do independent milk distributors flourish. Large combinations have arisen to dominate the metropolitan markets and to exclude or harass the products of others. Much as the Standard Oil monopoly was built up by domination of the refineries and the pipe lines, the new milk trust has built its control around the legally required pasteurization plants—the milk refineries.

In 1923 the National Dairy Products Corporation was organized; it initiated a program of acquiring or building pasteurization plants throughout the country. By 1938 it had acquired 360 dairy companies in key cities. Meanwhile the Borden Company, an older concern, followed a similar program in other cities, acquiring control of "gateways" through which milk commerce was forced to flow. By 1938 more than 110 agencies of these two firms dominated the milk industry of the state of New York. Much the same situation existed in Pennsylvania, Ohio, Michigan, and Wisconsin.

The milk monopoly, like the Roman god Janus, faced in two directions at one and the same time. It was both monopolistic and monopsonistic. The charges made for delivered milk to consumers were rigid and inflexible. Likewise, the prices paid to the farmers failed to follow the competitive pattern. The two majors imposed monopoly prices wherever their control permitted; in New York City the retail price for milk remained relatively rigid in both the boom and the depression years between 1923 and 1938. Retail prices dropped only 20 percent; during this same period, however, prices paid to farmers dropped 50 percent. The milk combination often paid two prices to the same farmer for the same quality of milk. The explanation given to the farmer was that he received a class 1 (or class A) price for that portion of his milk which was bottled and sold to the consumer and a class 2 (or class B) price for the rest of his milk which, according to the explanation given, was used by the processor in the manufacture of dairy products.[192] In reality, therefore, the milk company purchased milk at a net price considerably below the apparent (class 1) purchasing price. The class 1 price, however, frequently served to justify prices charged to consumers. Farmers had access to no audit to show whether they received the higher price on the total amount of their milk that was delivered to consumers. They had only the word of the monopsonist, and the weight

[192] For a discussion of class prices see *ibid.*, pp. 2778–2779, 2855–2856, 2888–2889.

of evidence indicated that the class prices often were manipulated to the financial disadvantage of the farmer as well as of the consumer.

As time went on the distributor tightened his grip upon both buying and selling prices. The farmer received less and less for his milk, and the distributor gained a larger and larger share.[193] Early in 1923, when the National Dairy Products Corporation was organized, the dairy farmer received 52 percent of the consumer's milk dollar, and the distributor, 48 percent; by 1933, however, the farmer's share had shrunk to 35 percent, and the distributor had succeeded in claiming 65 percent. In other words, while the farmer's share had declined by 33 percent, the distributor's share had increased by 40 percent.[194] It is not surprising, therefore, to learn that while dairy farmers endured depression conditions and while the country at large and business in general suffered severely from the economic turn of events following 1929, the two milk combinations prospered and returned substantial profits to their owners. During 1930, 1931, and 1932, when losses were generally characteristic of American industry, National Dairy averaged 13 percent profit on its invested capital. During the same period rather sumptuous salaries were paid to the corporation's executives. Milk processors paid higher executive salaries than processors of tobacco, flour, cotton, meat, bakeries, tanneries, etc. During the first six years of the depression a Philadelphia subsidiary of National Dairy returned 75 percent of its original cost to its owners.[195]

ADVERTISING

Advertising constitutes another barrier to free entry into the market and thereby lays the basis for monopoly. To the mind of the none-too-analytical layman advertising is a symbol of rigorous competition, but to the economically informed it is evidence of a restricted market. Obviously there are degrees of monopoly control, and there are degrees of product differentiation (intrinsic and imputed); this fact makes it difficult for the average citizen to comprehend the role of restraint which advertising performs. The owner of a product for which the price is competitively determined has nothing to gain from advertising. He can sell every unit he possesses at the market price, and were he to advertise "John Doe's field corn," he could sell no more and obtain no better price. The very purpose of advertising is either to carve out a monopolistic position for the

[193] *Ibid.*, p. 2797.   [194] *Ibid.*, p. 2800.
[195] *Ibid.*, pp. 2806–2807.

product or to perpetuate or strengthen the position already obtained.

Before the epoch of modern advertising, products could be established in the market by virtue of their reputation of quality and cost. Commodities formerly less complex and less a product of technology and chemistry could be analyzed more readily by the buyer. Consumers' goods and producers' goods, having become more complex, are sold less and less on the basis of tests which the consumer himself can apply and more and more in response to psychological appeal, ingenious presentation, colorful pretensions, and reputation built upon repetition. The eye, the ear, and the nose no longer can test the validity of claims and the efficacy of cures or discover the soundness of mechanical construction or the degree of freedom from harmful or worthless ingredients. That requires technical training and laboratory equipment beyond the reach of the consumer.

With the new pattern of technology, the new types of merchandising, the increased complexity of products, and the highly institutionalized and thoroughly organized advertising industry, the producer of a new product must run an expensive gauntlet before he can penetrate the market and reach the consumer. Ofttimes more important than the merits of his product and more expensive than his plant and equipment is the program of advertising which the producer must undertake to gain entry into the market. This barrier, though not insurmountable, is very substantial and frequently limits the field to the few who are able to finance such a program.[196]

THE TOOTH PASTE INDUSTRY [197]

A manufacturer of tooth paste described for the TNEC the all-importance of advertising to one attempting a start in that industry. In 1939 ten large manufacturers, producing ten branded products which through advertising had become household words, dominated the retail market. The new manufacturer proceeded to earn a place for his product—or attempted to do so—on its own merits without benefit of the heraldry and the psychological legerdemain of the advertising fraternity. The tooth paste he manufactured was based on a good formula and received the immediate approval of the American Dental Association (only one of the ten nationally ad-

[196] A striking illustration of this fact was the skillfully managed advertising campaign of a powerful and well-established soap manufacturer to place the new product—"Swan"—on the market during 1941–1942. This firm is reputed to have launched an advertising program costing more than $1,000,000 to secure entry into the market for its product.
[197] *Hearings before the Temporary National Economic Committee,* Part 8, pp. 3396–3412.

vertised products had received this endorsement). He had also secured government contracts, thereby meeting the rigorous standards usually required in the case of such purchases. Moreover, the product sold to consumers at substantially one-half the retail price ordinarily charged for a similar package of the ten nationally advertised products. If cost and quality were sufficient to sell it in open competition, it should have sold. Another fact to its advantage was that retailers were able to profit more from the sale of each unit, being allowed a markup of 100 percent as compared with only about 50 percent in the case of the advertised products.

This manufacturer thus had for his product virtually every quality which should result in an active demand—every quality but one, access to consumers. Consumers had been pre-empted, as it were; they belonged almost exclusively to certain producers, quite as though territories had been allotted by a pool or a cartel. Whenever the manufacturer sought retail outlets, invariably he was greeted with the same response: "You have a very good product, the price is right, your story is good, but bring customers to us. You bring customers into our stores to ask for your product and we will be very glad to carry it." [198] In other words, a good product is not enough. The producer must add another type of product differentiation; he must advertise to obtain a portion of the monopolized market. The producer literally found it necessary to buy his way into the market in order to have access to consumers. This approach he proceeded to investigate. After taking the matter up with several advertising firms, he discovered that it would cost $100,000 to make a preliminary survey to discover whether a national advertising program, if undertaken, would be successful. Such initial expense and the much greater costs which would follow to put the product across would be prohibitive, of course, to many producers, as it was to this one in particular. Monopolistic control of industry is, in part, a product of the inability of new enterprisers to enter the field; thus, heavy advertising costs have become an important barrier to free competition.

PATENTS

The monopoly problem today is more the product of a legal institution—the patent right—than it was in the days of pools, trusts, and combinations. From the patent laws there have evolved two classes of monopolies, one which was anticipated and planned for and the

[198] *Ibid.*, p. 3398.

other, unintended and unplanned. Patents, by legislative intent, grant their owners the exclusive right, for a limited period, to make, use, and sell the patented article. This grant of monopoly is made to stimulate the inventive process and to foster technological progress. Many testified that such a result had been achieved.[199]

Another social product of the patent system has been the fostering of predatory business units and combinations. The border line between the lawful and social use of the patent monopoly, on the one hand, and the unlawful or predatory use, on the other, is often indistinct, and to discover it requires careful examination and often the interpretation of the courts. The legal rights of the patent holder are not clear, and the distinction between the lawful and the unlawful must inevitably await the race between the prosecutor and the court, on the one hand, and the ingenuity of entrepreneurs, on the other.

The patent right has made possible a variety of practices in restraint of trade. One involves the advantage afforded to existing patent holders in purchasing patents on new processes as they are developed. This advantage is most pronounced in the case of an owner of a basic patent who ofttimes is the only one to whom patents on improvements may be sold. Intrenched by his ownership of a basic process, he may, by acquiring the rights to all improvements, extend his monopoly almost indefinitely. Moreover, as the monopoly continues it may fan outward, as wider sectors of the economy are embraced. Not only may complementary processes be acquired through purchase, but competing processes as well. This may be done either to centralize control or to assure that the competing process never reaches the market. Patents also permit their owners to extend their monopoly over the patented article, ofttimes a machine, to its product. Hence, the holder of patents has been able to control prices at which others sell not only the patented article but also its product. Often this is achieved by licensing or leasing to manufacturers the use of patented machines. Still another practice involves the tying contract, whereby the patent owner requires users of the patented article to purchase nonpatented materials as well, thereby extending monopoly control into areas not intended by the law. The patent pool offers another obstruction to competition. Owners of competing and complementary processes may combine and, by their claims to almost all phases of the productive process, successfully obstruct others from operating or force them to accede to whatever terms are imposed.

[199] *Ibid.*, Parts 2 and 3.

The patent-protected monopolist frequently has recourse to numerous instruments of duress to secure compliance by unwilling producers. At their worst these devices resemble racketeering, since threats are made, weapons used, and the victim often finds it necessary to buy "protection." The method of "terrorism" in this case is harassment by litigation. Threats of litigation are often sufficient, since legal contests usually are expensive; the victim frequently finds it less expensive to become a licensee of the patent which he is presumed to infringe than to continue to pay large annual fees for litigation. The patent system permits powerful units or combinations to destroy small competitors by endless litigation or by threats of litigation, regardless of the merits of the small producer's case or of his product. Infringement suits may thus be employed to coerce independent producers to resign their patent rights to stronger combinations. By the use of interference proceedings smaller firms may be forced to barter away their patentable rights even before the patent is granted.

THE GLASS CONTAINER INDUSTRY

Monopolistic practices within the glass container industry have been described in Chapter VII. This industry presents an illustration of the major abuses possible, with the patent system run riot for monopolistic ends. The Hartford-Empire Company, through the concentration of patent rights, had extended its monopoly hold throughout the glass container industry. Here was a corporation which made no bottles, produced no bottle-making machines, and sold no machines, but, through its patent control dominated 67 percent of the nation's glass bottle industry.[200] This concentration of power was achieved in a number of ways.

The refusal to license patents.—The president of Hartford-Empire candidly testified that the company followed a policy of restricting production by refusing to grant new licenses for the production of bottles. Patent rights could not be had even for a fee.[201] The industry was generally closed to new producers.

The blocking of potential patents.—The Hartford people declared that a main purpose of their policy was "to block the development of machines which might be constructed by others for the same purpose as" their own machines.[202] This represents the use of the patent system in a manner antagonistic to its purpose which, as set forth in the Constitution, is "to

[200] *Hearings before the Temporary National Economic Committee,* Part 2, pp. 380–383.
[201] See, for example, *ibid.,* pp. 619 ff.
[202] *Ibid.,* pp. 387, 776.

promote the progress of science and useful arts." The record shows that
the Hartford-Empire frequently made use of this policy.

The "fencing in" of patents held by potential competitors.—The process
of fencing involves the study of new inventions with the idea of surrounding them with numerous improvements to ensure that they can never
reach an improved stage and with the purpose of compelling the owner to
come to terms. He may even be compelled to license such improvements if
he is allowed to exploit his own device; he may be compelled to sell out at
the monopolist's terms; or he may be required, if he is permitted to enter
the business, to use the machines of his competitor.[203]

Patent interference.—A patent interference, like many other abuses, has
its legitimate use. It is designed to protect the inventor from others who
seek to patent a process for which he has a prior claim. Hartford used this
device as a means of harassing and delaying patent applications by the
inventors of competing processes. One of Hartford's letters described its
method and intent as follows: "we think it would be desirable, if possible,
to plant a series of traps for such possible Headley and Thompson divi-
sionals, the traps consisting of new applications to be filed to cover the
several subject matters which Headley and Thompson seem likely to
dominate." [204]

The litigation of patents.—The right of appeal to the courts to protect
a patent against infringement was designed and can only be defended
as a means of safeguarding the inventor's interest. On numerous occasions
the activities of Hartford-Empire illustrated how this objective of the law
has been perverted. Virtually all new inventions in the glass container
field were threatened or harassed with lawsuits.[205] With the power of
money against them, with the best-informed patent attorneys retained by
the monopoly, and faced with the heavy cost of litigation itself, the de-
fendent frequently was relatively helpless. Regardless of the superiority
of his claim, he was usually forced to terms. Thus, Hartford-Empire compelled independents to sell out to them.[206] The threat of litigation and
the heavy financial burden involved compelled even well-established firms
to pay royalties on their competitors' patents in order to escape litigation
fees.[207] The fate of less powerful competitors was even less merciful.

Extra legal extension of the life of the patent.—The laws provide that a
patent may be granted for a period of seventeen years. Hartford demonstrated that by using the defenses of the law, this monopoly grant may
be extended far beyond the period intended. By court delay, by interference suits—in this case instigated by owners of the patent—and by
appeals, the patent application may be held up for years. In one instance
a patent filed in 1910 was delayed so that it was not granted until 1937,
after which it had a life of seventeen years.[208] Thus, it would not expire

---

203 For a discussion of Hartford's fencing activities see *ibid.*, pp. 981–984, 986–987, 449
450, 460–461, 472, 558, 560.   204 *Ibid.*, pp. 455–456.
205 See the impressive list of suits initiated by Hartford, *ibid.*, p. 437.
206 *Ibid.*, pp. 524–525.   207 *Ibid.*, pp. 536–539.
208 *Ibid.*, pp. 439–441.

until 1954—forty-four years after the original application and thirty-five years after the inventor (who, rather than the Hartford monopoly, the law presumed to be the beneficiary) died.

THE HOLDING COMPANY

The power of the holding company and the prominent role it plays in American economic life is familiar to the average observer. Substantially every textbook which discusses monopoly devotes a section to the holding company. It is strange, in view of the fact that the TNEC was organized to conduct an investigation of concentration of economic power, that nowhere throughout the hearings was a systematic effort made to appraise adequately the social and economic impact of the holding company; neither can there be found an analysis of the success or failure of the antitrust laws to cope with this instrument of monopoly.

Only by more or less incidental treatment did the holding company enter the TNEC hearings, yet this was sufficient to emphasize the importance of this type of combination. The monopolistic practices of the iron and steel industry centered around the United States Steel Corporation, recognized as the greatest holding company of all times. Monopolistic practices in the whiskey and milk industries likewise were implemented through holding company arrangements.[209]

Experts who appeared before the Committee testified that "a good deal of our trouble is traceable back to the device of the New Jersey and Delaware and some other State laws which permitted holding companies, that our monopoly problem would not have been nearly as serious if it had not been possible for that to be done." [210] Others recommended that the holding company device be abolished altogether.[211]

INTERLOCKING RELATIONS

No systematic attempt was made by the TNEC to determine the role which interlocking corporate relationships play in American economic life. Nevertheless, a study as extensive as the hearings could scarcely avoid at least incidental treatment of such arrangements. Interlocking relationships, or "community of interest," as they frequently are called, result in corporate integration without formal

[209] *Hearings before the Temporary National Economic Committee*, Part 6, pp. 2460, 2507; Part 7.
[210] Dr. Frederic C. Howe, *ibid.*, Part 7, p. 2776.
[211] Dr. Frank A. Fetter, *ibid.*, Part 5, p. 1677; and John T. Flynn, *ibid.*, Part 5, p. 1831.

central control—such integration being effected through a common group of stockholders or directors. To assure unity of action by this method, it is not necessary for the common stockholders or the directors to represent a controlling interest in the firms.

Interlocking may take place between competing or noncompeting concerns. In either case it represents the concentration of economic power, and in the case of competing concerns it represents a ready avenue to monopoly. Interlocking directorships among competitors have become less frequent than they were prior to the Clayton Act, which has almost eliminated the practice.

Though apparently the antitrust laws have been effective in closing the door to this type of monopoly, they may merely have induced managers to adopt different methods of securing concerted action. To the monopolist, form is less important than content, and method is less a matter of concern than results. If interlocking directorships are forbidden, interlocking stockholders still may exert their influence to obtain the fruits of the forbidden method. Though it may be somewhat more inconvenient, there is little to prevent the interlocking stockholders from choosing directors who will serve as though the directors themselves interlocked. When, for example, in the glass industry it became necessary for a director of the Owens-Illinois Glass Company to resign as director of the Hazel-Atlas Glass Company, the same effect was readily achieved as was explained in a company memorandum.

Because of the recent publicity given Owens-Illinois and our investment in Hazel-Atlas in a letter read into the *Congressional Record* of March 8 by Mr. Borah, I advised Mr. McNash that it would probably be desirable for me to resign as a member of their board at either their April meeting or their July meeting, and we discussed the advisability of having Mr. George Quay, secretary of the company, elected in my place, with the understanding that he would be representing us and that I would receive through him the same type of information I now receive as a director. I will see you in the meantime and we will have a chance to discuss just what should be done in this connection.[212]

Interlocking directors, however, are common among noncompeting firms. The five largest life insurance companies interlock with 780 corporations, including 145 banks and 100 other insurance companies.[213] Similarly, fifteen directors of The National Distillers Prod-

[212] *Hearings before the Temporary National Economic Committee*, Part 2, p. 482.
[213] *Final Report and Recommendations of the Temporary National Economic Committee*, p. 582.

ucts Corporation (whiskey), through their commitments, caused that company to interlock with nearly 150 important corporations.[214]

Whereas the antitrust laws succeed fairly well in prohibiting the interlocking of competing corporations through directorships, they scarcely effect any control of the more subtle and less obvious combination through interlocking stockholders. This type of community of interest was prominent in the petroleum industry following the dissolution of the Standard Oil Company in 1892. In the investigation conducted soon thereafter by the Industrial Commission, witnesses testified that the various Standard Oil companies worked together in harmony because of their common ownership. It is not surprising, therefore, to discover that the interlocking of stockholders is still very prominent in the petroleum industry. In 1938 the Rockefeller family was influential in the control of five of the eighteen major oil producing companies, including the Standard Oil Company of New Jersey, the Ohio Oil Company, the Socony Vacuum Oil Company, the Consolidated Oil Corporation, and the Standard Oil Company of Indiana. Similarly, the Pew family, the Mission Corporation, and other prominent financial interests formed important links between the large oil companies.[215]

The majors themselves interlock in quite another manner through their ownership of the Great Lakes Pipe Line, the stock of which is owned by eight of the companies.[216] This is but one of many examples of the interlocking of the integrated oil corporations through stock ownership of other petroleum producing companies. Every one of the majors owns some stock in some other petroleum company in which another major has an interest.[217] To illustrate, the Pure Oil Company, the Standard Oil Company of Indiana, the Gulf Oil Corporation, the Skelly Oil Company, the Standard Oil Company of Ohio, the Shell Oil Company, the Atlantic Refining Company, the Standard Oil Company of New Jersey, the Consolidated Oil Corporation, Continental Oil Company, Mid-Continent Petroleum Corporation, the Texas Corporation, and Union Oil Company of California, all own a portion of the stock of the Hydro Patents Company.[218]

---

[214] *Hearings before the Temporary National Economic Committee*, Part 6, pp. 2493–2496, 2686; see also data on pp. 2513–2516 and 2695. A more comprehensive study of corporate interlocking through directorships is presented by the National Resources Board, *The Structure of the American Economy*, Part 1, chap. ix.
[215] *Hearings before the Temporary National Economic Committee*, Part 15, p. 8375; Part 14-A, pp. 7714–7715.
[216] *Ibid.*, Part 14-A, p. 7774.
[217] *Ibid.*   [218] *Ibid.*

Interlocking through stockholders among the integrated companies has been very common. Among the 120 largest stockholders of the 17 major companies in 1938, 14 owned shares in more than 11 of them, 48 owned shares in more than 6, and 58 in more than 2.

Seventy-seven of those in the group had interests in the Socony-Vacuum Oil Co., 69 in Standard Oil of New Jersey, 68 in the Ohio Oil Co., 67 in Standard of Indiana, 64 in the Consolidated Oil Corporation, 51 in Standard of Ohio, 49 in the Texas Corporation, 46 in the Pure Oil Co., 44 in the Atlantic Refining Co., 43 in the Continental Oil Co., 38 in the Phillips Petroleum Co., 37 in the Skelly Oil Co., 27 in the Shell Union Corporation and in the Cities Service Co., 26 in the Gulf Oil Corporation, and 25 in the Tide Water Associated Oil Co.[219]

Other illustrations of this method by which competing concerns arrive at a working relationship are found in the outboard motor and the glass industries. In 1935 two of the largest companies engaged in the manufacture of outboard motors were the Outboard Motors Corporation and the Johnson Motor Company. The three largest stockholders of the former, however, held 85 percent of the capital stock of the latter, and the relationship thus established came to the attention of the Antitrust Division.[220] Likewise, in the glass industry the Levis group had become stockholders in the Hazel-Atlas Glass Company, the Anchor Hocking Glass Corporation, the Thatcher Manufacturing Company, and the Kimble Glass Company.[221]

THE INTERNATIONAL CARTEL

In 1918, after listening to pleas by certain exporters that they were handicapped by the antitrust laws when competing with foreign combinations, the Congress passed the Webb-Pomerene Act.[222] By this measure competing producers are permitted to form combinations—associations, they are called—to engage in export trade, and as long as they restrict their joint activities to the foreign market, they are exempt from the antitrust laws. The law expressly provides, however, that if such an association by agreement or act artificially or intentionally enhances or depresses prices within the United States, it loses the protection of the act.

Perhaps the Congress was naïve enough to believe that combinations could be perfected to impose controls on the foreign market without

219 Temporary National Economic Committee Monograph No. 21, p. 191.
220 *Hearing before the Temporary National Economic Committee,* Part 5-A, p. 2385.
221 *Ibid.,* Part 2, pp. 478–479.
222 The Webb Export Trade Act; Act of April 10, 1918, Ch. 50, 40 U.S. Stats. 516.

influencing market supply and prices at home. Actually, however, no such cleavage is possible. The domestic market is in fact a part, and in the United States an important part, of the world market. If combinations of domestic producers are formed and if they, in turn, negotiate treaties and alliances with economic powers in foreign lands to manipulate the markets of the world, to divide territories, to control production, and to fix prices, it is pure fantasy to assume that such activities can be divorced from the domestic market. Presumably the government-endorsed cartel permits producers to combine in order to protect their interests in foreign markets; more often, however, it permits them to implement and perfect domestic controls by negotiating foreign alliances which leave them unopposed at home.

No thoroughgoing study has ever been made of the role which Webb-Export Associations have played as foci about which domestic markets have been subjected to control; a few interesting cases are available to show that the Webb-Pomerene Act has been used to foster restraints of trade in the United States. Industries which have established monopoly controls in the domestic market appear prominently among those which have employed the export associations; among these are the cement, sugar, copper, glass, and steel industries.[223]

THE STEEL EXPORT ASSOCIATION OF AMERICA

An illustration of the use of the foreign cartel to implement domestic controls is found in the Steel Export Association of America. This association, formed in 1928, embraced twelve of the leading steel producing companies of the United States; it was sponsored principally by the United States Steel Corporation and the Bethlehem Steel Corporation.[224] The Steel Export Association soon entered into alliances with European producers to control the market for various steel products,[225] to establish quotas, and to fix prices. As one representative of the association explained, "We divided up the world and said that this part of the world is American influence. . . . The rest of the world came under European influence." [226] It appears that an understanding between the International Steel Cartel and the Steel Export Association was reached to restrict exports from the United States to Europe as well as European exports to the United States. Thus, monopoly control by domestic producers over the United States market was enhanced by this guarantee of protection from external

[223] See the list of Export Trade Associations, *ibid.*, Part 25, p. 13349.
[224] *Ibid.*, Part 20, pp. 10922–10923.   [225] *Ibid.*, pp. 10925–10930.
[226] *Ibid.*, p. 10930.

invasion. Apparently the opportunity of insulating the American market from the products of foreign steel plants was a more important motive for the organization of the Steel Export Association than the desire to perfect export marketing methods.

Certain American producers declined to become parties to these controls, preferring to market their products independently and, of course, wherever possible to profit by the higher prices which the cartel agreements created.[227] In so doing they "invaded" the European market by underselling the members of the cartel. To the latter this constituted "dumping," despite the fact that it proved to be a profitable venture to the independents themselves. Threatened with these inroads upon its "sphere of influence," the European branch of the cartel protested to the Steel Export Association that unless the latter was able to control all exporters within its territory, it would become necessary for European producers to retaliate. They indicated that

if matters were not buttoned up . . . the International Cartel would take drastic steps toward lower prices and throw the world markets open. The inference was plain that such a low level of export prices would probably result in foreign makers attempting to share in the large and relatively high priced American domestic market.[228]

From this it is apparent that commitments had been made by European and American producers each to respect the monopoly rights of the other. But inasmuch as the Americans had not perfected 100 percent control of their export trade, the agreement threatened to disintegrate. The Steel Export Association reported to its members: ". . . more imminent, is the danger that the British and Continental parties will renounce the present tentative agreements unless they are made more satisfactorily effective. Such renunciation would inevitably be followed by an influx of low-priced foreign steel in domestic market." [229]

Not only was the export association employed to protect the home market from competition of foreign producers but also it served as a whip to compel independents to conform to the plans perfected by the combination. We find the members of the export association coaching the foreign branch of the cartel as to methods it should employ to destroy competition by independent American producers and to "eliminate" the latter from the market. This was revealed in a letter sent by one executive of the Export Association to another.

We have no quarrel with the Continentals or the British in quoting lower than £9.15.0 by means of the rebate system (as this is what we have been

227 *Ibid.*, pp. 10951–10956.   228 *Ibid.*, p. 10948.   229 *Ibid.*, pp. 10950–10951.

asking them to do for some time to eliminate the American outsider) if they have some real reason for not wanting a price lower than £9.15.0 to become *officially* known but, as partners, we consider that we are entitled to know what they are *actually* doing, because if what they are actually doing is sufficiently low actually to eliminate the American outsider, then we can properly judge the reports our members are constantly receiving as to prices being quoted by the American outsiders and whether or not they are securing any real volume of business.[230]

THE COPPER EXPORT ASSOCIATION

The activities of the Copper Export Association likewise illustrate the impossibility that domestic producers could combine to control world markets without such control being felt within the national market as well. This backwash of international combination is felt in two ways. First, the domestic price of products whose market is world wide inevitably reflects the world price; secondly, the association of producers brought about by the organization of export associations creates a focus for discussions, understandings, and arrangements which ultimately restrain competition in the domestic market.

The Copper Export Association, organized in 1918 as a Webb-Pomerene corporation, served as an export sales agent for its members. It functioned until 1927, when it was replaced by Copper Exporters, Inc. The association came into being primarily, it seems, because producers were concerned over the excess of copper stocks following the termination of the war. They sought an orderly means of liquidating these supplies. The Copper Export Association was granted the power to control the exports of its members as well as to fix export prices.

In 1921 the charter of the association was revised to permit it to purchase 200,000 tons of copper and withhold it from the market.[231] Members had displayed no little apprehension lest the existing stocks be offered for sale and had expressed the opinion that "unless some mode of relieving the strain is found, not only may the association break up and the members be driven to cut-throat competition with each other in dumping their copper into export markets, but some of the members may perhaps be overtaken by most serious financial difficulties." [232] Obviously control of the world market by the formation of such a pool indirectly would establish control over the domestic market. This was aptly expressed by a member of the Executive Committee of the Copper Association; when asked about the

[230] *Ibid.*, p. 10958.   [231] *Ibid.*, Part 25, pp. 13125–13128.
[232] *Ibid.*, p. 13126.

interrelation of the two markets, he said, "It would have applied to the copper market, irrespective of whether it was domestic or foreign, I would say." [233]

Although the control just described was officially sponsored by the association, further restraint of the domestic market was effected in 1921 by concerted action of its members, though not in the name of the organization itself. To forestall the possibility of rigorous price competition within the industry the major copper producers ceased operations. It is significant, however, that the shutdown by the various mines was simultaneous and that nonmembers of the association continued to produce, with substantially no variation of their productive output. It seems evident that the cartel formed the basis for domestic restraint of trade.[234]

Webb-Pomerene associations are presumed by law to impose no controls upon the domestic economy; in practice, however, they implement measures designed both directly and indirectly to restrain competition within the home economy and serve as media for the development of informal programs of restraint. These observations are succinctly pointed up by the following testimony relating to the Copper Export Association.

THE CHAIRMAN. Well, would you say that the effect of your arrangement through the Export Association was also felt in the United States?

MR. KELLEY. I don't think that there is any transaction of purchase and sale that doesn't affect a market.

THE CHAIRMAN. In other words, the world price is bound to be reflected in the domestic price.

MR. KELLEY. Right.

THE CHAIRMAN. Then would it not follow that whatever was done by the authority of the Webb-Pomerene Act through the policy of the Export Association would inevitably have an effect upon the domestic market as well as upon the foreign market?

MR. KELLEY. I think, to speak perfectly frankly, Senator, that you can't completely divorce the two markets.[235]

233 Ibid., p. 13127.   234 Ibid., pp. 13127-13135.
235 Ibid., pp. 13131-13132.

CHAPTER IX

THE PROBLEM OF
FULL EMPLOYMENT

THE TNEC was a creature of the Great Depression. President Roosevelt emphasized this fact in his monopoly message, which, after setting forth the duties of the Committee, he ended with the famous statement, "Idle factories and idle workers profit no man." The number one cause of this great undertaking and the number one problem it sought to solve was the depression. As Chairman O'Mahoney expressed it, the function of the TNEC was as follows: "We were asked to study the concentration of economic power and to find out, if we could, why, with all the unlimited resources nature affords, money, machines, and men have been idle, with consequent hardship and suffering to millions." [1] Dr. Lubin spoke for the Committee when he described its task: "We must make sure that never again does a catastrophe occur like that which overwhelmed us in the early 1930's." [2] This being the case, it is important that one section of this analysis be devoted to the findings of the TNEC with regard to the Great Depression.

In the "school" through which the TNEC members put themselves in the first few days of their activity it was emphasized that for many years recessions and depressions had been characteristic of the economy. One of the most "normal" attributes of the system has been this so-called "abnormal" deportment. Significantly enough, these periods of economic dislocation seem to be somewhat more common and more severe in the American economy than elsewhere. The world-wide crisis in 1929 apparently was most acute in the United States and Germany.[3] The economies of these two countries bore marked similarities. Both were advanced industrial nations. Both had employed high tariffs to protect favored industries, both had developed agencies to "rationalize" and "stabilize" industry—the cartel in Germany and the trade association in the United States, and both had

[1] *Final Report and Recommendations of the Temporary National Economic Committee*, p. 62.
[2] *Ibid.*, p. 527.
[3] *Hearings before the Temporary National Economic Committee*, Part 25, p. 13362.

developed inflexible price structures. These facts suggest some of the forces which generate the capitalistic crisis.

CHARACTERISTICS OF THE GREAT DEPRESSION

When the economy is analyzed according to its three component parts—the service division, the commodity handling division, and the commodity producing division—it is discovered that the depres-

TABLE 19. NATIONAL INCOME PRODUCED, 1919–1937, BY
ECONOMIC DIVISIONS FOR SELECTED YEARS
(In millions)

Year	Producing, Handling, and Service Divisions	Producing Division	Handling Division	Service Division
1920	$68,108	$31,423	$17,639	$19,046
1922	58,633	22,742	15,820	20,071
1924	67,893	27,306	17,696	22,891
1926	74,879	29,907	19,331	25,641
1928	77,602	30,031	19,660	27,911
1930	68,301	23,973	17,416	26,912
1932	40,015	9,517	10,564	19,932
1934	50,052	15,975	12,371	21,706
1936	63,465	22,577	14,647	26,241

Source: *Hearings before the Temporary National Economic Committee*, Part 1, p. 243.

sion was primarily a depression of the commodity producing division.[4] Employment and production were relatively stable in the service division and even in the commodity handling division. When the commodity producing segment of the economy is subdivided into its

TABLE 20. NATIONAL INCOME PRODUCED, 1919–1937,
COMMODITY PRODUCING DIVISION, FOR SELECTED YEARS
(In millions)

Year	Manufacturing	Agriculture	Construction	Mining
1920	$17,627	$9,026	$2,262	$2,508
1922	13,315	5,854	2,116	1,457
1924	15,266	7,357	2,993	1,690
1926	17,174	7,326	3,227	2,160
1928	17,771	7,314	3,313	1,633
1930	14,205	5,681	2,850	1,237
1932	5,621	2,442	978	478
1934	9,950	4,388	726	911
1936	14,261	5,883	1,221	1,212

Source: *Hearings before the Temporary National Economic Committee*, Part 1, p. 244.

[4] *Ibid.*, Part 1, pp. 145–147.

components—mining, construction, agriculture, and manufacturing —manufacturing proves to have been the most important; it is here the greatest fluctuations occurred. Thus, not only do depressions appear to be more acute in the great industrial economies but also their incidence is most severe in the industrial phases of those economies.

Another important characteristic of the Great Depression is that it was a durable goods depression.[5] The consumer's goods sector of the economy proved to be more stable than did that of producer's goods, which are increasingly important to an industrial economy. Durable goods are generally producer's goods and include automobiles, refrigerators, locomotives, machinery, and buildings; they include all the metals and materials which go into machinery, all transportation equipment, and iron and steel products such as hardware. Nondurable products, on the other hand, include articles such as food, meat products, leather, boots and shoes, paper, rubber products, textiles, and tobacco. Although producer's goods and durable goods are not synonymous, they are closely related, and both are highly characteristic of an industrial economy. It is here that the in-

TABLE 21. OUTPUT OF COMMODITIES, FOR SELECTED YEARS

Year	Percentage Durable Commodities	Percentage Nondurable Commodities
1879	31	69
1889	35	65
1899	36	64
1904	36	64
1909	37	63
1914	37	63
1919	38	62
1925	41	59
1929	44	56
1933	27	73

Source: *Hearings before the Temporary National Economic Committee*, Part 1, p. 201.

cidence of depressions is most acute. Durable goods have become increasingly more important. In 1879 they constituted 31 percent of industrial output, but by 1929 they were almost half, or 44 percent. An indication of their critical role during a depression is the fact that durable goods declined to 27 percent of the total industrial output in 1933. This role is further emphasized by the record of employment

5 *Ibid.*, pp. 27, 50.

statistics. Between 1923 and 1932 employment in the durable goods industries declined 53 percent as compared with only 28 percent for nondurable goods industries; similarly, pay rolls fell to about one-quarter of what they had been as compared to a decline of only one-half for nondurable goods industries.[6]

Another aspect of this problem is the wide fluctuation in production from year to year and the frequent disparity between practical productive capacity and actual output. This fluctuation is most marked in the durable goods industries and least marked in the con-

TABLE 22. PIG IRON PRODUCTION AND CAPACITY OF BLAST FURNACES, FOR SELECTED YEARS
(Millions of gross tons)

Year	Production	Practical Capacity
1910	27	33
1916	39	38
1921	17	44
1926	39	46
1929	43	46
1932	9	45
1935	21	44
1937	39	45

Source: *Hearings before the Temporary National Economic Committee,* Part 1, p. 207.

sumer goods industries. This is aptly illustrated by the production statistics for cement, pig iron, automobiles, and lumber. In the case of pig iron, annual production has fluctuated widely, varying from more than 100 percent of practical capacity in 1916 to less than 30

TABLE 23. ANNUAL PRODUCTION OF SHOES, 1919–1937
(Millions of pairs)

Year	Shoes	Year	Shoes
1919	331.2	1929	361.4
1920	315.0	1930	304.2
1921	286.8	1931	316.2
1922	323.9	1932	313.3
1923	351.1	1933	350.4
1924	313.2	1934	357.1
1925	323.6	1935	383.8
1926	324.5	1936	415.2
1927	343.6	1937	412.0
1928	344.4		

Source: *Hearings before the Temporary National Economic Committee,* Part 1, p. 208.

[6] *Ibid.,* p. 49.

percent in 1932. The production of nondurable goods, on the other hand, has been fairly stable, as in the case of shoes, cotton textiles, and cigarettes. The production of shoes, for example, held up remarkably well during the depression and remained stable throughout the most severe phases of the cycle.

It would appear, therefore, that if depressions are to be avoided and if an expanding economy is to be attained, attention must be given to the forces which maintain employment and production in the durable goods industries.

UNEMPLOYMENT FACTS [7]

The economy is capable of maintaining an expanding production if full use of both labor and technology is made. But owing to the manner in which the system is organized, we achieve neither the degree of expansion that is possible nor the full utilization of labor and technology. Unemployment, so critical after 1929, did not begin at that time; it was apparent as early as 1919. Prior to that, the industrial segment of the economy, including manufacturing, mining,

TABLE 24. EMPLOYMENT AND AVERAGE WEEKLY HOURS IN MANUFACTURING, MINING, AND STEAM RAILROADS

Year	Average Number of Wage Earners	Average Weekly Hours	Total Man-hours
1914	100	100	100
1919	126	93	118
1923	124	91	112
1924	115	87	100
1925	118	88	104
1926	120	90	108
1927	117	89	105
1928	115	89	103
1929	121	89	108
1930	106	85	90
1931	90	81	73
1932	76	76	58
1933	82	73	60
1934	94	69	64
1935	98	71	70
1936	105	75	80
1937	113	74	84

Source: *Hearings before the Temporary National Economic Committee*, Part 1, p. 222.

[7] *Ibid.*, pp. 43–65.

and railroads, found increasing use for workers; the number employed in those industries increased 26 percent between 1914 and 1919. In the boom which followed, however, the average number of wage earners employed declined almost continuously, and even the increase during 1928–1929 failed to bring it back to the 1919 level. Following 1929, of course, employment declined at an accelerated rate. The phenomenon of unemployment, therefore, was not new in 1930, but was an exaggeration of a trend long under way.

A striking illustration of this trend is found in the employment data for the expansion years of the twenties. Despite the fact that production increased markedly (25 percent) during this period, the total number of workers employed in manufacturing increased scarcely at all. In fact, industry was experiencing the equivalent of employing a gradually decreasing number of workers to produce a constant output. When the depression came, pay rolls declined more rapidly than the number of persons employed; later, when the depression was followed by recovery, production returned to its former high level, but did not bring pay rolls along with it.

The conclusion seems to be that a solution to the problems of the business cycle will not be found until a way has been discovered to give workers not only employment but also incomes sufficient to permit them to participate more abundantly in the productivity made possible by modern technology.

WASTED ECONOMIC RESOURCES [8]

The costs of the Great Depression were enormous. The human costs and the social costs (the costs in anguish and despair) can never be measured, but in terms of economic costs (sheer production costs) the total is tremendous. The economy broke down; the system failed to make the necessary functional adjustments to great structural changes. A period of stagnation and defeatism ensued. The economy with all the resources, skills, tools, man power, machines, factories, transportation facilities, technology, and experience necessary to sustain a high standard of living resigned itself to its functional imperfections and waited in stolid submission for the operation of the blind economic forces which were presumed in some teleological fashion to correct all ills. All the essential elements were at hand to sustain a prosperous economy, but the gears failed to mesh. The years from 1930 through 1938 were years of tragic waste of men and resources.

[8] See testimony by Isador Lubin, *ibid.,* pp. 12–74.

Employment lost.—During this nine-year interval 43,000,000 man-years were lost. This represents men willing and able to work, men

TABLE 25. EMPLOYMENT LOST DURING THE DEPRESSION
IN NONAGRICULTURAL OCCUPATIONS
(Man-years)

Year	Employment	Loss from 1929
1929	36,141,000	. . .
1930	33,925,000	2,216,000
1931	30,870,000	5,271,000
1932	27,661,000	8,480,000
1933	27,726,000	8,415,000
1934	30,259,000	5,882,000
1935	31,482,000	4,659,000
1936	33,201,000	2,940,000
1937	34,557,000	1,584,000
1938	32,153,000	3,988,000

Source: *Hearings before the Temporary National Economic Committee,* Part 1, p. 196.

who had been employed in 1929, but were set aside, idle, during the years of the depression. Forty-three million man-years constitutes a wastage of man power nearly 35 percent greater than the total man power utilized during our most prosperous year—1929.

Salaries and wages lost.—Idle men earn no pay and produce no goods. On the basis of 1929 wages and salaries, which totaled $50,000,-000,000, unemployment during the period 1930–1938 cost American wage earners $120,000,000,000. Wages lost were the equivalent of

TABLE 26. SALARIES AND WAGES LOST DURING THE DEPRESSION
IN NONAGRICULTURAL OCCUPATIONS

Year	Salaries and Wages Paid	Loss from 1939
1929	$49,260,000,000	. . .
1930	45,453,000,000	$ 3,807,000,000
1931	38,299,000,000	10,961,000,000
1932	29,941,000,000	19,319,000,000
1933	27,479,000,000	21,781,000,000
1934	31,138,000,000	18,122,000,000
1935	33,672,000,000	15,588,000,000
1936	37,418,000,000	11,842,000,000
1937	42,086,000,000	7,174,000,000
1938	38,500,000,000	10,760,000,000
Total loss, 1930–1938	. . .	119,354,000,000

Source: *Hearings before the Temporary National Economic Committee,* Part 1, p. 196.

240 percent of the total wages paid during the boom year of 1929. While workers lost these vast sums, society was denied the products of their labor.

Dividends lost.—Not only was it a workers' depression but a business man's depression as well. Profits in 1929 totaled $6,000,000,000. On the basis of that year the depression cost the owners of American industry $20,000,000,000 in profits which failed to materialize throughout the period 1930–1938.

TABLE 27. DIVIDENDS LOST DURING THE DEPRESSION

Year	Dividend Payments to Individuals	Loss from 1929
1929	$6,000,000,000	. . .
1930	5,800,000,000	$ 200,000,000
1931	4,300,000,000	1,700,000,000
1932	2,700,000,000	3,300,000,000
1933	2,200,000,000	3,800,000,000
1934	2,800,000,000	3,200,000,000
1935	3,000,000,000	3,000,000,000
1936	4,300,000,000	1,700,000,000
1937	5,000,000,000	1,000,000,000
1938	3,800,000,000	2,200,000,000
Total loss, 1930–1938	. . .	20,100,000,000

Source: *Hearings before the Temporary National Economic Committee,* Part 1, p. 196.

Farm income lost.—During the depression farmers lost more than 300 percent as much as their total income in 1929, when they received $12,000,000,000 for their produce. In 1932, the worst year of the depression, they received less than half that amount. Total losses for

TABLE 28. GROSS FARM INCOME LOST DURING THE DEPRESSION

Year	Gross Farm Income	Loss from 1929
1929	$12,000,000,000	. . .
1930	9,800,000,000	$ 2,200,000,000
1931	7,000,000,000	5,000,000,000
1932	5,300,000,000	6,700,000,000
1933	6,000,000,000	6,000,000,000
1934	6,800,000,000	5,200,000,000
1935	7,800,000,000	4,200,000,000
1936	9,000,000,000	3,000,000,000
1937	9,600,000,000	2,300,000,000
1938	8,400,000,000	3,800,000,000
Total loss, 1930–1938	. . .	38,400,000,000

Source: *Hearings before the Temporary National Economic Committee,* Part 1, p. 197.

the nine years were $38,000,000,000. The depression was no gaming table where some won and others lost and gains and losses canceled each other. The economic structure was out of gear, and the ledger showed only losses—wastage of men, resources, and machines.

National income lost.—In the banner year of 1929 the national income was $81,000,000,000. The economy had demonstrated its capacity to sustain an annual production of that amount. But in the nine years which followed, the average national income fell $15,000-

TABLE. 29. NATIONAL INCOME LOST DURING THE DEPRESSION
AT 1929 PRICES

Year	National Income	Loss from 1929
1929	$81,100,000,000	. . .
1930	70,000,000,000	$ 10,900,000,000
1931	60,500,000,000	20,600,000,000
1932	49,800,000,000	31,300,000,000
1933	55,200,000,000	25,900,000,000
1934	62,700,000,000	18,400,000,000
1935	67,500,000,000	13,600,000,000
1936	76,700,000,000	4,400,000,000
1937	81,000,000,000	100,000,000
1938	83,700,000,000	7,400,000,000
Total loss, 1930–1938	. . .	132,600,000,000

Source: *Hearings before the Temporary National Economic Committee,* Part 1, p. 197.

000,000 short of that amount. Thus, during the depression the American people lost nearly twice the income available to them in their most prosperous year.

Cost of the depression to the Government.—While men and machines wasted, while the economic system operated at less than full employment, problems of human personnel became critical. Society

TABLE 30. ESTIMATED TOTAL FUNDS USED FOR RELIEF AND
WORK PROGRAMS BY MAJOR PROGRAMS

(In millions)

Year	Total	Public Works	Works Programs	Direct Assistance
1933	$1,563	$ 464	$ 301	$ 609
1934	3,815	1,196	1,064	1,555
1935	3,954	1,054	944	1,956
1936	5,460	1,914	2,678	868
1937	4,771	1,647	2,133	991
1938	5,638	1,666	2,761	1,211

Source: *Hearings before the Temporary National Economic Committee,* Part 1, p. 225.

was not sufficiently callous to ignore the plight of millions thus plunged into distress; relief programs were organized. The Federal Government mortgaged its taxing powers in order to alleviate hunger and want. Relief—direct assistance, work programs, and public works— was organized on a scale never before attempted in human history; nearly 25,000,000 people were affected. These benefits to forestall human suffering (and probably civil disorder and revolution, as well) were costly. Thus, between 1929 and 1939 the failure of the economic system to function cost the Government nearly $30,000,000,000.

THE RELATION OF PURCHASING POWER TO FULL EMPLOYMENT

Witnesses who testified on this subject probably came closer to unanimity on the proposition that depressions have their root in a faulty system of distribution than was achieved on any other subject. Maldistribution, or widely uneven distribution of income, itself does not create a breakdown of the economic system, but it does set the stage and generate conditions which contribute to such dislocations. Among the more prominent experts who lent their support either directly or indirectly to this viewpoint were Isador Lubin, Commissioner of Labor Statistics; Willis J. Ballinger, economic adviser to the Federal Trade Commission; Leon Henderson, SEC commissioner; Mordecai Ezekiel, economic adviser to the Secretary of Agriculture; A. Ford Hinrichs, chief economist, Bureau of Labor Statistics; and Theodore J. Kreps, economic adviser to the TNEC.

One conclusion was clearly evident, not only to TNEC members but to laymen as well: the breakdown of American capitalism was due to no inherent weakness or incapacity of the productive mechanism. The weak link in the chain is purchasing power and the use made of savings. Productive instruments have suffered from no lack of ability to give consumers what they can pay for. On the contrary, the system bogged down for the very opposite reason; producers failed to find markets for goods which people sorely want and need. Purchasing power was produced, of course, but for various reasons it did not get to the market.

MALDISTRIBUTION OF INCOME

During the last two decades a number of studies have been made, all showing that there are wide inequalities in the distribution of income. A majority of the population receive low incomes, a small

minority enjoy large incomes, and an almost imperceptible few are the recipients of fabulous sums. The most important study of income distribution in recent years is that by the National Resources Committee made in 1939,[9] referred to on several occasions during the TNEC hearings.[10] According to its findings 8,000,000 families constantly were facing starvation; each received less than $750 a year, an average of $40 a month. This group included more than one-fourth of the families of the United States. American industry cannot find a satisfactory outlet for the products of mass production among families with such low incomes. After paying for the crudest type of shelter and food, they had substantially nothing left for radios or bathtubs, automobiles or telephones, washing machines or electric refrigerators.

Then there was a group of 11,000,000 families which received incomes between $750 and $1,500. These families were described as fighting poverty. After paying for modest shelter, for food, education, and the other minimum essentials of life, there remained little to create a demand for the products of modern large-scale, mass production industrialism. These two groups constituted nearly two-thirds of the nation's families.

Another group designated as the comfortable middle class included 8,000,000 families who received incomes between $1,500 and $3,000 per year. They constituted about one-fourth of all the families. Though their incomes were sufficient to purchase, at least modestly, the things which industry has to offer, they could not buy the automobiles, the plumbing fixtures, the television sets, and the automatic toasters which industry must sell in order to prosper on a mass production basis. The 8 percent who received more than $3,000 per year and the 2 percent who received more than $5,000 represent the few who were able to purchase but who could not have consumed the abundance which modern technology makes possible, just as those at the other end of the income scale represent the many who could have consumed, but were unable to purchase.

Thus, there were wide inequalities of income distribution. The poorest 4 percent of the families received only one-third of 1 percent of the total income, the poorest 14 percent received less than 3 percent of the income, and the poorest 27 percent less than 8. Half the population received only about one-fourth the income, yet it required more than 80 percent of the families to account for half of the income.

[9] National Resources Committee, *Consumer Incomes in the United States: Their Distribution, 1935-6.*
[10] See Part 11, pp. 5439-5440; see also Part 1, pp. 74-80.

At the other extreme, 1 percent of the population received 14 percent of the income, 5 percent received nearly one-fourth of the total, while 10 percent received nearly 40 percent.

THE STRATEGIC POSITION OF PURCHASING POWER

To Dr. Lubin a more equitable distribution of income is more than an ethical problem; it is a cornerstone upon which a prosperous economy may be erected.[11] The fundamental inability of a majority of the population to purchase goods was responsible for the disequilibrium between what modern technology was able to produce and what the owners of technology were able to sell in the market place. To this point Dr. Ballinger said that mass production "marks the highest level under man's productive programs" and that "we cannot have the economies of mass production save in an economy of mass consumption. Each is the condition of the other." [12]

The solution to the economic plight of the nation appears to be the expansion of domestic production. Vast wants still go unsatisfied for lack of purchasing power, and hence vast potential markets await producers should the lower income families find themselves in possession of a small supplement to their earnings. An increase of $2.00 per day to the incomes of the lower half of the population would increase the purchase of clothing by each family from $82 to $162 per year. Likewise, this income group would spend an additional $11,000,000 per year for oranges—and this in a land which destroys oranges for the want of a market. If these great unsatisfied wants were met, there would be no reports of excess capacity, but there would arise a definite need for expanded production.

These conclusions are similar to those drawn by others who have analyzed the problem. The Brookings Institution, after an exhaustive study,[13] concluded that if we were to supply incomes to people large enough so that all could enjoy a standard of living equivalent to that attained by those who enjoy a "liberal diet" and the other necessities and comforts ordinarily associated with it, it would be necessary to expand national production by nearly 80 percent above the peak of 1928–1929.

Thus, students of the problem have begun to say that there is a

[11] *Hearings before the Temporary National Economic Committee,* Part 1, p. 79.
[12] *Final Report and Recommendations of the Temporary National Economic Committee,* p. 619.
[13] Moulton, *America's Capacity to Consume.*

new frontier which may be developed in America and that the development of this frontier is one of the essentials of a prosperous economy. In the past, men have looked to foreign trade to supply a market for an expanding industrialism and to the undeveloped resources of the Western frontier as a fountainhead of prosperity; today we may find a similar frontier in the undeveloped markets of those whose unsatisfied wants may be transformed into effective demand through a more equitable distribution of purchasing power. To this point Dr. Kreps quoted a well-known magazine of business which reads strangely like the words of Adam Smith, that "consumption is the sole end and purpose of all production."

The tools and extensions of industrialization do not exist for their own sake. *They exist for . . . the consumer.* The entire producers' goods industry, for instance, whose purpose is the making of tools, is quite secondary to the real purpose of industrialization. That real purpose may be defined as an increase in the power to consume. . . .

The central economic problem is not a revival in the producers' industry, although that would help. Nor can it be a revival in "investment" in the old sense of the word. *The central economic problem is simply the conversion of a high potential power to consume into an actual power to consume:* a wider distribution of progress.

The great differential that links potential and actual consuming power is price; and what the new era cries for is a drastic decline in many lines of industrial prices.

Emphasis has been put on the need for confidence in making new investment; but . . . this emphasis is both unrealistic and academic. The realistic requirement is, rather, that the businessman should have confidence in the consumer; he must have confidence that if he decreases his prices and his profit margins he will get a corresponding rise in volume.

In the consumer lies the frontier. . . . By industrialization we built a new civilization. And during the last fifteen or twenty years, by further industrialization, we have created the possibility of an entirely new era for mankind. It is time now to get to work to make that era a reality.[14]

Moderately increased incomes for America's 19,000,000 families would create tremendous demands for the products of idle industrial factories. Mass production, however, will wait upon mass consumption, and mass consumption, upon mass purchasing power. Unless millions of people are placed in a position where they can purchase the fruits of modern technology, technology itself is liable to remain

[14] Quoted from "U.S. Industrialization," *Fortune,* February, 1940, p. 50, by the *Hearings before the Temporary National Economic Committee,* Part 30, pp. 16264–16265; italics supplied.

an unruly and unruled monster. That this problem is of more than academic interest and of more than broad social policy was evidenced by the testimony of the president of the Ford Motor Company.

> DR. ANDERSON. In other words, if you could see a market for 1,000,000 to 2,000,000 cars a year, say at $500, you could produce the car?
> MR. FORD. We could produce the car all right; yes.
> THE CHAIRMAN. Now just to repeat what I understand you to have said, an increased market for technological advance depends upon an increase of purchasing power; is that correct?
> MR. FORD. Mass purchasing power.
> THE CHAIRMAN. Mass purchasing power?
> MR. FORD. I believe so.
> THE CHAIRMAN. That is the essential need for further technological improvement?
> MR. FORD. I believe so.[15]

THE RELATION OF PRICES TO PURCHASING POWER

Not all income finds its way back into the economic stream. This fact takes us afield into the processes of savings, investment, and hoarding which will be discussed later. But the key to the economic problem is the wide inequality of income distribution. Many factors combine to create this maldistribution, as it is quite properly called. A major cause is the fact that production has ceased to be production principally by human labor but has become production by factory, tool, and machine. These instruments of technology are owned, and the right of ownership is recognized to carry with it a right to the productivity of the capital instrument. Instruments of capital, instruments of technology, are highly productive, but the increased productivity does not ordinarily go to the worker, and the ownership of capital goods is concentrated. Likewise, the ownership of land is concentrated. Hence, wide inequalities of income distribution occur. Technology is synonymous with invention, and under the operation of the patent system and large-scale industry the rewards of invention often fail to be widely distributed.

In a sense, what has been said is that machines, land, and inventions have been monopolized or partially monopolized, with resulting maldistribution of income. This leads to the point of emphasis of this section—the role of monopoly and monopoly prices in the uneven distribution of purchasing power. Something has happened to prices since World War I, making it increasingly difficult to bring the benefits of technology and mass production to the masses. This was

[15] *Hearings before the Temporary National Economic Committee*, Part 30, p. 16330.

so aptly developed by the Brookings Institution that it would be redundant to elaborate it here.[16] Rigid, inflexible prices have obstructed the flow of benefits from technological change to the consumer, resulting in increased maldistribution and "overproduction." Through monopoly prices the gains from technology have been retained by a few; when these gains have become overconcentrated, they have brought disillusionment even to their owners, though perhaps not so devastatingly as to those at the lower end of the income scale.

A partial solution to this problem, posed by the Brookings Institution, found favor before the TNEC.[17] The price reduction method of increasing purchasing power among the masses was recommended as one of the best ways of passing along the benefits of technology. It was described as a means of achieving the desired end with a minimum of group and sectional friction and of giving every consumer a larger return for his money. It was held to be one of the most effective ways of promoting the fullest use of and the expansion of the national economy. But in various ways monopoly prices stand as impediments to this painless program of distributing purchasing power; this impediment was described by the Brookings Institution as follows:

The basic economic policy which we are enunciating does, however, definitely attack what we regard as a serious abuse of the profit system and the institutions of private capital which have grown up in modern times. This is the tendency to centralize economic advantage, to protect existing business enterprises by protecting the price structure. For more than 50 years this tendency has been developing through the devices of corporate consolidations, pools, trusts, cartels, trade associations and code authorities. Particularly since the World War, and often with the active assistance of government, efforts have been going forward to stabilize existing business situations, and to underwrite the prosperity of individuals, corporations, or large business groups by attempting to stabilize prices. We believe the evidence is clear that such attempts, however well intentioned, are dangerously short-sighted.[18]

Likewise, the Federal Trade Commission, with its long association with business, similarly had denounced monopolistic price techniques which block the road to wide distribution of income and to extensive participation in the gains of modern technology. In 1921 the Commission set forth the following as causes of the business decline of that year.

[16] Moulton, *Income and Economic Progress.*
[17] *Final Report and Recommendations of the Temporary National Economic Committee,* pp. 620–623.
[18] *Ibid.,* p. 621.

1. The excessive price of many basic commodities, prominent among which is coal, which vitally affects the cost of other commodities.

2. The existence of the typical corporate monopolies and agreements in violation of the antitrust laws.

3. Open price associations in many cases not yet challenged by the law, yet tending to bring about and maintain unduly high prices.

4. Interference with the channels of trade by distributors, trade associations, particularly by activities tending to maintain an unnecessary number of inefficient regular dealers while shutting out new dealers seeking to sell at lower prices.[19]

Thirteen years later, in 1934, the Federal Trade Commission called attention once more to the role and responsibility of monopoly prices during an even more disastrous depression. On this occasion it cited the following joint declaration by 127 of the nation's leading economists.

The most competent economic opinion, as well in Europe as in this country, can be cited in support of the view that a strong contributing cause of the unparalleled severity of the present depression was the greatly increased extent of monopolistic control of commodity prices which stimulated financial speculation in the security markets. There is growing doubt whether the capitalistic system, whose basic assumption is free markets and a free price system, can continue to work with an everwidening range of prices fixed and manipulated by monopolies.[20]

MALDISTRIBUTION NO EXPLANATION FOR DEPRESSIONS

Convincing as is the theory that lack of purchasing power in the hands of the masses is the cause of depressions, it is not a satisfactory explanation. Merely because the majority of the people find themselves inadequately rewarded, it does not suffice to show that a portion of the total income fails to find its way back into the economic stream. It is possible, at least theoretically, for income to be very unevenly distributed, yet for all of it to find its way back to the market place, with the result that all resources and all factors are employed. That, in fact, was the manner in which Say, in his law of the markets (*loi des débouchés*), and the classical economists dismissed the need of considering the capitalistic crisis.

But unfortunately for Say and for humankind, recurring economic crises do occur, and men such as Lauderdale, Marx, and Hobson,[21]

[19] *Ibid.*, p. 622.
[20] Quoted from the Federal Trade Commission, *Report to the President, November, 1934*, p. 39, in the *Final Report and Recommendations of the Temporary National Economic Committee*, p. 623.
[21] To this list must be added Owen, Chalmers, Sismondi, Malthus, Rodbertus, Foster and Catchings, Veblen, Douglas, Strachey, Ezekiel, and others.

who have spoken of the relation of overproduction (underconsumption, oversavings, and maldistribution) to depression, have all pointed, though inexpertly at times, in the right direction or have fumbled like amateurs with the right tools.

DISTRIBUTION AND FULL EMPLOYMENT

The processes which result in maldistribution of purchasing power, as it is called, give rise at the same time to other changes which divert income from the economic stream; the diverted income thus becomes sterile and thereby useless to the economy and constitutes a focal point at which the system breaks down.

Capitalism is distinguished from the types of economic organization which preceded it by the volume of savings and the volume of investment which take place under its regime. The TNEC conducted no exhaustive analysis of the pattern of savings; [22] a brief presentation, however, did emphasize the great amount of annual savings which takes place, as well as the extent to which these savings are concentrated. Concentration of income, it was found, almost inevitably results in concentration of savings. The wealthier 10 percent of America's families save 86 percent of the savings, and the poorest 80 percent account for only 2 percent of the savings. Institutional savings have become more and more characteristic of the economy; people save automatically through routine contributions to programs such as life insurance, social security, and annuities. Vast sums are thus produced which seek profitable employment. In fact, the dynamics of capitalism requires continuous investment of these great reserves. Such investment is essential to an expanding economy and to increased standards of living.

Income received may be diverted into either of two streams—consumption or savings. If spent for consumer's goods, it automatically finds its way back into the economic stream and stimulates commercial and industrial activity. A high consumption economy would tend to avoid depressions and to operate at full employment. If income is diverted into savings, these savings may take either of two forms—investment or hoarding. If savings are invested (by the creation of new capital goods—plant expansion, etc.), once again the effect is to stimulate business. Income is hoarded, however, when it is neither spent for consumption nor invested.

[22] For a more thorough treatment attention is called to Temporary National Economic Committee Monograph No. 37.

As inequalities of income distribution increase and as incomes become concentrated in the upper brackets, the proportion of income saved likewise increases. Recipients of large incomes find it increasingly difficult to place investment, and hence, unwillingly, they are forced to hoard. The opportunities for investment themselves are, in part, a reflection of the ability of the underlying population to exercise its purchasing power to buy the products of the new capital outlays. When income is hoarded, it is lost to the economic stream, with the result that employment is restricted and the industrial spiral turns downward. Underemployment of men, resources, and machines follows in the wake of the hoarding process.

The testimony already placed before you has shown conclusively that the chronic low industrial production in our economy has not been due to any lack of ability to make goods. Every time that demand has increased, industrial production has increased promptly and swiftly. . . . We know all about how to make the goods, and how to organize production. But we don't yet know how, in times of peace, to keep the buyers supplied with enough purchasing power to provide markets for all the goods and services we can make.

Other testimony before you has shown that the weak link in the purchasing power chain lies in the use made of savings. At each individual transaction, the amount paid by the purchaser for goods exactly equals the amount received by the seller. For all transactions added together, the sums spent must equal the sums received. But as our economy is now organized, a considerable proportion of the funds received by sellers are not respent, but are set aside as savings. Our distribution of income and savings habits are such that as national income rises, the amount set aside as savings increases much faster than the national income itself increases. Savings make markets for goods only when somebody actually takes the savings and invests them, by spending them for machinery or plant or other new capital goods. As our economy now functions, however, the effect of a rising national income on the willingness to invest is much less marked than the effect on the willingness to save.[23]

THE ROLE OF SAVINGS AND INVESTMENT

The most important witness before the Committee in this phase of its work was Professor Alvin H. Hansen, of Harvard University.[24] Dr. Hansen's views were well known to economists, and the TNEC thus became a sounding board for his analysis and proposals. The two streams, savings and investment, are the foci of the economic dis-

[23] From a statement by Mordecai Ezekiel in the *Final Report and Recommendations of the Temporary National Economic Committee*, pp. 418–419.
[24] *Hearings before the Temporary National Economic Committee*, Part 9, pp. 3495–3520, 3538–3559, 3837–3859.

organization and dislocations of the day. The keystone of the capitalistic structure is the investment process. The health of the system depends directly upon the continuous placing of large capital expenditures. In order to keep the economic stream flowing on a high level, the portion of the national income which is saved must be returned to the economy through the channel of investment. This involves the making of capital outlays—the purchase of plant, machinery, commercial or industrial construction, houses, office buildings, or public works. Savings need to be employed, and investments are the really dynamic portion of national income.

Under our system of capitalistic industrialism, with its mass production, high per capita income, unequal distribution, and concentrated incomes, we have developed a high savings economy. This has given rise to problems never before encountered and has created an urgent need to find opportunities for continuous capital investment. The failure to accomplish this in the late twenties—in other words, unplanned, unwilling, and unforeseen hoarding—was the basic cause of the great economic collapse.

The depression which had saddled itself upon the land in 1929 was a more or less unique phenomenon, unlike other depressions which had preceded it; it is not to be explained in terms of traditional business cycle analysis. A fundamental change in the pattern of economic life itself seems to have taken place. This was a structural change, marking for the nation the end of a long period of economic expansion. The old forces which brought to an end previous depressions have disappeared with the new structural framework. The formative period of capitalism has passed; an era of economic maturity seems to have arrived. The rapid expansion which brought about the industrialization of the West and the opening up of vast new territories is terminating. Rates of population growth are declining, and a stable population appears in the offing. The old order, with its dynamic pace and its intense demands for new capital outlays, has passed.

But the new order is more capable than ever of creating great reservoirs of savings, which must either find outlets in investments or serve as millstones to a suffering economy. A way must be found to repatriate this share of the income stream and to release its energy for the maintenance of a healthy and an expanding economy. Hoarded incomes create unemployment in the heavy industries; this reduces consumption expenditures, which in turn reduces capital outlays.

The nation is caught thereby in a wicked cycle of economic dislocations. The solution is more capital outlays; it is highly important that
a way be found to offset all savings. Recovery and full employment
depend upon a constant expansion of capital outlays. Failure to find
that solution can mean only economic stagnation and continuous unemployment of men, materials, machines, and resources.

PROCEDURES TO ACHIEVE FULL EMPLOYMENT

This, then, is the Hansen thesis; gloomy as it is, it is an attempt to
face facts and trends analytically and realistically. But Professor Hansen offered a number of more positive suggestions for consideration
by the TNEC. To him there is no simple solution to the modern economic crisis, but some very concrete things can be done. The system
may be reformed so that it does not make such heavy inroads upon
consumption. Whenever private investment fails to absorb the stream
of savings, public investment must fill the breach. It is possible to
choose various kinds of public investment, and among the more advantageous the following were suggested: (1) private capital outlays
—expansion of plant and equipment, commercial manufacturing,
mining, railroad, public utility, and residential construction; (2) public investment—self-liquidating, or other, public projects directly or
indirectly productive and contributing to a higher standard of living;
and (3) community consumption—by increasing the standard of living of the masses in the form of social services, public health, public
recreation, low-cost housing, and so forth, and thereby developing a
high consumption economy.

In his final recommendations to the Committee Dr. Mordecai Ezekiel proposed a fivefold program designed to maintain the economy
as an expanding industrial mechanism operating near full employment.[25] If such a goal is to be attained, it cannot be achieved by insisting upon the continuation, with superficial modifications, of the
same pattern of organization from which generated the Great Depression and earlier crises. Neither can it be achieved by maintaining
the fiction of a free economy while perpetuating the rigidities and
the impediments of monopolistic privileges. Basic forces are operative
which are sufficiently fundamental to create a periodic, if not a permanent, collapse of the economy. These forces should be harnessed,
and fundamental changes may be necessary if the economy is to func-

[25] *Final Report and Recommendations of the Temporary National Economic Committee,* pp. 417–439.

tion and if capitalistic societies are to avoid wholesale revolution, peaceful or otherwise. The fivefold program of reconstruction suggested by Dr. Ezekiel follows.

Government spending . . . is not the only possible method of maintaining buying power. Several different procedures can be used, either alone or in conjunction with one another. By moving far enough along these lines, either individually or in combination, we can so modify our capitalistic economy as to make it capable of maintaining full employment and full production even after the defense expenditures come to an end.

The several lines of action may be broadly grouped, as follows:

(1) Government spending to counterbalance the excess savings, including—
   (a) Spending based on borrowing;
   (b) Spending based on interest-free money; and
   (c) Spending based on taxation.
(2) Taxation to reduce the excess savings and increase investment by—
   (a) Reducing the willingness to save; and
   (b) Increasing the willingness to invest.
(3) Procedures to increase individual security and reduce the pressure to save, such as adequate social security against old age, unemployment, dependency, and all forms of disability.
(4) Modification of business practices to make income more evenly distributed, and to insure that profits do not increase out of proportion to pay rolls in periods of prosperity. These include—
   (a) Possible voluntary action of business and labor.
   (b) Antitrust pressures on monopolistic or semimonopolistic industries to enforce competition, and Government yardstick competition.
   (c) Concerted action for larger industrial output, lower prices, and higher wages, with the democratic participation of business and labor, under governmental oversight.
   (d) Action to give labor a bargaining power equal to that of employers, and to establish minimum-labor standards.
(5) Measures to increase the consuming power of low-income groups, by giving their dollars a greater buying power than the dollars of higher-income groups.[26]

HARMONY OF ETHICS AND ECONOMICS

There appears to be a close harmony between the measures which, if adopted, would promote economic justice among people and those which would increase the efficiency and productivity of the economic system. Ethical standards call for a greater equality of treatment, a narrowing of the gulf between the haves and the have-nots, and a

[26] *Ibid.*, pp. 420–421; for a more extensive discussion of these recommendations see the section on "Hoarded Income" in Chapter XI.

more equitable distribution of the fruits of production. Standards of economic efficiency, on the other hand, seem to call for measures which will increase purchasing power at the bottom of the social scale, eliminate hoarding at the top, and promote investment throughout the economy. It is not at all strange that these two objectives are found to be in harmony. In nature, health and beauty are closely related; in architecture, engineering, and athletics, symmetry and grace correlate with efficiency. Possibly there is an analogy. Apparently an economic system best adapted to serve the needs of the entire population will function most smoothly. It would appear that when the economy fails to distribute its benefits widely, we have collapse and depression; when it fails the ethical objective, it fails the economic objective.

CHAPTER X

DISCLOSURES BY THE TEMPORARY NATIONAL ECONOMIC COMMITTEE

"I KNOW you are looking for all the dirt you can find and you are trying to find it" was the troubled and self-censoring response to a question posed by a TNEC examiner.[1] This, however, was an acceptable characterization of neither the motive nor the approach of the TNEC. Again and again its members emphasized the fact that the Committee was not a "grand jury," that it was "not conducting a trial," and that the hearings did not constitute a search for wrongdoing.[2] Nevertheless, it was obviously impossible for the TNEC to perform the task it had been asked to undertake without uncovering certain shortcomings in the organization of the economy, violations of public trust, circumvention and evasion of the law, and willful abuse of power and privilege.

Some of its disclosures relate to life insurance selling practices as they affect the unwary and indigent purchasers of industrial policies, some to the predatory exploitation of the national patent system, to ingenious ways by which the Banking Act of 1935 and the Clayton Act had been evaded, to the abuse of their trust by corporate officials, to racketeering practices in the oil, poultry, and milk industries, and to corporate control of state legislatures, and others to the shortcomings of life insurance election machinery. In some instances these disclosures represent merely a confirmation of conditions which were already common knowledge; in others, the gravity of their social implications was startling, and in at least one instance they led to an investigation for criminal action. Only a few case studies of industry were undertaken, but the abuses uncovered by those inquiries were sufficient to suggest that there are similar practices in other segments of the economy.

[1] *Hearings before the Temporary National Economic Committee*, Part 12, p. 5687.
[2] *Ibid.*, Part 2, p. 378; Part 6, pp. 2420, 2445–2446; Part 8, p. 3287; Part 10, pp. 4544–4546; Part 15, p. 8206; Part 17, p. 9459; Part 18, p. 10381; Part 23, pp. 11859–11860; Part 25, p. 13110.

THE ABUSE OF INDUSTRIAL INSURANCE

One of the most pitiful, and at times most sordid, disclosures had to do with the sale of industrial life insurance. These policies are usually sold to people with low incomes who are quite unable to inform themselves concerning the quality of the commodity offered and often are in dire need of the benefits so glowingly described. The scruples of those who have managed the sales campaigns frequently have fallen to the level of the medieval robber barons who pillaged the product of other men's toil. Three classes of life insurance are commonly sold by legal reserve life insurance companies: ordinary, group, and industrial insurance. This discussion is limited to industrial insurance.[3] In terms of their face value, industrial policies usually are small and frequently are paid for on a weekly basis to a company agent who acts as collector. Premiums usually are computed on a weekly payment plan, and the policy is written in units on the basis of what five cents a week will purchase. As noted, these contracts ordinarily are sold to people with very low incomes, usually living in urban and industrial centers. These people constitute a group quite unable to take advantage of the lower net cost higher denomination policies represented by the various types of ordinary life insurance; to them industrial policies constitute a burial fund eked out of their earnings, often at considerable sacrifice.

Fortunately, the most flagrant abuses discovered by the TNEC were not characteristic of all companies engaged in the business. Nevertheless, there were companies, one suspects, which deliberately and designedly exploited irregularities to the limit of their profitableness, stalking their prey as did the patent medicine racketeers and the blue-sky buccaneers of the past.

INADEQUATE PROGRAMMING

Characteristic of industrial life insurance is the almost complete absence of programming. In recent years the more progressive old-line companies selling ordinary life insurance have attempted to tailor life insurance programs to suit the needs of the individual client. Some policies are better adapted to a given situation than others, and individuals in different circumstances are advised to carry different programs. Many industrial insurance concerns, however, are primarily hawkers and collectors of premiums and apparently have little regard for the client's needs or his ability to pay; the basic objective, almost

[3] *Ibid.*, Part 12, pp. 5597–5604.

to the exclusion of the client's welfare, has been to make the sale. One of the best-known companies in the business instructed its agents as follows: "We hear a lot about programming life insurance for clients. Ninety-five out of every one hundred of your prospects, of your clientele, don't need programming. They need just old-fashioned common life-insurance sales presentation." [4] With little guidance from the representative of the company and with little ability to make the proper selection of a policy, the buyer takes what the pressure of events brings to him. By comparison with those who can afford the lower net cost ordinary-life policies, he is ignorant; his selection, if it can be called that, often is ill adapted to the purposes which ought to be served.

Agents themselves are under pressure to sell. There is constant pressure from the home office, there is pressure because of the commission basis of sales promotion, as well as the necessity of "beating the other fellow to the sale." One aspect of this bad selling and bad programming is overselling the client. This point is aptly summarized in the following report by a New York legislative committee:

The pressure exercised on the agents in the sale of industrial policies has driven them to the point where they have been forced to depart from the ethics of their calling. . . . The pressure upon the agents has caused an enormous sale of industrial policies to those who are unable to maintain them.[5]

Agents revealed that they often employed the crudest devices to coerce reluctant prospects into line. This practice was described by one agent in the following picturesque manner:

Since the bulk of mine are Negroes, I will metaphorically draw a hearse up in front of his door and park it there until he signs. . . . I will have to paint pictures of the Grim Reaper and everything else to frighten the person into believing that unless the person is actually covered with insurance, death might take place almost momentarily.[6]

Overselling, therefore, becomes common. In one instance a woman who had a wage of $7.50 per week had been sold policies by one company alone which required $2.42 from her weekly income for insurance; moreover, she was found paying equally as much to other companies. Similarly, one man was paying $1.75 to one company out of a weekly wage of $10; in addition he received regular calls from two other companies for similar amounts.[7]

---

4 *Ibid.*, Part 12, p. 6128.   5 *Ibid.*, p. 5864.
6 *Ibid.*, p. 6068.   7 *Ibid.*, p. 6069.

Even the indigent were persuaded to buy. No particular care seems to have been exercised not to overburden clients with contracts which they could not maintain; on the contrary—as will subsequently be developed—such a policy may well have been encouraged by some companies. One agent testified that more than 75 percent of the people on his collection route were at that time on relief. Apparently they, too, were overloaded; the agent stated that on premium collection days it was a race between himself and collectors from other industrial companies to reach the client first.[8] Another agent verified this by relating that there were times when as many as 100 percent of his clients were in arrears. This utter lack of planning or regard for the insuree's welfare is an important factor contributing to the excessive lapse ratio in the industrial insurance business.

In addition to overburdening the policyholder, ofttimes the insurance is maldistributed with regard to the family. An insurance counsellor testified that he did a thriving business correcting and adjusting the errors arising from the lack of industrial insurance programming.[9] His experience indicated that more often than not the bulk of the protection on each family unit was not on the bread winner but on the dependents. It was common to find no insurance on the head of the family and all of it on the wife and the children. People who came to the counsellor for aid were paying nearly 15 percent of their income for industrial insurance and frequently were insuring the lives of great aunts and great uncles as well as boarders or complete strangers. About one case in five represented speculative insurance where the insurable interest was highly doubtful. The counsellor found 98 percent of the insurance written on the endowment plan. Apparently this situation prevailed, not for any reason connected with the purchaser's welfare, but principally because the salesman usually received a higher commission by writing this type of policy.

Industrial insurance has its "Kallikak family," whose record threw into bold relief this utter disregard for planning and programming. It was found that they were paying $927 per year to an army of weekly collectors; this represented more than 50 percent of the total income of the family. It had been sold a total of $18,000 of insurance; altogether it was paying premiums on forty-four policies, four ordinary and forty industrial. During every year but one between 1919 and 1936 this family purchased from one to eight industrial policies. The father was insured for more than $6,000 by fifteen policies costing

8 *Ibid.*, p. 6154.   9 *Ibid.*, pp. 5811–5813.

$295 per year and the mother, for nearly $4,000 by thirteen policies at a cost of $275 a year. The rest of the insurance was distributed between a son and the father's brother.[10] When this unusual situation was called to the attention of the three major insurance companies involved, they apparently had nothing to suggest for the welfare of the family.

VICIOUS ASPECTS OF THE AGENCY SYSTEM

The plight of many who purchase industrial policies ill-advisedly is traceable directly to the agency system, sponsored by the companies, in which the agents are wanting in scruples and social consciousness. Life insurance companies themselves assert that protection is a service which, like medicine or dentistry, should be rendered in accordance with the needs of the client and performed only by adequately qualified professionals. Without such assistance the layman is quite as unable to prescribe for his own insurance needs as he is to determine his requirements of insulin, sulphanilimide, or vitamines. Lacking professional advice, he often falls prey to charlatans and quacks. The latter, aware of the consumer's helplessness, frequently has exploited it to the fullest.

High-pressure sales techniques have characterized the industrial life insurance agency system. The citizens who usually purchase this type of policy are especially vulnerable: their incomes are low, their experience restricted, and their understanding limited. As amateurs, they find themselves pitted against professionals—not professional experts willing and able to diagnose and prescribe, but professionals in the art of selling and extraction. The art approaches a racket in some agency systems, and the welfare of the purchaser is often utterly ignored. The following instructions by one company to its sales force too often are characteristic of industrial insurance practices:

Try to close early in the interview. Remember when your mother was baking how she used to tèst the cake with a straw? If it came out sticky she put the cake back in the oven and applied more heat.

Do not hesitate to test your prospect early in the interview. If he begins to ask questions during your presentation try him out. . . .

When the response to such a feeler indicates your prospect is not yet ready, turn on some more heat.[11]

Above the purchaser stands the agent; over the agent hangs the agency system. The "heat" is applied constantly. Drive, drive, drive for new business is the unceasing pressure upon the sales force. This

10 *Ibid.,* pp. 5813–5816.   11 *Ibid.,* p. 5947.

is typified by a letter sent by the vice president of one company to a member of his sales staff. Along with other telling remarks he said, "You can depend upon my hounding the life out of you throughout the entire year unless your district is keeping pace." [12] Since little mercy is shown by the company to the agent and his representatives, there is little room for mercy and considered programming by the agent to the purchaser.

A common means of exerting pressure upon agents is the allotment of quotas; the company's mandate appears to be "Fill the quota or get out." [13] Men are told, "Each district is going to be given an allotment which will have to be met," and "All of the men shall be more thoroughly impressed than ever before that the quota is a positive expectation of management from them." In a moment of Freudian inadvertency a high official of one company spoke quite picturesquely of the system as a "sweat quota."

Other pressure stratagems are regularly employed to keep the sales force keyed up. The holding of frequent pep meetings for the sales staff is a common technique. [14] In conjunction with these a wide variety of contests are conducted currently to keep the salesmen on edge. [15] But management often has recourse to other pressures: to baubles such as contests and quotas have been added various other goads. Agents told of the open ridicule and the public discomfiture to which men are put who fail to reach the quotas established for them. [16] But pressures do not stop here; agents frequently are subject to intimidation and threats of dismissal unless they continue to set new records of achievement. These admonitions seldom are either subtle or idle. [17]

As a result of all this a great deal of new business is added. "Heat" is applied to the agent, and in the field the agent applies it to the "prospect" to obtain new signatures on policy applications. This "frenzy business," as it is sometimes called, often is bad business, especially for the insured; [18] applicants soon escape from the atmosphere of the sales situation or perhaps awake to realities of their earning capacity, and hence many policies lapse. Company representatives testified that they make little attempt to ascertain how much of the business thus obtained under duress remains with the company. [19] In fact, one suspects that in the light of the vested interest which some companies have in lapsed policies the whole program may have been

12 *Ibid.,* p. 6032.
14 *Ibid.,* pp. 6025, 6033, 6085.
16 *Ibid.,* p. 6100.
18 *Ibid.,* p. 6010.

13 *Ibid.,* pp. 6033, 6060, 6099, 6110, 6126, 6155.
15 *Ibid.,* pp. 6031, 6044, 6061, 6064, 6081, 6108, 6160.
17 *Ibid.,* pp. 6026–6027, 6034, 6035, 6085, 6099.
19 *Ibid.,* p. 6100.

inspired, in part, to ensnare such guileless purchasers. But the buyers of policies are not the only victims of the system. In order to meet quotas and to establish sales records agents often have felt compelled to pay from their own pockets for policies, which have come to be known as "tombstones" and "lamp posts." When removed from the spell and the sawdust trail of the company evangelist, these policy-holders, like the more legitimate ones, soon become "backsliders"— the policies lapse.

Agents engaged in the industrial insurance business are generally poorly paid and poorly trained for their work.[20] Moreover, there is a continual turnover among them. A turnover as high as 65 percent a year is not at all uncommon, and frequently it runs as high as 100 percent.[21] Poor agents lead to poor service, poor programming, and a high lapse ratio.

Many factors combine to cause policyholders to let their policies lapse. Not the least important of these are high-pressure methods of business solicitation. When one considers that many industrial com-panies are stock companies (not mutual companies) in which policy-holders do not participate in the profits, and when one realizes that lapsed policies are an important source of profit to such companies, it is apparent that they have a vested interest in conditions which lead to policy lapsing.[22]

Between 1928 and 1937, 187,000,000 industrial policies terminated. Not all of them lapsed; 4 percent terminated because of death, and the beneficiaries received the contracted protection; 20 percent were surrendered; 71 percent, however, lapsed because of nonpayment of premiums. This represented more than 135,000,000 policies.[23]

The lapse record for individual companies is astounding. Out of eighty-four companies in 1938 nearly 80 percent had lapse ratios in excess of 75 percent. In other words, 75 percent of the policies in force lapsed within the year. Insurance men refer to this as "squirrel-cage activity" wherein many policyholders experience loss and disillusion-ment year after year. Most of the lapses occur during the first year. Several representative companies testified that their lapse ratio for the first year ran nearly 50 percent.[24]

In 1938 the three leading industrial companies (all mutuals) had

20 *Ibid.*, pp. 6042, 6044, 6147–6149.
21 *Ibid.*, pp. 5852, 5855, 5943, 5944, 6001, 6044, 6056, 6063, 6087, 6091, 6096, 6112, 6124, 6147.   22 *Ibid.*, pp. 5608–5609.
23 *Ibid.*, Part 10, pp. 4304–4305, 4739; Part 12, pp. 5608–5609.
24 *Ibid.*, Part 12, pp. 5952, 6027, 6066, 6101.

lapse ratios of 49, 54, and 63, respectively, in relation to new policies written during the year, and 5, 6, and 10 percent in relation to total policies in force. These three companies found lapsing to be an impor-

TABLE 31. POLICIES LAPSED FOR NONPAYMENT OF PREMIUMS, 1938

(FOR SELECTED INDUSTRIAL COMPANIES)

	Name of Company	Percentage Ratio of Number Lapsed to New Issues	Percentage Ratio of Number Lapsed to Number in Force December 31, 1938
M a	Metropolitan	49	5
M	Prudential	54	6
M	John Hancock	63	10
S b	National Life & Accident	75	23
S	Western & Southern	58	8
S	Life Insurance Company of Virginia	68	13
S	Industrial Life & Health	94	150
S	Monumental Life	66	17
S	Peoples Life	85	54
S	Sun Life	65	11
S	Baltimore Life	76	18
S	Commonwealth Life	69	21
S	Interstate Life & Accident	89	68
S	Kentucky Central Life & Accident	97	105
S	Southern Life & Health	90	77
M	Home Friendly	90	42
S	Supreme Liberty Life	96	142
S	American Life & Accident of Kentucky	91	104
S	Home State Life	76	32
S	National Burial	89	135
S	Southern Aid Society	96	44
S	Lincoln Income Life	95	162
S	Mammoth Life & Accident	82	53
S	Globe Life	362	10
S	Alta Life	235	43
M	Cincinnati Mutual Life	102	267
S	Guaranty Income	11	13
S	American Union Life	22	13
S	Security Life	200	77
S	Continental Assurance	16	19

Source: *Hearings before the Temporary National Economic Committee*, Part 12, pp. 6172–6173.
a M indicates mutual companies.   b S indicates stock companies.

tant source of income, amounting to $46,000,000 during the ten-year interval between 1928 and 1937. One company, however, the Globe Life Insurance Company, had 362 lapsed policies in 1938 for every 100 it sold that year, and the Cincinnati Mutual, 267 for every 100 it had in force at the end of the year. Few communities would stand for slot machines where the odds were so uneven. The record of the Western and Southern Life Insurance Company was by no means the worst, yet in 1937, a representative year, 7 percent of all new policies lapsed after two weeks, 13 percent after five weeks, 20·percent after ten weeks, 30 percent after one-half year, and 39 percent by the end of the year.

TABLE 32. INDUSTRIAL PERSISTENCY
LAPSE RATIO FOR INDIVIDUAL WEEKS OF ISSUE IN THE
WESTERN AND SOUTHERN LIFE INSURANCE COMPANY
(*For selected years*)

	AFTER PREMIUMS HAVE BEEN PAID FOR THE FOLLOWING NUMBER OF WEEKS							
Year	2	4	6	8	10	12	26	52
1932	18	28	35	40	44	47	62	73
1934	11	17	21	25	27	30	39	46
1936	8	12	16	19	21	23	30	36
1937	7	11	15	17	20	22	30	39

Source: *Hearings before the Temporary National Economic Committee,* Part 12, p. 6305.

Disillusionment resulting from the intentional, though often reluctant, lapsing of policies is but one of the hazards to the industrial policyholder. By custom and practice the representative of the company calls regularly to collect the premium; ofttimes this is the policyholder's only contact with the company. Should the representative, either by negligence or design, fail to make the collections, the contract lapses. Some of the less scrupulous companies apparently make frequent use of this opportunity to abrogate the rights of their clients. One company sent instructions to its agents as follows: "We were certainly unfortunate in issuing a policy to this young man. . . . The quicker you can get rid of this case the better it will be. Make special note of it and watch for an opportunity." [25] Thus, at the very moment when the insured is most in need of protection and when the contractual obligation of the company to its client becomes most vital, he finds himself "pushed overboard."

[25] *Ibid.,* pp. 6012–6013. In this case the company sold both industrial life and casualty insurance.

A former agent of another company, with headquarters in the nation's capital, testified that his field manager had taken the initiative in lapsing the policy of an insuree suspected of having acquired a serious ailment. After several years, during which the insured had paid for protection, the agent was instructed not to collect. The following statement is revealing: "Yes; we went by the house one day when the woman was on the porch with the money and the book waiting for us and although she hollered to me I was told that I didn't hear anything, it was just the wind, and we kept on walking and the policy did lapse." [26] In still another case the company instructed the agent as follows: "The only thing I can do is to try and get her in a lapsed condition and cancel her policy." [27] One agent complained to his company with respect to such practices: "He has ordered me to lift several policies which I do not feel should have been. I am working for the company, but I believe in being fair both to the company and the insured." [28]

Possibly the most hypocritical and sanctimonious piece of literature presented to the TNEC embodied the same kind of instructions from a company official to the agent; it said,

We are afraid this poor woman is gradually but surely drifting toward closing out her life. Since we feel assured the impairments noted were on hand when the policies were issued, the Claim Department has suggested that I write you to be on the watch for an opportunity to let these policies appear on the pink lapse sheet. Deal justly, considering what is best for all concerned. We wait your attention to this.

Apparently "justice" was done, for scarcely two months later the agent replied, "the above-mentioned policies lapsed with a D.L.P. of 12–6–37." [29]

THE HEAVY COSTS OF INDUSTRIAL INSURANCE

Industrial insurance often is spoken of as "the poor man's protection." Individuals in better circumstances more frequently purchase, and are better able to pay for, ordinary life insurance. It is unfortunate that those who need it most receive the poorest protection and pay disproportionately more for such protection when they contract for industrial life insurance.

Table 33 shows the net costs of carrying both industrial and ordinary insurance for an individual at age 25. Although industrial insurance carried with the other companies listed costs more than with

[26] *Ibid.*, p. 6073.   [27] *Ibid.*, p. 6142.
[28] *Ibid.*, p. 6101.   [29] *Ibid.*, p. 6014.

TABLE 33. COMPARISON OF NET COSTS OF WHOLE LIFE POLICIES ISSUED BY SELECTED INDUSTRIAL AND ORDINARY LIFE INSURANCE COMPANIES

INDUSTRIAL LIFE INSURANCE
($250 POLICY ISSUED IN 1939 AT AGE 25)

Name of Company	Annual Premium	Twenty Annual Premiums	Twenty Years Dividends	Twenty Years Premiums Less Dividends	Twenty Year Cash Value	Twenty Year Net Cost
Home Beneficial	6.70	$134.00	None	$134.00	$45.62	$88.38
John Hancock	6.77	135.40	25.78	109.62	61.49	48.13
Metropolitan	6.77	135.40	21.75	113.65	61.49	52.16
Monumental Life	6.50	130.00	None	130.00	52.15	77.85
Sun Life	6.63	132.60	None	132.60	47.93	84.67

ORDINARY LIFE INSURANCE
($1,000 POLICY ISSUED IN 1939 AT AGE 25)

Name of Company	Annual Premium	Twenty Annual Premiums	Twenty Years Dividends	Twenty Years Premiums Less Dividends	Twenty Year Cash Value	Twenty Year Net Cost
Aetna	20.48	409.60	90.87	318.73	231.00	87.73
Equitable, Iowa	20.14	402.80	101.32	301.48	231.00	70.48
John Hancock	19.89	397.80	89.33	308.47	233.00	75.47
Metropolitan	19.04	380.80	96.66	284.14	244.86	39.28
New York Life	21.49	429.80	155.08	274.72	230.00	44.72
Northwestern	20.55	411.00	131.32	279.68	230.50	49.18
Union Central	20.33	406.60	80.76	325.84	230.00	95.84

Source: *Hearings before the Temporary National Economic Committee*, Part 10-A p. 284, and Part 12, p. 6306.

either the John Hancock or the Metropolitan companies, a comparison brings out the high cost of industrial insurance. To purchase $250 of industrial insurance involves a total net cost (twenty-year experience) of $48.13; to purchase $1,000 of such insurance, therefore, would cost $192.52. The same company, however, is selling ordinary life ($1,000) at a net cost of $75.47. This latter figure—$75.47—is interesting, since it approximates the average cost of purchasing only $250 of insurance with most industrial concerns. The Metropolitan charges $39.28 per $1,000 for ordinary whole life; yet the same amount of industrial insurance would cost $208.64 ($52.16 × 4).

THE PROFITS OF INDUSTRIAL INSURANCE

Quite apart from selling practices and costs to the policyholders, industrial insurance has been an unusually profitable venture for the owners of many companies. This has been particularly true of stock companies, where disregard for the client's welfare is most pro-

nounced. Although most industrial policies are carried with mutual companies, forty-four stock companies write 15 percent of the business.[30] Most of these companies were organized after 1900; their total paid-in capital amounted to about $6,000,000. By 1938 these firms had prospered handsomely; $32,000,000 had been declared in stock dividends, $44,000,000 had been added to surplus, and $66,000,000 had been declared in cash dividends. These gains represent an aggregate total of nearly $143,000,000, or about 2,500 percent of the original paid-in capital.[31]

In the case of the Home Beneficial Association, an original paid-in capital of $5,000 in 1899 had returned to stockholders nearly $1,000,000 in capital stock, $4,500,000 in cash dividends, and $1,800,000 in surplus.[32] The record of the Western and Southern Insurance is also interesting. It is the largest stock company in the business. In 1888 its promoters, two brothers, saw "great possibilities" in industrial insurance. They organized a firm and kept the ownership strictly within the family. It became a veritable gold mine; from an original paid-in investment of $100,000 the company grew through its profits to a concern with capital stock of $15,000,000 and surplus of $9,000,000. By 1938 the company had declared $15,000,000 in stock dividends in addition to nearly $20,000,000 in cash dividends. But this does not represent all the benefits received by the family. The company paid rather munificent salaries to its officers, including the two brothers and a number of relatives. Not only that, it paid out nearly $6,000,000 for the personal income taxes of its officers, directors, and stockholders.[33]

The disturbing aspect of this record of high profits is that they are made not only at the expense of the economically defenseless and those with low incomes, but they result from high-pressure sales techniques, overselling, bad programming, and excessive lapse ratios rather than from high-quality service at low cost. It appears to represent a callous disregard by the industry for individual welfare and a lack of concern by society for the plight of those who suffer an exploitation quite as serious as that now outlawed by pure food and blue sky laws.

[30] Representing more than 90 percent of the total industrial insurance in force with stock companies.
[31] *Hearings before the Temporary National Economic Committee*, Part 12, pp. 5612–5615, 6174.
[32] *Ibid.*, pp. 6039, 6174.
[33] *Ibid.*, pp. 5929–5932.

THE HARTFORD-EMPIRE COMPANY; A PATENT MONOPOLY

A second revelation by the TNEC involved the Hartford-Empire Company. Here it was demonstrated how a corporation might rise to a position of power and monopoly, not through efficiency or through managerial skill, but by manipulating privileges granted under the patent laws. The Hartford-Empire manufactured no bottles, produced no machines for the bottling industry, and sold no machines to producers, yet through its control it effected a near monopoly of the glass bottle industry. By leasing the machines to manufacturers and by collecting royalties therefrom, it controlled the production of more than two-thirds of the industry, and by "treaties" with other producers it influenced the rest. It maintained control over production and prices more complete than that exercised by most public utility commissions; yet it was responsible to no public authority, legislative or administrative. Its securities were listed on none of the great security exchanges, it periodically made public no balance sheet or report of its operations, and no report of its standing was to be found in the private rating manuals, such as Moody's or Poor's.[34] It represented great concentration of power, derived from a public grant (patents), without public responsibility.

The source of the Hartford-Empire strength is its patent control of a basic process. In 1911 an engineer in Hartford, Connecticut, developed a method of feeding glass; the Hartford-Empire owns this patent—the automatic gob feeding machine. The only competitive process of importance is owned by the Owens-Illinois Glass Company, with whom Hartford has an alliance. No one may use this process—which means no one can engage in the business on an economic basis—without a permit from Hartford-Empire. It will sell no machines, but under its leasing system it has extended its control wherever its machines go—in fact, even beyond that, since by threat of litigation it has determined where other machines may be employed. Its patent ownership, however, extends to improvements beyond the basic patents. As technology improved, Hartford-Empire perfected its control by obtaining title to patents covering improvements of its own and other processes. A few cases are illustrative. The phase-change patent and the shaping or stuffing patent constituted the basis by which Hartford sued and overcame many of its competitors in the early

[34] *Ibid.,* Part 2, p. 397.

years of its development.[35] By harassing competitive processes in the courts and by the purchase of foreign patents, the alliance between Hartford and Owens cleared the field for themselves.[36] They shared litigation expenses and presented a front so powerful with regard to legal talent and financial power to sustain a campaign of litigation that few ventured even to defend themselves when challenged. Control extended even to patents unborn, since the agreement to license bottle-making machinery usually provided that all improvements upon the machines should revert to the Hartford-Empire.[37]

HARTFORD-EMPIRE EXTENDS ITS CONTROL

Control of the industry was effected through the process of licensing machines to glass bottle producers. These manufacturers, of course, paid royalties for the privilege. Those who used other processes— whose claims might have been as good as those of Hartford had they possessed the ingenuity and the financial strength to prosecute their cases in the courts—did not readily or willingly become vassals and pay tribute to the Hartford combination. Yet one by one they were brought to terms.

Eventually the Hartford-Empire Company and the Owens-Illinois Glass Company controlled practically 100 percent of the bottle-producing business. Hartford, through its licenses, dominated the operations of nearly thirty plants, and Owens-Illinois operated fifteen plants on its own account.[38] The battle against many of the smaller concerns involved no great difficulty for this combination. Some applied willingly for the use of its machines; some, who had machines which they considered legally their own and not infringements on the Hartford patents, submitted reluctantly in order to avoid litigation and to remain in business; some succumbed only under threat or pressure of litigation; others dared to fight.

Both the Hartford-Empire and the Owens-Illinois Glass Company owned patents covering machines which were equipped to accomplish the same results. When these two challenged each other with litigation, the cost threatened to be enormous.[39] Rather than permit this to happen, they came to terms and formed an alliance too powerful for others to combat. From that time the two firms shared litigation expenses, thereby increasing the odds against a successful defense by those charged with infringement.[40] Under this agreement the two con-

---

[35] *Ibid.*, p. 437.   [36] *Ibid.*, pp. 520–521.
[37] *Ibid.*, p. 592.   [38] *Ibid.*, pp. 384–385, 474, 762–763.
[39] *Ibid.*, p. 496.   [40] *Ibid.*, p. 521.

cerns benefited from a mutual cross-licensing arrangement, the Owens people continued to produce the finished product, Hartford proceeded to license other producers, and the profits from royalties were divided. As a result Owens's competitors in the glass bottle business, through their licenses with Hartford, were in effect paying rebates to the Owens firm, or, as representatives of the latter described it,

Our negotiations with Hartford-Empire Co. and others, so far as our patent situation and royalty income is concerned, should be to attempt to secure a position whereby we pay no royalty on any item we produce and we attempt to force all others to pay royalty on every item they produce, we participating with anyone else in the royalties they receive.[41]

The Hazel-Atlas Company had been engaged in the business of manufacturing glass containers for fifty years prior to 1938—long before the Hartford-Empire was conceived.[42] It had its own machines, including a feeding device with which it was satisfied, and saw no need to pay or any advantage in paying royalties to lease the Hartford process. Furthermore, it did not believe its processes to be in violation of the Hartford patents. Nevertheless, in 1926 it was sued together with a number of other producers. This litigation continued until 1932, when the Atlas concern received an adverse decision in the Federal Circuit Court; at that moment it had to decide whether to continue to defend its case up to the Supreme Court or to come to terms with the monopoly. According to Atlas officials, it was decided that it would be advantageous to discontinue its outlay for litigation and to pay royalties instead. These legal expenditures had amounted to nearly $150,000 annually, making no accounting for the additional cost of time consumed by managerial personnel and the consequent disruptions of organization.

The Hartford people, likewise, found it to their advantage to come to terms, since they could not be certain that the Supreme Court would decide the case in their favor. Their position was described as follows:

I think the thing that disturbed Hartford-Empire was we were going to make every effort to get to the Supreme Court of the United States. I think in addition to that, they fully realized the resourcefulness of our organization and experience in the practical application of feeding devices of all kinds.[43]

Thus, with a healthy mutual respect for the financial strength and litigation capacity of each other, the two firms entered into an al-

[41] *Ibid.*, p. 501. [42] *Ibid.*, pp. 536–550. [43] *Ibid.*, p. 540.

liance whereby Atlas agreed to pay royalties on its own machines and Hartford agreed to share its earnings with its former competitor. The divisible income of Hartford was thus to be split in three ways, one-third to Atlas, one-third to Owens, and one-third to be retained by itself. Though Atlas reluctantly agreed to pay royalties to Hartford, it fared much better than did many smaller firms who could not afford to litigate their rights. Atlas was strategically in a better bargaining position and thus obtained rights to share royalties actually paid by its competitors.

But the stakes for which Hartford played were larger than a mere alliance with Atlas. At the same time a group of smaller glass companies were being sued for infringement. These firms were waiting to learn the outcome of the Atlas suit, but when Atlas capitulated, their defense collapsed, and a substantial number of these firms became licensees of Hartford, but not on such favorable terms.

Another company whose capitulation strengthened the monopolistic role of Hartford and which, because of its position, was able to secure more favorable terms was Ball Brothers of Muncie, Indiana.[44] The capitulation by Atlas was an important factor in the decision of the Ball firm to come to terms with Hartford, which it did in 1933. Ball had been notified that it was infringing and thereby subject to suit. Wishing to escape the difficulties and the costs of litigation, it sought terms. Mr. Ball described his decision thus: "We wanted to escape any such unpleasant litigation, and any claims that they might make for past damages." [45]

But Ball drove for special favors in return for its compliance and its royalty payments. It was the chief producer of fruit jars and sought to limit the production of that commodity. In this it was successful. Hartford agreed not to grant any further licenses in the United States which would permit anyone to make fruit jars. Moreover, Ball succeeded in obtaining an informal agreement with Atlas, the other principle producer, to curtail production. Licenses already granted to certain smaller concerns were terminated.

An interesting sidelight on these hearings is the fact that some of the participants in this oligopolistic combination learned for the first time the full nature of the "rules of the game" under which they worked. Ball did not know until the TNEC informed him that a part of the royalties he paid went through Hartford to his chief competitor.

[44] *Ibid.*, pp. 551–582.   [45] *Ibid.*, p. 555.

Mr. Cox. Mr. Ball, under this contract which was made in 1933, you pay royalties to the Hartford-Empire Co., that is right, isn't it?

Mr. Ball. It is.

Mr. Cox. Mr. Ball, were you ever told before you signed this contract that those royalties were going to be divided with Owens-Illinois and Hazel-Atlas?

Mr. Ball. No, sir; we had no idea of it.

Mr. Cox. When did you find out about that, Mr. Ball?

Mr. Ball. Read it in the newspaper a couple of days ago.[46]

There were, however, many producers of glass bottles who were not in a position to bargain on terms as satisfactory as these. The annual outlay of thousands of dollars to defend their patent rights against the combined strength of Hartford-Empire and Owens-Illinois was more than many could endure. Their case seemed hopeless, since, as Assistant Attorney General Arnold put it, "resources and persistence and an army of experts and counsel are as important in a patent fight as they are in any other kind of war." [47]

Whenever independents did not readily submit and request a license from Hartford-Empire, the *modus operandi* usually followed a common pattern—persuasion, then pressure, finally suits for infringement on the basic patents, and following that "an invitation to Hartford." Quite as artless as the proverbial bidding of the spider to its prey were these "friendly" summonses to independents, who thereafter valiantly struggled within the mesh of the web. A few cases will illustrate. Five smaller concerns had associated themselves for the purposes of marketing their product and to obtain other advantages to be had from managerial centralization. They were producing with machines manufactured by a company holding patent rights different from those of the Hartford-Empire. Hartford soon took an interest in their case, threatened them with suit, invited them to Hartford, and upon their arrival presented them with a claim for past royalties amounting to two-thirds of a million dollars. Ultimately, in order to stay in the business, these independents were forced into a settlement involving the payment of $100,000 plus royalties; at the same time they were required to relinquish their fruit jar trade to the Ball people and to restrict production in other lines.

A firm in Texas and another in Detroit, which had purchased machinery to produce bottles, were "invited to Hartford," were refused licenses to operate, were harassed by suits, and, later, found that their

[46] *Ibid.*, p. 560.   [47] *Ibid.*, p. 590.

customers were driven away when the latter, too, were sued for infringement. In order to do business, glass bottle producers in effect had to obtain "a certificate of convenience and necessity" from the combination which had as its center the Hartford-Empire.

Both the record of its activities and a memorandum taken from its files point to the fact that the Hartford-Empire Company had exploited the patent system for purposes quite antagonistic to the objectives of public policy. The patent laws are designed to foster the arts and the sciences; yet the Hartford-Empire turned them into instruments of suppression and monopoly. They described their purposes of seeking patents in the following manner: (1) to prevent the duplication of its machines by other companies, (2) to block the invention of other machines, and (3) to get patents on all possible improvements of competing processes to prevent their reaching a stage of perfection. Evidence bore testimony to the fact that this policy had been fully implemented by the practices and deeds of the company.[48]

PRODUCTION AND PRICE CONTROL

Monopoly in the glass industry branched in two directions. Not only did the Hartford-Empire alliance maintain control over the licensing of machines essential to producing glass bottles, but through these licenses controls were instituted to effect a monopoly over the final product (glass bottles) as well. Practically all licenses to manufacturers were restricted, usually with respect to the type of bottles which could be produced as well as to the quantities.[49] Hartford people described this policy as follows:

Consequently we adopted the policy which we have followed ever since, of restricted licenses; that is to say, (a) We licensed the machines only to selected manufacturers of the better type, refusing many licensees who we thought would be price cutters; and (b) we restricted their field of manufacture in each case to certain specific articles with the idea of preventing too much competition; (c) in order to retain more complete control of the situation, we retained title to the machines and simply leased them for a definite period of years, usually 8 or 10 years, with the privilege of renewal for a smaller additional term.[50]

Only two unrestricted licenses were granted, and these were in the possession of the two large producers.[51] Licenses were restricted in two ways—first, not all who applied could obtain them and, second, those who did obtain them were not free to produce as they wished

48 Ibid., pp. 386–387.   49 Ibid., pp. 405, 421, 425, 426.
50 Ibid., p. 417.   51 Ibid., p. 423.

or to sell for prices they pleased. Moreover, a license usually carried a provision that it could be canceled: "It can be cancelled tomorrow if we see fit." [52] By means of these licenses production was restricted and prices were controlled. Such control was readily admitted by the Hartford managers, but, in the words of Senator O'Mahoney, they preferred to speak of it in the more "euphonious way" [53] as "price stabilization." [54]

Thus, under the cloak of the patent laws the industry had succeeded in imposing planning and control upon both itself and the consumers, but without public sanction or consent. It had created what Chairman O'Mahoney called an AAA for milk bottles, but its spokesmen insisted they had used it "intelligently." "We reserve judgment, but, generally speaking, when the producing capacity is way in excess of consumption, we do not and would not grant licenses." [55] Managers of the industry displayed little faith in free enterprise or rugged individualism; a planned economy—at least the glass segment of it—is preferable to a free competitive economy, and the control is best placed, not in the hands of public authority, but with the beneficiaries of the monopoly. "Who is better able to say whether we shall have 1,000 licenses or 500 or 200 or 50? We know the trade." [56]

THE EMASCULATION OF SECTION 7 OF THE CLAYTON ACT

Another of the many instances in which the Supreme Court has by a bare majority struck down important pieces of social legislation is found in connection with Section 7 of the Clayton Act.[57] After attempting for many years to control monopolies under the Sherman Act, Congress in 1914 undertook to strengthen that legislation by means of the Clayton Act. Section 7 prohibits a corporation from acquiring the capital stock of another if by so doing it leads to monopoly or substantially lessens competition. This provision of the law reads as follows:

That no corporation engaged in commerce shall acquire, directly or indirectly, the whole or any part of the stock or other share capital of another corporation engaged also in commerce, where the effect of such

---

[52] *Ibid.*, pp. 405, 409.   [53] *Ibid.*, p. 427.
[54] For many evidences and admissions of price control see *ibid.*, pp. 415, 417, 418, 419, 421, 423, 426, 427.
[55] *Ibid.*, p. 413.   [56] *Ibid.* See also pp. 421–422, 426.
[57] *Ibid.*, Part 5, pp. 1771–1788; and *Final Report and Recommendations of the Temporary National Economic Committee*, pp. 273–283.

acquisition may be to substantially lessen competition between the corporation whose stock is so acquired and the corporation making the acquisition, or to restrain such commerce in any section or community, or tend to create a monopoly of any line of commerce.

. . .

No corporation shall acquire, directly or indirectly, the whole or any part of the stock or other share capital of two or more corporations engaged in commerce where the effect of such acquisition, or the use of such stock by the voting or granting of proxies or otherwise, may be to substantially lessen competition between such corporations, or any of them, whose stock or other share capital is so acquired, or to restrain such commerce in any section or community, or tend to create a monopoly of any line of commerce.[58]

Section 7 was directed at the usual method by which consolidations and combinations had been effected. With the passage of this law Congress thought that it had created an instrument which would provide the desired control. Such, however, did not prove to be the case. As so often has happened to remedial legislation, able and ingenious lawyers soon contrived ways to do legally what the law forbids them to do, and a sympathetic court looked to the letter, not to the intent of the law—considered the form, not the effect of the lawyers' stratagems. Ways were found to circumvent Section 7, and as a result of favorable court decision this portion of the Clayton Act was emasculated.

Three methods were soon devised to bring about corporate consolidations once it became illegal to do so through the ordinary method of one corporation acquiring the capital stock of a competitor. The Federal Trade Commission, which has been charged with the enforcement of Section 7, has described these methods as follows: [59] (1) One corporation might acquire control of a competitor through the purchase of its voting stock and thereby use the stock to obtain the physical assets, (2) it might create a holding company to purchase the voting stock of a competing company and then vote the stock to obtain title to the assets and thereby effect a consolidation, or (3) it might purchase the factory, equipment, and good will of the competitor. The latter method—consolidation by purchase of the physical assets or merger of properties—is not prohibited under the Clayton Act. The first two, however, use the illegal purchase of stocks in order to achieve the legally permissible acquisition of assets.

[58] *Hearings before the Temporary National Economic Committee*, Part 5, p. 1773.
[59] *Ibid.*

Three important cases which came before the Federal Trade Commission and eventually to the Supreme Court illustrate the manner by which Section 7 was nullified; these involved Swift and Company,[60] the Thatcher Manufacturing Company,[61] and the Arrow-Hart-Hegeman Electric Company.[62] The procedure was similar in all these cases: the company illegally purchased the stock of a competitor; it proceeded thereafter through such control to acquire control of the property. In each case the Federal Trade Commission ordered the respondent to divest itself of both the assets and the stock, since an order merely to divest itself of the stock would be an empty gesture and a mockery. In each of these cases the lower court sustained the order of the Commission, and appeal was thereafter taken to the Supreme Court. The Court held that although the Clayton Act had been violated by the acquisition of stock ownership and although through this method the respondent had acquired control over the assets of its competitor, the Federal Trade Commission was powerless to do anything about it. Inasmuch as the companies had "legally" gained control of the assets prior to action by the Federal Trade Commission, the latter had acted beyond its authority to require the company to divest itself of control. The Court was divided in each case, four justices, including the Chief Justice, dissenting.

But the law had been made—in this case unmade; Section 7 of the Clayton Act has been rendered quite impotent except as a "make work" project for the lawyers. Acquisition of assets has become the usual method of consolidation,[63] and mergers once thought prohibited by Congress have gone on quite unabated.[64]

IRRESPONSIBILITY OF CORPORATE STEWARDSHIP

Corporations are creatures of the state and as such are presumed to serve some public purpose. Corporations have stockholders and are presumed to promote their interests. Corporate managers, in principle, are selected to represent their owners and are presumed to be rewarded more or less in proportion to their efficiency and loyalty in prosecuting that purpose. In fact, however, managers may, by their stewardship, so direct the activities of a corporation that it will create benefits for any one of three different groups or any combination of the three. Corporations may be managed efficiently to the end that

60 *Ibid.*, p. 1775.   61 *Ibid.*, pp. 1775–1776.
62 *Ibid.*, pp. 1776–1777.   63 *Ibid.*
64 *Final Report and Recommendations of the Temporary National Economic Committee*, pp. 280–281.

consumers—the public—may enjoy better quality at lower prices. On the other hand, corporations may be managed to the end that greater profits will accrue to the owners—the stockholders. Or they may be operated, either run efficiently or manipulated and mismanaged, to create profits of various kinds for the managers—profits which arise from efficient production, manipulative profits, promoter's profits, or stock market profits.

A study of the folkways of American business would be illuminating. Army officers who violate their basic responsibilities ordinarily are court-martialed. Public officials who renege the mandates given them at the polls may be cast aside by the voters. But corporate managers who ignore their obligations to stockholders are not so readily disciplined. Apparently there has developed a code which permits the exploitation of corporate stewardship for personal gain. The ordinary requirements of integrity and trust usually demanded of lesser men, and in little things, too frequently have been set aside when dealing with big things involving large sums.[65] Defended by the ablest attorneys who devise the circumventions to be employed in order, technically, to stay within the law, the code achieves the sanctity of legality and respectability. The TNEC made no attempt to penetrate into this most interesting aspect of American economic life, but inevitably the hearings revealed illustrations of such abuse of trust. A few case studies will be presented.

More than one industrial insurance company was subjected to the scrutiny of the TNEC, but the Monumental Life Insurance Company of Baltimore, Maryland, probably represented the industry nearly at its worst. Among its activities may be found most of the abuses within the industry.[66] It started out as a mutual company, with the usual benefits of a mutual accruing to the policyholders. In 1928, however, the insiders, the management of the firm, conceived the idea of transforming it into a stock company. When the transformation was complete, the managers had become the principal owners—stockholders—and had retained themselves as the officers of the new firm. As a mutual, the company had built up a surplus of more than one-half million dollars. Legally, and of course actually, this surplus belonged to the policyholders. When the conversion was complete, however, they had lost all tangible equity.

---

65 This issue is raised in a rather forceful manner in the *Hearings before the Temporary National Economic Committee*, Part 17, p. 9682.
66 *Ibid.*, Part 12, pp. 5617 ff.

When such a comprehensive change affecting the economic interests of thousands of policyholders is made, it would be expected that the latter would be given ample notice and an opportunity to approve or reject the plan. For all practical purposes the policyholders in this case were neither informed nor consulted. The law, as is customary, required that they be notified, so an inconspicuous notice was put in the Baltimore papers. Apparently no other attempt was made to inform the policyholders that the company as well as the character and the extent of their equities were being radically altered. In a series of swift moves the transformation was completed before they could become aware of it. The minimum letter of the law—and that only—was observed. That this was the shrewd intent of the promoters seems apparent from their oft-repeated assertions: "We followed the statute," "We were proceeding under the statute," and "That was approved by the Insurance Commission." That the promoters assiduously cut the line closely at this point seems to be clear.

Ratification by the policyholders had to be obtained, so in a few short weeks the agency managers and their agents were mobilized to collect the requisite proxies. Agents were given printed proxies and allowed only a few days in which to obtain the necessary signatures and to return them to the managers. In addition to the ordinary pressure upon the agents to get the job done, each was paid a bonus (the moneys for which came from the policyholders' own funds) to mobilize the needed proxies. Irregularities seem to have been common: few policyholders knew what they signed, if, indeed, they did sign; many proxies were signed for them—"forged" is the term which was used in the testimony—by the agents who were given a "must" and a time limit. No independent audit was ever made of the final count when the ballots were assembled, and no attempt was made to verify their authenticity. Those responsible for the count took orders directly from the officers who were to benefit thereby. When the TNEC sought to examine the ballots several years later, they had been destroyed. But everything had been done "legally"!

Policyholders were not informed of their right to subscribe for shares in the new company. A few who learned of it were "taken care of," but most of them signed away their rights in the proxies or had them voted away at the annual meeting. Most of the shares stayed in the hands of the promoting managers.

Little opposition—or, seemingly, interest—was encountered from the office of the State Insurance Commissioner. This, one suspects,

was directly related to the fact that several important officials of that office were "taken care of"; they ended up with substantial blocks of shares and, by circumvention, had the purchase money supplied for them by the promoters. The Insurance Departments of other states in which the company did business might have been expected to take an interest in behalf of their citizens who were policyholders. But little time was allowed for that. Shortly before the conversion became a *fait accompli* the promoters wrote the authorities in other states describing that all was being done "with the knowledge of the Insurance Commissioner of Maryland" and "in strict accordance with the statutes of this State." [67]

Most of the unfavorable practices associated with industrial insurance previously discussed were employed by this company after the new managers took over. The company made very high profits and at the same time used the usual pressure techniques to obtain business. It had a high lapse ratio and apparently promoted lapsing. It had a high turnover among its agents and made little attempt to train its employees.

MANIPULATING THE SURPLUS ACCOUNT

In recent years a new method of manipulating the corporate balance sheet has been developed which apparently has not been employed for productive or social purposes. This method was called to the attention of the TNEC in its study of the petroleum industry. Many of the large oil companies had availed themselves of a privilege, granted to them in the corporate charter, to revalue their assets and to make a restatement of capital stock. A purpose which might be served by this method would be to scale down capital assets to conform with real values and to revalue the certificates of ownership to conform with the new valuation. But the method employed was quite the reverse; capital stock was revalued at a much lower figure than necessary, and the remainder of the value of the assets was reflected by a substantial increase in capital surplus. [68]

This creates an accounting illusion; a corporation with a large surplus appears to be a profitable concern which has accumulated large earnings. The procedure is tantamount to the watering of stock —but in reverse. By such methods the management places the corporation in a position where it may pay dividends—out of the "mongrel" surplus—even though its earnings do not warrant such dividends.

[67] *Ibid.*, p. 5633.   [68] *Ibid.*, Part 17, pp. 9613–9645.

This offers a great temptation to managers, since it enables them to perpetuate their control without challenge from the stockholders who usually are content as long as dividends are forthcoming. This, indeed, appears to be the purpose of such revaluations of assets with their resultant "revaluation" surpluses. There seems to be no secret about it. The Corporation Trust Company, in soliciting business and encouraging corporations to obtain their charters from the liberal state of Delaware, advertised that this was one of the benefits obtainable from the lenient statutes of that state. In a booklet entitled *The Delaware Corporation* the promoters say, "Payment of dividends may be paid out of net assets in excess of capital as well as out of net profits, a useful power in certain kinds of business." [69]

The "useful power" appears to be the opportunity which it offers to managers to perpetuate themselves in office by maintaining a steady record of dividends regardless of earnings. Representatives of the great oil companies testified that less than 1 percent of the stockholders ordinarily are represented at the annual meetings; thus the management, as the only practical participator, usually controls.[70] With the ability to maintain a steady stream of dividends, even out of capital, managers need have little fear that stockholders thus lulled into a sense of security will vote other than to sign perfunctory proxies.

Between 1929 and 1938 eight of the large oil companies restated their capital stock, and a substantial amount of the dividends declared thereafter represented a liquidation of capital rather than a reflection of earning capacity. A typical case was that of the Consolidated Oil Corporation, which had recourse to this device in 1932.[71] It restated the value of its capital stock and transferred to surplus all equity in excess of a nominal value of $5.00 per share for the outstanding no par value common stock. The ostensible purpose of this maneuver was to permit a revaluation of capital assets to conform with "economic conditions." Nevertheless, the very large item of $221,000,000 created as capital surplus, as compared with $31,000,000 of capital stock,[72] created an illusion of great earnings and strength.

Several disadvantages flow from this manipulation of the balance sheet other than the opportunity of control which it offers to insiders and the possibility of declaring dividends out of fictitious earnings.

[69] *Ibid.*, p. 9616; see also revised edition of the booklet *The Delaware Corporation,* The Corporation Trust Company, May, 1941.

[70] *Hearings before the Temporary National Economic Committee,* Part 17, pp. 9618, 9641; see also Part 14. p. 7105.

[71] *Ibid.*, Part 17, p. 9621.   [72] Previously, capital stock was $251,000,000.

Particularly, the cushion which protects the bondholders and preferred stockholders is weakened. If, for example, a corporation has $100,000,000 in capital stock before revaluation and $25,000,000 in that account afterward, as well as $75,000,000 in the "synthetic" surplus account, this latter figure may, through the issuance of dividends, dwindle away and with it the protection available to senior creditors. Another weakness is that managers may be able to conceal the financial position of the corporation and by adjusting the surplus account may maintain a semblance of strength when such is not the case.

BORROWING COMPANY FUNDS

The officers and directors of a corporation are in reality the trustees of the assets belonging to the stockholders. Theirs is a moral and legal responsibility to husband and manage these assets. It is of questionable propriety for individuals in such positions to employ the moneys of the corporation for their own personal use. In fact, many state laws, especially those affecting banks and insurance companies, have provided that borrowing by an officer or director is illegal and subject to penalty.

Ways may be found, however, to defeat the purposes of the law; the insurance studies before the TNEC offer examples of such stratagems. In the case of the Travelers Insurance Company, loans which legally could not be made directly were openly but indirectly made in opposition to the purpose and the intent of the law.[73] The Travelers Insurance Company organized and operated a number of subsidiaries, including two banks—The Travelers Bank and Trust Company and The Connecticut River Banking Company. In each case its ownership was sufficient to control the policy of the subsidiary, representing 100 percent ownership in the first and 71 percent in the latter.[74] With this control the company proceeded through loans to enable officers, directors, and key employees to purchase its stock. Although the borrowing of company funds is illegal, the law was circumvented by causing the controlled subsidiary to do what the parent corporation could not do. From 1912 to 1939 the Connecticut River Bank granted more than 500 loans to the officers and directors of the parent corporation, including the president. These advances amounted to more than $3,000,000; individual loans ranged from $150 to $110,000.[75] At times as much as 40 percent of its loans outstanding were of such character.

[73] *Hearings before the Temporary National Economic Committee*, Part 13, pp. 6364–6420.
[74] *Ibid.*, Part 13, p. 6366.   [75] *Ibid.*, p. 6405.

One suspects that this is only one of many holding company arrangements which have been devised for the convenience of managerial manipulation. During the same period loans to employees by the Connecticut River Bank totaled more than $600,000. Meanwhile the second alter-ego of the Travelers Company was engaged in similar operations; during the shorter period between 1930 and 1939 the Travellers Bank and Trust Company had granted to the managers twenty loans totaling more than $300,000.

Another artifice was that employed by the Monumental Life Insurance Company.[76] Flagrant as the procedure was in this case, apparently it was used upon the considered advice of legal counsel and may have been within the law. The company granted loans to the chairman of the board, but instead of their being made directly to him, they were made to a subordinate, his secretary. The charter of the corporation forbade loans "either directly or indirectly" to any director or officer; yet more than $120,000 was advanced in this manner. No reports were ever made to the supervisory authorities concerning the character of these transactions; in fact, specific questions on formal reports were answered in a manner which could be judged to be false or deceptive.

DIRECTORS WHO DO NOT DIRECT

A serious problem has been the negligence or inability of stockholders to exercise their legal rights of electing corporate directors. This makes possible a continuation of control by a few, often with little or no feeling of responsibility to stockholders. A problem of almost equal moment, but less familiar, is the indifference of many directors and the negligence of their obligations at directorship meetings. If directors take their responsibilities lightly and fail to attend regularly, managers may become doubly irresponsible and serve only their own interests.

That such negligence is not uncommon is illustrated by the record of the Metropolitan Life Insurance Company—one of the largest corporations in the world.[77] Here, at least nominally, the directors are responsible to, and represent, policyholders rather than stockholders. This corporation has a board of twenty-five members. Between 1929 and 1938 attendance was far from regular, and ordinarily about 40 percent were absent. Never was attendance at board meetings higher than 80 percent, and it was rarely that. One director attended

[76] *Ibid.*, Part 12, pp. 5663–5668, 5681–5688.   [77] *Ibid.*, Part 4, pp. 1265–1279.

only three meetings out of eighty-three during a period of seven years; another, two meetings out of 108 in eight years; still another, nine meetings out of about 125 in ten years; another attended no meetings at all in five years. Notable was the record of one director who attended no meetings in sixteen years of "service." When it became apparent that the TNEC was interested in this fact, the chairman of the board requested his resignation. At times the directors of this great corporation met and actually conducted business without a quorum.

If the economy is to serve the broad national interest and if corporations are to serve the interests of both the public and their stockholders, means will have to be found to ensure the accountability of corporation managers; present practices of both stockholders and directors are poorly designed to achieve that end.

DIRECTORS WHO EXPLOIT THEIR FIDUCIARY POSITIONS

Corporate managers are chosen, at least in theory, to promote the interests of the owners; by the same token directors are elected to represent those interests. It seems, however, that these assignments frequently have been regarded, not as positions of stewardship, but as vantage points of exploitation for individual benefit. The commercial world, which has not looked askance at holding companies which milk their subsidiaries or at industrial managers who manipulate the market value of their corporations' securities, has often countenanced a philosophy which encourages directors to place their trustee and fiduciary functions secondary to personal gain.

The theory and the ethics of corporate management, and usually the law, require that directors shall not be "pecuniarily interested in transactions" of the corporation.[78] It seems apparent, however, that corporate directorships are eagerly sought because of the opportunities of personal gain which they offer and frequently are exploited for that purpose. This was particularly evident during the hearings relating to the life insurance industry.[79] In 1937, for example, the New York Life Insurance Company maintained deposits of $63,000,000 with commercial banks. It developed that a substantial number of the larger of these balances were with banks with which New York Life interlocked; the Chemical Bank and Trust Company, the New York Trust Company, the National City Bank, and the Northern Trust Company all had representatives on the New York Life board of directors. Large deposits of this character, upon which no interest was paid,

[78] *Ibid.*, pp. 1412, 1446.   [79] *Ibid.*, pp. 1412–1478.

seem to have been profitable to the banks, and for that reason they were favors to be sought. Once on the board, directors went to work for their banks; one thinks of them, not as representatives of the policyholders, but as representatives of the banks who were looking first of all after their peculiar interests. We find one director writing to the insurance company as follows: "I would appreciate very much the designation of this company as the depositary of the funds of the company." [80] This letter evoked the expected results. In a number of similar instances representatives of the insurance company claimed that the placing of large deposits shortly after a banker became a director was "purely a coincidence."

The same situation obtained in the case of another large insurance company, the Mutual Life Insurance Company of New York.[81] Apparently it had followed the policy of placing its commercial deposits with interlocking banks. In 1938 it held such deposits with the National City Bank, the Central Hanover Bank, the First National Bank, the New York Trust Company, the Citizens Union National Bank, the Guaranty Trust Company, the Chase National Bank, and others.[82] The largest deposit—amounting at one time to $23,000,000 —was placed with the bank with which the company had the largest number of interlocking directors. Apparently there was no reluctance on the part of directors to solicit such business. As one banker-director phrased it, "as I make my living as president of the First National my first interest is to build up its business." [83] As a result of the claims set forth in the correspondence which supplemented this statement, his bank received a very sizable deposit. Other directors put in claims for their banks for similar favors and apparently obtained results. As TNEC member Arnold remarked in view of the many letters placed in evidence, "There is a tone in some of these letters of expectation on the part of persons who are directors, or trustees, of your company that by virtue of that position they will get certain advantages by way of deposits." [84]

The distribution of corporate patronage did not stop with banker-directors, however. Lawyers, advertising men, commercial representatives, brokers, and underwriters were some of the directors who exploited their positions with the great life insurance companies to obtain special dispensations for their firms. An attorney who became a

80 *Ibid.*, p. 1431.　　　　　81 *Ibid.*, pp. 1453–1472.
82 *Ibid.*, pp. 1462–1464.　　　83 *Ibid.*, p. 1454.
84 *Ibid.*, p. 1463.

director for the Metropolitan and who confessed that he taught legal ethics saw nothing improper in the fact that his firm received nearly $400,000 in legal fees during his connection with the company.[85] Many preferential contracts were awarded in this manner. New York Life awarded advertising contracts amounting to several hundred thousand dollars a year to the firm of one of its trustees,[86] while a prominent politician and former candidate for the Presidency, who solicited business while he was a director, was awarded an oil contract involving millions. In the latter instance the oil firm was even permitted to alter its bid in order to obtain the contract.[87] A director of the Mutual Life Insurance Company was successful in routing some of the bond brokerage business of that company to his relatives. The following excerpt throws some light on the code of stewardship which seems to have evolved.

You were good enough at my suggestion to instruct the treasurer of the Mutual Life to send some business to my brother-in-law . . . and I understand that he has always attended to his commissions satisfactorily.

At present he is not having an easy time in bringing sufficient business to that brokerage house to justify his continuance and this is a matter of great concern to me. If he can just round this bad corner until times improve, he will have plenty of business, for he is a man of great energy and resourcefulness. Therefore, if at this time you could have our treasurer drift a little business toward Mitchell, it would come as a very timely aid to him.

Of course he can buy and sell bonds on the stock exchange, as well as stocks, and I do hope that you can give him some encouragement at a time when he very sorely needs it. I will regard it as a favor done to me.[88]

A revealing illustration of this practice involves another director of New York Life; even though he received a direct commission of 10 percent on all premiums paid to his firm by New York Life, a representative of a casualty insurance firm openly solicited its business while a director.[89] Evidently these efforts were successful; in 1938 his company wrote the public and elevator liability insurance, the workmen's compensation insurance, steam boiler insurance, power plant insurance, surety bond insurance, and a variety of other contracts for New York Life. He seems to have been able even to obtain the termination of existing insurance arrangements and to have the business channelized to his firm.[90]

85 *Ibid.*, pp. 1412–1414.
87 *Ibid.*, pp. 1435–1436.
89 *Ibid.*, pp. 1433–1434, 1472–1477.

86 *Ibid.*, p. 1439.
88 *Ibid.*, p. 1465.
90 *Ibid.*, p. 1474.

THE AMERICAN INCLOSURE MOVEMENT

The technological revolution of the twentieth century, which in agriculture is represented by the tractor, the combine, the mechanical corn picker, and the truck, has had an impact upon the rural worker of America similar to that of the industrial revolution upon the rural worker of England during the eighteenth century. Now, as then, land holdings are being combined to form large units, and great portions of the rural population are being dispossessed, with resultant unrest and distress.

Everywhere in America a trend is under way which is evidenced by larger farms, fewer farmers, more machines, and greater production per man. The trend is the same whether one looks at the wheat, the corn, or the cotton belt. The situation is pronounced in the wheat belt; in Oklahoma it is reported that the combine harvester reduced the employment of men during the harvest season from 11,000 in 1921 to 165 in 1932.[91] In the same state an owner purchased 100 quarter sections of land, and after introducing machinery he continued to operate with one man on each quarter instead of the former two to four. A similar trend exists in the state of Washington, where one farmer described the new process as follows: "We no longer raise wheat here in eastern Washington; we manufacture it. With large tractors, gang plows, seeders and combines for production and trucks for transportation . . . we have virtually a factory system of production." [92] With the loss of workers and farmers from the rural areas comes also the demise of the small towns and the disappearance of their populations. In North Dakota the new type rubber-tire tractors, which propel larger plows, disks, harrows, and seeders, are said to have displaced two out of every three to five men formerly employed during the harvest season. Many small farmers and scores of laborers have been displaced. They have become a submerged economic class, unable to find livelihood on the farm or to earn a place for themselves in the cities, already cursed with unemployment.

With regard to the corn belt the situation is no more favorable.[93] A single machine—the mechanical corn picker—has eliminated the jobs of nearly 20,000 workers in the state of Iowa. But the mechanization of the farm and the use of power-driven machinery is not limited

91 *Ibid.*, Part 30, pp. 17049–17051.
92 *Ibid.*, p. 17049.
93 *Ibid.*, pp. 17051–17053.

to the corn picker; other devices include power-driven corn planters and cultivators. In 1939 it was estimated that nearly 6 percent of Iowa's farm families had been deprived of their livelihood in a three-year period.

The plight of the share cropper in the cotton regions has been made even worse by the new mechanical techniques.[94] Share croppers are being replaced by machines, and wage workers are being swept from the plantations. "They crowd the towns of the Delta and choke the slums of Memphis, Tenn." In the western South great numbers have turned to the coastal regions, but as yet no substantial Westward migration of Negro workers has begun. In Mississippi it was estimated that nearly 50 percent of the Delta farm workers would presently be displaced by machines. A striking illustration of the process is the case of a planter who purchased twenty-two tractors and thirteen four-row cultivators and dismissed 130 out of 160 share-cropper families. Similar conditions were found in the Texas cotton belt. In that region popular resentment at times has reached a high pitch, as is indicated by the following editorials from rural newspapers:

The land hog is all-powerful. He may buy a tractor and get possession of all the land in a community and, with a little hired help, farm all the land and thereby drive all his neighbors off the land to starve—just for his own private gains.

The big landowner does wrong in discharging his tenants and working his land with hired labor, but since that is the only way he can get a fair compensation he can't be blamed. This situation is causing more people to be without work than anything else.[95]

In California a modification of this trend is evident; [96] here corporation agriculture is becoming dominant. The fruit and vegetable lands are coming under the control of large corporations including packing companies. One company alone controls 20,000 acres, in addition to 47,000 acres in other states. It is said that the term "farm" is becoming obsolete in California.

These illustrations are sufficient to portray the wide sweep of this great movement. Mechanical progress, however beneficial in the long run to the country as a whole, has created countless thousands of human wrecks. Landless men, great armies of "Joads," constitute a festering sore on the social and political body and contribute a poor foundation to a political democracy. The picture would not be so

[94] *Ibid.*, pp. 17046–17049.   [95] *Ibid.*, p. 17042.
[96] *Ibid.*, pp. 17062–17067.

distressing if the increased productivity arising from the new machine techniques found its way back to the workers and to consumers in the form of lower production costs and wider consumption. But since the control of the machine and the factories is highly concentrated and the prices of farm machinery monopolistic in character, the increased productivity is drained from the economy and, in the form of hoarded income, becomes sterile, constituting an impediment to productive progress.

THE IMPACT OF ECONOMIC CONCENTRATION UPON REPRESENTATIVE GOVERNMENT

The success of democratic institutions depends upon the ability of voters to choose legislators who will exercise their judgment to promote the welfare of all the people. Likewise, it depends upon the responsiveness of legislators to the popular will and the ability of the people to recall from office representatives who fail to fulfill these responsibilities. But the rise of the great corporations and the concentration of economic power within these agencies has facilitated the mobilization of financial resources and of the instruments for controlling public opinion, with the result that pressures may be put upon the elected representatives to obtain legislation favoring those who control the corporations. So well organized are the methods of "reaching" the legislature and so easily are the desired responses obtained that business men often look upon this method as the normal, legitimate, and expected mode of governmental performance. Without comprehending that they do so, frequently they look upon the legislature as their legislature whose function it is to serve their interest. Popular government becomes government by pressure groups, and legislation tends to serve special interests rather than the common good.

This mode of behavior on the part of business is illustrated by the activities of the Association of Life Insurance Presidents. The methods used by this organization in surveillance of and lobbying before state legislatures demonstrate how difficult it is to obtain legislation for the general welfare if perchance some powerful interest is mobilized to defeat it and, equally, how difficult it is to defeat legislation sponsored by special interest groups, inasmuch as public opinion is not so readily mobilized and the necessary funds with which to do so are seldom available.

Lobbying activities by the large insurance companies are not new;

in 1906 the famous Armstrong Investigation exposed and denounced such practices.

Nothing disclosed by the investigation deserves more serious attention than the systematic efforts of the large insurance companies to control a large part of the legislation of the State. They have been organized into an offensive and defensive alliance to procure or to prevent the passage of laws affecting not only insurance, but a great variety of important interests to which, through subsidiary companies or through the connections of their officers, they have become related. . . . Enormous sums have been expended in a surreptitious manner. Irregular accounts have been kept to conceal the payments for which proper vouchers have not been required. This course of conduct has created a widespread conviction that large portions of this money have been dishonestly used.

. . .

The pernicious activities of corporate agents in matters of legislation demand that the present freedom of lobbying should be restricted. They have brought suspicion upon important proceedings of the Legislature, and have exposed its members to consequent assault. The Legislature owes it to itself, so far as possible to stop the practice of the lavish expenditure of moneys ostensibly for services in connection with the support of or opposition to bills, and generally believed to be used for corrupt purposes. The Legislature should free itself from the stigma which now attaches to the progress of measures affecting important interests. The laws against bribery and corruption, offenses which are difficult of proof, are sufficiently stringent, but an effort should be made to strike at the root of the evil by requiring under proper penalties full publicity with regard to moneys expended in connection with matters before the Legislature. Corporations should be required to keep accounts and vouchers in which all such payments should be fully detailed and receipted for, and an adequate statement regarding them should form a part of such reports as may be required.[97]

Apparently, the Association of Life Insurance Presidents maintained a "watch dog" over each state legislature.[98] The task of this representative was to keep the industry informed of measures which, if enacted into law, might affect life insurance. The lobby manager for the industry in Georgia frankly told the TNEC that his effectiveness was increased if his operations were clandestine.

I am a marked man, [he said]. I have the privilege of the floor and I have been down to the legislature several times, possibly a dozen or more. The speaker of the house has made the public statement that he does not wish any member to accept any invitation given by any person who has any interest in legislation before the house.[99]

[97] *Ibid.*, Part 10, pp. 4802–4803.   [98] *Ibid.*, pp. 4396–4405.
[99] *Ibid.*, p. 4405.

Consequently it became necessary for him to appoint an emissary who would operate in disguise; this was done by inducing a newspaper man to do the undercover work. This man had "access to the floor of the house and a partner, so to speak, on the floor of the senate." Thus, he was able to ferret out important information to enable the life insurance interests to anticipate measures which were about to be introduced in the legislative chambers. Members of the legislature and their sentiments toward the industry were kept under constant surveillance.

Once it becomes apparent that a measure is to be introduced which the industry does not want, there are several ways by which it may be opposed. The most effective, according to the testimony, is to destroy it before it materializes. Pressures are brought to bear.

We try to get hold of the man to introduce it and argue the question on its merits and get him to withdraw it. I might say to you, sir, if you will let me diverge a minute, we rather believe in that, like the dutch man at the boarding house where there were tough roosters. He said he ate them when they were eggs.

Since the description given here is that of an interested witness, one suspects that there have been many occasions when the owner of a "tough rooster" has been able to tell of methods employed to kill a bill by means other than "on its merits." Should this strategy fail, the next attempt made is to kill the bill in the committee.

We make an effort in advance . . . to have friends on the committee and to have the meetings at the proper time and under favorable environment. This has frequently worked out.

Failing this, the next most effective method is organized obstructionism.

If we do not succeed in getting a bill adversed, we try to introduce another bill, hoping the whole thing will wind up in a row, to be plain about it. If a bill passes either house and goes to the other house, we try to repeat the above tactics.[100]

REACHING THE LEGISLATORS

But the task of controlling state legislation has just begun with these stratagems. The legislators themselves, compositely and individually, are subject to minute observance to discover, if possible, how their actions may be influenced. In 1935 a card index of the members of the Florida legislature was compiled; a careful itemization

100 *Ibid.,* p. 4399.

was made covering personal data for each, indicating the approaches which might prove effective. It was considered best that some of the personal data thus collected should not be entered on the card index, but should be kept on separate memoranda, suggesting a willingness on the part of the lobbyists to employ almost any method to obtain their ends.

Another course was to establish legislative contacts; these seemed to range from working through interested parties who knew the legislators to entertaining them personally. Entertainment may take place at the time important legislation is under consideration or it may pay larger dividends when done currently, regardless of the imminence of any particular measure.

We might mention in passing that we believe in killing a bill before it gets on the floor, or before a committee, if possible. It is much easier to handle one man or two men alone than it is to argue with a whole committee and it is impossible to argue with the whole house. This money has been spent in invitations to those of whom we wished to make friends, and seeing that their wives and daughters were looked after properly and courteously; and a large portion of it in giving a dinner after the session was over to all of those who were good enough to favor us. We have been told that one reason we are kindly received is that we do not forget favors after we get them.[101]

There are various ways of bringing pressure to bear upon legislators to restrain them from voting as their judgment and their conscience might dictate. One way is to deluge them with calls, letters, and telegrams from a presumably aroused public to obtain the defeat of a given bill. This may easily be accomplished, since life insurance companies are conveniently organized to mobilize the "opinion" of their policyholders. There are many agents in the field, and if each agent solicits "10 letters from policyholders," legislators quickly feel the pressure. The Association of Life Insurance Presidents employed such a procedure in Florida in a successful attempt to control legislation in that state; letters, telegrams, and phone calls were inspired and, in fact, paid for to arouse this "spontaneous" expression of public opinion.[102]

It is thought wise that there should be as many telegrams and telephone calls as possible to reach these members from their respective home communities. This, of course, is a matter with which you are thoroughly familiar. Furthermore, it is advisable to have as many communications as possible from policyholders. These, of course, are details concerning which you will use your own judgment.[103]

[101] *Ibid.*, p. 4401.   [102] *Ibid.*, pp. 4385–4386.   [103] *Ibid.*, p. 4385.

An effective method such as this is not likely to be neglected. The same technique was used in Pennsylvania to defeat a bill which would have authorized savings bank life insurance:

I am pleased to inform you that the Wilkes-Barre Association of Life Underwriters, which represents all the "old line" companies, and which are approximately 500 in number, were very much in accord with your letter, and immediately contacted all State senators, and each member of the house of representatives, including the chairman of the insurance committee, and protested strongly against House Bill No. 883.

Undoubtedly, such an avalanche of telegrams and personal calls has never before been received by these individuals. We have had definite assurance from them that the bill will be strongly opposed.[104]

Another type of duress is to work through certain financial interests; industrialists, bankers, and contractors often are in a position to influence the lives of state legislators, and their wishes are not to be lightly ignored. Ofttimes the quiet word of these key citizens will carry a stronger influence than obviously inspired letters. The life insurance company presidents found this device useful and effective, as is illustrated in certain self-explanatory letters written during a successful attempt to influence the Georgia legislature:

The easiest way to handle this bill is to kill it. I think that has been done. The First National Bank, of Valdosta, Ga., is the financial backer of the Honorable Nelson, who introduced the bill. I hand you a copy of a telegram that was sent to Senator Nelson yesterday by this bank, at the instance of one of our agents . . . I have an idea that the bill will now be withdrawn.[105]

Please let me write you in a personal way. Last week I went to Rome, Ga., and invited to lunch 20 men, whom I happen to know, large policyholders. Every one of them in our company, and, of course, with other companies, too, some of them. The 20 men carry a million and a half of life insurance.

I talked to them some about the taxation of premiums, as I am sure we are going to have a world of trouble with the next legislature. We have laid some foundation, I think, on which to build, to stall this. But what I want to say is, that I asked these men (and repeat, in a most personal way, they understanding that no company had anything whatever to do with it, but that I was inviting them and meeting them as a fellow policyholder) what they would do if it were indicated that this, that, or the other man would vote to increase the tax on their premiums. Their response was, to name the man who would do that and they would do the best they could to keep him from going to the legislature again. This is a straw.[106]

But often control by means of lobbying and pressure upon individual legislators is too cumbersome, too obvious, and perhaps too

[104] *Ibid.*, p. 4427.   [105] *Ibid.*, p. 4414.   [106] *Ibid.*, p. 4407.

expensive. More efficient ways are available. Human nature is the same in legislatures as on the school playground; a few leaders often are influential enough to determine what is to be done and the manner in which it is to be done. The life insurance companies were realistic enough to recognize this fact and to capitalize upon it; key men, policy-determining men, were reached wherever possible. Influential men, men who possessed talent of leadership or a voice of authority, were sought out and put under obligation to the companies. Later, when their turn came to vote, knowing "on what side their bread was buttered" or, perhaps more accurately, having acquired certain predilections and convictions, their weight was placed where the companies wished it to be. The following instructions by the vice president of one large company to the effect that certain legal fees be channeled to a key legislator illustrates this type of approach.

He is one of two men to whom the legislature listens with the greatest respect, and has been on the law committee at every session that he has attended. We are going to need him in the legislature to cover the constitutionality of an act depriving municipalities of the right to levy taxes, and that is the principal reason why I would like to see him in this *Lannie Thompson case,* aside from the fact that, as I said in my letter of March 1, I believe that the respect in which he is held will be a material factor in securing a change in the point of view of our appellate court, one of whose judges did me the honor to discuss that situation academically yesterday.[107]

Representatives of the insurance companies apparently saw nothing reprehensible in this method of influencing legislation.[108] It was part of the code—the folkways of business. Sometimes, too, it was found effective to place the people's representatives under obligation to the trade—favors extended, even at financial cost, may return handsome dividends, even though the legislator finds it unecessary to make any outlay in repaying his debt. Upon the advice of a willing accomplice in the office of the state insurance commissioner of Georgia, the lobbyist for the companies paid the occupational tax of an insurance agent who, hardly by coincidence, was also chairman of the committee on insurance, appointed at the "instance" of the companies. That these favors were extended with the expectation of reciprocity is obvious from a letter presented in testimony.

A few days ago I had a call from Mr. Harold Dobbins, who seems to have an agency contract with you and who is very much concerned about the payment of his occupational tax, although it had been my previous under-

107 *Ibid.,* p. 4411.   108 *Ibid.,* p. 4414.

standing that the company takes care of such matters for its agents. In any event, Mr. Dobbins gave me the impression that he was called on to pay this tax and that by reason of his inability so far to close some business, although he said he had some under way which he expected to close if he could hang on, he found himself unable at this time to pay the tax levied against him, and asked whether or not it could be allowed to run along for a little while unpaid.

My plan was rather to take it up with you, in the thought that under all of the circumstances you might feel that it would be a good "investment" for the company to meet this expense, at least for the time being, in view of the fact that Mr. Dobbins is again scheduled, I understand, for the chairmanship of the insurance committee and his good will might be worth keeping.

Think it over, and destroy this letter when you have its contents in mind.[109]

Another illustration of this policy of placing important committee members under obligation to the industry concerns the chairman of the controlling committee on life insurance in the Rhode Island legislature, who owed fealty to the industry as it was organized. As in the instance of the commissioner already referred to, commissioners of other states have served as plenipotentiaries of the companies rather than as tribunes of the public. In Rhode Island the Governor's report affecting an important issue was even written for him, through this channel, by the insurance companies. "Pressure was brought upon our Governor for favorable action on the savings bank life insurance legislation, and he naturally turned to the chief of the division of banking and insurance for information." [110] The result was quite as TNEC member Henderson summarized it:

MR. HENDERSON. Mr. Crane sent some material to Mr. White, of the Puritan Life. Mr. White gave it to Mr. Cummings, who had requested it, I gather. Mr. Cummings then made a report to the Governor, as chief of the division of banking and insurance. Then he gave a copy of that to Mr. White, and then he sent it to the various insurance commissioners. . . . So in effect this has been a sort of an adaptation of your idea . . . and it goes out now under the imprimatur of the chief of the division of banking.[111]

Thus, more than thirty years after the Armstrong Investigation, life insurance companies openly and effectively were lobbying to determine the course of legislative policy. In addition to their success in Florida, the defeat of savings bank insurance plans in other states

---

109 *Ibid.*, p. 4415.   110 *Ibid.*, p. 4430.
111 *Ibid.*, p. 4432.

was due to them. In 1935 such bills were defeated in five states, and in 1936 in seven.

If lobbying by life insurance companies is looked upon as a case example, representative of what business men have come to consider a customary, natural, and approved method of procedure, it reflects truly a divergent course in the evolution of the free enterprise system and of representative government as these institutions were conceived of in the nineteenth century. Such practices, indeed, may be so out of harmony with both free enterprise and free institutions that they become the fruit which destroys the tree. We now have the phenomena of corporations that have little or no responsibility to the states wherein they are most active (having received their charters—often ultra-liberal charters—from foreign states) and show little evidence of responsibility to their stockholders so mobilizing their resources of finance, of legal talent, and of publicity as to determine the action of the elected representatives of the people. When substantially all the pressure, suasion, duress, and publicity is in one direction, legislators often willingly or unwillingly yield, and consciously or unconsciously alter representative government to a system of control by the dominant pressure groups. It appears that a pattern is being established; few business men seem to challenge it from an ethical standpoint or to have thought it out to its ultimate impact upon free institutions. No doubt many would brand as subversive anyone who might have the temerity even to raise the issue.

CHAPTER XI

RECOMMENDATIONS

ULTIMATELY the Temporary National Economic Committee rendered its final report and recommendations. Its proposals reflected the experiences and predilections of the members themselves, as well as the thinking of the depression decade. The Committee was actuated, however, by the testimony it had heard, by the facts it had collected, and by the recommendations which had been brought to its attention. Recommendations were principally of two types: those presented during the hearings and those offered by TNEC members and the staff.

SUGGESTIONS FROM THE HEARINGS

The TNEC members looked upon their organization as a factfinding body; there are surprisingly few suggestions throughout the thousands of pages of testimony which could be described as recommendations. The Committee did not solicit such proposals,[1] and consequently few were received. Those which were offered will be described. Generally, however, they do not represent carefully prepared or studied programs for action. If they appear to have been presented in an incidental, informal, and random manner, it is because they were so presented, for the most part. They do not, therefore, constitute a considered and an organized effort to submit a comprehensive program or to suggest solutions to the basic problems with which the TNEC had to grapple.

THE PATENT SYSTEM

Inasmuch as the social utility of the patent system had been subject to scrutiny, a number of recommendations were made for its improvement. Suggestions came principally from three sources: eminent patent attorneys, the Science Advisory Board, and the United States Patent Office. There seemed to be general agreement that existing legislation could be made to function more satisfactorily if the staff of the Commissioner of Patents were enlarged to permit a more ade-

---

[1] Except in the final sessions—see the section on "Public Sessions to Consider Recommendations."

quate and expeditious examination of applications.[2] Few seemed to favor the suggestion that the patent holder be compelled to license his invention "to anybody who paid a reasonable compensation." [3] It was suggested by some, however, that compulsory licensing offered a way of protecting the public from the suppression of useful improvements and of assuring that new techniques be made available to all.

Many of the shortcomings and abuses of the patent system stem from delays and interferences which lengthen the interval between the original application for a patent and the final expiration of the monopoly granted.[4] The Commissioner of Patents proposed that the net life of the patent be limited to a maximum of twenty years. The seventeen-year monopoly under the present law would remain unaltered by the adoption of this proposal, except that the patent would expire twenty years after the date of filing. Thus, under the twenty-year rule, dilatory tactics to prolong the life of the patent would be self-penalizing. Inasmuch as interference proceedings—intended primarily for the protection of legitimate patentable rights—are often filed in the Patent Office for the express purpose of delay, suggestions were made to correct such abuse. The Commissioner proposed that the decision of the Examiner of Interferences (or possibly an Interference Board) be final.[5] Patents would thus be issued immediately after the examiner's decision. In order to curb another type of delay in the Patent Office, it was proposed that renewal applications be abolished. Under existing regulations an applicant may prosecute his application up to point of allowance and then let the matter lapse by failure to pay the final fee. Nevertheless, he is permitted thereafter to renew the application and resume prosecution.[6] Two other recommendations were made by the Commissioner of Patents to speed up the issuing process. The law permits an inventor to make public use of his invention for two years before filing an application; it was proposed to reduce this from two years to one. Similarly, the law allows an applicant two years after the issuance of a patent in which to assert the priority of his invention; it was suggested that this also be reduced to one year.[7]

In 1935 the Science Advisory Board recommended the establishment of a single court for patent appeals; [8] during the hearings this

2 Hearings before the Temporary National Economic Committee, Part 2, pp. 267, 282; Part 3, p. 861.

3 Ibid., Part 2, pp. 278, 297.   4 Ibid., p. 282.

5 Ibid., Part 3, p. 862.   6 Ibid.

7 Ibid.   8 Ibid., pp. 860, 892–893, 1142.

reform received support from several quarters. Such a court would have appellate jurisdiction over all appeals involving patents. Its advocates believed that it would lessen conflict with respect to patent laws, that it would reduce both time and cost in litigating patents, and that it would enhance the presumptive validity of patents, once issued.

INTERSTATE TRADE BARRIERS

Probably in no other section of the TNEC hearings were recommendations for remedial action solicited and received as they were in those relating to interstate trade barriers. Suggestions came from practical business men, such as the chairman of the National Federation of Sales Executives, who avowed a "selfish interest" in trade barriers which constitute impediments to business.[9] Suggestions, likewise, came from scholars, such as a professor of government at Harvard University who had made a broad study of the effects of interstate trade barriers.[10] They came from numerous commissions on interstate co-operation created by state legislatures,[11] from the American Standards Association, representing many national organizations interested in promoting uniform standards,[12] and from the Council of State Governments, representing the high officials of the forty-eight states including the Governors' Conference, the National Association of Attorneys General, and the National Association of Secretaries of State.[13]

Proposals for the elimination of harmful trade barriers may be grouped as follows: those which require action by the states (or between the states), those which require Federal and state co-operation, those which may be achieved by Federal action, and those which involve resort to the courts. The simplest method of freeing the nation of interstate trade barriers would involve, of course, persuading legislatures either to refrain from initiating such laws or to repeal those already enacted. But often it is difficult to obtain the removal of barriers by unilateral action. As in the case of international trade restrictions, state barriers are created by unilateral measures and are multiplied by imitative and retaliatory action. To obtain their removal, however, it often is necessary to find a common basis for co-operation and reciprocity.

The work of the Council of State Governments and the State Commissions on Interstate Cooperation offers a practical illustration of

9 *Ibid.*, Part 29, p. 16081.
10 *Ibid.*, pp. 16087 ff.
11 *Ibid.*, pp. 15892 ff.
12 *Ibid.*, pp. 15987–15995.
13 *Ibid.*, p. 15738.

what can be done by the states themselves. In April, 1939, the Council of State Governments called a National Conference on Interstates Trade Barriers—discussions and plans related to the elimination of barriers.[14] Many tangible results were achieved. Public opinion was aroused, and state legislators were made aware of the broad social interest in contrast to the urgings of special interest groups. Due, at least in part, to these efforts, no additional barriers were erected during the legislative year of 1939; moreover, a number of states removed existing barriers.[15]

Another positive step was the formation in forty-four states of commissions on interstate co-operation to discover, diagnose, and combat trade barriers.[16] The activity of the Indiana Commission demonstrates the practicability of states negotiating reciprocity treaties to respect each other's standards of inspection and to remove burdens which have been heaped upon products of interstate commerce such as milk, liquor, eggs, fruits, and vegetables.

Both the executive director of the Council of State Governments and Professor Elliot of Harvard believed that constructive results could be achieved by the creation of a Joint Federal-State Commission on Intergovernmental Problems,[17] organized "like the TNEC," having representatives from the Senate, the House of Representatives, the Administrative branches of the Federal Government, and the state legislatures, to explore means of preventing and eradicating barriers. Such a committee would have a permanent staff and would have these functions: (1) to engage in research and to analyze problems as they arise; (2) to serve as a clearing house for hearing complaints and gathering facts relating to their merits; and (3) to refer such complaints, when justified, to the states, with suggestions for appropriate action.

Many felt that there was an important area in which the Federal Government could contribute to the removal of barriers. One of the simplest ways by which it might assist is by continuing certain studies and projects already undertaken, such as the researches and publicity programs of the Department of Justice, the Department of Agriculture, the State Department, and the United States Marketing Laws Survey.

There appears, however, to be a need for more than research and publicity; congressional action, too, seems appropriate. Congress

14 *Ibid.*, pp. 15745–15746; see also p. 16110.
15 See *ibid.*, p. 15747 for an impressive list of laws repealed in 1939.
16 *Ibid.*, pp. 15892–15894.   17 *Ibid.*, pp. 15751, 16091, 16110.

alone has power "to regulate commerce among the several States. '
The Constitution prohibits the states from laying any impost or
duties on imports or exports. Although the Congress has the authority
to control interstate traffic, in numerous instances it has not exercised
that right. In the absence of congressional action it has long been
the practice of the courts to permit the states to exercise a substantial
measure of control over interstate commerce.[18] Numerous barriers,
either intentional or unplanned, have resulted, and their elimination
appears to be possible only through the vigorous exercise of the
powers of Congress. Such also appears to be the conclusion of various members of the Supreme Court. Members of the Court, though
reluctant to "legislate" themselves, have pointed the way by citing
the rights of Congress. On one occasion this viewpoint was presented
as follows:

Maintenance of open channels of trade between the States was not only of
paramount importance when our Constitution was framed; it remains today a complex problem calling for national vigilance and regulation. . . .
Congress alone can, in the exercise of its plenary constitutional control
over interstate commerce, not only consider whether such a tax as now
under scrutiny is consistent with the best interests of our national economy, but can also on the basis of full exploration of the many aspects of
a complicated problem devise a national policy fair alike to the States and
our Union. . . . But the remedy, if any is called for, we think is within
ample reach of Congress.[19]

Thus, the Court has clearly defined the position of Congress. The
latter has "plenary" power over interstate commerce, and the remedies to many barriers are within its "ample reach." The exercise of
that power requires a systematic analysis of barriers and legislation to
combat them.

One of the many opportunities for helpful Federal legislation is
in the field of standards. What constitutes "fresh eggs," "a barrel," or
"marketable fruit" are matters which many states have attempted to
define. Because of the multiplicity and diversity of these and numerous other standards they have ofttimes become interstate barriers.
Moreover, at times they have been deliberately manipulated for the
purpose of erecting barriers. A realistic approach would recognize the
simple fact that markets for many products have ceased to be con-

18 *Ibid.*, pp. 15748, 16088.
19 Dissenting opinion of Justices Black, Frankfurter, and Douglas in McCarroll v. Dixie
Greyhound Lines, Inc. (U. S. Sup. Ct. decided Feb. 12, 1940); see also *ibid.*, Part 29, pp.
15750, 15782–15784, 15787.

fined to local communities, and that more and more they involve interstate trade. To facilitate such trade, national standards are needed as well as adequate and effective inspection procedures for plant, animal, and dairy products and for the interstate traffic of motor vehicles. In the absence of Federal standards some progress has been made through the leadership of such organizations as the American Standards Association. By promoting scientifically designed standards, uniform practices among states have been established, and the basis has been laid for reciprocity in recognizing each other's inspection certificates. The establishment of acceptable minimum standards by the Federal Government would facilitate reciprocity among states where there is a will to co-operate and would immediately identify practices deliberately designed to burden commerce.[20]

It would appear, therefore, that legislation is needed both to facilitate interstate co-operation and to penalize deliberate discrimination. The suggestion was made that the Federal Government be authorized to issue certificates of inspection which would serve as interstate passports for the goods inspected.[21] No further inspection, therefore, would be required for the interstate movement of such products as milk, fruit, vegetables, and meat. States desiring to impose restrictions more rigorous than those required by Federal inspection might be permitted to do so, but only if the same rigorous standards were applied to the marketing of intrastate products. Moreover, special penalties might be necessary to punish state officials who, in the administration of the law, discriminate in favor of products of domestic origin.

The system of grants-in-aid has been employed in numerous instances by Congress as an instrument to promote useful social ends and to obtain uniformity among the states. This system offers a partial solution to the problem at hand. Obstructions placed in the way of interstate motor carriers may be taken as illustrative. Inasmuch as aid already is granted through the Federal highway system, the grants-in-aid method may readily be adapted to promote uniformity of taxes, of rules relative to truck size, weight, height, and length, and of other regulations involving the right to use the highways. In all probability, careful analysis will suggest ways to employ similar methods to eliminate barriers in other fields.[22]

---

[20] Various suggestions proposing Federal standards may be found throughout Part 29 of the Hearings; attention is called particularly to pp. 15772, 15777, 15987, 16110.
[21] Ibid., pp. 16101–16103.   [22] Ibid., pp. 15752, 16097–16106.

No attempt was made to outline the complete pattern of Federal legislation which would be required; rather, the recommendation was made that an over-all study be conducted to discover what action would be helpful and to plan specific legislative measures. It was proposed, nevertheless, that the powers of the Interstate Commerce Commission be broadened so that it shall be permitted to prescribe reasonable regulations with respect to vehicle weight, size, height, length, etc., for all state highways whenever a responsible Federal or state agency alleges that existing regulations are unreasonable and constitute barriers to interstate commerce.[23]

There remains another approach to the interstate barrier problem, namely, action through the courts. Although the Supreme Court has refused to "legislate," it has indicated that recourse to the courts is an appropriate procedure. Since the powers of Congress over interstate trade are plenary, the constitutional provision that no state may burden interstate commerce must be interpreted in the light of congressional intent as measured principally by the action of Congress or by its failure to act. Nevertheless, the Court in the *Baldwin v. Seelig* case, said that no state may place itself in economic isolation. Comprehensive and effective measures to remove the manifold interstate obstructions must await action by the states themselves and by Congress; nevertheless, resort to the courts, though a less satisfactory approach, might be employed to good purpose more frequently than it has been.

TECHNOLOGICAL UNEMPLOYMENT

The monumental document containing the hearings on *Technology and the Concentration of Economic Power* includes an impressive collection of data relating to the impact of machine technology upon employment. The hundreds of workers thrown temporarily (or permanently so far as the lives of some of them are concerned) out of work by the adoption of new production techniques may be one of the less significant aspects of the total unemployment problem, but such unemployment, nevertheless, is of major consequence to the individuals involved. Despite the interest of the TNEC and the magnitude of the hearings, however, no comprehensive body of recommendations was presented. A few suggestions were offered, either directly or by inference, though upon analysis some appear to be somewhat superficial.

23 *Ibid.*, p. 16096.

Some of the proposals by labor leaders were reminiscent of spread-the-work, make-work fallacies. Both Mr. Whitney of the Railway Brotherhoods [24] and Mr. Green [25] of the American Federation of Labor proposed shortening the working day or week. To the extent, of course, that such a proposal would enable workers to share a larger portion of the productive output of new machine processes, it presumably has merit, but to the extent that it offers a way of restricting the potential output of both men and machines, it is self-defeating.

Mr. Green advanced a fivefold program for dealing with technological unemployment, including: (1) the assembling of more complete and detailed facts about employment, wages, hours, etc., to make possible an intelligent analysis of the problem; (2) shortening the working week so as to make possible the reabsorption of displaced workers into industry; (3) increasing the national income to make re-employment possible; (4) assurance to workers that they will share in the return from technological improvements; and (5) an exhaustive study of employment opportunities. Some of these suggestions are somewhat nebulous and constitute aspirations only rather than a blueprint for procedures.

A bit more specific were the recommendations of Mr. Murray of the CIO dealing directly with the problem of technological unemployment. His plan contained five parts: (1) companies installing labor-displacing techniques should reabsorb the displaced workers in the regular turnover of employees; (2) workers should be notified in advance of actual displacement, during which time they should be given vocational guidance and training by the company to fit them for other posts; (3) workers for whom such jobs are unavailable should be employed in some capacity, and their wages should be charged to the cost of installing the new equipment; (4) workers who suffer a reduction of 10 percent or more of their earnings as a result of being absorbed at lower paying jobs should be given job compensation equal to a percentage of their total earnings with the company before the new techniques rendered their skills obsolete; and (5) wherever it is impossible thus to absorb workers on other jobs, they should be paid a dismissal wage based in part on the length of their service.[26]

It would appear that the most specific and, perhaps, the most practicable proposal for dealing with technological unemployment is the dismissal wage, which was supported by industrialists, labor leaders,

24 *Ibid.*, Part 30, pp. 16906, 16915.   25 *Ibid.*, p. 17134.
26 *Ibid.*, pp. 16506–16507.

and economists. The president of the American Roller Mill Company described the policy his company adopted in 1929 when substituting new finishing mills for the old-style hot-mill production. When the conversion was made, the company announced that it would place as many of the men as possible in the new mills. Men who could not thus be placed, except those who had been with the company less than one year, were guaranteed half pay (but not less than $50 per month) for as many months (not to exceed six months) as they had spent years in service. The company reported that it had placed most of the men and in addition had paid separation allowances totaling nearly $300,000 to about 600 workers. Moreover, a good many of these men eventually obtained jobs at the new plant.[27]

Severance pay had also been guaranteed in labor union contracts negotiated between the American Communications Association (CIO) and some of its employers. The Mackay Radio and Telegraph Company guaranteed to retrain workers at company expense to aid them in acquiring the skills necessary to operate the new installations. The R.C.A.C. (Radio Corporation of America Communications) agreed to give six months' notice in advance of proposed mechanization changes, during which time opportunities for retraining would be available and no new employees would be added in the departments affected. In a later contract the Mackay Radio and Telegraph Company guaranteed that an employee dismissed because of technological changes would be given severance pay in proportion to his years of service.[28] Although other unions have obtained similar clauses in their contracts, those which have been described appear to have been the most comprehensive with respect to technological displacement; [29] they may point the way to a more general approach to the problem.

The schemes involving the dismissal wage thus far discussed depend either upon voluntary action by the employer or upon the bargaining ability of the union to obtain such a concession. Commissioner Lubin voiced the consideration, however, that the technological displacement of labor is one of the costs incidental to an improving technology and that such costs should fall, not upon the laborers, but upon consumers—in other words, upon the public, the real beneficiaries of a more productive economy. To provide for a more equitable system of social bookkeeping Mr. Lubin proposed that severance pay be made compulsory. He contended that the social

[27] *Ibid.*, p. 16448.   [28] *Ibid.*, p. 16750.   [29] *Ibid.*, p. 16756.

effects of such a program would resemble those of workmen's compensation laws, which not only have provided protection for workers but, also by throwing the responsibility upon employers, have tended to prevent the occurrence of the very situation for which protection was sought.

THE CONSUMER

A portion of the hearings was devoted to problems of the consumer, during which witnesses outlined reforms they would like to see initiated. Because of the selection of the witnesses, including leaders from various consumer groups, there was general agreement as to what ought to be done. The Consumer's Counsel of the Department of Agriculture summarized these recommendations as follows:

1) That standards of consumer goods whereby their quality and usefulness for consumers may be accurately described be made available for use in the sale of such goods . . . that the definition of such standards should be undertaken by the Government.

2) That the sizes of packages in which foods are sold to consumers be standardized to eliminate confusion and deception.

3) That the committee ascertain and make known to consumers the effects of resale price maintenance legislation upon retail prices and upon the other factors involved.

4) That this committee investigate and make known to consumers the facts concerning the performance of commodity rating agencies, the use of advertising material in the schools, and the purposes, financing and programs of organizations which are, or which purport to be, organizations of consumers.

5) The proposal made in February, 1938, by a number of consumer spokesmen that a central agency of consumer services be established in the Federal Government was placed before the committee.[30]

The emphasis throughout the consumer hearings was upon the first two points, involving the need for reliable standards to guide the buyer and to aid him in getting his money's worth. It is an old story with which many are familiar—the inability of consumers to rely upon brand names as tests of quality or upon price as a measure of worth; it is a story of the unreliability of advertising claims and the general meaninglessness of labels. Hence, the witnesses asked for measures to end confusion among consumers and to supply reliable tests for the things which they buy.

THE PROBLEM OF DEPRESSIONS

The TNEC met nearly a decade after the beginning of the Great

30 *Ibid.*, Part 8, p. 3454.

Depression and was called into being by the Recession of 1937. It is not too much to say that finding a solution for the puzzle of depressions constitutes the chief economic problem of the century and was by far the most outstanding confronting the TNEC. Despite this fact one looks through the hearings in vain for a comprehensive body of recommendations for coping with these crises. A number of proposals directed toward this problem were made, however, including those of Professor Hansen.

Income distribution.—During the first few days of the hearings the suggestion was made by Commissioner Lubin that there should be a more equitable distribution of income. Since mass production is dependent upon mass consumption, the success of capitalism, he said, depends upon mass distribution of purchasing power. Too small a portion of the nation's population, however, receive incomes sufficient to provide a market for the abundance of goods which the economy is capable of producing. The economic system broke down in 1929, not because of any inherent structural defect, but from faulty operation. Mr. Lubin said:

To me it is a problem of keeping the gears of the economic machine constantly in mesh. I don't know any other way of keeping them in mesh than by so distributing our income that it will pull into our homes, through a higher standard of living, the goods, that is, the clothing, food, entertainment, education, and so forth, which our economic machine must turn out at a rate considerably higher than at the present time, even if we were to get back to a standard no higher than that of 1929.[31]

If the incomes of the 10,000,000 families in America receiving less than $1,250 a year (in 1935–1936) were raised by the equivalent of $2.25 a day, according to the pattern of American consumption habits they would expand their purchases in an almost unbelievable fashion.

They would buy $800,000,000 worth of food more than they buy now; they would increase their purchasing of clothing by $416,000,000; they would increase their purchase of housing or rents by $613,000,000; they would spend $213,000,000 more on fuel, light, and refrigeration; they would spend $385,000,000 more on transportation, automobiles, etc.; they would spend $73,000,000 more on personal care; they would spend $234,000,000 more on recreation; they would spend $208,000,000 more on medical care.[32]

Were incomes raised above that level, a point soon would be reached where the productive capacity of the country would need to be materially expanded. Thus, although a wider distribution of the incomes

[31] *Ibid.*, Part 1, p. 79.   [32] *Ibid.*, p. 76.

and purchasing power may not offer the ultimate and complete solution to the phenomena of the business cycle, it would constitute a more secure foundation for a stable economic structure.

The capital market.—As might be expected, a number of witnesses who understood the implications of the trade cycle were more concerned with the breakdown of investment and its relation to savings than with the breakdown of purchasing power, however closely related the two may be both in cause and consequences. Typical of the proposals to deal with the problem of lagging investments were those offered by the Superintendent of Banks of the State of New York, by the Assistant Secretary of State, by a Minneapolis bank executive, and by Professor Hansen.

The Superintendent of Banks of the State of New York had a suggestion which, though it did not constitute a solution to the over-all problem, might offer partial relief.[33] He called attention to the fact that there are many savings banks and trust institutions throughout the country with large reservoirs of savings seeking investment. Moreover, economists have shown that the failure of investments to equal savings has been an important factor in the generation of economic crises. Savings institutions throughout the country are required by law to limit their portfolios to a select list of bonds, principally those of the Federal, state, and municipal governments, railways, and public utilities. In order to "keep open the channels by which savings flow into capital investments," he suggested that the legal powers of these financial institutions be broadened to permit the purchase of a wider variety of securities. This, he said, could be done, without relaxing the standards by which eligible bonds are chosen, by enabling the banks to invest in fields hitherto closed to them, such as industrial bonds, or by giving bank directors broader powers of discretion, such as they already enjoy in Massachusetts.

One of the boldest proposals for the development of new construction was that offered by Assistant Secretary of State Berle; he recommended the creation of capital banks—or a public works finance corporation—to provide a type of banking for new investment and construction which would function as satisfactorily as commercial banks do in their field.[34] What is needed, Mr. Berle thought, is a new division of the banking system to handle capital matters—one which would defray its own expenses, pay a nominal return on its own capital, but quote interest rates sufficiently low to encourage worth-while

33 *Ibid.*, pp. 3792–3809.   34 *Ibid.*, pp. 3809–3835.

and needed construction. Such an institution would not be guided by the desire to show handsome profits. It could operate soundly, but at low profits, as do the Federal Reserve banks and mutual life insurance companies, and it could establish service as a test of efficiency. The interest rate would be controlled "to get work done," lowering it "when you want more work done, raising it when you don't want it done, exactly as the Federal Reserve Banks do with their commercial banking rates." [35] Thus, whenever any person, corporation, or governmental agency needs capital to construct useful additions to the capital plant of the country, lower rates would be available, but if anybody wanted capital for a use which would pyramid inflation, he would be turned down regardless of the rate offered.

There are plenty of opportunities, said Mr. Berle, for capital outlay. High interest rates, however, deter the construction of many useful projects. Noncommercial business such as hospitals and semicommercial business such as low-cost housing cannot afford to pay commercial rates of interest. Hence, despite the need for new investment and despite the problem of idle savings, such projects are not undertaken. There are plenty of outlets for capital, but the necessary avenues for financing have not been developed. The new banks would have the dynamic task of helping to balance investment to savings. Mr. Berle described this task as follows:

. . . it seems to me that our first concern ought to be to work out a banking system which can quote a rate of interest which will take the business. If that rate happens to be a nominal one for something which isn't going to make any profit, then that is the rate to quote. If it happens to be, let us say, a 1- or 1½- or 2-percent rate for the middle-class or lower-middle-class housing which is not being built by anybody today, then quote that rate. If it happens to be a commercial enterprise, making the standard commercial profit which can pay a standard commercial rate, then quote that rate. For after all, what is this money that we are using? It is the creation by a banking system of currency under a Federal license, and the only reason for quoting any interest rate at all is to induce the bank to function.[36]

In other words, what is needed is a banking institution which, on a self-sustaining basis, quotes a capital rate equal to what the project can pay. Mr. Berle implied that our economy—which has both the need for capital investment and the men and materials with which to supply it—may someday be so constituted that saying "you haven't the money for it" will merely be a comic remark.

35 *Ibid.*, p. 3821.   36 *Ibid.*, p. 3820.

Another approach to the problem created by the disequilibrium between savings and investment was presented by Ralph W. Manuel, president of the Marquette National Bank of Minneapolis.[37] He proposed that individuals be compelled to use the full amount of their income. The total money value of all income received and of all things produced balance, of course. But if some people neglect to return to the market the full amount of money income received, purchasing power is drained off, and falling prices and deflation follow.

The stream of money income may be returned to the market either through the process of spending for consumption or through investment. The latter involves savings. Saving, however, may take place without investment, and when it does, purchasing power is lost to the stream. This process frequently is referred to as hoarding. The most common method of hoarding is idle commercial bank balances (amounting in 1939 to about $4,000,000,000). Something must be done to discourage hoarding, since, when it occurs, it dams up the economic stream and creates crises. Something must be done to assure that all who receive income shares from the economic system exercise those shares by taking them in the forms of goods and services. Especially is it necessary to provide that income saved comes back through the money markets.

Mr. Manuel would make a direct attack upon hoarding. Using the income tax system as a vehicle, he would require each taxpayer to account for all income received and thereby disclose whether or not any part of it had not been returned to the stream of income.[38] If the income recipient could show that all income had been consumed or invested or placed with third parties who had assumed that obligation for him, no penalty would attach. If, however, certain portions had been withdrawn from the stream—hoarded—some form of tax, or escheat, would apply. A tax somewhat less than 100 percent probably would suffice. Thus, instead of attempting, as has been the practice, to make investment so attractive that it will lure risk capital to activity, it may be necessary in our highly industrialized system of private ownership, to penalize hoarding. To fail to do so is to run the risk of an inevitable imbalance between savings and investment and consequent economic collapse.

Offsets to savings.—The TNEC got closer to the core of its problem with the testimony presented by Dr. Alvin H. Hansen than at any

---

[37] *Ibid.*, pp. 3706–3726.   [38] *Ibid.*, p. 3711.

other time.[39] Two aspects of America's foremost economic problem are the recurrence of depressions and the underemployment of men and resources. Because of the high development of our production techniques and the fact that our economic institutions permit not only private property but also a marked degree of concentration of ownership of the means of production, we have developed a high production economy and, even more important, a high savings economy as well. Remarkable as has been the progress of production, our economy is, no doubt, even more notable because of the proportion of the social income which is saved. Inasmuch as savings may be either invested or hoarded, the possibility of hoarding has become a perpetual threat to the health of the economic system.

The basic problem is to keep the income stream flowing. Consumption and investment out of income do so, automatically. Hoarding, however, dries up a portion of the stream and provokes an economic crisis. In a high savings economy, therefore, the key to full employment is continuous capital outlay—continuous investment of savings. Professor Hansen said, "It is necessary to have an offset for all saving. Otherwise, you will have a decline of national income." [40] Capital outlay for the expansion of plant and equipment is the dynamic factor in the income stream. The rise and fall of such expenditures causes income to be high or low, and the rise and fall of consumption is a result of the rise and fall of employment incident to the rise and fall of capital outlays on plant and equipment.

. . . money spent or withheld for capital outlays is high-powered money . . . a high savings economy will remain a highly dynamic economy so long as it is able to experience periodically great bursts of capital outlays on plant and equipment. It is then a dynamic, rapidly expanding, and progressive economy, despite its instability. But if such an economy fails to find adequate investment outlets in plant and equipment for its new savings and for its depreciation allowances, it will lose its dynamic quality and become a depressed and stagnant economy, with a large volume of chronic unemployment. The high-savings economy can escape a fall in income and employment only through the continuous development of new outlets for capital expenditures on industrial plant and equipment and on commercial, residential, and public construction.[41]

Thus, if we are to enjoy full recovery and full employment, says Professor Hansen, we must have outlays for capital goods expansion sufficient to absorb all our savings. Such outlays or investments may be either private or public. It is doubtful, however, whether with

[39] *Ibid.*, pp. 3538 ff.   [40] *Ibid.*, p. 3539.   [41] *Ibid.*, p. 3503.

existing economic institutions private investment will ever be sufficient to absorb all the savings. Hence, Hansen believes that public outlays will be necessary to supplement private and to keep the income stream flowing.[42]

Large outlays of public capital may be necessary as a permanent feature of the economy if we are to enjoy an expanding economy and avoid depressions. Such expenditures need not, of course, be like those made by the Nazis in Germany to build and maintain a military regime, or like those forced upon the United States by the Axis conquests, which did, nevertheless, suddenly produce recovery and full employment. There are many useful projects for which public outlays may be made—projects which will expand the patrimony of the state, which, themselves, will produce income or broaden the social and cultural benefits to the population as a whole. Such opportunities for public investment would include projects such as roads, dams, schools, rural electrification, hospitals, sewerage projects, low-cost housing, etc.[43] Some of these undertakings, of course, would be self-liquidating.

An alternative, or, more accurately, a method complementary to public investment, would be the use of public expenditures to create a high consumption economy.[44] This might be done by subsidizing the consumer and increasing private consumption by providing a wider variety of public services in the field of health, recreation, housing, and the like.

To provide these services and to make the requisite public investments involves policies of public finance. But such policies would be involved even were there no necessity for increased governmental expenditures. Hansen recommended a thoroughgoing study of the tax system to adapt it to the needs of the business cycle.[45] Taxes, he said, should bear more heavily upon savings,[46] not upon consumption, so that when used for public investment they would offset savings, and when used otherwise, would create a high consumption economy. Our present tax structure—Federal, state, and local—by bearing too heavily upon consumption is one of the numerous factors causing depressions.

CONCENTRATION AND MONOPOLY

In view of the fact that the TNEC was chartered by Congress to conduct a study of monopoly and the concentration of economic

[42] *Ibid.*, pp. 3546 ff.   [43] *Ibid.*, p. 3548.   [44] *Ibid.*, p. 3838.
[45] *Ibid.*, pp. 3543-3544.   [46] *Ibid.*, p. 3554.

power, it was to be expected that a few proposals would be directed to this aspect of economic life. At least three recommendations dealt with monopoly in particular industries—one in the milk industry and two in the petroleum industry. Inasmuch as the great milk combinations in the eastern sections of the United States had, to a very substantial extent, established their control through the ownership of pasteurization plants, it was suggested that these plants be given the status of public utilities. Since the law often requires pasteurization as a public health measure and the plants thereby constitute unavoidable gateways to commerce, it seems appropriate that, like the historic grist mills, they be required to serve all who come and at reasonable rates. Only thus would independent distributors be able to operate and only thus would a semblance of free competition be maintained.

That the great integrated petroleum companies dominate the oil industry was quite evident. That by their unified control over oil wells, refineries, pipe lines, tankers, and marketing organizations they are able to drive independent refiners and retailers from the field also seemed evident. Their ability to do so developed, sometimes, not from efficiency, but from their ability to use the resources at their command to the disadvantage of independents. The integrated producers appeared to be using the profits from pipe lines (part of which profits were contributed by receipts from the independents themselves) to subsidize refining and retailing activities. Against this competition independents could not endure, leaving the field, more and more, to the control of the large companies.

Hence, the representatives of the independent oil retailers asked the TNEC to initiate measures to require compulsory divorcement of the various stages of petroleum production.[47] Each stage of production would thereupon be required to stand on its own feet and, through competition, to justify its existence. Only thus, it was felt, could independent retailers or refiners prove their worth and remain in business, since their competitors could no longer rely upon profits contributed from other stages of the production process.

A series of related suggestions called for the divorcement of the pipe lines from other stages of the petroleum industry and for the extension of effective public utility control over them. The reasoning by which these proposals were supported was as follows: pipe-line profits are high [48] and frequently are employed to subsidize other

47 *Ibid.*, Part 16, pp. 8852–8861, 8898.
48 *Ibid.*, Part 14, pp. 7106, 7233–7241, 7262, 7337–7343, 7376.

branches of the industry owned by the integrated companies. Moreover, although pipe lines technically are public utilities, they are not so in effect.[49] Although their costs of transportation are relatively low,[50] pipe-line charges and published tariffs ordinarily are no lower than those of the railroads.[51] Hence, even though independents may avail themselves of the service of the pipe lines, they are not permitted to enjoy the economic advantages of this low-cost type of transportation—the benefits accruing to the integrated companies as owners. Consequently, payments by independents to pipe lines are, in effect, drawbacks or rebates which their competitors receive for the transportation of their products.[52] The proposal was made, therefore, that pipe lines be required to disassociate themselves from corporations engaged in other branches of the industry. As had been done thirty years earlier in the case of the railroads by the means of the commodities clause, pipe lines would be denied the right to haul their own products. Only thus, it was felt, would their public utility status be made effective.[53] Pipe-line corporations could then be required to serve all comers at reasonable rates and could be compelled to declare their dividends directly to stockholders so that these funds would not be available as a war chest to be employed to the detriment of the independents and to perfect market control.

In addition to recommendations relating to monopoly in specific industries, a number of general proposals were made. The most important of these was the suggestion that antitrust prosecution be pursued more vigorously. Chairman O'Mahoney pressed his plan for Federal charters for corporations engaged in interstate commerce.[54] He believed that corporations could be constrained through their charters, and through the power to annul them, from engaging in harmful monopoly practices. Another suggestion involved broadening the powers of the Federal Trade Commission by permitting it to aid the Judiciary by acting as a master of chancery in antitrust cases.[55] Then, there was the proposal mentioned in a previous chapter that the right to organize holding companies be abolished.[56]

More rigorous prosecution of the antitrust laws commended itself to several who appeared before the TNEC. One of America's foremost authorities on monopoly, Dr. Fetter, stated the monopoly laws

[49] *Ibid.*, pp. 7199, 7235, 7251, 7271, 7275, 7329, 7385.
[50] *Ibid.*, pp. 7178–7180, 7252.   [51] *Ibid.*, p. 7251.
[52] *Ibid.*, pp. 7233, 7235, 7256, 7262, 7275, 7338, 7377, 7386.
[53] *Ibid.*, pp. 7236, 7249, 7275, 7377–7378.   [54] *Ibid.*, Part 5, p. 1849.
[55] *Ibid.*, Part 11, p. 5155.   [56] *Ibid.*, Part 5, pp. 1677, 1710.

had "been very inadequately enforced without earnest purpose and without adequate means." [57] The Antitrust Division of the Department of Justice seldom has had more than fifteen lawyers, whereas large corporations brought to trial often have maintained a large staff of fifty or sixty. The most persistent advocate of antitrust action was TNEC member Thurman Arnold, the Assistant Attorney General.[58] To him the antitrust suit is not an end in itself but has for its objective the establishment of a "free and independent economy." Nor is it the policy of the Antitrust Division or the courts to use such prosecution to strike down all combinations and monopoly. "Combinations which are necessary in a machine age to create efficient mass production or distribution, and which pass the savings on to consumers, are not unreasonable under the antitrust laws." [59]

Mr. Arnold held that the proper approach to the monopoly problem is by litigation rather than by the issuance of declaratory judgments. However much business men may desire advance rulings concerning the legality of contemplated practices, to him such a procedure is quite as unfeasible as asking the umpire at a baseball game to rule in advance of the play whether or not the runner was out. To the Department of Justice the proper procedure is the case method, approaching each situation as it arises and being guided by the facts which apply. Either of two types of suit is available to the Government—criminal or equity. The latter is preferred, because it makes possible the use of the civil or consent decree, thereby opening the door "for any group which wishes to propose a constructive solution for the problems of its industry." [60]

The civil decree differs from the declaratory judgment in that it renders no advance ruling on business practices, but works out a solution to an actual problem which has arisen. The consent decree is not a device "for smuggling unlawful cartels into American economic life, nor for freeing offenders from penalties." [61] It does, however, offer a means of ending violations of the law and of safeguarding the public against the continuation of monopolistic practices. The Department of Justice does not attempt to tell industry what it should do, nor does the law permit it to.[62] Mr. Arnold described the Department's position thus: "A dog talks by barking and we talk

[57] *Ibid.*, pp. 1979–1980.
[58] *Ibid.*, Part 11, pp. 5144–5161.
[59] *Ibid.*, p. 5146.
[60] *Ibid.*, p. 5154.
[61] *Ibid.*
[62] Representatives of the Department of Justice oppose any law which would give it such power.

through litigation." [63] Once litigation has begun and the pertinent facts have been revealed, however, should the representatives of the industry come forward and say, "We are under constant attack, we don't like the present situation," [64] and then offer a plan to correct the practices about which the Justice Department complains, the latter will give their proposal careful consideration, and if deemed in the public interest they will recommend to the court that a civil decree be issued. The industry, in effect, is thus permitted to write its own injunction, which becomes effective only if approved by the department and the court. The decree constitutes an order of the court, and its violation is punishable as an act of contempt.

Somewhat opposed to a policy of vigorous antitrust prosecution is the suggestion that some agency in the Government, such as the Federal Trade Commission or the Department of Justice, be empowered to render advance opinions with respect to contemplated business practices which might, if adopted, run afoul of the monopoly laws. The idea is not new; President Wilson supported such a policy when recommending the legislation resulting in the Clayton and the Federal Trade Commission acts. He felt that there should be some authority to which business could go for an advance opinion—a declaratory judgment—rather than wait for decisions of the court after a lengthy and expensive period of litigation. [65] This policy found favor with several who appeared before the Committee, including TNEC member Jerome Frank [66] and Charles Hook, [67] former president of the National Association of Manufacturers. A declaratory judgment would be issued only after a formal hearing before a public body at which all interested parties would be heard and only after an analysis of the relevant facts. Business men, when acting in good faith, so it was claimed, would then be free from uncertainty and fear and would be adequately forewarned if their proposition were contrary to the law and to the public interest.

The agencies of the Government having first-hand experience with monopoly control were inclined to look with disfavor upon the issuance of declaratory judgments. Both the Department of Justice and the Federal Trade Commission opposed the plan. One infers that they fear the proposal is not made in good faith by some of its proponents. There are numerous decisions of courts as well as many

[63] *Hearings before the Temporary National Economic Committee*, Part 11, p. 5160.
[64] *Ibid.*, p. 5159.   [65] *Ibid.*, Part 5, p. 1789.
[66] *Ibid.*, pp. 1791, 1811.   [67] *Ibid.*, Part 20, p. 10811.

rulings by the Federal Trade Commission for those who seek guidance with respect to proposed combinations and practices. Ofttimes, it was held, men know what the law is, but seek new avenues of circumvention. From such an authorizing agency apparently they desire to discover in advance, not how to conform with the spirit of the law, but how far they can go,[68] or perchance to obtain a green light or a blank check for specific practices unrevealed.[69] Moreover, these agencies did not believe that a Government body could foresee all the contingencies and ramifications of the policies upon which they might be called to render advance judgment. Guidance from precedent was held to be a more satisfactory approach than endorsement of the unknown.[70]

A materially different approach to the monopoly problem would substitute self-rule in business for government control. Many witnesses representing business and industry, either by practices they had adopted or by proposals they made, indicated their endorsement of the principle of self-rule. Such a policy would, in effect, involve the repeal of the Sherman Act and other monopoly laws. The president of the Anaconda Copper Mining Company advocated their outright repeal; he proposed that business firms be permitted to get together to "co-operate" in the production, sale, and distribution of their products. Moreover, the Government should be authorized "to compel industry to conform" with the decisions made. Thus, industry would "be subject to regulation, but not regulated by" the Government. According to a former president of the National Association of Manufacturers the members of an industry should be permitted wider freedom "to get together to discuss costs and price without fear of prosecution." This, he indicated, would involve arriving at some decision as to what constitutes a "fair price" and as to the methods by which such a price should be maintained.[71] He endorsed the posted price system as an effective means of securing the desired unity.

PUBLIC SESSIONS TO CONSIDER RECOMMENDATIONS

Nearly a year after the last general hearings the TNEC held public sessions for the consideration of recommendations. During the interval between January 15 and March 11, 1941, twelve sessions were held "at which the TNEC virtually talked to itself." [72] Those who

[68] Ibid., Part 5, p. 1809.   [69] Ibid., pp. 1805–1806, 1809–1811.
[70] Ibid., Part 5, p. 1811.
[71] Hearings before the Temporary National Economic Committee, Part 20, pp. 10812–10816.   [72] Business Week, March 22, 1941, p. 22.

offered statements were principally TNEC members or staff members from the administrative branches represented on the Committee. In a few cases others appeared, presenting viewpoints endorsed by the department members. Proposals by representatives of business—industrialists, bankers, and merchantmen—were not, therefore, presented, nor were there recommendations by experts in the fields of public finance, money and banking, cycle theory, and business organization. When the TNEC was first organized, it was generally understood that the final hearings would constitute something of an open forum where all who desired to be helpful might be heard. Hearings of such a nature did not materialize.

Chairman O'Mahoney was careful to say that the views presented were for consideration only and did not, therefore, represent those of the Committee.[73] Almost every speaker thereafter indicated that his remarks represented personal convictions and hence did not commit either his department or the Administration. The statement of Assistant Attorney General Arnold is typical: "these recommendations simply represent my own ideas and the ideas of the economists and lawyers on the whole staff. They cannot even be considered as recommendations of the Department of Justice." [74] The views of those who spoke varied as widely as do laissez faire and mercantilism. Some proposed leaving things to "God's laws," while others urged positive reforms relative to monopoly, insurance, patents, the consumer, and the business cycle.

Vice Chairman Sumners offered no formal statement; nevertheless, his remarks, interspersed now and then, left little doubt as to his position, which came very close to unqualified laissez faire. He spoke of a plan of nature and a living God whose designs ought not to be disturbed. He said, "It seems to me that He could have made everything all right so nobody would have had to do anything, and there wouldn't have been any necessity to struggle." [75] As an appropriate corollary to this, the vice chairman repeatedly spoke of the inappropriateness of Federal action and of the importance of moving "the power and the responsibility back toward the people." [76]

What business is it of yours up here at Washington [asked Mr. Sumners] to tell my people down in Texas what to do? . . . There are people down in the State, they have a State legislature, they have their merchants and mercantile business. What business is it to Washington messing up with

[73] *Final Report and Recommendations of the Temporary National Economic Committee,* p. 97.   [74] *Ibid.,* p. 98.
[75] *Ibid.,* p. 601; see also p. 287.   [76] *Ibid.,* p. 601.

those people? . . . I would like to see you gentlemen of the Federal Government stay out and let them take care of their mustard plaster.[77]

One of three recommendations offered by the Department of Commerce was that a program of business and economic research be undertaken. This might constitute an elaboration of what President Roosevelt referred to in his original TNEC message when he called for a Bureau of Industrial Economics. As conceived of by the Department of Commerce, the agency would function under its direction and would provide for a flow of current data on the national economy —on production, orders, inventories, productive capacity, resources, movement of goods, business practices, and business fluctuations.[78] It was felt that if business men could operate with more complete knowledge of the contingencies they face, the economic system would operate more smoothly. Such a program of fact finding would not, of course, remedy the more fundamental dislocations of the economy, but it would furnish a more dependable basis for the formulation of national economic policy.

MONOPOLY

Various measures were proposed to deal with the problems of monopoly and the concentration of industry. Vigorous enforcement of the monopoly laws was endorsed more widely than any other suggestion. Championed, of course, by Mr. Arnold of the Department of Justice, such a policy was supported by others including the Consumers' Counsel,[79] the Federal Trade Commission,[80] the economic adviser to the Department of Agriculture,[81] as well as TNEC members O'Connell [82] and Pike.[83] Dr. Ezekiel warned, however, that antitrust action would not remedy the basic dislocations of the economic system. He emphasized the fact that much of the economic concentration which characterizes such industries as automobiles, steel, and aluminum is the result of inevitable economic laws and the ability of the large concerns to produce at lower cost than small concerns. He declared, "We can't restore small units of production [and force] giant concerns to operate like thousands of individually competing small concerns or to break them up without serious loss of economic productivity."

Many agreed with Mr. Arnold that vigorous antitrust action was

[77] Ibid., p. 133.
[78] Final Report and Recommendations of the Temporary National Economic Committee, p. 329.
[79] Ibid., p. 441.
[80] Ibid., p. 311.
[81] Ibid., p. 425.
[82] Ibid., pp. 643, 651.
[83] Ibid., p. 493.

called for.[84] He recommended an increased appropriation for both the Antitrust Division and the Federal Trade Commission.[85] He pointed out, however, that this would impose no additional burden on the Treasury, since the Antitrust Division generally brings in more revenue than it receives. It was further recommended that the budget of the Antitrust Division should permit the enlargement of its staff to follow up decrees issued by the courts. Mr. Arnold proposed, moreover, that "listening posts" be established in each state to hear consumers' complaints and to maintain a watchful eye over the effectiveness of the antitrust laws.

A more important role was urged for the Federal Trade Commission. This would involve performing existing functions more effectively as well as the extension of its duties. It was indicated that the Commission's staff is insufficient to handle the wide variety of cases before it, particularly restraint cases.[86] A larger staff, principally of trial attorneys and trial examiners, is necessary. Representatives of both the Department of Justice and the Federal Trade Commission agreed that the Federal Trade Commission Act should be amended to permit the Commission to act as master of chancery for the court, and to aid it by hearing evidence, making findings, and suggesting the appropriate form of decree in equity cases.[87] These increased responsibilities for the Commission would, of course, necessitate an increased budget.

Proposal to amend Section 7 of the Clayton Act. — Another proposed revision of the law related to Section 7 of the Clayton Act. In this instance the Federal Trade Commission merely reaffirmed the position it had taken in the earlier hearings which had been supported in the Preliminary Report of the TNEC.[88] The Commission proposed:

1) That Section 7 of the Clayton Act be amended so as to render unlawful, not only the acquisition of the stock, but also the acquisition of the assets of a corporation or corporations where one or more of the effects specified in Section 7 of the act, as now in effect, may follow.

2) That paragraph 2 of the Section . . . be amended so as to cover the acquisition of the stock of one or more corporations, instead of two or more as in the present form. This paragraph covers acquisitions by a holding company, and it is manifest that if the holding company acquires the stock of a company in substantial competition with one of its subsidiaries,

84 *Ibid.*, pp. 98–142.   85 *Ibid.*, pp. 117–118.
86 *Ibid.*, pp. 299, 308–311.   87 *Ibid.*, pp. 137, 311.
88 S. Doc. 95, 76th Cong., 1st sess., 1939.

there is or may be the same restriction or destruction of competition as in the acquisition of two competing companies.

3) That the Section be further amended so as to prevent its being effective to close what may be the only available market for the assets of a corporation in bankruptcy or in immediate danger of bankruptcy. A competitor of the corporation in financial difficulties may often be the only available market for its assets and it is believed that permitting an acquisition under such circumstances will not defeat the purposes of the paragraph, provided the provision is so safeguarded as to prevent the bringing about of a competitor's financial difficulties by collusion for the purpose of evading the prohibitions of the paragraph.

4) If Section 7 is amended as above proposed, it will be necessary also to amend Section 11 by inserting the words "or assets" after the word "stock," so that the Federal Trade Commission may be authorized to order a corporation found to have violated Section 7 to divest itself of both stock and assets unlawfully acquired.[89]

Federal charters for corporations.—It would be expected that Chairman O'Mahoney would recommend what he and Senator Borah already had proposed to the Congress—the requirement of Federal charters for corporations engaged in interstate commerce.[90] In this he was supported by those who spoke for the Department of Justice [91] and the Federal Trade Commission.[92] Though Chairman O'Mahoney did not press his reasons, he indicated that Federal charters would eliminate state competition resulting in the lax granting of charters which, under the "equal rights" clause, were tantamount to national charters without national responsibility. The chairman argued that Federal charters were necessary to control corporate concentration, which otherwise would result in greater concentration of Federal powers. Such charters, it was claimed, might serve as an effective restraint against monopoly and unfair methods of competition, since they can be so devised that if the chartered corporations violate certain designated regulations, they automatically will lose their right to continue in business.

Compulsory registration of mergers.—The chief counsel of the Federal Trade Commission and the Assistant Attorney General, as well as Representative O'Connell, agreed that compulsory registration of mergers would lend material support to antitrust enforcement.[93] Corporations should be required by statute to register in advance with some agency, such as the Federal Trade Commission or

[89] *Final Report and Recommendations of the Temporary National Economic Committee*, pp. 293–294.
[90] *Ibid.*, pp. 632, 681–683.　　　　[91] *Ibid.*, p. 284.
[92] *Ibid.*, p. 294.　　　　[93] *Ibid.*, pp. 122, 294–297.

the Securities and Exchange Commission, any contemplated change by means of which a given percentage (e. g., 50 percent) of the national output of any commodity is brought under a single control. Registration would be required thirty days in advance of the merger, during which time the Department of Justice and the Commission would be authorized to require the submission of any information relevant to the public interest. Such action, it was felt, would be salutory, making it possible to restrain combinations before harm is done. Moreover, it would obviate the necessity of "unscrambling the eggs in the industrial omelet" after such an assignment has been rendered difficult, if not impossible. Once a merger has been consummated and a going industrial concern has been established, dissolution becomes difficult and cannot be effected without harm and perhaps injustice to some. In view of these difficulties courts often are reluctant to grant a dissolution as complete as would be necessary to give adequate public protection. Moreover, dissolution can be effected only after a long period of litigation and only after a plan has been approved by the court. A more satisfactory method would be to require advance registration with a period for public examination during which the Department of Justice would be able to announce its intent of prosecution or agree to a consent decree.

Regulate trade associations.—Only TNEC member Mr. O'Connell presented a program to control the powerful trade associations.[94] He advocated that they be required to register with an agency selected by the Congress and that they be obliged to make periodic reports relating to their organization and activities. Registration statements and reports would thus "assure open covenants openly arrived at" and would serve to simplify issues of law and fact; they would also assure a social orientation of trade association objectives and facilitate government intervention when the public interest required it. Mr. O'Connell would have the Congress define more clearly the permissible activities of trade associations and provide a clear-cut demarkation between what is prohibited and what is not. Certain practices should be specifically outlawed. He would require that the statistical activities of trade associations be given wide publicity to inform buyers as well as sellers. In fact, he would create a government agency, perhaps a Bureau of Industrial Economics, to aid business in the collection, analysis, and dissemination of such data.

Repeal the Miller-Tydings Act.—Several, including Mr. Arnold

94 *Ibid.,* pp. 642–645.

and the Consumers' Counsel, recommended the repeal of the Miller-Tydings amendment to the Sherman Act,[95] which has served as a charter for the so-called "fair trade" statutes of the forty states. Mr. Arnold denounced "fair trade" laws as antagonistic to the antitrust laws and as cloaks for many conspiracies in restraint of trade. The Antitrust Division filed a statement presenting, more or less in full, the case against resale price maintenance.[96]

Joint Federal-State Committee on Inter-governmental Relations. —In the earlier hearings the executive director of the Council of State Governments proposed the organization of a mixed legislative and administrative committee "something like the TNEC" to study economic problems relating to interstate trade barriers. The Department of Commerce, through the medium of the Interdepartmental Committee on Interstate Trade Barriers and the Council of State Governments, commended this plan to the TNEC for its approval.[97] This approach was endorsed by the Assistant Attorney General,[98] the Secretary of Agriculture,[99] and Dr. Ezekiel.[100] Such a committee would be organized principally to investigate the hundreds of laws now contributing to interstate trade barriers and to conduct comprehensive economic research with respect to all laws tending to impede the flow of commerce between the states. It would make recommendations jointly to the Federal and state governments and proposed measures by which such barriers could be removed.[101]

Small business clinics.—Related to the problem of monopoly and concentration is the plight of the small business establishment. The Securities and Exchange Commission and the Department of Commerce were particularly concerned with this problem. Commissioner Pike advocated the establishment of small business clinics, or a Bureau for Small Business, to aid the small business man to survive and to preserve the vigor of the competitive system.[102] His plan was endorsed by Senator Mead.[103] These clinics might be modeled after one already proven effective in Baltimore. Their aim would be to preserve small enterprises. At very little cost the Federal Government could provide for the establishment of these service companies from which small enterprisers might obtain expert advice regarding management problems, methods of financing, marketing programs, and other as-

95 *Ibid.*, pp. 121, 232, 391, 441.   96 *Ibid.*, pp. 243–249.
97 *Ibid.*, pp. 336–355.   98 *Ibid.*, p. 341.
99 *Ibid.*, p. 342.   100 *Ibid.*, p. 418.
101 *Ibid.*, p. 346.   102 *Ibid.*, pp. 479–499.
103 *Ibid.*, p. 502.

pects of their business. It already had been demonstrated in Baltimore that such clinics could be largely self-supporting and materially helpful at the same time.

INSURANCE

Securities and Exchange Commissioner Pike alone presented recommendations with respect to life insurance. His program provided: first, that the states undertake a program to strengthen the existing machinery for regulating and supervising life insurance; second, that the Federal Government assist the states in these efforts by rendering advice, by disseminating information, and by exercising supervisory powers on its own account; third, that industrial life insurance, with its accompanying abuses, gradually be eliminated by making available superior benefits and services through the social security program and postal savings.[104]

Principally, Commissioner Pike urged improving the state machinery to supervise life insurance; many of the essential reforms, he thought, could be attained in this manner. He outlined a tenfold program as follows:

1. Insurance commissioners should be appointed by a responsible executive (in all cases subject of course to confirmation by the proper State body) and their selection should only be made with regard for the appointee's experience and qualifications.

2. The tenure of office of the insurance commissioner should be increased substantially and insofar as possible competent commissioners should be continued in office regardless of their political affiliation.

3. The salaries of insurance commissioners should if possible be substantially increased.

4. Insurance commissioners should not be obliged to undertake any duties other than the regulation and supervision of insurance companies.

5. There should be substantial increases in the budget for insurance departments of most States.

6. The personnel of most insurance departments should be increased. The work of an insurance department should be undertaken only by fulltime qualified employees whose pay is sufficient to make them conscious of their responsibilities and free from insurance company or political influence. The employment of special outside examiners should be discontinued.

7. State insurance supervisory officials should strengthen examination procedures particularly in respect of companies domiciled within their State. The desired improvement would include more frequent examinations in some States, more competent examiners, greater publicity to and

104 *Ibid.,* p. 600.

full release of all examination reports, and the undertaking of examination which would give greater attention to the insurance operations as contrasted with the purely financial aspects of the business.

8. Closer regulation and supervision of agency practices is required. Agents should be required to show more adequate training, better prospects for financial success, and greater knowledge of the life-insurance business. Furthermore, State supervisory officials should give more attention to such matters as company courses, sales contests, compensation arrangements, and so forth.

9. The number of policy forms should be reduced and greater attention given to establishing standardized policy forms or policy provisions acceptable in all States.

10. State supervisory officials should more closely scrutinize activities of officers and directors and generally make more thorough checks on the competence and activities of company managements.[105]

Commissioner Pike offered other suggestions for improving state supervision of life insurance companies. He proposed that the states give serious consideration to liberalizing their laws to permit investment in common stocks. A second proposal was designed to ensure competition among insurance companies and to place state supervisory authorities in a position to "police inter-company agreements restricting competition." The earlier hearings had demonstrated that "gentlemen's agreements" had been negotiated among companies without either representation or supervision by the public. Mr. Pike proposed that state laws be altered to provide such representation and to give adequate publicity to the character of the agreements reached. A final suggestion had to do with giving policyholders greater representation on the boards of both stock and mutual companies. The states were urged to develop techniques to achieve mutuality in fact as well as in principle. Policyholders might be permitted to elect at least a minority of the directors of stock companies. Mutual companies might be encouraged or required to adopt the most effective methods already in use to assure representation and participation of policyholders.

Despite the fact that Commissioner Pike would leave the essential controls in the hands of the states, he indicated that there is an area in which the Federal Government might be helpful and in which Federal supervision is needed.[106] The scope of their activities makes life insurance companies national in fact, hence the broad national interest in them cannot be ignored. Possibly the greatest contribution which the Federal Government could make would be as collector

105 *Ibid.*, pp. 566–567.   106 *Ibid.*, pp. 587–597.

and distributor of information. Related to this was the proposal that
a Federal agency be constituted with well-defined visitatorial powers
over all life insurance companies doing interstate business. Such an
agency could give adequate publicity to practices employed and
would be able to report on the efficiency of state supervision. It might
be authorized to make investigations of companies when requested by
the insurance commissioners of two or more states. It could require
reasonable reports and develop uniform reporting standards. As a
functionary of this Federal agency an Insurance Advisory Council
might be created to assist state regulatory officers. The regular reports
of such an agency would serve to advise insurance company executives
of conditions requiring their attention. They would also aid by directing public attention to areas where state supervision needs
strengthening in order to promote sound insurance practices. Finally, this agency could keep the state legislatures and the Congress
advised of conditions requiring legislative correction.

Mr. Pike likewise felt that certain specific Federal measures would
be helpful. These would include a Federal law to prohibit insurance companies from selling policies either directly or indirectly in
states in which they had not been authorized to do business. The
national bankruptcy laws might be amended to permit state insurance commissioners or a designated Federal insurance agency to
apply to the United States District Court to order a company's
liquidation or reorganization. Finally, the Federal Government could
provide legislation to restrain officers and directors of insurance
companies from exploiting their positions for personal gain or for
ulterior purposes.

THE PATENT SYSTEM

In the hearings relating to the patent system, sponsored by the Departments of Justice and Commerce, certain recommendations had
been made which were summarized in the preliminary report of the
TNEC in 1939.[107] These proposals had received the endorsement of
the Committee, and some of them had been enacted into laws. Those
presented in the final hearings were in large part a reaffirmation of
the stand previously taken.[108] As originally presented, there were
seven recommendations by the Patent Bureau; five of them had already been enacted into laws by the Seventy-sixth Congress.[109] The

[107] S. Doc. 95, 76th Cong., 1st sess., 1939.
[108] *Final Report and Recommendations of the Temporary National Economic Committee*, pp. 357–380.   [109] *Ibid.*, p. 358.

Commissioner urged the enactment of the other two—proposals one and two of those which follow.

1. The creation of a single court of patent appeals, having jurisdiction coextensive with the United States and its Territories. The purpose of such a court would be to replace the present 11 different and independent jurisdictions by a single appellate tribunal, so as to prevent conflicts in decisions and to secure uniform treatment of patents, and to reduce the time and the cost of patent litigation.

2. The limitation of the life of a patent so that it shall expire not more than 20 years from the date of filing of the application, and thereby obviate the possibility of prolonging the patent monopoly by keeping an application pending in the Patent Office a long time. Under this proposal the term of a patent would not be greater than 17 years, but would be correspondingly reduced if the application were kept pending in the Patent Office more than 3 years.

3. The simplification of interference procedure in the Patent Office by eliminating one of the appeals, within the Office, thus providing for only a single decision in the Patent Office and a prompter issuance of a patent to the winning party.

4. Abolishing renewal applications, thus eliminating an unnecessary procedure and removing a means for prolonging the pendency of applications.

5. Reducing from 2 years to 1 year the period of public use and publication allowed to an inventor before an application for patent need be filed.

6. Reducing from 2 years to 1 year the period within which an applicant may copy claims from an issued patent for the purpose of asserting priority of invention.

7. Giving the Commissioner of Patents authority to require an applicant to respond to an Office action within less than the normal statutory period of 6 months.[110]

The Assistant Attorney General, Mr. Arnold, pressed the recommendations made in the preliminary report by the Department of Justice, which were designed to prevent the abuse of patents for monopolistic purposes. This was to be achieved, principally, by limiting the right of patent owners to grant restricted licenses and by preventing the use of infringement suits as instruments of economic aggression. The Commissioner of Patents, however, was unwilling to support these proposals. A summary of the suggestions by the Justice Department follows.

Briefly, we recommend that the owner of a patent be required to grant unrestricted licenses if he grants licenses at all, and not to impose restrictions upon the buyer in sales of patented articles. We recommend a requirement that sale or assignment of patents or patent rights be recorded

110 *Ibid.*, pp. 357–358.

in writing and that a copy of the document be filed with the Federal Trade Commission. We recommend the imposition of such limitations upon suits for infringement as would prevent the use of such litigation as a weapon of business aggression rather than as an instrument for adjudicating honest disputes. Finally, we recommend that violators of these requirements forfeit their patent rights to the United States.[111]

THE CONSUMER

The Consumers' Counsel appeared before the TNEC once more to repeat recommendations made in the earlier hearings to promote the welfare of consumers and to "enlarge the opportunities of our people to build an economy in which the principle of monopoly is displaced by the principle of abundance." [112] He endorsed the proposals for a more effective program of antitrust action, for repeal of the Miller-Tydings Act, and the suggested reforms of the patent system. He commended to the TNEC the recommendation made by the CIO that industrial councils be created to assure full use of industrial capacity. Moreover, he called for the organization of a central agency in the Government to "foster, promote, and develop the consumer welfare of the people of the United States." Such an agency would be authorized by the Congress (1) to represent the interest of consumers in all functions of the Government, (2) to furnish expert advice to the administrators of Government programs involving the consumer interest, and (3) to review and report on the activities of the Government from the point of view of their effect upon the consumer's welfare. This agency would be an independent functionary and would not, therefore, constitute a branch of any existing agency created principally to promote the interest of a particular producer group. One of its chief tasks would be to counteract, at least in part, some of the pressures on the Government by special interest groups.

Another proposal related to the development of quality standards for consumer goods and the requirement of informative labeling. The earlier consumer hearings had emphasized these needs. The Consumers' Counsel urged the creation of a consumer standards board to co-ordinate the many activities of Government already engaged in the development of standards, as well as to undertake research to promote such ends. It would draft tentative standards and propose the same to the proper authorities for adoption.[113]

111 *Ibid.*, p. 269, and S. Doc. 95, 76th Cong., 1st sess., pp. 17–18.
112 *Ibid.*, pp. 439–452.
113 See also the testimony by the Department of Agriculture, *Final Report and Recommendations of the Temporary National Economic Committee*, p. 399.

FULL EMPLOYMENT

However much its members may have desired to evade the fact, the problem of full employment and the recurrence of depressions was the principal issue before the TNEC. Even Chairman O'Mahoney voiced such an opinion when he said, "We are asked . . . to find out . . . why, with all the unlimited resources nature affords, money, machines, and men have been idle, with consequent hardship and suffering to millions." [114] Nonetheless, no systematic attempt was made to outline a program for achieving full employment. The proposal that came nearest to such an attempt was that made by Dr. Ezekiel.

Purchasing power.—Fittingly enough, some echoed the belief, common since 1929, that the collapse of the economic system was due to the breakdown of purchasing power. Chairman O'Mahoney,[115] Dr. Ezekiel,[116] and Mr. Ballinger [117] all spoke of the strategic importance of consumer purchasing power. The economic adviser to the Federal Trade Commission, Mr. Ballinger, found the key to the depression in the way in which income is distributed. Though not inconsistent with the thesis of "hoarded income," and perhaps a bit more naïve than that approach, his explanation of the economic crisis was faulty distribution.

There are a number of competent economists [he said] who believe that the fundamental trouble was lack of buying power among the great majority of American families. These families simply did not have sufficient income to buy more goods. Our economic system will not produce more goods unless such goods can be bought. . . . Mass production "marks the highest level under man's productive programs." However, "we cannot have the economies of mass production save in an economy of mass consumption." [118]

The way to avoid depressions, accordingly, and the way to full employment is to devise means by which income may be distributed more widely and more abundantly to assure that a large proportion of the national income goes to, and is used by, consumers. It is necessary, in other words, to create an economy with a strong propensity to consume. Consumer incomes might be increased in several ways; wages might be raised and methods might be developed to reduce the prices of commodities which consumers buy. The latter proposal is consistent with the programs previously discussed for restrain-

114 *Ibid.*, p. 62.
116 *Ibid.*, pp. 418–425.
118 *Ibid.*, pp. 618–619.

115 *Ibid.*
117 *Ibid.*, pp. 619–623.

ing monopoly and perfecting the system of competitive pricing.

Hoarded income.—Perhaps at no other time did the TNEC get down to fundamentals as well as it did when Dr. Mordecai Ezekiel, economic adviser to the Secretary of Agriculture, submitted recommendations.[119] Nowhere throughout either the hearings or the final sessions was as comprehensive an attempt made to analyze the causes of the trade cycle and to suggest a program for remedial action.[120] Dr. Ezekiel had no quarrel with those who seek a more equitable distribution of purchasing power. He endorsed the proposals to eliminate interstate trade barriers. Moreover, he supported those who would protect consumers from monopoly exploitation. Nevertheless, he did not believe a program of antitrust action would provide a solution to the basic ills of the economy.[121] Something materially more fundamental is involved, which cannot be rectified by breaking up monopoly combinations.

The breakdown of the capitalistic economy is traceable, he said, to the breakdown in purchasing power, and "the weak link in the purchasing power chain lies in the use made of savings." [122] This, of course, is the familiar thesis of Dr. Hansen, Commissioner Henderson, and others. Not that there is insufficient purchasing power to permit the economy to thrive, but due to the structure and the organization of our economic institutions, a critical portion of the stream of income becomes sterilized. This income is neither spent for consumers' goods nor invested in new plant. There is a tendency within the economy to save more than is invested. Call this "oversaving" or "hoarding." To a very considerable extent this condition results from the fact that the ownership and control of industry is concentrated, and hence incomes are concentrated. Savings run ahead of investment, the stream of income becomes clogged, and the economy bogs down.

For the economic system to function at full capacity requires that the income stream be kept open—every aspect of oversaving must be corrected, the hoard must be harnessed, and an offset be found for all savings. There are several feasible alternatives, any or all of which may be employed to release the dammed up stream of income and to

---

[119] *Ibid.,* pp. 417–439.
[120] An exception to the above statement might be made in the case of the testimony of Alvin H. Hansen and associates during the Savings and Investment hearings.
[121] *Final Report and Recommendations of the Temporary National Economic Committee,* pp. 429, 437.
[122] *Ibid.,* p. 418.

return the hoard to the functioning economy.[123] These alternatives include: (1) borrowing hoarded savings and spending them, (2) taxing hoarded savings and spending them, (3) increasing individual security and reducing the pressure to save, (4) providing a more even distribution of income, and (5) increasing the consuming power of the underlying population. Dr. Ezekiel said that we might choose between any of these lines of action or follow several of them. From the standpoint of maintaining full employment it makes little difference which line is followed so long as the complete gap between savings and investment is filled and the aggregate effect is sufficient. Nevertheless, certain lines of action are socially more desirable than others, and some more than others will contribute to a healthy, vigorous expansion of economic activity.

The first suggestion involves the government's borrowing the hoard and spending it. Such an expedient will work only so long as it is continued and should, therefore, be considered only as a temporary measure to be supplemented by more fundamental correctives.

The second involves taxing the hoard and spending it. If the instrumentality of taxation is employed to revive the ailing economy, it is important that the entire tax system be surveyed and revised to assure that all its aspects promote so far as possible, or impede as little as possible, full employment of national economic resources. When taxes which fall heavily and regressively upon those with low incomes are employed to finance government spending, they do little to offset oversaving—they merely substitute public consumption for private. At present, too large a proportion of public revenues are of this type. Income, estate, and corporation taxes, however, bear principally on those income groups which account for a large share of the total savings. "Government spending based on such taxes does help put money into use that otherwise might lie hoarded and idle, and so helps to increase the level of activity." [124] Dr. Ezekiel would use tax instruments to reduce excess savings and to increase investment both by reducing the willingness to save and by increasing the willingness to invest. Thoughtful planning would be necessary to achieve these ends.

Just as there are many ways of taxing, so are there of spending; some are socially more desirable than others, and some contribute more than others to a vigorous and productive economy. Government spending may be for consumption or for furthering production (in-

[123] *Ibid.,* pp. 420–421, 434–435.　　　　[124] *Ibid.,* p. 423.

vestment). Many useful public works might be undertaken to lay the basis for a broader economy. If public expenditures are for immediate consumption, they should be made with discrimination to secure maximum social benefits. Expenditures to improve public health and to increase the standard of living would be most justified—such as those "for education, child welfare, and medical facilities." [125]

The third suggestion was to invoke procedures to increase individual security and reduce the pressure to save. Measures to achieve this goal would include the expansion of social security benefits to lessen the distress of old age, unemployment, dependency, and other forms of disability. Although this, perhaps, would aid in closing the gap between savings and investment, it would in the writer's opinion be of little importance, inasmuch as its effects would be most pronounced among those who ordinarily save little. Coupled with and financed by a system of progressive taxation, however, such a program would contribute toward an economy with a higher propensity to consume.

Measures to provide a more even distribution of income might be employed to achieve equilibrium between savings and investment. This, too, would contribute to a high consumption economy and thereby toward full employment. Various means might be employed to secure this end, including the voluntary raising of wage levels by business, the establishment of minimum wage standards, the raising of wages through collective bargaining, antitrust action to restrict the concentration of income resulting from monopoly exploitation, and a concerted policy of lowering prices to permit a broader popular participation in the benefits of modern technology. Finally, Mr. Ezekiel recommended the adoption of measures to increase the consuming power of low-income groups. These would include certain programs previously described, together with measures to enhance the position of consumers "by giving their dollars greater purchasing power."

Other proposals.—Various suggestions were directed either to the over-all problem of the business crisis or to the mitigation of distresses created by it. The economic adviser to the Federal Trade Commission emphasized the necessity of reducing prices as the "most effective way . . . to promote fullest use and expansion of our economic system." He described the practical difficulties which an ever-widening range of prices, fixed and manipulated by monopolies, creates when at-

[125] *Ibid.*, p. 422.

tempting to maintain the present economic system with "free markets and a free price system." [126] Senator Mead proposed that the lending powers of the Federal Reserve banks be liberalized to facilitate the granting of working capital to business and that a system of loan insurance by the Reconstruction Finance Corporation be developed to guarantee business loans.[127] Commissioner Lubin advocated that the dismissal wage be adopted as a national policy to deal with the problem of technnological unemployment.[128]

FINAL REPORT AND RECOMMENDATIONS

On March 26, 1941, the TNEC met to vote on proposals prepared by its executive committee and its secretary, Dr. Dewey Anderson.[129] The recommendations which were adopted fill the first forty-three pages of the final report. The war which had broken out in Europe was in full swing, and its significance to American institutions had begun to preoccupy the thinking of American leaders. Conversion of the American economy to a war economy was under way, and problems of defense were paramount. It is not surprising, therefore, that the final report takes on an air of a war document, even though the United States had not yet been plunged into the conflict.

The final report frequently alludes to the fact that "the form of political and social organization which we call democracy is at bay throughout the world," and speaks of powerful forces having arisen that are antagonistic to the principles of free government and free enterprise. The Committee's task, as they conceived it, was to propose measures to preserve democratic institutions on this continent; they saw in the concentration of economic power a challenge to these institutions. In setting forth their philosophy and in defining their objectives the Committee declared that democracy could not remain only a political concept, but must take cognizance of economic realities as well.

If democracy is really to survive [their report said] then all organizations through which man operates—industrial, social, and political—must also be democratic. Political freedom cannot survive if economic freedom is lost.[130]

Public institutions, political and economic, must be made to serve the entire community.

Governments are instituted among men to serve men; men are not created

126 *Ibid.*, pp. 620–622.   127 *Ibid.*, pp. 500–501.   128 *Ibid.*, pp. 551–556.
129 *Ibid.*, p. 79.   130 *Ibid.*, p. 7.

to serve government. . . . Like government organization, business organization has no right or function to control the activities and the lives of men.[131]

With this statement of premises and purposes the Committee proclaimed the necessity of re-examining the "elementary factors of our faith in democracy." They declared that the economic dislocations following 1929 had resulted from the failure of leadership to comprehend the realities and needs of the economy. "It will not do," the Committee declared, "merely to drift, as unfortunately we have been drifting, nor to putter around with patchwork remedies intended to restore an economic structure already dead." [132] After these courageous words one was prepared for bold and sweeping proposals to rectify the far-reaching maladjustments which were responsible for the creation of the TNEC. No sweeping program for reconstruction was forthcoming, however. The Committee said:

The members of the committee are not rash enough to believe that they can lay down a program which will solve the great problems that beset the world, but they are convinced that the information which this committee has assembled, when eventually properly analyzed and disseminated, will enable the people of America to know what must be done if human freedom is to be preserved.[133]

The final report of the TNEC is essentially an anti-monopoly document, and most of its recommendations are intended to foster free enterprise and to prevent concentration of economic power. The anti-monopoly proposals will be discussed first; [134] other recommendations relate either to the general economy or to specific industries, such as insurance.

FAITH IN FREE ENTERPRISE

This committee recommends the maintenance of free, competitive enterprise by the effective suppression of the restrictive practices which have always been recognized as evil.[135] [Approved without objection.]

In the earlier hearings Chairman O'Mahoney had said, "I believe . . . that our final report should begin with a definite and unequivocal declaration of our faith in free enterprise." [136] Such a declaration was forthcoming in the following words: "The Temporary National Economic Committee, therefore, avows its faith in free enterprise." [137]

---

131 *Ibid.*, p. 5.   132 *Ibid.*, p. 24.   133 *Ibid.*, p. 4.
134 The order in which the recommendations are presented does not follow that used in the final report.
135 *Final Report and Recommendations of the Temporary National Economic Committee*, p. 9.
136 *Ibid.*, p. 672.   137 *Ibid.*, p. 7.

Moreover, the Committee indicated that its proposals would be directed to that objective and that it was opposed to regimentation either by government or by industrial combinations.

PASSING ON TECHNOLOGICAL GAINS

We insist that a free competitive system offers the best opportunity for the widest participation in such gains [from technological change] achieved through a reduction in prices of goods, in stimulation of new industries and extension of existing ones, fuller employment, reduction of working hours, increase in consumers' purchasing power, and a more equitable distribution of the value added by manufacture.[138] [Approved without objection.]

This is the nearest the TNEC came to presenting an over-all plan to achieve full employment and to prevent major economic dislocations. The Committee, as a whole, apparently was unable to see any other important cause for depressions than the "evils of monopoly" and therefore was unable to agree upon any other approach to the problem.

DECENTRALIZATION OF INDUSTRY

We therefore submit to all public and private bodies responsible for industry location the desirability of decentralizing industry to the end that the maximum economic benefits can be secured from plants operating at their most efficient size, the depressing aspects of the factory system be prevented, and the American way of life be preserved.[139] [Approved without objection.]

The immediate problem prompting the Committee at this point involved the location of war-born industries. The hearings had developed no data relating to the relationship between plant size, location, and efficiency.[140] That such studies would be helpful is apparent. This somewhat innocuous admonition to business and government to seek the optimum size plant should meet with little opposition. But other than an exhortation, it offers little positive aid, inasmuch as no standards are suggested, and no machinery is provided to implement the policy proposed.

STIMULATING COMPETITION

In this period of Government aid for defense purposes, it is urged that Congress and the President allocate funds in such a manner that monopoly control of basic products be eliminated to insure an adequate supply at competitive prices, so that, furthermore, competition may develop which

138 *Ibid.*, p. 22.   139 *Ibid.*, p. 23.
140 See, however, Temporary National Economic Committee Monograph No. 13.

will prove effective in the peacetime period following the defense effort.[141] [Approved without objection.]

The Committee, concerned as it was with monopoly and concentration as underlying causes of the ills of the economy, was particularly disturbed because it believed that defense industries were being created which would remain in years to come to intensify the monopoly problem. No facts were developed during the earlier hearings, however, to support this belief; the opinion flowed from the everyday experiences of the TNEC members.

THE BASING-POINT SYSTEM

We . . . recommend that the Congress enact legislation declaring such pricing systems [basing-point systems] to be illegal.[142] [Approved without objection.]

One by one the Committee proposed specific reforms to strengthen the traditional American struggle against monopoly and to bolster the system of free enterprise. Extensive hearings had been held on the basing-point system demonstrating that it had been employed to control prices and to restrain competition in many fields including iron and steel, cement, lumber, brick, asphalt, glass, white lead, metal lath, floor tile, bolts, salt, and sugar. The Committee had come to the conclusion that the basing-point system is uneconomic and wasteful and should, therefore, be specifically outlawed as other practices had been in the Clayton Act.

RESALE PRICE MAINTENANCE LAWS

We recommend to the Congress the repeal of the Miller-Tydings Enabling Act.[143] [O'Mahoney, Sumners, Reece, and Taylor dissenting.]

It had been shown that "fair trade" laws had enabled marketing groups to perpetrate monopolistic schemes and price fixing conspiracies. Such resale price maintenance contracts had been legalized in interstate commerce by the Miller-Tydings Act. The Committee, therefore, proposed that the Federal Government decline to champion such practices.

INTERSTATE TRADE BARRIERS

We . . . recommend that the Congress enact legislation establishing a continuing committee on Federal-State relationships which shall be charged with the responsibility of collecting current information as to trade practices between the States, and of devising ways and means of

141 *Final Report and Recommendations of the Temporary National Economic Committee,* p. 24.
142 *Ibid.,* p. 33.   143 *Ibid.*

preventing or restraining uneconomic barriers to trade.[144] [Approved without objection.]

The formation of such a committee had been proposed both in the original hearings and in the public sessions to consider recommendations. The TNEC quite accurately characterized trade barriers in the following manner: "While isolated cases do not loom large in the national economy, the aggregate effect is detrimental."

GOVERNMENT PURCHASING

The committee urges that the purchasing function [of the Government] be centralized in one agency to the greatest extent possible, and that procurement be planned, as to time, place, and amount, in such manner as to obtain the needed goods at the lowest price and without dislocating the general economy.[145] [Approved without objection.]

Although this suggestion was offered, in part, as an economy measure and to improve public administration, the intent of the TNEC was to assure that public buying practices do not foster monopolies. The evidence before the Committee had indicated that the Government often had been imposed upon by combinations and conspiracies among sellers through the submission of identical bids and other collusive practices. Co-ordination of purchasing agencies would protect the Government, restrain monopolists, and assemble a record of practices to aid in the formulation of public policy.

NATIONAL STANDARDS FOR NATIONAL CORPORATIONS

The Temporary National Economic Committee . . . endorses the principle of national standards for national corporations and recommends that Congress enact legislation to that effect.[146] [Sumners, Reece, O'Connell, and Pike dissenting.]

From the outset it was apparent that Chairman O'Mahoney would press for compulsory Federal charters for large corporations engaged in interstate commerce. Despite the fact that substantially no testimony was offered relating to such a policy or to the regulations which would be employed, this "brain-child" of the chairman was featured most prominently in the final report of the TNEC. It was argued that a national law would be able to prohibit interlocking directorships and thereby eliminate one of the major methods of concentration. Laws might be devised to make corporation directors trustees in fact, as well as in name, and to restrain directors from using their positions for personal gain at the expense of the stockholders and the public. Corporation officers and directors might be held personally

144 *Ibid.*, p. 34.　　　　145 *Ibid.*　　　　146 *Ibid.*, p. 29.

liable for violations of the antitrust laws, and the scope and financing practices of subsidiary corporations could be defined.

Four members of the TNEC were unwilling to endorse "national standards for national corporations." Despite the reasons advanced, one gathers that for the most part they were opposed to such a policy in principle. They objected, however, that the implications of the recommendation were not really apparent, that the objectives were not clear, and that the proposal falsely implied that it would "solve all the problems involved in the concentration of economic power." They asserted, moreover, that mere legislative proscription is not sufficient to eliminate undesirable corporate practices. As a result of the position thus taken, the dissenters are left in the position of tacitly conceding that there is need for action, of having struck down a partial solution to the problem or, perhaps, the essentials of what might develop into a more complete solution, and of offering no alternative plan to fill the need.

THE ANTITRUST LAWS

The committee therefore recommends the vigorous and vigilant enforcement of the antitrust laws.[147] [Approved without objection.]

This is the essence of the TNEC report. Substantially all recommendations set forth thus far have built up to this approach, and most of those which follow are designed to strengthen the "trust-busting" technique. One gathers that, as a whole, the Committee felt that there are few problems of the economic order which would not correct themselves if monopoly control were eliminated.

FUNDS FOR ENFORCEMENT

We strongly urge the absolute necessity of providing funds for these agencies [the Department of Justice and the Federal Trade Commission] adequate to the task which confronts them.[148] [Approved without objection.]

This proposal is a corollary to the preceding recommendation. It has been the contention of some that the existing monopoly laws, in themselves, are adequate to provide most of the essential safeguards if only there were the administrative will and sufficient funds to enforce them. Without an adequate budget to finance the requisite activities and to employ the needed personnel, few statutes, however desirable, can be enforced.

147 *Ibid.,* p. 9.   148 *Ibid.,* p. 35.

LEGISLATIVE CHANGES OF ANTITRUST LAWS

The committee believes that legislation is clearly indicated as necessary in order that the struggle against monopoly and the uneconomic concentration of economic power in private hands be carried on with better effect than heretofore. Our suggestions follow: [149]

Some of the proposals already listed relate to public policy affecting monopoly. The Committee felt, however, that sharper definition and certain specific changes of the law are needed, particularly with respect to patents, trade associations, mergers, civil penalties, and the powers of the Federal Trade Commission.

The Committee held that the privilege accorded by the patent monopoly has been "shamefully abused." It therefore offered amendments involving both procedural and substantive changes. These were to supplement recommendations made in the preliminary report already enacted into law.[150]

Patent Laws

Licensing of patents.—We recommend that the Congress enact legislation which will require that any future patent is to be available for use by anyone who may desire its use and who is willing to pay a fair price for the privilege.[151] [Sumners and Taylor dissenting.]

Such a measure would restrict the power of a corporation to purchase and suppress patents controlling important technological improvements. Although it would permit the owner of the patent to retain a "monopoly profit" from his invention, it would in effect assign that monopoly the status of a public utility by requiring the owner to serve all who come at reasonable rates. The Committee proposed that machinery, either judicial or administrative, be set up to determine what constitutes a reasonable royalty.

Unrestricted licenses.—We recommend that the owner of any patent be required to grant only unrestricted licenses, and that he not be permitted to impose restrictions upon the buyer in sales of patented articles.[152] [Approved without objection.]

The purpose of this proposal is to limit the monopolist's power to the invention itself and to restrain him from extending such monopoly to areas never intended by the law. The holder of the patent would not be permitted to restrict a licensee with respect to the quantity of any

[149] *Ibid.*, pp. 35–36.   [150] S. Doc. 95, 76th Cong., 1st sess., 1939.
[151] *Final Report and Recommendations of the Temporary National Economic Committee*, p. 36.
[152] *Ibid.*, pp. 36–37.

article he may produce, the price he may charge, the use to which the product is put, or the area in which it is sold.

Recording of transfers and agreements.—We recommend that any sale, license, assignment, or other disposition of any patent be evidenced by an instrument in writing and that the same be required of any condition, agreement, or understanding relating to any sale or disposition of any such patent, and that in any such case a copy of such written instrument be filed with the Federal Trade Commission within 30 days after execution.[153] [Approved without objection.]

Apparently the purpose of this requirement is to guarantee "open covenants openly arrived at" and to assure that the terms of such agreements are consistent with public policy. The Committee indicated that there should be a substantial monetary penalty for failure to file as required.

Limitation on suits for infringement.—We recommend legislation which will provide that no action, based upon a charge of infringement of any patent, whether for damages, for an injunction, or for any other relief shall be permitted against any licensee under a patent or against any purchaser or licensee or any article unless the plaintiff has previously secured a judgment against the grantor of the license or the manufacturer of the article for infringement in connection with the granting of such license or the sale of such article.[154] [Approved without objection.]

This provision should prove effective in restraining those who employ patent suits to harass those who are using the product of competitive patents in order to coerce them to become licensees. Without such protection potential licensees frequently become the pawns and "property" of the firms which display the greatest capacity and propensity for litigation.

Forfeiture of patent for violation.—If any person who owns any interest in or right under a patent violates any of the prohibitions described in paragraphs (*a*) and (*b*) above, his interest therein should be forfeited, such forfeiture to be brought about in a civil action against such person by the United States. Any patent or interest therein so forfeited should become a part of the public domain.[155] [Taylor dissenting.]

Single Court of Patent Appeals.—. . . we recommend the creation of a single Court of Patent Appeals with jurisdiction co-extensive with the United States and its territories.[156] [Approved without objection.]

The latter measure had been advocated and generally approved throughout the earlier hearings. Such a court would replace existing independent jurisdictions and would, it was felt, speed up court

---

[153] *Ibid.,* p. 37.   [154] *Ibid.*
[155] *Ibid.*   [156] *Ibid.*

action, assure more uniform treatment of patents, and reduce the cost of litigation.

Limitation on period of patent monopoly.—The life of the patent should be so limited that it will expire not more than 20 years from the date of filing of the application.[157] [Approved without objection.]

The earlier hearings had shown that through the application of the patent laws, or through their manipulation, the legal life of patents (technically, seventeen years) sometimes has been stretched to last more than twice as long. The proposed twenty-year limit would obviate the possibility of prolonging the patent monopoly by keeping the application pending in the Patent Office for long periods and would thereby remove a major motive for one type of litigation.

Foreign patent controls.—The further recommendation is made that the patent laws be strengthened so that no application for patent may be filed in a foreign country until specific permission has been obtained from the proper agency in this Government.[158] [Approved without objection.]

This recommendation was made separately from the other patent proposals; its purpose is to protect the national economy from monopolies deriving their power from international agreements based on patent controls and cross-licensing arrangements. Through the interchange of patents, American and foreign firms had cartelized various industries including beryllium, magnesium, optical glass, and chemicals and thereby had divided the world market among themselves.

Trade Associations

We recommend that all trade associations whose participating members are engaged in interstate commerce be required to register with an appropriate Federal agency and to file periodical reports of their activities.

The committee also believes that the time has come to make a clear legislative proscription of certain types of activity on the part of trade associations.[159] [Approved without objection.]

Thus, the TNEC recognized the far-reaching power which trade associations had attained over the economic activities of the nation. Rather than outlaw such combinations and thereby eliminate whatever constructive contributions they make or perchance drive them underground, the TNEC would subject them to supervision and would seek to assure "open covenants" by giving publicity to their activities. Specific collusive and monopolistic practices by trade associations would be outlawed.

[157] *Ibid.*   [158] *Ibid.*, p. 32.   [159] *Ibid.*, p. 38.

Corporate Mergers

The committee again urges [160] . . . that section 7 of the Clayton Act be amended so as to include within its prohibitions the acquisitions of assets of competitors under conditions applicable to stock under the existing law. . . . We propose that the Federal Trade Commission be given authority . . . to forbid the acquisition of the assets and property of competing corporations of over a certain size unless it be made to appear that the purpose and apparent effect of such consolidation would be desirable. . . . It is suggested . . . that no such merger should be permitted unless its proponents demonstrate—

a) That the acquisition is in the public interest and will be promotive of greater efficiency and economy of production, distribution, and management;

b) That it will not substantially lessen competition, restrain trade, or tend to create a monopoly (either in a single section of the country or in the country as a whole) in the trade, industry, or line of commerce in which such corporations are engaged;

c) That the corporations involved in such acquisition do not control more than such proportion of the trade, industry, or line of commerce in which they are engaged as Congress may determine;

d) That the size of the acquiring company after the acquisition will not be incompatible with the existence and maintenance of vigorous and effective competition in the trade, industry, or line of commerce in which it is engaged;

e) That the acquisition will not so reduce the number of competing companies in the trade, industry, or line of commerce as materially to lessen the effectiveness and vigor of competition in such trade, industry, or line of commerce;

f) That the acquiring company has not, to induce the acquisition, indulged in any unlawful methods of competition or has not otherwise violated the provisions of the Federal Trade Commission Act, as amended.

The committee further recommends an outright prohibition on the acquisition of stock in or holding company control of competing companies with suitable exceptions for bona fide investments and the control of true subsidiaries by parent corporations.[161] [Approved without objection.]

These modifications of the Clayton Act were proposed because ingenious methods had been devised to circumvent the law. The Clayton Act forbids the acquisition of stock in competing companies when the effect is to lessen competition. It does not forbid the acquisition of assets under similar circumstances, and it has been construed to permit the acquisition of assets via the illegal route of stock acquisition.

160 See the Preliminary Report, S. Doc. 95, 76th Cong., 1st sess., 1939.
161 *Final Report and Recommendations of the Temporary National Economic Committee*, pp. 38–39.

The TNEC members believed that these amendments would outlaw both stock acquisition and the holding company as a means of monopoly control without impairing the more legitimate uses of the holding company. Moreover, the Committee believed that these changes would substitute prevention for punishment by requiring advance approval of combinations rather than subsequent compulsory dissolution after public harm has resulted.

Penalties

The Committee . . . urges . . . the enactment of legislation which would subject corporations and corporate officers violating the antitrust laws to more stringent civil penalties than exist at the present time.[162] [Approved without objection.]

Federal Trade Commission as a Master in Chancery

The committee recommends that the Federal Trade Commission Act be amended to provide that on request of the Attorney General, the Commission or any member thereof, may hear evidence and make findings of fact and conclusions of law in any pending antitrust proceedings.[163] [Approved without objection.]

According to this plan the Federal Trade Commission upon request would hear evidence, make findings of fact, and render conclusions at law in antitrust proceedings. This will be recognized as the proposal made earlier by the Assistant Attorney General.[164] Such activities by the Commission would be advisory to the courts and should relieve many burdens now imposed upon them, as well as lend continuity and uniformity to antitrust procedure.

Although the final report of the TNEC was preponderately a monopoly document, it extended to other problems of the economy as well. These included the relief from poverty, the need for economic research, the problem of investment, and the insurance industry.

THE LOWER THIRD

We commend such efforts as the food stamp plan, slum clearance, and low-cost housing, the extension of hospital and medical facilities, and the development of vocational and cultural programs for the less privileged of our people, to the end that they may become as speedily as possible fully participating, responsible members of the community.[165] [Approved without objection.]

The Committee emphasized the fact that the plight of the lower third of the population—people with meager incomes, unstable employment, unhealthful living conditions, and limited cultural opportuni-

---

162 *Ibid.*, p. 40.
164 *Ibid.*, pp. 137–138.
163 *Ibid.*
165 *Ibid.*, p. 22.

ties—constitutes an insecure foundation for democracy. It endorsed, therefore, remedial measures to improve the lot of this portion of the population.

BUSINESS AND ECONOMIC RESEARCH

We recommend . . . that the work of the Department of Commerce in the field of business and economic research be developed to provide for an adequate flow of current data on our national economy. . . . Further, we recommend that essential research in other agencies necessary to provide a comprehensive and integrated record of the current functioning of the economy . . . be adequately supported and provision made for filling any essential gaps.[166] [Approved without objection.]

In his message to Congress on April 29, 1938, President Roosevelt had called attention to the need for more adequate data concerning business trends. When business policy perforce is formulated in ignorance of prevailing conditions and trends, mistakes frequently are made which disrupt the economy. The TNEC held that fact-finding should be continuous to render essential economic information available to business men, to the Government, and to the public. Fact-gathering activities would relate to "production, orders, inventories, productive capacity, and related matters."

STIMULATING INVESTMENT

We reject as un-American and unrealistic the belief that the limits of economic achievement have been reached in the United States.[167] [Approved without objection.]

Although this in itself does not constitute a positive recommendation, it represents an important position taken with respect to policy. The Committee would have no truck with those who adhered to a mature economy theory or with those who suggested that the capitalistic system had reached a stage at which business is no longer able to absorb the savings of the country or to expand sufficiently to provide employment for all. This frightened interpretation of Professor Hansen's testimony had caused no little concern among commentators, the repercussions of which had reached many who held high political office. Although a great deal of attention had been given to Dr. Hansen's ideas in the earlier hearings, there was nothing in the record which challenges or refutes them. Nevertheless, this statement of faith by the Committee was generally heralded as a rejection of the Hansen thesis as "un-American and unrealistic." [168]

166 *Ibid.*, pp. 31–32.   167 *Ibid.*, p. 30.
168 *Newsweek*, XVII (April 7, 1941), 41 and XVII (April 14, 1941), 84.

INSURANCE

Our studies have disclosed conditions which lead to the following recommendations which are respectfully made for the consideration of the several States in which these companies are domiciled:

1. Insurance commissioners should be appointed by a responsible executive (in all cases subject of course to confirmation by the proper State body) and their selection should only be made with regard for the appointee's experience and qualifications.

2. The tenure of office of the insurance commissioner should be increased substantially and insofar as possible competent commissioners should be continued in office regardless of their political affiliation.

3. The salaries of insurance commissioners should if possible be substantially increased.

4. Insurance commissioners should not be obliged to undertake any duties other than the regulation and supervision of insurance companies.

5. There should be substantial increases in the budget for insurance departments of most States.

6. The personnel of most insurance departments should be increased. The work of an insurance department should be undertaken only by full-time qualified employees whose pay is sufficient to make them conscious of their responsibilities and free from insurance company or political influence. The employment of special outside examiners should be discontinued. The development of a civil service in State insurance departments is highly desirable. Companies should no longer be required to pay the salaries of examiners. If they must be charged for examination the necessary amount should either be collected by a lump-sum charge set in advance and paid by the company directly to the State treasury or preferably be collected through an appropriate State Tax.

7. State insurance supervisory officials should strengthen examination procedures particularly in respect to companies domiciled within their State. The desired improvement would include more frequent examinations in some States, more competent examiners, greater publicity to and full release of all examination reports, and the undertaking of examination which would give greater attention to the insurance operations as contrasted with the purely financial aspects of the business.

8. Closer regulation and supervision of agency practices is required. Present laws for licensing agents are all too frequently administered purely as revenue measures. Agents should be required to show more adequate training, better prospects for financial success, and greater knowledge of the life-insurance business. Furthermore, State supervisory officials should give more attention to such matters as company training courses, sales contests, compensation arrangements, etc.

9. The number of policy forms should be reduced, and greater attention given to establishing standardized policy forms or policy provisions acceptable in all States. The present confusion in this field is most undesirable.

10. State supervisory officials should more closely scrutinize activities of officers and directors and generally make more thorough checks on the competence and activities of company managements.

11. The life-insurance business should be conducted on a competitive basis, with emphasis on management efficiency rather than sales promotion. No intercompany agreements should be permitted the effect of which is to prevent any company from developing actuarily sound service and sales techniques.

12. A fundamental change in the conduct of industrial insurance should occur. Otherwise, its eventual elimination may be necessary. The primary responsibility for the change lies with the companies issuing such insurance and the States which supervise them. [Approved without objection.]

. . .

Without interjecting the Federal Government into the general field of insurance regulation, it is possible to utilize Federal powers in a direction which will strengthen State regulation and make it more effective. There are admittedly areas where State regulation is severely handicapped by reason of the interstate character of the life-insurance business. If forthright steps are not taken now to plug the gaps where State regulation cannot do an effective job and to prevent relaxations of regulatory standards in several States such as have occurred in the past to the disadvantage of numerous policyholders, State regulation may eventually decay and all-inclusive Federal control will be required. Accordingly:

1. A Federal statute is recommended preventing life-insurance companies from using the mails, the radio, or other means or instrumentalities of interstate commerce to sell insurance in a State where they have not been lawfully admitted to do business.

2. The National Bankruptcy Act should be amended to permit any State insurance commissioner to apply to the appropriate United States district court to bring about the liquidation or reorganization of a life-insurance company. If a company should be adjudicated bankrupt, the designated Federal agency or its nominee should be appointed to act as conservator and advisor during the readjustment of the company's affairs.

3. Officers and directors of insurance companies operating in more than one State should be prohibited by Federal statute from using their positions for improper personal gain either directly or indirectly. The statute should also declare life insurance officials not only in fact but in the eyes of the law trustees required to adhere to the strictest fiduciary standards, and appropriate civil and criminal penalties should be provided.

4. It is recommended that an appropriate committee of Congress or some designated agency of the Federal Government be directed to conduct a thorough investigation of all forms of fire, casualty, and marine insurance.[169] [Approved without objection.]

[169] *Final Report and Recommendations of the Temporary National Economic Committee*, pp. 41–43.

The TNEC chose not to support a program of Federal supervision and regulation of insurance. Control, it was felt, should remain with the states, but they should be exhorted to improve their procedures. Federal intervention, thus, would be limited to measures which would strengthen regulation by the states, but would not supplement or replace it by Federal controls.

Commissioner Pike would have preferred to have the report of the TNEC go farther. He recommended liberalizing investment laws to permit life insurance companies to invest a portion of their funds in common stocks.[170] This the Committee did not endorse. Moreover, in a statement which accompanied the final report and with which TNEC members O'Connell and Hinrichs concurred, Mr. Pike advocated extending a substantial degree of Federal supervision over life insurance companies.

1. A designated Federal agency should be enabled to obtain adequate information concerning the operations of life insurance companies, so that it may assemble detailed reports and information which it would have authority to disseminate for the benefit of companies, policyholders, and State and National officials.

2. A designated Federal agency should be empowered, with the approval of the President, to prohibit insurance companies from paying surrender values of the policy benefits during a limited period, not to exceed 90 days, or to place restrictions on such payments. This moratorium power should be exercised only in times of serious economic stress resulting in dislocations of the entire banking and financial structure.

3. A designated Federal agency should be given reasonable and clearly defined visitorial powers over all interstate life insurance companies, to the end that it may effectively coordinate and advise on insurance problems and assist States other than the State of domicile in the examination of interstate companies.

4. An Insurance Advisory Council, whose duties should be to advise the Congress and the appropriate State authorities, should be created to function in close cooperation with a designated Federal agency. The council should consist of representatives of State insurance commissioners, company officials, policyholders, and a designated Federal agency. In addition to its advisory duties, the council should be required to submit a written annual report to the Congress on the state of the insurance business, and to assist the States whenever possible in strengthening their own regulatory activities.[171] [O'Connell and Hinrichs concurring.]

SUPPLEMENTAL STATEMENTS

In addition to the dissenting and the supplemental statements referred to, other statements accompanied the final report, setting forth

[170] *Ibid.*, p. 42.   [171] *Ibid.*, p. 45.

the personal views of TNEC members Lubin, Henderson, Hinrichs, Sumners, and O'Mahoney. The most important of these is the joint statement by Messrs. Lubin and Henderson.[172] Though agreeing with the general tenor of the report, they felt that it should have gone much farther in its recommendations. They insisted that the TNEC was not organized as a mere "monopoly committee" and that a revived program of trust busting would fail to go to the heart of the American economic problem.

We do not believe [they said] that the program which this report presents would, in itself, have prevented the great depression of the thirties. . . . Surely, it should be possible . . . to formulate more clearly our national economic objectives and . . . to offer a concrete program geared to the needs of our times.

In the body of the final report Mr. Hinrichs, Acting Commissioner for the Bureau of Labor Statistics, inserted his "minority report," offering proposals to mitigate the distresses caused by technological innovation. These suggestions, which were similar to those presented by TNEC member Lubin in the preliminary deliberations, were as follows:

1. Industry and labor organization should develop joint studies of the means of effecting technological change with minimum hardship to the workers involved. They should mutually provide for advance notices of dismissal in labor contracts.

2. Legislation should be enacted providing for the payment of dismissal wages and retraining programs for technologically displaced workers.

3. The social-security laws should be immediately amended to extend unemployment compensation to cover more adequately the dismissal of workers from defense industries.[173]

Representative Sumners repeated his objections to the stand taken by the Committee with respect to the Miller-Tydings Act and the Federal licensing of corporations engaged in interstate commerce. In fact, he opposed any measure which would increase the jurisdiction of the Federal Government. To the Congressman the solution of these pressing problems must be left to the states, to the people, and to natural processes.

We seem to have forgotten [said he] that there is a living God whose laws control everywhere, guiding, directing, and compelling human beings to be governed by them in their economic and political government, as distinguished from being governed by the theories of men.[174]

172 *Ibid.*, pp. 51–52.   173 *Ibid.*, p. 23.
174 *Ibid.*, p. 50.

Chairman O'Mahoney, likewise, made a personal statement. It is significant that he neither took exception to the recommendations set forth nor offered any specific proposals in addition. More than to anyone else, the final report was due to him and the policies endorsed were chiefly his suggestions. Senator O'Mahoney concluded, however, with a proposal somewhat surprising in nature and unintentionally frank in its implications.[175]

Therefore I recommend that the Congress by an appropriate statute call a national conference of the various organizations representative of business, labor, agriculture, and consumers, which have for years been working on the diverse phases of the economic problem. The duties of such a conference would be twofold, first, to define the nature and democratic responsibility of such organizations—business, labor, agriculture, and all—and, second, to define a formula for stimulated production under the impetus of peace rather than war.[176]

[175] Discussed in the following chapter.
[176] *Final Report and Recommendations of the Temporary National Economic Committee,* p. 48.

CHAPTER XII

AN APPRAISAL

THE OUTBREAK of the second World War, in 1939 followed by the defense program in the United States and its eventual entrance into the war altered the role which the Temporary National Economic Committee might otherwise have played in the evolution of American economic institutions. The creation of a war economy, unfortunately, represents the only speedy way by which in recent years Western peoples have been able to mobilize their resources to achieve full employment. With the coming of the war, the conditions responsible for the organization of the TNEC, for the time being, disappeared. Had there been no war, however, it is doubtful whether the influence of the TNEC would have been profound. The hearings failed to concentrate sufficiently on any one subject to have a profound effect on public opinion. Some of the suggestions in the final recommendations showed little relevance to materials developed in the hearings, and slight attention was given to many problems posed therein. Despite its magnitude, it probably never would have ranked with the great inquiries of the past, such as the Armstrong, the Pujo, the Pecora, and the public utility investigations. In many respects it takes its place along with the Industrial Commission, its counterpart in so many ways, which has had little effect upon American legislative and economic history.

THE CONTRIBUTION OF THE TNEC

Notwithstanding its failure to justify the hopes of those responsible for its creation, the TNEC made a number of positive contributions and will, no doubt, retain a place in American economic history. Its full influence, probably its major influence, will be intangible—reflected in the thinking of the populace, of scholars, and of those responsible for designing and administering public law. Whatever the extent of this contribution, it will, of course, be incapable of measurement. It is possible, however, to point more directly to certain tangible and, in part, measurable contributions which the Committee already has made. These include assembling a great variety of data on pertinent economic problems, giving widespread publicity to these

facts and issues, bringing about voluntary reforms on the part of business management, and causing Congress to initiate laws to correct certain abuses.

Because of its mandate the TNEC initiated one of the most extensive and most fundamental investigations ever undertaken by any agency of its kind. The responsibilities assigned to it by the Congress and by the President related more vitally to the foundations of American economic life than those ever delegated to any other committee. The scope of its duties, the breadth of its task, and the burden of its obligations were tremendous, coming into existence as it did nine years after the collapse of the economic system in 1929 and confronted with the stark reality that the riddle of unemployment remained as yet unsolved.

The Committee assembled much varied information relating to the structure and functioning of the American economy. These materials relate to the organization and operation of many industries, such as steel, investment banking, petroleum, glass, milk, insurance, beryllium, whiskey, and copper. The pattern of the economy has been defined more clearly by focusing light upon the objectives, performance, and effects of numerous economic policies and institutions, including basing-point systems, holding companies, identical bidding, price leadership, trade associations, "fair trade" laws, racketeering self-government in industry, interstate trade barriers, monopoly laws, and patent policy. The implications and significance of important economic problems are developed with recommendations here and there for their solution; such problems include the irresponsibility of corporate management, the inequality of income distribution, the inadequacy of consumer purchasing power, the failure of investment processes to absorb savings, the helplessness of consumers, and the plight of those technologically unemployed.

In this collection of facts, trends, and opinions scholars and historians will find the raw materials of research from which to interpret recent American economic life; statesmen and legislators may find guidance for the formulation of policies to govern the economy; and in it, no doubt, demagogues will discover texts and slogans to support their causes.

But it would be quite possible, as already has been done by some who have written on the subject, to misjudge and to overemphasize this "storehouse of new information" role of the TNEC hearings. One might easily be awed by the three-foot shelf containing thirty-seven

volumes and 17,000 pages and be impressed by the audacious scope of an undertaking which tackled at one time substantially all the most trying economic problems of our time.

There is, however, relatively little that is new in the TNEC. Often it tells a story that has been told before. Though much valuable information has been assembled, most of it was already available in the standard publications of the day. Treatises on holding companies, business cycles, the corporation, banking and finance, monopoly, and related matters have dealt with the same problems which one encounters in the hearings and ofttimes have done so in a more analytical and a more comprehensive manner. No doubt a more thorough description and analysis of the same practices and problems might have been obtained by a judicious selection of materials from the leading encyclopedia devoted to the economic and social sciences. Nevertheless, because of the magnitude of the undertaking and because of the prestige which government investigations and reports command, the TNEC hearings and report will often be cited as a fountainhead of authority. Like the writings of Adam Smith, the Bible, and the epigrams of Confucius, they will be invoked by men with little knowledge to awe and convince others of equally limited understanding.

A significant contribution of the TNEC, however, is not that it revealed the existence and described the operations of certain economic practices, but that it brought the record up to date. That cartels, holding companies, "fair trade" laws, patent abuses, racketeering, basing point systems, collusive bidding, and other devices have been employed to regiment the market is scarcely new knowledge. That the TNEC cut a cross-section of American economic life in 1939, however, that it revealed these practices to be employed in full vigor long after they had become textbook material and after fifty years of anti-monopoly legislation, and that it gathered together some of the materials essential to a complete analysis of these devices and of their effects on the economy is in itself a major contribution. That the TNEC presents little that is new undoubtedly is a fact, but that it describes how today business men continue to resort to devices and practices which several decades ago were branded as contrary to public policy is also a fact which should not pass unnoticed.

Two important functions of government investigations are the discovery and the publicizing functions. Even if the TNEC had revealed nothing new with respect to the organization of the economy or to the causes of maladjustments, it has performed an educative service by

bringing to the attention of legislators and the public many pertinent facts relating to modern problems and by focusing attention upon the various solutions which were proposed. The hearings served as a basis for hundreds of newspaper articles and editorials and for numerous discussions in current periodicals. Thus, it became the center of a great forum of discussion and debate—a process vital to democratic institutions. Though this service to public enlightenment is unmeasurable, it should be listed high among the contributions of the TNEC. Moreover, the hearings served as a sounding board for many who urged the adoption of particular programs to correct various aspects of economic life. Mr. Arnold employed it to obtain popular support for a more aggressive antitrust program; Chairman O'Mahoney used it to develop sentiment for national charters for corporations. One after another the spotlight of public attention was focused on other issues. The frequent expenditure of large sums for no other purpose than to foster an alert and informed public opinion might prove to be of inestimable value in promoting an orderly evolution of the economic pattern.

Other accomplishments of the TNEC, however, have been somewhat more tangible. Even before the adoption of the final report, members of the Committee were able to point to a number of changes in business practices resulting directly from its activities. Although such reforms can be considered neither extensive nor especially fundamental to the basic problems which called the TNEC into being, they involved modifications of pricing policies on the part of some industries, abandonment of certain monopolistic practices by others, increased public administrative activity to control similar practices, and the passage of laws relating to certain issues dealt with in the hearings.

Examples of altered pricing policies are found in the beryllium, steel, and building material industries. The beryllium hearings were begun in May, 1939; scarcely more than one month later the leading producer in this industry announced a series of price reductions amounting to nearly 15 percent. In the steel industry prices were cut even before the hearings got under way; business journals, rightly or wrongly, attributed the reduced prices to the forthcoming investigation and gave it credit a year later for the announcement that steel prices in general would remain at the revised levels.[1] That the TNEC served, at least temporarily, to restrain price-fixing activities in other

---

[1] See, for example, *Business Week,* July 2, 1938, and December 2, 1939.

industries was evidenced by confidential correspondence circulated among building material manufacturers, warning against "undue" raising of prices and advising that the Monopoly Committee was in a position to make investigation of price structures.[2]

Industrial policy was altered in a number of other ways. After testimony has been presented condemning the "Iowa Plan" in the petroleum industry as a monopolistic device by which the integrated oil companies extended their control over the retail branch of the industry, the president of one large company which had used this plan recommended its abandonment.[3] Similarly, after the completion of the patent hearings and as a result of action brought by the Department of Justice, the Hartford-Empire Company and other large producers of glass containers announced their willingness to grant unrestricted licenses of glass-producing machinery.[4] Following the tin-plate investigation, producers of that product negotiated new contracts with canners on a more liberal basis. The life insurance hearings disclosed that large life insurance companies frequently had elected to their boards of directors individuals who rarely, if ever, attended board meetings; when it became evident that the TNEC was interested, steps were taken to alter the practice.[5]

The vigorous activities of the Antitrust Division, under the leadership of TNEC member Thurman Arnold, has been attributed in part to the moral support which they received from the TNEC and to the degree of popular support the latter had created for such a policy. The extent to which this is true is, of course, immeasurable; both the TNEC hearings and the increased activity of the Antitrust Division are part of the same socio-economic complex, but it is true, nevertheless, that the Antitrust Division assumed an increased importance during these days.

Attributable also to the work of the Committee were numerous bills presented to Congress. At the time the final report was made, fourteen bills were before Congress dealing with matters raised by the TNEC, seeking to curb monopoly, to investigate foreign holdings within the country, to determine the impact of technology upon long-term unemployment, and to study measures for dealing with post-war problems.[6] The most important action which had been taken by

[2] *Final Report and Recommendations of the Temporary National Economic Committee*, p. 82.   [3] *Ibid.*, p. 81.   [4] *Ibid.*, p. 127.
[5] "Legal Economic, Social aspects of Monopoly," *Commercial and Financial Chronicle*, CXLVII (November 26, 1938), 3248.
[6] *Final Report and Recommendations of the Temporary National Economic Committee*, pp. 68, 75.

Congress at this time related to patents; five of the seven recommendations made by the Committee in this connection [7] had been enacted into law. These statutes simplified interference procedure, abolished renewal applications, shortened the period of public use allowed to an inventor prior to application for a patent, shortened, similarly, the period during which a claimant may assert priority of invention, and authorized the Patent Office to adopt methods to speed up patent procedure.

THE SCOPE OF THE HEARINGS

The mandate given to the Temporary National Economic Committee was broad, calling as it did for a twofold analysis of the causes, character, and effects of the concentration of economic power and of monopoly and the reasons why the "business system does not provide employment and produce and distribute goods in such a way as to sustain an acceptable standard of living." [8] Perhaps this mandate was too comprehensive, presenting thereby too great a task for the Committee. Despite the character of the hearings and the thoroughness with which some subjects were covered, there are several important areas which the Committee could have been expected to explore which it neglected or to which it gave only passing and incidental attention.

A brief appraisal would be appropriate at this point, showing the extent to which the TNEC fulfilled the assignments delegated to it. The task of the Committee, which was outlined by the presidential message of April 29, 1938,[9] and by the joint resolution creating the TNEC,[10] required investigations and recommendations along the following lines.

Improvement of antitrust procedure.—The TNEC performed this portion of its assignment quite effectively. Monopolistic situations were analyzed, and in substance the final report became a recommendation for revitalizing antitrust activities.

Mergers and interlocking relationships.—One finds little throughout the hearings, either in an organized approach to the subject or in incidental treatment, which presents an analysis of facts, trends, and social implications relating to these types of combinations.

Financial controls.—Although valuable studies were made relating to savings and investment, to insurance companies, and to investment banking practices, the broad subject of financial controls and their effect upon

[7] See the *Preliminary Report*, S. Doc. 95, 76th Cong., 1st sess.; see also *ibid.*, pp. 137–358.
[8] Presidential Message of April 29, 1938, S. Doc. 173, 75th Cong., 3d sess.
[9] S. Doc. 173, 75th Cong., 3d sess.   [10] Public Resolution 113, 75th Cong.

the economy was given no systematic treatment. Specifically, the President requested a study of (a) investment trusts and (b) bank holding companies. Such treatment as they received was incidental.

Trade associations.—There is a great deal of material scattered throughout the hearings giving witness to the far-reaching operations and influence of trade associations. Scarcely anywhere, however, does the Committee make the trade association the subject matter of its direct attention—to discover its character, extensiveness, growth, *modus operandi,* and its general effect upon economic and political institutions. Although the trade association was the subject of certain recommendations presented in the final report, these did not flow from materials developed in the hearings.[11]

Patent laws.—Probably on no other subject was the TNEC more direct and more thorough than it was in this portion of its assigned task. The patent hearings are revealing, and the final recommendations constitute a straightforward attempt to deal with the problems raised.

Tax correctives.—Fundamental as the tax problem is and far-reaching as were the opportunities for an effective analysis of fiscal policy and for suggesting constructive reforms of the tax structure, this segment of the proposed study was either neglected or evaded by the TNEC. At about this time an analysis and a set of recommendations made by the staid magazine of businessmen, *Fortune,* went to the heart of the problem,[12] whereas the TNEC fell short of its opportunity.[13]

Bureau of Industrial Economics.—The creation of such a bureau at no time became the subject of formal discussion nor was testimony introduced detailing the functions such an agency might perform, the opportunities it might have for service, or possible objections to it.

It is remarkable in a study as extensive as was that undertaken by the TNEC into the "concentration of economic power" that so few of the important questions relating to concentration were analytically or systematically explored. The hearings began and ended with the assumption that concentration is becoming increasingly characteristic of the economy, and it was continually implied that such a trend is undesirable. Yet nowhere was the matter the subject of careful scrutiny. Just what concentration is or how it is measured was left unanswered. The extent to which concentration is characteristic of the economy was left to conjecture. Quantitative measures of the trend, decade by decade, during the last half century were lacking. Broad generalizations and inferences were compounded without

11 Temporary National Economic Committee Monograph No. 18 presents a comprehensive analysis of trade associations, but this study was not available to the Committee in the preparation of its final report.
12 "The Second Fortune Round Table," *Fortune,* XIX (May, 1939), 67 ff.
13 Three monographs were eventually published relating to fiscal policy: Temporary National Economic Committee Monographs Nos. 3, 9, 20.

factual foundation. The question whether concentration is inevitable, beneficial, and desirable from the standpoint of productive efficiency and the use of modern technology went quite unexplored. Whatever the degree to which concentration exists, little attention was given to its effect upon economic, social, and political life, and in particular upon the distribution of income, the mechanism of investment, the stratification of social classes, and the stability of democratic institutions. It would seem that a searching exploration of these and other issues basic to the question of concentration would have been called for before a final report could be written.

Some issues, such as taxation and fiscal policy, were neglected; others were evaded. In a study of concentration and monopoly all relevant factors merit an objective and dispassionate examination. Someone might well have been assigned to assure that a comprehensive examination of the more important issues pertinent to its assignment was made by the TNEC. Many such questions received a critical and judicious examination, but the fact that a number of others did not leaves either the methods or the objectivity of the Committee subject to censure. Two examples will serve to illustrate: the relationship of tariffs and of advertising to concentration and monopoly did not become subjects of Committee inquiry.

In the case of advertising the very suggestion that it merited consideration brought prompt rebuke from the Committee's chairman. When a witness called attention to the vital role which advertising plays in monopolistic competition, he immediately discovered that he was on forbidden ground.[14] An impartial tribunal investigating the forces which lead to concentration and monopoly would have welcomed information relating to the role of advertising. But the chairman indicated his disapproval in such a manner that a leading journal of business described him as the "champion of advertising." [15] An attempt to reveal certain facts was designated as an "attack on advertising." [16] Although the Committee had lent an attentive ear to many other "attacks," this one was to be avoided. This is strange reasoning, inasmuch as the Committee, through its chairman, had repeated frequently that the purpose of the TNEC was to conduct "a careful, serious, and constructive study of the causes which have brought

[14] *Hearings before the Temporary National Economic Committee*, Part 8, pp. 3397–3412, 3453–3456.
[15] *Business Week*, May 20, 1939, p. 44; see also *Printer's Ink*, CLXXXVII (May 18, 1939), 30.
[16] *Hearings before the Temporary National Economic Committee*, Part 8, p. 3408.

about the concentration of economic power." [17] Nevertheless, the chairman refused to permit testimony relating to advertising unless malefaction could be proved. The pith of the chairman's remarks are as follows:

> I confess that I see nothing wrong about advertising.[18]
> That seems to do away with the whole testimony of the witness because you brought him here to make an attack on advertising but when he is brought face to face with that he denies the attack on advertising. . . .[19]
> You know, it just strikes me, Mr. Montgomery, that there are enough illegitimate practices in the economic world for us to try to solve and not bother ourselves with legitimate things which in the very nature of the human being you can't control.[20]

This conception of the task of the TNEC that it should listen to facts only when illegitimate practices are found violates a fundamental principle originally laid down by the Committee; in fact, the chairman himself had described the TNEC as a fact-finding agency, not a grand jury,[21] as conducting a hearing, not a prosecution,[22] as engaged in the study of economic conditions, not of wrongdoing.[23] The suggestion that the TNEC confine its attention to situations in which it can be shown that illegitimate practices exist precludes the possibility of an examination of the rules of the game, as such, to discover whether or not such rules might be altered to the advantage of the general economy and of society at large. If the Committee seriously desired to analyze the forces resulting in monopoly, monopoly prices, and concentration, it could not ignore the effects of advertising, false or faithful. What the Committee said, in effect, was that certain areas of economic life are sacrosanct and that consideration of the principles by which they operate and the manner in which they function is forbidden territory.

THE QUEST FOR A PANACEA

A note of pathos pervaded the hearings; it was evidenced by the oft-expressed or oft-implied hope that in some manner, after piling up a mountain of facts, some formula or panacea would emerge from

---

[17] *Congressional Record*, Vol. LXXXIV, Part 14, p. 3496; the Committee by unanimous resolution had declared "that its function and purpose is to collect and analyze . . . available facts pertaining to the items specified in Public Resolution 113 (75th Cong.), in an objective, unbiased, and dispassionate manner" (*ibid.*, Part 1, p. 2).
[18] *Hearings before the Temporary National Economic Committee*, Part 8, p. 3400.
[19] *Ibid.*, p. 3408.   [20] *Ibid.*, pp. 3409–3410.
[21] *Ibid.*, Part 17, p. 9459.   [22] *Ibid.*, Part 15, p. 8206.
[23] *Ibid.*, Part 23, p. 12075; Part 17, p. 9724.

the amorphous collection thus assembled. As one witness expressed it, "We have long hoped that out of the great store of information amassed by various Government agencies, concerning the American economy, there would come some practical conclusions pointing the road toward the elimination of the Nation's No. 1 problem: unemployment." [24]

However valuable facts and recorded information may be and despite their importance to the formulation of workable policy, they do not, in themselves, provide the answers to basic economic problems. The formulation of economic policy—as distinguished from the more or less chance evolution of economic institutions—depends upon a rather clear understanding and agreement as to the objectives sought. This requires a modicum of agreement, tacit or otherwise, as to what interests economic processes should serve, which institutions should be employed and which should give way, and what interest groups should be shorn of vested positions for the common benefit. Without reasonable agreement upon these and other objectives, the clear-cut delineation of social and economic policy becomes quite impossible.

No such common understanding existed among the members of the TNEC. This, of course, is not surprising, since the Committee reflected the general indecision of the American people. Quite obviously, even had it been able to agree upon a common and consistent set of objectives and had it elaborated a policy leading to the right, to the left, or staying in the middle, it may not have been able to muster any substantial support in Congress or elsewhere.[25] The Committee was made up in part of conservative defenders of the *status quo,* some of whom wanted no TNEC organized in the first place and who saw little need for social change. Others were liberals who desired to "make capitalism work." Some of these were "one solution" men, with preconceived plans and thereby relatively blind to the broader aspects of other problems. A few were men with inquisitive minds, willing to lend considerate attention to bold plans if they gave evidence of mitigating the dislocations of the American economy. All could agree with the chairman in his desire to preserve the democratic system, the system of private enterprise, the profit system, the free utilization of capital, and the achievement of full

[24] *Ibid.,* Part 30, p. 16899; see also pp. 15614, 16817.
[25] This is not to deny that the Committee had an obligation and possessed a remarkable opportunity to exercise leadership and to lend its support to the eventual creation of a body of public opinion which would support a program designed to make the economy function more satisfactorily.

employment.[26] Beyond these generalities there was little agreement.[27]

In this manner, then, the TNEC ended more or less as it began —as a fruitless quest for a panacea. The mountain of facts produced no magic formula, principally, perhaps, because the formula sought in the composite mind of the members was one which would take care of everything and yet leave things as they are; one which would alter none of our basic institutions, affront few of our vested interest groups, change little in the organization and the pattern of economic society, yet at the same time adjust its most far-reaching dislocations and solve its most fundamental problems.

MONOPOLY ESCAPISM

The TNEC "Investigation of Concentration of Economic Power" was in effect a monopoly investigation, and the final recommendations were concerned almost exclusively with the restoration and preservation of the competitive market. From the very beginning an inherent weakness of the approach was the acceptance of basic assumptions which should have been the subject of continuous and rigorous examination. The investigators began with the postulates that monopoly was the basic cause of the economic ills to which the economy succumbed after 1929 and that monopoly, *per se,* is bad. Starting with these two propositions and without submitting their validity to investigation, the majority of the Committee found in them the basis of its final conclusions. The three years which had intervened, the million dollars which had been spent, the many witnesses who had appeared, and the 30,000 pages of testimony did not yield replies to many fundamental queries which these two assumptions provoke. That they did not is due in large part to the fact that such answers were not sought. Hence, there was a tendency for the testimony assembled to become a mass of substantiating data rather than to present an analysis of the forces resulting in economic dislocation and maladjustment.

There is something appealing and satisfying to the doctrinarian— whether he be a follower of Marx, Adam Smith, Ricardo, or of some

26 *Congressional Record,* Vol. LXXXIV, Part 14, p. 3496.
27 One critic characterized the TNEC as follows: "The schisms within the Monopoly Committee simply reflect the organized indecision of the middle class. . . . As tribunes of the middle class the monopoly investigators find themselves paralyzed with doubts. . . . If the Monopoly Committee has not gone very far beneath the surface and shows no signs of wanting to do so, it is not for lack of brains or money. It is simply that it doesn't dare to." MacDonald, "The Monopoly Committee, a Study in Frustration," *The American Scholar,* VIII (July, 1939), 295–308.

medieval theological sect—in finding in his dogma a set of first causes and ultimate answers. A body of established principles often precludes the necessity of exhaustive analysis and renders possible the discovery of simple solutions for complex answers. There is an element of such escapism in the almost exclusive monopoly approach to the problems which called the TNEC into being. It is as though men yearned for the simple life which prevailed when there were no great problems of social readjustment created by a dynamic society, by modern technology, and by mass production—when there were no corporations and no locomotives. The antimonopoly tradition is deeply imbedded in our folklore; it has an emotional appeal, and it has a political appeal. For centuries "monopoly" has been an ugly word and monopolists have been considered the agents of diabolical plots; men in public life may, therefore, denounce monopoly without jeopardizing their political careers and at the same time feel a sense of righteousness for doing so.

Questions left unanswered by the monopoly probe include the following: What was the relationship of monopoly to the depression? What is the relationship of monopoly to economic efficiency? Is a substantial amount of monopoly organization inevitable and desirable? What can be learned from fifty years of antitrust action? Aside from its economic aspects, what is the relationship of monopoly to constitutional democracy? There is a tacit assumption running through both the hearings and the final report that the depression was in large part the fruit of economic concentration and monopoly. Nowhere, however, was a case developed to show this causal relationship. No doubt a good case could have been made that monopoly prices and concentration were important aggravating factors in the breakdown of the economy in 1929, but the weight of testimony by Messrs. Hansen, Lubin, Henderson, Ezekiel, Altman, Manuel, and Davenport would indicate that, important as protection of the public against monopoly is, it does not present the solution to the basic maladjustments creating "idle men and idle machines."

The relation of monopoly and of bigness (concentration) to economic efficiency went quite unexplored. That a definite and positive relationship exists in an appreciable area of the economy is certain. At times modern technology, mass production, integrated organization (horizontal and vertical) of plant facilities, wide area marketing, and numerous other techniques making for product quality at lower costs are in themselves adjuncts of bigness and of concentration and,

since monopoly is a matter of degree, of monopoly. Technology has permitted a new productive efficiency, and an economic institution— the corporation—has made possible the assembling of capital equipment to implement the new technology. Bigness, with its concomitant, monopoly (oligopoly), has given us automobiles, locomotives, telegraphs, electric-light bulbs, radios, steel, and many other products. There is, therefore, an area in which monopoly, and oligopoly, are the more efficient modes of economic organization. How to achieve, preserve, and harness such bigness to promote the social welfare merits the most critical attention of this generation.

A corollary to the question of efficiency is whether a further trend toward monopoly is desirable or inevitable. Professor Beard, after studying trends for the 200 years since the beginning of the industrial revolution and the 50 years since the passage of the Sherman Act, speaks of certain fundamental elements in the process of human history which are inexorable and with which we must work whether we like them or not.

As to myself, my conviction is clear and positive. After reading tons of trust-busting literature, briefs of lawyers in trust cases and judicial decisions and thousands of pages of testimony and recommendations, after listening to any number of anti-trust speeches by honest men and demagogues, after suffering from the frightful din and racket of more than fifty years, after reading statistical studies, such as John Moody's and Berle's and Means', I have come to the conclusion that ours is now and in the nature of things is destined to be a great continental, technological society and the trust-busters, however honest and honorable, are just whistling in the wind . . . are unwillingly the foes of getting our economic machine in full motion, and are destined to defeat besides.[28]

Frequently we have recognized the social desirability of monopolies and have insisted upon them. We have invented social institutions to harness them. By means of the public utility fiction we harnessed grist mills, grain elevators, railroads, electric light and gas companies, and numerous other producing agencies. Other monopolies have been created and have been made subject to the social will in other ways, as in the case of the postal system, the Tennessee Valley Authority, and Boulder Dam. Probably few can be found who would object to the program proposed by the TNEC to conduct a relentless campaign against the abuses of monopoly, but such a program, however valuable, should not be allowed to deter us from the search for an

[28] "The Anti-Trust Racket," *The New Republic*, XCVI (September 21, 1938), 184.

effective harness for modern technology or to lull men to the belief that it alone constitutes a complete solution.

It would have been fruitful for the TNEC to have made an analysis of the record of antitrust action since 1890, and, indeed, it would seem to be essential before recommending the continuation and the intensification of the trust-busting campaign. Why, after fifty years, should there be occasion for a monopoly investigation? To what extent is the failure of the antimonopoly program due to defective laws, to indifference of administrative leaders, to inadequacy of the budget, and to other factors? To what extent should antitrust policy be the sole social approach to monopoly, and to what extent should it merely be auxiliary to other, more fundamental, more comprehensive, and perhaps more heroic, approaches?

A less tangible and in all probability a materially more basic aspect of the impact of monopoly upon the social order is its relation to the political system. Whether or not monopoly, some or all of it, may be shown to be more effective from the standpoint of economic efficiency, it may be destructive of certain civic values which men hold in higher esteem than the fruits of a more productive economy. Is a regime of monopoly compatible with democratic institutions? Is political centralization an inevitable fruit of economic centralization, as TNEC members were prone to assert? What is and will be the impact of monopoly and centralization on the middle class, so often described as the *sine qua non* of democratic institutions? What relation exists between concentration and monopoly and an increase of the so-called proletariat, and what are the implications of this relationship to capitalistic institutions and democratic government? And this, no doubt, raises once more the crucial questions: "If monopoly, in what areas, to what extent, for whom, and by whom?" Truly, these are trying problems, and perhaps they are incapable of solution, but nothing will be gained by failure to recognize them.

THE NEGLECT OF BASIC ISSUES

The final report of the TNEC, absorbed as it was with monopoly, circumvented fundamental problems with which both the Committee and the nation were faced. The problem of "idle factories and idle workers," the devastating impact of the economic crisis, received scant consideration. This is somewhat astonishing in the light of the opening sessions of the TNEC, when in the "Economic Prologue," Mr.

Henderson, Commissioner Lubin, and Dr. Thorp so lucidly and so unequivocally outlined the basic maladjustments of the economy and detailed the task which the Committee was called upon to perform. "The over-all question," said Mr. Henderson, "seems to be, Why have we not had full employment and full utilization of our magnificent resources?" [29] That the Committee offered no program relating to the achievement of full employment is the more surprising in view of the fact that it had listened to the testimony and suggestions of Professor Hansen, Dr. Ezekiel, and others. The promise of the TNEC was never fulfilled. The Committee's original conception of its task contrasts strikingly with the pattern which ultimately emerged in the final report. None the less, the original conception could scarcely be more aptly expressed than by the following composite description pieced together from declarations of the chairman:

It cannot be too often repeated that unemployment—unemployment of capital as well as unemployment of men—is the central question mark that rises before us all.[30]

. . . the Temporary National Economic Committee begins this hearing to develop . . . why it is that in a world of inexhaustible natural resources, inhabited by men who know more about the physical and chemical secrets of nature than all the generations which have preceded them, we still have not learned how to apply the wonders of technology to the abundance of nature in such a fashion as to provide decent jobs for the millions of idle who are able and willing to work.[31]

The resolution by which the committee was created, and the message of the President which was the cause for the creation of the committee, were both directed to the fundamental problem of how we can solve the question of unemployment, unemployment both of labor and of capital.[32]

The end to be sought is a stable society in which the individual members have an opportunity to live with a certain degree of security and have the opportunity to pursue the activities which appeal to them.[33]

We seek the formula by which we may enable the people to increase production and to distribute goods and services more equitably and effectively than ever before. We seek to foster and encourage private business.[34]

I think it is not only appropriate, but important, to call public attention to the fact that the failure of leaders throughout the world to answer the questions which were propounded to us was the fundamental cause of the present world crisis.[35]

[29] *Hearings before the Temporary National Economic Committee*, Part 1, p. 180.
[30] *Ibid.*, Part 14, p. 7098.   [31] *Ibid.*, Part 30, p. 16208.   [32] *Ibid.*, Part 15, p. 8165.
[33] *Final Report and Recommendations of the Temporary National Economic Committee*, p. 437.   [34] *Ibid.*, p. 672.   [35] *Ibid.*, p. 62.

In the first few paragraphs of the final report the Committee prepared its readers for bold and comprehensive proposals dealing realistically with the functional and structural aspects of twentieth-century economic life. One is unprepared, however, for the simple suggestion, reminiscent of Say's theory of the markets, that a return to free competition is all that is required. In fact, the Committee said,

It will not do . . . to putter around with patchwork remedies intended to restore an economic structure that is already dead. . . . The upheaval in which this generation is caught proceeds from the failure of leadership, here and throughout the world, to comprehend that the nineteenth century is as completely an era of the past as the eighteenth. Efforts to solve our problems of unemployment and underinvestment by the means and methods of the past were foredoomed to collapse, not because the principles on which leaders acted were wrong, but because the methods were not suited to the times.[36]

Probably the most severe critics of the final report were two members who not only signed that document but also expressed "complete agreement" with most of its recommendations. Although concurring in the views that the essential basis of the economic system is free private enterprise, that the abuses of monopoly should be curbed, and that totalitarianism, in the form of "big government" and of "big business," is untenable, both Commissioners Lubin and Henderson expressed their disappointment with the perspective and performance of the Committee. In a separate statement they said, "We feel . . . that the report should go further and fully take into account the fact that . . . the economic world of tomorrow will be a very different kind of world than that which we have known in the past." [37] They reminded the Committee that all of its members had agreed that it was not to be, as was popularly supposed, merely a "Monopoly Committee." [38] Messrs. Henderson and Lubin went on to say that the report emphasizes the avoidance of monopoly more than the broader and more fundamental approach. An apt summary of their position is as follows:

The Temporary National Economic Committee was charged with the fundamental problem of devising ways and means of utilizing fully our men, our machines, and our materials so that the economic paralysis of the early 1930's could not occur again. . . . We do not believe that the pro-

[36] *Ibid.*, p. 24.   [37] *Ibid.*, p. 51.
[38] Frequently in public statements and in Congress Chairman O'Mahoney protested against calling the TNEC a monopoly committee. On one occasion when the inquiry was so characterized he remonstrated that it is "not anti-monopoly, damn it" [*Nation's Business*, XXVI (September 28, 1938), 15].

gram which this report presents would, in itself, have prevented the great depression of the thirties. Likewise such a program will not be adequate to meet the problems of tomorrow.[39]

The testimony and the suggestions offered by Professor Hansen were denounced as un-American and unrealistic; the analyses by Messrs. Henderson, Lubin, and Thorp in the preliminary hearings were forgotten; the approaches outlined by Dr. Ezekiel and others were disregarded. Throughout the hearings influential members of the TNEC seemed reluctant to entertain the idea that fundamental functional dislocations had developed requiring equally fundamental but new approaches; they appeared to fear the implications of most of the testimony relating to problems of the business cycle. It is as though Committee members, not liking their essential task, solved it by assuming the problem not to exist.

Apparently the Committee was not completely unaware of this basic deficiency. It has been noted that in the final report it said:

The members of the committee are not rash enough to believe that they can lay down a program which will solve the great problems that beset the world, but they are convinced that the information which this committee has assembled, when eventually properly analyzed and disseminated, will enable the people of America to know what must be done if human freedom is to be preserved.[40]

To a hopeful citizenry, the victims of an ailing economy, the TNEC thus made its final bequest—not a courageous, comprehensive, and realistic program for action but a mass of material to be "properly analyzed" by someone to discover what might be done Pandora's box without a key.[41] Some day, Committee members appeared to hope, someone would accept the challenge and formulate a plan before it is too late. The chairman gave testimony to his "abiding faith that

39 *Final Report and Recommendations of the Temporary National Economic Committee,* pp. 51–52; see also pp. 526–527.
40 *Ibid.,* p. 4.
41 Current press reactions to the final report reflected the general disillusionment experienced by those who had expected more tangible results from the inquiry. Professor Beard, writing in *The New Republic,* XCVI (September 21, 1938), 182, had anticipated such a report when he said, "If all we can do is snap at the heels of business, while the economic machine runs at 50 percent of efficiency and ten or twelve million people sink into the degradation of permanent unemployment, then we might as well give it up and go whistling, not in the wind, but in the graveyard." *Business Week* (March 22, 1941), p. 22, spoke of the report as a "magnificent failure," "a colossal dud." *Time,* XXXVII (April 14, 1941), 85, characterized the recommendations as follows: "The Committee rattled a rusty BB gun into place and pinged at the nation's economic problems." I. F. Stone, writing in *The Nation,* CLII (April 19, 1941), 463, summarized the work of the TNEC thus: "It spent three years digging up the facts, and then reinterred them with as much dispatch as was decently possible."

the patriotism and ability of the people of America is equal to the task." [42] To do what the Committee had failed to do, the chairman in his supplementary statement to the Final Report proposed calling together a national conference of the representatives of business, labor, agriculture, and consumers, to find "a formula for stimulated production." [43]

FACTORS ACCOUNTING FOR THE CHARACTER OF THE HEARINGS AND THE REPORT

That the TNEC initiated its inquiry with a sense of responsibility, a measure of zeal, and reasonably high aspirations seems evident. That its final achievements were not commensurate with what was expected of the Committee seems equally manifest. Although a complete analysis of the underlying reasons for this outcome would encompass all the elements contributing to the socio-political complex of the depression decade, it is possible to suggest a few factors which were important in shaping the course taken by the TNEC. These include the character of the Committee itself, the predilections of its members, its loss of personnel, the absence of a purposive and dominating leader, the fear of business antagonism, the tremendous scope of the Committee's task, the lack of integrated organization, and its failure to operate as a forum for constructive proposals.

The composition of the Committee did not contribute to its effectiveness. It was large; it was hybrid; it was responsible to diverse authorities; as a corollary to all these facts, its members represented divergent areas of social thinking. There were twelve members on the TNEC; generally, effective committees are smaller, so that concerted action can more readily be achieved and individual members may feel a sense of responsibility for shaping committee policy. The TNEC was a hybrid committee, being neither senatorial, congressional, nor executive. None of the outstanding investigative bodies of the past were so constituted. The TNEC was a departure from precedent; only the Industrial Commission had employed this device. Despite the fact that the latter was the greatest undertaking of its kind prior to 1939 this blood brother to the TNEC produced little that was tangible or measurable. Its report, widely described as timid and vague,[44] was shelved by Congress.

[42] *Final Report and Recommendations of the Temporary National Economic Committee,* p. 687.
[43] *Ibid.,* p. 48.
[44] Charles A. Beard, writing in *The New Republic* ["The Anti-Trust Racket," XCVI

Members of the Congress, veterans of the investigative process, had warned that this type of committee was not the best machinery to do the job. As a joint committee, it suffered from a split personality.[45] Senator Wheeler, speaking before the Senate, said:

I think we are setting a very foolish precedent . . . I think the investigation should be made either by the Senate, or by the Departments, and we should not have a joint committee.[46]

Similarly, Senator Norris expressed his doubts about this type of organization.

This resolution provides for a committee to be composed of three members of the Senate, three members of the House of Representatives, and five members of the different departments . . . I do not believe . . . that much good will be accomplished by a three-headed investigation of that kind.[47]

There is no way of estimating what effect the loss of personnel had upon the ultimate contribution of the TNEC. Only half the original Committee members who assembled at the first hearings remained to write the final report; two-thirds of the Senators were gone, one-third of the Congressmen, and one-half of the original executive appointees. Moreover, the Committee lost the full-time services of its energetic and provocative executive secretary. Seven out of thirteen had left the Committee, and these included some of the best minds and most influential leaders in public life. These changes, however, represent only about half of those which took place, since some who replaced original members likewise departed. More serious, perhaps, than the actual loss of personnel were the disruptions to Committee procedure which such changes entailed. Unavoidably, members were called upon to propose a program relating to issues discussed in hearings which they had not been privileged to hear. The continuity of thought and the deliberation and discussion which the Committee process makes possible was not shared by the new members.

The disruption of Committee personnel was in part the result of the time element. The final report was presented almost four years

---

(September 21, 1938), 182.] characterized the Industrial Commission as follows: "The Commission engaged experts, heard witnesses, inquired into trusts and combinations in restraint of trade and otherwise, and heaped up thousands of pages of testimony. At the close it made a few pious recommendations . . . . the mountain groaned and out came, not a mouse, but a squeak."

45 "Its frustration and impotence are caused by a severe case of schizophrenia."—MacDonald, "The Monopoly Committee," *The American Scholar*, VIII (July, 1939), 303.
46 *Congressional Record*, Vol. LXXXIII, Part 8, p. 8590.
47 *Ibid.*, p. 8500.

after the President's monopoly message to Congress and nearly three years after the first hearings. With the passage of time there was opportunity for interest and zeal to wane, a process which was not remedied by loss of membership. Added to this is the fact that the economic orientation of the nation was rapidly altering. War was imminent, and the problem of national mobilization had begun to challenge men's minds and served to de-emphasize the motives which had called forth the inquiry.

A salient characteristic of the more prominent and successful inquiries of the past has been the role played by certain able men selected by the committees to plan and direct their activities. Great economic investigations have tended to be one-man shows, and their success has depended in large part on the ability, zeal, fearlessness, and energy of some outstanding man into whose hands the committee placed the conduct of the investigation. Ordinarily such men have been employed as counsels; as such they have been able to devote full time and full attention to their task. They have been unencumbered by many of the pressures and issues of expediency which attach to the careers of men in political life; they have been relatively young men with the prospects of establishing a reputation in public life. At the turn of the century Charles Evans Hughes guided the Armstrong Investigation to a conclusion resulting in many reforms of insurance laws; Samuel Untermyer dominated the Pujo probe of finance banking which led to the Federal Reserve, Federal Trade Commission, and Clayton Acts; and Ferdinand Pecora engineered the activities of the Banking and Currency Committee which resulted in the Securities and Exchange Act. No Hughes, no Untermyer, and no Pecora rendered similar service to the TNEC. An undertaking as comprehensive as was that of the TNEC was perhaps in greater need of such leadership than were the many inquiries which preceded it.

One of the Committee's greatest assets became an intrinsic weakness. Members were determined that this should be an objective, impartial investigation without any punitive characteristic or intent. Under continuous pressure and subject to skillfully planned publicity, Committee members permitted (perhaps unconsciously, but at least for expediency's sake) this laudable purpose to divert them from undertaking a fearless inquiry into the fundamental causes of economic dislocations and from attempting to formulate a program to rectify them. Even before the bill creating the TNEC was passed, the inquiry was labeled on the floor of Congress "an attack on busi-

ness," "a reign of terror" which would "wreck the nation." These accusations were particularly significant, since the Administration, because of its reform program, had been under continuous attack for being hostile to business. Before the first hearings were held, members of the Committee were apologizing for its program and giving out press interviews assuring the nation that its intentions were honorable and that it did not intend to undermine established institutions. How closely that committed it in advance to an innocuous final report is, of course, difficult to say. But a continuous verbal barrage reached the Committee and members of Congress protesting against the political deviltry which the inquiry was supposed to represent. Some ingenious press agent characterized the undertaking as a "witch hunt," an epithet which was repeated frequently while the Committee was getting off to a bad start. Business men warned each other of the danger that the "mouse might lie down with the lion." Hostile editors of business journals spoke of "fishing expeditions" and "headhunting excursions" and accused the Congress and the Administration of fostering a plot which would "disturb business" and "delay recovery."

A striking illustration of such pressure developed during the life insurance study. Long before the Committee had time to digest the testimony, a concerted broadside was unloosed prejudging its decisions and denouncing its presumed recommendations. Insurance company employees and policyholders were informed that their interests were being jeopardized; "spontaneous" policyholders' meetings were held throughout the land, and the Congress was deluged with letters denouncing the plot and demanding protection.[48] When the final report eventually was completed, the TNEC had little to propose after all its studies of life insurance practices but to exhort the states to do a better job of regulation.

Perhaps the TNEC was overzealous in not prosecuting anyone. Perhaps the desire to appease and placate business set aside the serious purpose of conducting a thorough and scrutinizing investigation into the country's fundamental economic problems. There is a distinction between indiscriminate muckraking and purposive analysis of problems, just as there is a difference between a punitive expedition and an impartial but fearless inquiry. Political expediency and pressure-group psychology seem to have obscured that difference. There is, in fact, despite the odious label, nothing inherently wrong

48 See, for example, *Congressional Record,* Vol. LXXXVI, Part 1, pp. 909–911; *ibid.,* Part 2, pp. 1852–1854.

about "witch burning" if it is conducted in a purposive manner with the intent of securing necessary information. This point is aptly brought out in the following statement by Dwight MacDonald.

Successful investigations . . . are all alike in one respect—they all have been "witch burning expeditions." They have been conducted in an unfriendly and aggressive manner, usually by a special counsel who relentlessly pursues the witnesses as though they were defendants in a court of law.[49]

Contributing to the ultimate ineffectiveness of the final report was the all-encompassing character of the TNEC investigation itself. Embracing as it did not only the problems of monopoly and full employment but also the patent system, life insurance, investment banking, cartels, interstate trade barriers, wartime inflation, consumer problems, and other matters, it became difficult, if not impossible, for the Committee to co-ordinate and integrate the elements of so comprehensive an undertaking into one unified report directed toward one central objective. Successful inquiries have usually related to one problem, such as life insurance (Armstrong), finance banking (Pujo), commercial air transport (Black), and banking practices (Pecora). In these investigations the attention of committee members was undivided, and the public mind could be focused on one problem. The TNEC, in undertaking an inquiry involving a multiplicity of related problems, resembles the attempt of the Industrial Commission, and so far as its final report is concerned, the fruits were similar. A cartel inquiry might have been more effective in its sphere; a separate consumer investigation scarcely could have produced so little as did the TNEC with respect to that problem; the same might be said for other matters subject to inquiry. An out-and-out study of either antitrust policy or the problem of full employment would have permitted a singleness of purpose and a clarity of objectives which were never attained. Particularly is it unfortunate that the study of full employment was hampered by a preconception as to its relationship to monopoly. The comprehensive scope of the investigation, therefore, constituted an impediment to the successful termination of the Committee's assignment. In essence, if not in design, like the great investigations which had preceded it, the TNEC became a one-purpose investigation—a monopoly investigation.

The attempt to interrelate the many complex problems involved in the breakdown of the economic system should not be disparaged.

49 "The Monopoly Committee," *The American Scholar*, VIII (July, 1939), 301.

Nevertheless, there was an element of planlessness about the organization of the TNEC hearings which probably contributed no little to their final form. However impressed one may be with the magnitude of the hearings and the importance of the materials developed, one is at loss, at times, to discover the objectives toward which they were directed. Opportunism seems to have been an important factor in the selection of certain areas for investigation and in the omission of others. Inquiries usually were conducted by one of the departmental branches represented on the Committee. No central staff was maintained which co-ordinated, integrated, or directed the over-all approach. Apparently Departments selected for study certain segments of economic life in which they were particularly interested and at times when it was known that they had a particular program to recommend. The TNEC became, therefore, a sounding board for certain economic crusades. As a result of its many managers and the diversity of its hearings, the product often suffered from lack of totality and direction.

The diverse characteristics of the members and the preconceptions which they brought to the Committee were, of course, reflected in the final report. Eagerly and sincerely desiring to obtain the endorsement of their own favored scheme of reform, they were thus less able to attend to the broader aspects of public policy, and some of them, because of their own social theory and predilections, were led to obstruct what others might propose. In other words, the final report became what it was partly because Senator O'Mahoney came to the Committee as a champion of "national charters for national corporations," because Representative Sumners saw a return to natural law as the only hope, because Mr. Arnold had an impelling conviction that rigorous antitrust action was called for, because Senator King saw little need for change in the structure and performance of existing economic institutions, and because representatives from the Department of Commerce conceived their role on the Committee to be that of defenders of business practices as they are.

A procedure which the TNEC employed in one or two instances might advantageously have been followed more frequently. In the case of patents, for example, experts from government agencies and from industry were interviewed who, in addition to supplying relevant facts, outlined proposals for remedial action. After weighing these suggestions the Committee formulated its patent program, much of which was almost immediately enacted into law. This represents

one of the few cases in which experts were encouraged to propose plans and likewise one of the few instances when constructive changes resulted from TNEC initiative. Had this pattern been followed more often, the contribution and influence of the TNEC might have been greater. Members of the Committee were busy men, occupied with legislative and administrative responsibilities which did not permit full or uninterrupted attention to the overwhelming problems with which the TNEC dealt. Neither was there a full-time staff which could perform this function for them. The Committee, after hearing the testimony, might profitably have constituted itself as a deliberative body to receive and appraise recommendations; men well qualified in the fields of cycle theory, investment, insurance regulation, cartels, monopoly, public finance, industrial management, banking theory, and related problems might have been invited to pose problems, analyze causes, and propose solutions. The Monetary Commission found this procedure to be particularly fruitful in 1912. From such a forum might have developed a final report relating more closely to the testimony heard and attempting to offer more adequate solutions to the troublesome problems which were raised.

APPENDIX

THE ROLE OF CONGRESSIONAL INVESTIGATIONS

THE TEMPORARY NATIONAL ECONOMIC COMMITTEE was one of many committees created by the United States Congress which have investigated virtually every aspect of economic, social, and political life. It takes its place among the great investigations of the English-speaking democracies; in magnitude and scope perhaps it is the greatest. Congressional investigations are as old as the United States; in fact, the idea of government inquiries is much older. Its origin dates back to the first royal commissions in the fifteenth century in England, when the power of Parliament to conduct investigations became established. The first subject for study by that body was election disputes. Later, the expenditure of parliamentary appropriations became a matter for frequent probing.

It was natural that a tradition so well established should be transferred to America; many examples of legislative inquiries by the colonial assemblies are recorded.[1] Since the first meeting of the Federal Congress, in 1789, nearly 500 investigating committees have been created. They have been divided almost equally between the United States Senate and the House of Representatives; about twenty-five were joint committees of both Houses.[2] For the first thirty years the House was the chief investigative body, the Senate conducting only three investigations.[3] The activities of the Senate gradually increased; from 1900 to 1925, of the sixty investigations conducted, the Senate was responsible for forty; the House, twenty.

It would be impossible to determine the cost of all these investigations; it is estimated that Congress appropriated approximately $5,500,000 directly to committees prior to 1938.[4] This does not include costs incurred by various bureaus and departments and, more recently, by the WPA. From 1900 until the beginning of the first World War, Congress appropriated an average of $30,000 a year for investigations. The sum has increased from $250,000 in 1920 to more than $500,000 a year.[5]

A discussion of what is meant by an investigating committee is appropriate at this point. A congressional investigating committee is a committee authorized by a resolution passed by the House or the Senate or both to investigate matters concerning which information is not regularly or readily obtainable. It may be a standing or a select committee, and its purpose must be inquisitorial. Special funds are generally appropriated for its activities. The rights and duties of the committee are generally care-

[1] Dimock, *Congressional Investigating Committees,* p. 54.
[2] *Congressional Record,* Vol. LXXXIII, Part 11, p. 2311.
[3] *Ibid.* [4] *Ibid.* [5] *Ibid.,* p. 2312.

fully circumscribed in the resolution. The ultimate test of an investigating committee is whether it has been authorized by Congress and whether it is inquisitorial.

There are few problems of public interest which have not been subject to inquiry by governmental committees. The list includes immigration, commercial banking, unemployment insurance, communist propaganda, railroad consolidation, lobbying, Post Office leases, conservation of wild life, the Alaskan Railroad, Indian affairs, treaties with China, campaign expenditures, animal feeds, and the price of shoes. Congressional committees have kept watch on the functioning of Federal bureaus, departments, and establishments and have inspected the affairs of private citizens and corporations.[6] Probes of the conduct of the Administration have been frequent; during Grant's term there were thirty-seven such inquiries.[7] The permanent agencies have been subject to their share of investigations; the United States Shipping Board, the Federal Trade Commission, the War Finance Corporation, the Tariff Commission, the Veterans Bureau have all been investigated in the past two decades. The War Department has been the most frequently investigated branch of the Federal Government, with the Treasury Department next, followed by the Interior Department. The conduct of each war engaged in by the United States has been probed by committees of Congress.

INVESTIGATING COMMITTEES CLASSIFIED

Committees of investigation may be classified in six different categories.

1. The most common and the most prominent today are the senatorial committees, recent examples of which are the investigations of Teapot Dome, beginning in 1923, and of stock exchange and banking practices, by the Senate Banking and Currency Committee in 1933.

2. By far the most frequent in earlier days, but of lesser importance today, are the House committees. These are illustrated by the Pujo Committee, created by the House in 1913, and the Tolan Committee of 1942.

3. Joint committees composed of both Senators and Representatives are much less common. The Wade Committee, which kept a watch over the conduct of the Civil War, and the committee which investigated Muscle Shoals are examples.

4. Temporary administrative commissions are appointed by the President and are composed of members outside the Congress or the Administration. The so-called Wickersham Commission, the National Commission on Law Observance and Enforcement, of 1931, and the Industrial Relations Commission of 1912 are examples of this type. Temporary administrative commissions resemble the royal commissions of England; they are empowered to carry on their work, if necessary, beyond the life of the Congress. They are usually composed of technical experts or authorities in the field under investigation.

6 Ford, *Representative Government*, p. 255.
7 Galloway, "The Investigative Function of Congress," *The American Political Science Review*, XXI (February, 1927), 47.

5. Joint congressional and administrative committees, such as the TNEC, the Industrial Commission of 1898, and the War Policies Commission of 1930, are more rare; the writer knows of none of consequence except the three mentioned. These committees are composed of members from the House and the Senate as well as the Administration.

6. Semi-permanent or permanent governmental agencies, whose purpose is inquisitorial, are doing more and more of the work formerly done by the congressional committees. They include the Federal Power Commission, the United States Coal Commission, the United States Railway Labor Board, the National Resources Planning Board, the United States Tariff Commission, and the Federal Trade Commission (in some of its activities).

AUTHORITY OF CONGRESS TO CONDUCT INVESTIGATIONS

Congress has no authority specifically enumerated in the Constitution to make investigations; but through long-continued practice, to do so has become an implied power, and, next to the legislative function, investigation is recognized as its chief function. "The powers of Congress in respect to investigation and legislation are not absolutely identical, but the power of investigation is the wider and extends to matters on which Congress could not constitutionally legislate directly, if they were reasonably calculated to afford information useful and material in the framing of constitutional legislation." [8]

The frequent use of investigations may be attributed chiefly to the type of government which functions in the United States. In Great Britain, where the Ministry is responsible directly to the Parliament, fewer probes seem necessary. The Prime Minister and Cabinet members appear in person on the floor of Parliament to answer questions and to account for their actions. Long ago, however, the British royal commissions became a recognized and essential aid to the Government. In the United States, where the executive and the legislative departments are separate, some technique is needed to hold the Administration to strict accountability. One authority on government has taken the position that "the legislative investigation is the American method of achieving ministerial responsibility without reducing power. It is one of the checks in a system of checks and balances." [9] Likewise, John Stuart Mill once wrote: "The proper office of a representative assembly is to watch and control the government; to throw the light of publicity on its acts; to compel a full exposition and justification of all of them which anyone considers questionable; to censure them if found condemnable, and if the men who compose the government abuse their trust, or fulfill it in a manner which conflicts with the deliberate sense of the nation, to expel them from office and either expressly or virtually appoint their successors." [10]

[8] The Constitution of the United States of America (Annotated), Washington, D.C., 1938, p. 95.
[9] Galloway, "The Investigative Function of Congress," *The American Political Science Review*, XXI (February, 1927), 64.
[10] John Stuart Mill, *Considerations on Representative Government*, New York, 1874, pp. 115–116.

Congressional investigations, at times, have become substitutes for impeachment, which is laborious and cumbersome at best. There have been only four impeachments in the history of the Congress which have resulted in a verdict of guilty and removal from office. Revelations brought out by investigations, however, if they indicate undesirable conditions, frequently result in the removal of derelict individuals from office or in voluntary resignations. Hence, the procedure of impeachment is rarely attempted; more satisfactory results seem to be obtained by investigations.

Witnesses have not always been willing to appear or to present evidence before congressional committees. Occasionally, when they did appear, they refused to give the requested information. Gradually, however, Congress has assumed the right to conduct compulsory investigations. The opposition has been strong, but when cases involving the summoning of witnesses or demanding of evidence have appeared before the courts, the latter have upheld the Congress. The courts have been restrained by the Fourth and Fifth Amendments to the Constitution, but they have been liberal in their interpretations. Until 1820 the power to punish for contempt went unchallenged, but at that time a decision of the Supreme Court [11] unanimously found that power to be possessed by Congress by necessary implication. No further controversy occurred until 1880, when the Supreme Court held that Congress may fine or imprison a contumacious witness if his examination is necessary for the framing of legislation or the exercise of the power of impeachment.[12] In 1897 the Court affirmed the power of Congress to look into the conduct of its members.[13] That the "power of investigation is an essential corollary of the lawmaking function" was established by a decision of the Court in 1927.[14] There seems to be little to limit the scope of congressional investigations if a legislative intent is expressed in the resolution of authority.

The powers of the TNEC to compel witnesses to give testimony were the same as those granted to the Securities and Exchange Commission in an Act of Congress, August 26, 1935.[15] Any member of the Committee was "empowered to administer oaths and affirmations, subpena witnesses, compel their attendance, take evidence, and require the production of books, papers, correspondence, memoranda, contracts, agreements, or other records which the . . . [Committee] deems relevant or material to the inquiry. . . . In case of contumacy by or refusal to obey a subpena issued to any person, the . . . [Committee] may invoke the aid of any court of the United States . . . in requiring the attendance and testimony of witnesses and the production of books, papers . . ."

THE BRITISH ROYAL COMMISSIONS

The forerunner of the congressional investigation in the United States, as well as its counterpart in England, is the British royal commission. Ref-

[11] Anderson v. Dunn, 6 Wheat. 204 (1821).
[12] Kilbourn v. Thompson, 103 U.S. 168 (1881).
[13] Re Chapman, 166 U.S. 661 (1897). [14] McGrain v. Daugherty, 273 U.S. 135 (1927).
[15] *Congressional Record*, Vol. LXXVIII, Part 2, p. 2269.

erence has been made to the early activities of the royal commissions during the sixteenth century. In 1571 a committee of Parliament was appointed to look into election disputes, which became the chief subject of inquiry by such committees for many years. Royal commissions have three functions: (1) to formulate legislative policy, (2) to inquire into the activity of the administrative departments, and (3) to study social conditions.[16] In contrast to investigations in the United States, the royal commissions rarely have a political motive. They are usually held behind closed doors and receive little publicity.

A royal commission is distinguished from other British committees of investigation by having a royal warrant of appointment. Hence, it has more prestige than other British committees or congressional investigations in the United States. It is considered a high honor to serve on royal commissions; outstanding men and women readily have given their time without compensation for that purpose. Usually the members are laymen, appointed by the Ministers. Eminent individuals who have thus served include the Webbs, E. H. Tawney, Sir William Beveridge, J. M. Keynes, and H. J. Laski. As in the case of congressional committees, the commissions have the power to summon witnesses only when specifically granted; other British committees of investigation do not receive such grants. While the royal commissions are *ad hoc*, they are usually of greater duration than a congressional committee, the average life being one and one-half years. Their size varies from one commissioner, as in the case of Lord Durham's appointment to investigate difficulties in Canada in 1837, to twenty-one, as in the English Liquor Licensing inquiry in 1929.[17]

There are three types of royal commissions: (1) *Representative*. The representative type is the largest and frequently consists of politicians; hence, it is more partisan. (2) *Expert*. As the name implies, the expert royal commissions are used for advisory purposes in technical matters, such as public health and local government administration. It is removed from politics, but not necessarily open-minded. (3) *Impartial*. The members on this type of commission must be trustworthy, have sound judgment, and be persons whose recommendations carry weight.

The British royal commissions have been responsible for most of the major internal reforms in England in the past 150 years. "Nearly every important measure of reform has been preceded by an inquiry by a Royal Commission or a Parliamentary committee or a Department Committee or by independent ministers." [18] Also, "almost all the great reforms of the nineteenth century in internal administration, taxation, education, labour protection, and other social questions, have been based on the full investigations made by the Royal Commissions . . ." [19] The scope of their activities in social life deserves special emphasis. They have investigated

16 Clokie and Robinson, *Royal Commissions of Inquiry*, p. 2.
17 *Ibid.*, p. 157.
18 Gosnell, "British Royal Commissions of Inquiry," *Political Science Quarterly*, XLIX (March, 1934), 84.
19 Dimock, *Congressional Investigating Committees*, p. 35.

conditions of the poor in the British Isles, the results of public and private education, the effects of punishment upon criminals, and the extent of illiteracy in England.[20] It has been asserted that "the history of British democracy might in considerable measure be written in terms of the history of successive Royal Commissions." [21] Investigations of recent years have been made of a wide variety of subjects, including the coal industry in 1919 and 1926, transportation in 1928, unemployment insurance in 1930–1932, local government in 1923–1929, and the income tax in 1920. All these have resulted in legislation designed to improve conditions prevailing when the studies were made. A few of the royal commissions have become permanent, such as the civil service, crown lands, forestry, charity, railways and canals, historical manuscripts, and church estates.

The number of royal commissions has been gradually declining. They reached their greatest prominence in the middle of the nineteenth century. In the decade from 1901 to 1910 they averaged five a year; between 1935 and 1940 they averaged two a year. This decline is not necessarily the result of a decreased need for investigations, although a better organization of the Government and the expansion of civil service have tended to reduce that need somewhat. Rather, it has been the result of the employment of other methods of conducting inquiries and of obtaining information. In addition to the types mentioned above, there are many supplementary committees always at work, making frequent reports.[22] Because of their influence, however, it is not likely that the royal commissions will completely disappear.

FUNCTIONS OF CONGRESSIONAL COMMITTEES OF INVESTIGATION

Congressional investigations perform numerous functions, and because of considerable overlapping, each inquiry may accomplish several, either directly or indirectly. They may serve (1) to assist in the formulation of legislative policy, (2) to control the Executive, (3) to carry out administrative policies, (4) to mold public opinion, (5) to judge the qualifications of members of Congress, (6) to further the political ambitions of persons or parties, (7) to thwart the misdeeds of individuals or groups, (8) to provide a continuous check on the actions of those in positions of power, and (9) to educate the public.

Probably the most important function is to assist in the formulation of legislative policy. It is essential that Congress have some means of obtaining facts for intelligent drafting of laws. In recent years many, if not most, investigations have been conducted for this purpose. Studies designed to aid Congress in drafting legislation have involved the stock exchange, banking, insurance, and railway financing.

It has frequently been the function of congressional committees, particularly during the administrations of Presidents Wilson and Franklin D. Roosevelt, to carry out administrative policies. Probes into tariffs during

20 Clokie and Robinson, *Royal Commissions of Inquiry*, p. 2.
21 Frankfurter, *The Public and Its Government*, p. 162.
22 Clokie and Robinson, *Royal Commissions of Inquiry*, p. 203.

President Wilson's administration prepared the way for the Underwood Tariff revision. The investigation into lobbying by public utilities during President Franklin D. Roosevelt's administration facilitated the passage of laws restricting holding companies. The studies of the stock exchange and banking, begun during President Hoover's administration and concluded during President Roosevelt's, were very fruitful of legislation. Similarly, the TNEC was designed to create receptiveness to objectives of New Deal policies.

The third function is to control the Executive. All administrative departments, with the exception of Commerce and Labor, have been investigated by congressional committees. The President and his Cabinet were subjected to inquiries twenty-three times up to 1930. Significant examples are the probes of the banking situation during President Jackson's administration, the Hayes-Tilden election controversy, the Credit Mobilier scandal, and the Teapot Dome case; a more recent illustration is the activity of the Dies Committee relative to the existence of communism in the Roosevelt administration.

The molding of public opinion is almost a duty of Congress. A democracy assumes a continuous and active public opinion, and since this too rarely exists congressional committees occasionally are appointed to serve that purpose. Senator McCormick of Illinois saw this need when, in offering a resolution for an investigation of railway strikes, he said, "What is needed . . . is some body of men which may bring the facts to public attention. There is no other possible means of mobilizing that public opinion which may induce men to return to work." [23]

Official investigations may serve as antidotes to lobbies. The lobby inquiries of 1935 demonstrated the power of congressional committees to counteract the influence of pressure groups; these inquiries opened the way for the enactment of laws restricting holding companies and regulating public utilities. [24] The investigative body is in effect the people's lobby; it becomes a sounding board for facts and often is the only means by which the public interest can be mobilized to secure essential legislation.

Since early colonial history judging the qualifications and conduct of members of Congress has been recognized as a proper function of congressional committees. The Pennsylvania assembly, in 1742, conducted an inquiry into riots resulting from election disputes. An investigation of the elections of 1920 resulted in the passage of a bill in Congress regulating the publication of campaign expenditures. Outstanding examples of the refusal by Congress to seat a member are those involving Vare, Newbury, and Smith.

Congressional investigations may be employed to further the political ambitions of an individual or a political party. Few inquiries are entirely free from personal or partisan purposes. The first congressional investigation—that of the defeat of General St. Clair in 1792—was initiated in part to influence public opinion against the selection of Hamilton for a second

[23] McGeary, *Developments in Congressional Investigative Power*, p. 30.
[24] *Ibid.*, p. 39.

term as Secretary of the Treasury.[25] In election years the inquisitorial device may be employed to aid the party in power. To refer to the lobby investigations again, a Senate committee developed from the testimony of the Crusaders, the Farmers' Independence Council, the Sentinels of the Republic, and others that a number of organizations hostile to the New Deal had received funds from the same individuals, some of whom were wealthy industrialists and financiers.[26] Certainly the investigation of the Teapot Dome scandals under the leadership of Democratic Senator Thomas Walsh was not without political implications. But this does not represent a criticism of investigations, since abuses are often revealed and remedial measures invoked; it does, on the other hand, emphasize one of the advantages of the two-party system. Congressional inquiries provide a safeguard against the abuse of public trust.

The very threat of an investigation may serve to discipline individuals or groups and to prevent abuses which might otherwise occur. Probes bring the facts into the light, penalties are invoked, and the results serve as an example of what faces other malefactors. "Publicity is the sunlight of God's truth" is a truism which is particularly applicable to the record of achievement by congressional investigations. Even before the TNEC had an opportunity to investigate, steel and oil companies modified certain contracts with the trade which otherwise might have proved embarrassing.

Another important function of legislative investigations is to provide a continuous check on the actions of those in positions of power. Professor Ford has said, "The essence of representative government is this: that a watch is kept on the behavior of those entrusted with power." [27] On another occasion he stated, "The difficulty of making a representative system really representative centers in the fact that commonly when any set of persons get opportunity they are naturally inclined to use it for their own advantage." [28] Where there is suspicion of malfeasance or corruption or evidence of malpractice, it becomes a vital function of the Government to investigate and to act.

The educative function is seldom, if ever, a prime motive for a congressional investigation. But inquiries such as those which dealt with the public utilities, the stock exchange and investment banking, and those such as the Industrial Relations Commission and the TNEC created a national forum for the mobilization of public opinion. While much of the valuable information revealed may not immediately be utilized in the legislative process or lead to immediate administrative action, it often lays the groundwork essential to the development of public policy.

CRITICISMS OF CONGRESSIONAL INVESTIGATIONS

The critics of congressional investigations are numerous, and their criti-

25 Claude Bowers, *Jefferson and Hamilton,* Houghton Mifflin, 1925, p. 175.
26 McGeary, "Congressional Investigations during F. D. Roosevelt's First Term," *The American Political Science Review,* XXXI (October, 1939), 683.
27 Ford, *Representative Government,* p. 200.   28 *Ibid.*

cisms are frequently justified. Rarely is an inquiry conducted which does not warrant some censure. Many critics hold that investigations are a costly device, that they consume too much of the time of busy Congressmen, that they are inefficient and are ill-prepared, hence, superficial. Because they are often partisan or dominated by pressure groups, they are likely to be organized to promote some special point of view. Another criticism has been that more attention and better treatment are often accorded to favorable witnesses. Moreover, politicians often feel they must further the interests of the party which elected them, sometimes at the expense of objectivity or facts. Committee members may use the investigation as a springboard for the propagation of their own ideas. Private lives of individuals and the affairs of innocent persons occasionally are probed, and as a result legislative inquiries gain the reputation of being witch hunts, fishing expeditions, and ghost dances. One critic described investigations thus: ". . . that legalized atrocity, the Congressional investigation, where Congressmen, starved of their legitimate food for thought, go on a wild and feverish man-hunt, and do not stop at cannibalism." [29] Some committees have sought newspaper headlines, bringing out the most sensational revelations just before the last edition goes to press. However, most of the greater investigations, those which stand out as having accomplished worth-while results, are essentially free from most of these faults.

As a result of these criticisms and for less laudable reasons serious objections have often been raised to the authorization or selection of committees of investigation. Most of the inquiries proposed fail to receive the necessary majority of votes. Those which do, usually have to combat the opposition of the individual or group to be investigated. The utilities lobby furnished an excellent example of organized and concerted efforts to prevent or control an investigation. Though the lobby failed to prevent authorization of the investigation, through its efforts the undertaking was put into the hands, not of Congressmen, but of the Federal Trade Commission, which was considered "safe." Under the guise of preventing the members from turning an inquiry into a "pleasure jaunt," opponents sometimes restrict its effectiveness by limiting its sphere of activity to the District of Columbia. Another device is to limit the funds for carrying out the objectives of the committee so that little, if anything, can be accomplished.

DIFFICULTY OF OBTAINING TESTIMONY

Once the inquiry is under way, the committee is faced with the problem of securing information. Noncommittal answers prove to be a stumbling block; questionnaires often remain unanswered; and often the evidence simply is not obtainable. Various impediments are sometimes invented to obstruct the efforts of the committee. Many documents examined in the munitions investigation had written across them "confidential by order of the War Department"; in this particular case, however, the committee

29 Walter Lippman, *Public Opinion*, Harcourt, Brace, 1922, p. 289.

ignored this.[30] In another probe the admission was made: "You will find nothing in our files. We were not born yesterday. We have not handled any matters of policy except by telephone for years." [31] In the Banking Committee's investigation of securities and banking Mr. Pecora, when the Stock Exchange refused to send out the questionnaires to secure the information he wanted, threatened to summon them to produce all their records in the Senate building. Faced with this alternative, they co-operated, reluctantly.

OUTSTANDING INVESTIGATIONS

Congressional investigations have played a vital role in the evolution of American economic institutions and in the formulation of national legislative policy. Some of the more important inquiries in recent decades dealing with social and economic conditions will be described. The contribution and influence of the investigative technique was quite significant even prior to 1890. In 1792 a committee of the House conducted an inquiry into the defeat of General St. Clair by the Indians of the Northwest. It resulted in improvement of the organization of the War Department.[32] The first Senate committee of inquiry of importance investigated Andrew Jackson's conduct in the Seminole War of 1819–1820. This resulted in the first challenge before the courts of the powers of the Senate to summon persons and papers.[33] During the Civil War the Wade Committee, the first joint House and Senate committee, took over part management of the War. An excellent example of the exposure of fraud and collusion, both in private and public places, is the investigation which involved the Credit Mobilier affair. Inquiries into conditions in state governments disclosing political patronage and the spoils system resulted in the organization of the Civil Service in 1886. In 1872, when the question of regulation of transportation was before the public, the Senate appointed a committee to investigate certain phases of the railroad problem. The Windom report, revealing "extortionate charges and unfair discrimination" and recommending Federal construction and operation of railways was made in 1874. In 1886 the Cullom Committee, appointed to make a thorough investigation of the railroad question, reported, favoring a mild system of regulation; the Interstate Commerce Act of 1887 was based largely on this report.

The Industrial Commission (1898).—A vital problem which confronted the nation near the end of the last century was the rise of trusts and their attendant evils, also the labor problem. Congress established the Industrial Commission to investigate questions pertaining to immigration, labor, agriculture, manufacturing, and business, and "to suggest such laws as may be made the basis of uniform legislation by the various states of the

30 Black, "Inside a Senate Investigation," *Harper's Magazine*, CLXXII (February, 1936), 280.
31 *Ibid.*, p. 281.
32 Williams, "Probes by Congress Check Government," *The Washington Post*, April 6, 1935, p. 7.　　　　33 Anderson v. Dunn, 6 Wheat. 204 (1821).

Union, in order to harmonize conflicting interests and be equitable to the laborer, the employer, the producer and the consumer." [34] The Industrial Commission has been compared to the royal commissions on labor, of which there have been several. The Commission was a joint committee of five members from the House, five from the Senate, and nine from civil life, appointed by the President. Those from the House were appointed chiefly from its labor committee, and, although the Presidential appointees were from all walks of life, three were representatives of organized labor. The Commission was notable for its use of experts, especially economists. J. R. Commons and W. Z. Ripley were the Henderson and Frank of the Temporary National Economic Committee.

The hearings, lasting more than two years, were conducted in an impartial and scholarly manner. The reports, reflecting the work of economists throughout, comprise nineteen volumes, ten of which deal directly with labor. The trusts and industrial combinations received attention next in importance; taxation and transportation were given some consideration. The report favored the establishment of a commission with supervisory powers over industry, and the creation of a Bureau of Corporations (the forerunner of the Federal Trade Commission) followed in 1903. It was a well-written, conservative document, but it produced little in the way of legislation and social reform that was tangible or measurable.

The Armstrong Investigation (1905).—In response to requests for an investigation of insurance companies, the Armstrong Insurance Committee was authorized in 1905. There was widespread apprehension over the practices and the powers of insurance companies, and certain specific abuses needed correction. Most of the large insurance companies were centered in New York, and they had accumulated assets exceeding $1,500,-000,000. The problems which faced the committee included the issue of placing restrictions on the expansion of capital resources, the manner in which insurance surpluses should be invested, how control by policyholders in a mutual company might be made effective, how "deferred dividend" policy should be dealt with, and how evils arising from the political activities of life insurance companies might be prevented.[35]

The committee spent four months studying the major New York companies. Its counsel, Charles E. Hughes, was able and courageous and conducted the hearings objectively, making no attempt to give sensational publicity to the findings. The report, a volume of 300 pages, contained a summary of the hearings and recommendations for legislation. Most of the recommendations were enacted into law which still provides practical safeguards for the interests of policyholders. The investigation resulted in the resignation or removal of the presidents and other executives of the three largest companies.[36] Moreover, the insurance business in New York was reorganized on a more secure and satisfactory basis.

[34] North, "The Industrial Commission," *The North American Review*, CLXVIII (June, 1899), 709.   [35] "The Insurance Report," *The Nation*, LXXXII (March 1, 1906), 170.
[36] MacDonald, "The Monopoly Committee; a Study in Frustration," *The American Scholar*, VIII (July, 1939), 301.

The Monetary Commission (1912).—As a result of the panic of 1907 the Aldrich-Vreeland Emergency Currency bill provided for a Monetary Commission "to secure an organization of capital and credit by which confidence can be firmly established and credit maintained under all circumstances and conditions." [37] The Commission was composed of nine Senators and nine members of the House, with Senator Aldrich as chairman. Few hearings were held; the Commission relied chiefly on specialists, such as professors, bankers, economists, and other authorities on monetary problems in the United States and foreign countries. Representatives of the Commission visited most of the countries of Europe, as well as Canada, Mexico, and Japan. Directors and managers of leading banks were interviewed, and reports were written with the aid of banking authorities of the various countries. Men such as Professor O. M. Sprague, Paul Warburg, and Francis Hirst wrote monographs on banking conditions both here and abroad. The reports, published in 1912, consisted of twenty-three volumes, three-fourths of which were monographs by experts. The bill resulting from the report was called the "Aldrich Plan," but it never was reported out of committee. It was condemned by both parties in the platforms of 1912, but there was general agreement that some reform was necessary. Another bill which was a direct result of the report, however, emerged as the Federal Reserve Act of 1913.

The Industrial Relations Commission (1912).—In 1911 the Congress directed the President to appoint an Industrial Relations Commission to look into the conditions of labor in the principal industries of the United States, to discover the basic causes of dissatisfaction, and to report its conclusions; half a million dollars was appropriated to make the investigation. This step was taken largely as a result of violent labor demonstrations, particularly the dynamiting of the Los Angeles *Times* building. President Taft left the appointment of the Commission to President Wilson. There were nine members; three employers and three representatives of labor.

Mr. Frank Walsh, who was made chairman, believed that "the philosophy, the opinions, the errors, the prejudices of men were the determining factor in industrial relations"; [38] hence, he made little use of experts and devoted much of the committee's time and money to public hearings. He had a deep-seated hatred for the misery, the stupidity, the complacency, the accumulated wealth, and the waste of our economic system. The hearings received daily publicity, and it was a new experience for labor to have its cause championed. It undoubtedly bolstered the labor movement.

The report by John R. Commons, although it received little publicity, was a major part of the final report. He decried the appalling conditions of labor and recommended the creation of a Federal fund for social welfare and the creation of an industrial commission for each state and for the United States. Mr. Walsh had made of the Commission a very different

[37] Mitchell, "Review: The Publication of the National Monetary Commission," *The Quarterly Journal of Economics,* XXV (May, 1911), 563.
[38] "Industrial Conflict," *The New Republic,* IV (August 28, 1915), 89.

body from that which Congress had planned; hence, the Commons report recommending a permanent industrial commission was looked upon with suspicion. A large number of recommendations were made, but Congress was not inclined to act on any of them. The major part of the final report was ill-organized and indicated a lack of agreement on the part of the Commission; there seemed to be only one unanimous declaration: a definition of the terms "open" and "closed" shop.

The Newlands Committee (1912).—In 1912 the Senate authorized a committee to investigate regulation of interstate commerce. This Committee undertook to investigate and to recommend changes in the laws regulating and controlling firms engaged in interstate commerce. It heard lawyers, publicists, economists, and businessmen; the result was 3,000 pages of hearings. There was little harmony or agreement among the members of the Committee. Senator Newlands, the chairman, advocated an interstate trade commission which would absorb the Bureau of Corporations. No direct legislative action was taken, but the Federal Trade Commission Act, enacted two years later, displayed evidence of the influence of the Newlands Committee.

The Pujo Committee (1913).—The Pujo Committee, organized in 1913, was concerned with the "concentration of banking control in the hands of a few men." [39] It is an example of an investigation to advise the Administration; President Wilson desired information for legislation to check the rise of monopolies by outlawing certain practices not specifically covered in the Sherman Act. The Committee was composed of seven Democratic and four Republican members of the House and had the very able Mr. Untermyer as counsel.

The hearings received considerable publicity and served to arouse public discussion. Mr. Untermyer, in discussing the investigation, said, "I take this opportunity of assuring you that the only purpose of this inquiry is as a basis for a wholesome, remedial, and constructive legislation. Every effort has been made, as far as I am concerned, to keep it as free as possible from sensationalism and to pursue the investigation in as conservative and unemotional a manner as the facts to be disclosed will permit." [40] The report of the Committee presents an excellent account of the workings of finance capital in the United States. It contains many constructive recommendations, some of which have been put into legislation. Other tangible results of the Pujo report were the ban on interlocking directorates in the Clayton Act and its contribution to the Federal Reserve Act.

The Public Utilities Investigation (1928).—Senator Thomas Walsh introduced a resolution in 1928 recommending an investigation of public utility companies. There had been an earlier investigation (1925–1927), but the evils within the industry continued, and further action seemed in order. The purpose of this inquiry was to study and report on the growth of capital assets and liabilities of public utility corporations doing inter-

[39] C. S. Tippetts, and Shaw Livermore, *Business Organization and Control*, Van Nostrand, 1941, p. 512.
[40] "The Untermyer Inquiry," *Review of Reviews*, XLVII (February, 1913), 137.

state business and to gather facts concerning the issuance of securities and the operation of holding companies. The commission also was directed to report on the publicity or propaganda activities of public utilities.

Probably never before had any proposal been subjected to such a storm of high-powered propaganda and lobbying as did this one.[41] But when it became apparent to the power companies that an investigation could not be averted, they managed to have it put into the hands of the Federal Trade Commission, which during the administration of President Coolidge was considered friendly to big business.

Judge Healy, from Vermont, was selected to make the study, and the results were far from what the utility companies had anticipated. "Armed with the authority of the Federal Government to compel the attendance and testimony of witnesses and to subpoena important and telltale documents and records, the Commission has hewn its way through the maze and intricacies of designed confusion and the bewildering mass of material to the very heart of our modern monopoly system and laid it bare." [42] For more than four years the Committee studied the utility companies and produced 100 volumes of hearings and reports.

The investigation contributed to the legislation embodied in certain sections of the Securities Act of 1933 and the Securities and Exchange Act of 1934. It led directly to the Public Utilities Act of 1935 which included the Holding Company Act; it also aided in the formulation of the Natural Gas Act of 1938. Another, less tangible, result was the revival of popular interest in public ownership of the utilities. Several Midwestern and Western states passed laws during and after the study making it possible for public authorities to generate and distribute electric current in competition with private concerns; [43] the Tennessee Valley Authority was created in 1933 to supervise the development and use of Muscle Shoals and other Tennessee Valley water-power enterprises.

The Wickersham Commission (1931).—When Herbert Hoover was President he used the device of *ad hoc*, semi-public commissions to study scores of problems with which the country was faced during his Administration. So common were they that they became the target for witticisms.[44] One of these commissions was the National Commission on Law Observance and Enforcement, more commonly known as the Wickersham Commission, appointed in 1931. Its purpose was "to study many aspects of the subject of crime in the United States and not to stop until it had made ac-

[41] Black, "Inside a Senate Investigation," *Harper's Magazine*, CLXXII (February, 1936), 275.

[42] Carl D. Thompson, *Confessions of the Power Trust*, Dutton, 1932, Foreword.

[43] William E. Mosher, "Utility Regulation at the Bar," *The New Republic*, LXXV (June 7, 1933), 90.

[44] "Once to every man and nation, comes the moment to decide,
In the strife of truth with falsehood, for the good or evil side.
But the case presents no problem to the White House engineer;
He appoints a big commission to report some time next year."
—George Norris

Quoted by Silas Bent in "Mr. Hoover's Sins of Commissions," *Scribner's Magazine*, XC (July, 1931), 9.

curate determinations of 'fact and cause' and had followed these with 'constructive, courageous conclusions, which would bring public understanding and command public support.' " [45] Half a million dollars was appropriated by Congress to the Commission, which consisted of ten lawyers and one woman—the president of a women's college.

The final reports (there were fourteen) included the works of the chairman, Roscoe Pound, and Newton D. Baker. Unfortunately the Commission became involved in a bitter national dispute—prohibition—thus, much of its work was discredited. Public opinion was so aroused on the matter of prohibition that although but one of the fourteen reports dealt with that subject the others were relegated to the background and received little attention. The conclusions expressed on the various aspects of crime were not revolutionary; in fact, they were but a repetition of the contentions and points of view of critical observers for many years. They received inadequate and incompetent publicity. There is little evidence of concrete benefits resulting from the investigation.

The Pecora Investigation (1933).—The inquiry of the Senate Banking and Currency Committee into stock exchange and banking practices, better known as the Pecora Investigation, was authorized in 1933. The banking collapse of 1932–1933 demonstrated the need for an inquiry and furnished an opportunity for reform. Mr. Pecora, as counsel, proved to be very able; he succeeded in drawing needed information from noncommittal financiers and in revealing "scandalous" conditions. The investigation was as fruitful of legislative results as any have been; the Banking Act of 1933 or the Glass-Steagall Banking Act, the Banking Act of 1935, the Securities Act of 1933, and the Securities and Exchange Act of 1934 were all directly or indirectly based on the findings of the Committee. Its exposures also contributed to the resignation of the chairman of the National City Bank of New York and to the discontinuance of the Chase National Bank's life pension of $100,000 annually to the ex-chairman of the board. It forced many business organizations to clean house. The Investment Bankers Association adopted a code to correct certain practices exposed by the investigation. Elimination of methods of income tax avoidance, described before the Committee, was provided by a later revenue act.

The Munitions Investigation (1934).—An investigation in 1934 by the Senate had for its avowed purpose to inquire into the manufacture and sale of munitions of war. However, political motives were, perhaps, a greater inspiration than in most inquiries. The offer of the resolution was based partly on the theory that "the commercial motive is one of the inevitable factors often believed to stimulate and sustain wars." [46] The resolution was introduced by Senators Nye and Vandenberg. A committee of twelve members was appointed by the Vice President; this Committee conducted hearings for more than a year and made two suggestions for legis-

[45] Winthrop D. Lane, "Crime and the Wickersham Report," *The Survey*, LXVII (November 1, 1931), 134.
[46] "Efforts by Congress to Write a Permanent Neutrality Law," *Congressional Digest*, XVIII (October, 1939), 228.

lative action: rigid control of loans and credits to belligerent governments and revision of the American position on armed merchant ships. These hearings contributed to the Neutrality Act of 1935 and the Johnson Act of the following year.

GENERAL CONCLUSIONS

Congressional investigating committees have acquired a permanent and salutary place in American political life. Many of the criticisms raised against them are valid, but the benefits derived from these probes outweigh the undesirable aspects. One must take an over-all view to appreciate the value of investigations. Many constructive changes have been effected in political, economic, and social life, and committees of investigation have contributed notably to these adjustments. The results are very frequently indirect or delayed; reforms often are not effected immediately, but the facts and the recommendations produced may serve as a basis for legislation years later. As an example, a select committee of the Senate held hearings on crop insurance in 1923; this led indirectly to the Federal Crop Insurance Corporation in 1938. Another committee of the Senate studied unemployment insurance systems in the United States and foreign countries in 1931; this aided in the formation of the Social Security Act of 1935. That interest in committee reports still exists is indicated by the strong demand for reports of the Public Utilities investigation, the Wickersham Commission, the stock exchange and banking hearings, and the Temporary National Economic Committee. Facts thoroughly established and charges carefully sifted are a great help to those seeking to define issues, clarify objectives, crystallize social thinking, or formulate policies.

The benefits of congressional investigations have been evidenced in various other ways: (1) investigations have served to mold public opinion; (2) remedial legislation frequently has resulted, either directly or indirectly from committee findings and recommendations; (3) congressional investigations often lead to more vigorous law enforcement; [47] (4) fear of public exposure or of subsequent regulation at times has evoked voluntary reform measures.

Financial returns from investigations often have more than repaid the Government the amount it has spent for them. The committee investigating stock exchanges and banking stated: "Assessments for deficiencies and penalties have been levied by the Bureau of Internal Revenue in a sum exceeding $2,000,000 as a direct result of the revelations before the subcommittee." [48] The Teapot Dome oil investigation netted the Government $3,000,000 in taxes from the estate of Edward Doheny and several

[47] The Senate Civil Liberties Committee, studying conditions in Harlan County, Kentucky, in 1937, exposed the use of murder, kidnap, and arson to prevent miners from joining labor organizations of their own choosing. Consequently, the Department of Justice made a study which resulted in the indictment of "24 executives of coal miners, 21 mining operators, and 23 law enforcement officers" (McGeary, *Developments in Congressional Investigative Power*, p. 90).

[48] McGeary, *Developments in Congressional Investigative Power*, p. 92.

millions from other sources. The Black Air and Ocean Mail Committee estimated that it saved the Government $10,000,000 in overpayments which would have been made if the contracts had not been exposed.[49]

Perhaps the most beneficial aspect of investigations is their contribution to the vigor of democratic processes. Committees are made up from the people themselves or their representatives. They are effective in restraining those who seek or exercise special privileges. Vested-interest groups and the beneficiaries of special privilege may be expected to continue their opposition to the method of legislative investigation, knowing that disclosure and publicity weakens their power.

[49] *Congressional Record,* Vol. LXXXIII, Part 11, p. 2311.

BIBLIOGRAPHY

Because of the character of the subject matter treated in this volume, the principal source materials have naturally been the *Hearings* before the Temporary National Economic Committee, and *The Final Report and Recommendations* of the Temporary National Economic Committee. Other valuable references which originated with the TNEC are the *Final Report* of the Executive Secretary to the Temporary National Economic Committee on the Concentration of Economic Power in the United States, and the forty-three Monographs, each one devoted to a special problem vital to the national economy.

"Anti-trust Inquiry," *Newsweek*, XII (July 4, 1938), 8–9.

"Background of the Anti-Monopoly Investigation," *Business Week*, December 24, 1938, pp. 21–25.

Batchelor, Bronson. "Business under the X-Ray," *The Atlantic Monthly*, CLXVII (January, 1941), 98 ff.

Beard, Charles A. "The Anti-Trust Racket," *The New Republic*, XCVI (September 21, 1938), 182–184.

Belair, Felix, Jr. "New Deal Opens Fight on Big-Business Front," *The New York Times*, January 2, 1938.

Berle, A. A., Jr. "Memorandum: Investigation of Business Organization and Practices." July 12, 1938. Mimeographed.

Berle, A. A., Jr., and G. C. Means. The Modern Corporation and Private Property. New York, Macmillan, 1933.

"Berle's Confidential Memorandum," *Commercial and Financial Chronicle*, CXLVII (August 27, 1938), 1279.

"Berle Monopoly Report in Full; 'Must' Reading for Advertisers," *Printer's Ink*, CLXXXIV (September 1, 1938), 15–17.

Black, Hugo L. "Inside a Senate Investigation," *Harper's Magazine*, CLXXII (February, 1936), 275–286.

Bowen, Howard R. "The Impact of the War upon Smaller Manufacturing Plants," *Survey of Current Business*, XXIII (July and September, 1943), 19 ff.

—— "Trends in the Business Population," *Survey of Current Business*, XXIV (March, 1944), 8–13.

Brady, R. A. "Reports and Conclusions of the TNEC," *Economic Journal*, LIII (December, 1943), 409–415.

Bratter, Herbert M. "Meet the Monopoly Committee," *Banking*, XXXI (September, 1938), 23–24.

"Business Heads Score Taxes as TNEC Enters Main Phase," *Newsweek*, XIII (May 29, 1939), 37–38.

"Case for Insurance, The," *Nation's Business*, XXVIII (January, 1940), 69.

Chamberlain, Edward. The Theory of Monopolistic Competition. Cambridge, Harvard University Press, 1938.

Chase, Stuart. "Capital Not Wanted," *Harper's Magazine*, CLXXX (February, 1940), 225–234.

Chase, Stuart. "Shadow over Wall Street," *Harper's Magazine,* CLXXX (March, 1940), 364–374.

Clark, John. "Monopolistic Tendencies and Their Consequences," Academy of Political Science, *Proceedings,* XVIII (January, 1939), 124–131.

Clokie, Hugh, and J. William Robinson. Royal Commissions of Inquiry. Stanford, Stanford University Press, 1937.

"Code for Investigators," *Business Week,* September 3, 1938, p. 44.

Cohen, Jerome B. "The Forgotten TNEC," *Current History,* September, 1941, pp. 45–50.

Corey, Herbert. "O'Mahoney Wants Facts, Not Scalps," *Nation's Business,* XXVI (September 28, 1938), 15–16.

Crumbaker, C. "Note on Concentration of Economic Power; Review Report," *The Journal of Political Economy,* L (December, 1942), 934–944.

Cummings, Homer. "Extracts from an Address by the Attorney General on the Unsolved Problem of Monopoly, November 29, 1937," *Congressional Record,* 75th Cong., 3d sess., Vol. LXXXIII, Part 1, p. 23.

Davenport, Walter. "What Price Henderson," *Collier's,* CVIII (September 6, 1941), 18 ff.

Dimock, Marshall Edward. Congressional Investigating Committees. Baltimore, The Johns Hopkins Press, 1929.

Douglas, P. H. Controlling Depressions. New York, Norton, 1935.

Fetter, Frank A. The Masquerade of Monopoly. New York, Harcourt, Brace, 1931.

Flynn, John T. "Bigger and Better Monopolies," *The New Republic,* XCVI (October 26, 1938), 333.

Ford, Henry T. Representative Government. New York, Henry Holt, 1924.

Frankfurter, Felix. The Public and Its Government. New Haven, Yale University Press, 1930.

Galloway, George. "The Investigative Function of Congress," *The American Political Science Review,* XXI (February, 1927), 47–65.

George, Edwin B. "Conundrums before the National Economic Committee," *Dun's Review,* XLVI (November, 1938), 22–28.

—— "The Personnel of Our National Economic Jury," *Dun's Review,* XLVI (October 15, 1938), 8–18.

Glenn, Frank. Thunder and the Dawn. New York, Macmillan, 1932.

Gosnell, Harold F. "British Royal Commissions of Inquiry," *Political Science Quarterly,* XLIX (March, 1934), 84 ff.

Gubin, E. K. "Congressional investigations, June 2, 1938," *Congressional Record,* 75th Cong., 3d sess., Vol. LXXXIII, Part 11, pp. 2311–2312.

Hobson, J. A. Economics of Unemployment. London, Macmillan, 1922.

"Insurance Report, The," *The Nation,* LXXXII (March 1, 1906), 170.

Johnston, Eric. America Unlimited. Garden City, N.Y., Doubleday, Doran, 1944.

Keynes, John Maynard. General Theory of Employment, Interest, and Money. New York, Harcourt, Brace, 1936.

Kreps, Theodore. "Not an Antitrust Racket," *The New Republic,* XCVI (October 5, 1938), 243.

Leven, Maurice, Harold Moulton, and Clark Warburton. America's Capacity to Consume. Washington, D.C., The Brookings Institution, 1934.

"Life Insurance—and TNEC," *Business Week,* March 16, 1940, pp. 50–60.

Lubell, Samuel. "The Daring Young Man on the Flying Pri-cees," *The Saturday Evening Post,* CCXIV (September 13, 1941), 84 ff.

MacDonald, Dwight. "The Monopoly Committee; a Study in Frustration," *The American Scholar,* VIII (July, 1939), 295–308.

McGeary, Martin Nelson. Developments in Congressional Investigative Power. New York, Columbia University Press, 1940.

McKee, Oliver, Jr. "Monopoly Investigators," *The Commonweal,* XXIX (November 4, 1938), 35–37.

Mitchell, Wesley C. "Review: The Publication of the National Monetary Commission," *The Quarterly Journal of Economics,* XXV (May, 1911), 563 ff.

Moley, Raymond. "Business in the Woodshed," *The Saturday Evening Post,* CCXII (April 6, 1940), 224 ff.

—— "Hit and Run," *Newsweek,* XIII (February 27, 1939), 52.

—— "The Great Monopoly Mystery," *The Saturday Evening Post,* CCXII (March 30, 1940), 9 ff.

—— "The Odyssey of TNEC," *Newsweek,* XVII (April 14, 1941), 84.

—— "Sharpshooting at Insurance," *The Saturday Evening Post,* CCXII (April 20, 1940), 244 ff.

"Monopoly and the U. S. System," *The Commonweal,* XXIX (December 16, 1938), 214–215.

"Monopoly Inquiry Holds Out Far-Reaching Possibilities," *Newsweek,* XII (July 18, 1938), 32.

Moulton, Harold G. America's Capacity to Consume. Washington, D.C., The Brookings Institution, 1934.

—— Income and Economic Progress. Washington, D.C., The Brookings Institution, 1935.

—— The Formation of Capital. Washington, D.C., The Brookings Institution, 1935.

Murray, James E., "Has Small Business a Future?" *Vital Speeches,* IX (May 15, 1943), 473–477.

North, S. N. D. "The Industrial Commission," *The North American Review,* CLXVIII (June, 1899), 709 ff.

Nourse, Edwin G. "Monopolistic Practices and the Price Structure," Academy of Political Science, *Proceedings,* XVIII (January, 1939), 124–131.

—— and Associates. America's Capacity to Produce. Washington, D.C., The Brookings Institution, 1934.

"Now Is the Time," *Printer's Ink,* CLXXXIV (August 25, 1938), 86.

"Off to a Good Start," *Business Week,* December 10, 1938, p. 48.

O'Mahoney, Joseph C. "Fear and Force—or Facts?" *Dun's Review,* XLVII (April, 1939), 5 ff.

O'Mahoney, Joseph C. "It's an Economic Study," *Printer's Ink*, CLXXXV (October 6, 1938), 21–22.

"Papers Relating to the TNEC," *The American Economic Review*, XXXII (June, 1942), 1–135.

Parkinson, Thomas I. "A Call to Action," *Printer's Ink*, CLXXXV (October 13, 1938), 11–13.

"Patent System Probe First on Monopoly List," *Newsweek*, XII (December 5, 1938), 34.

"Propaganda Glossary," *Time*, XXXIII (June 19, 1939), 65–66.

Robertson, A. W. "That Devil Monopoly," *Printer's Ink*, CLXXXVI (February 9, 1939), 33 ff.

Robinson, Joan. The Economics of Imperfect Competition. London, Macmillan, 1933.

Rogers, Lindsay. "The Inquiring Congressmen," *Survey Graphic*, XXVIII (January, 1939), 5–8.

Scaville, John, and Noel Sargent. Fact and Fancy in the T.N.E.C. Monographs. Washington, D.C., National Association of Manufacturers, 1942.

Schmidt, Emerson P. Small Business, Its Place and Problems. Washington, D.C., Chamber of Commerce of the United States, 1943.

"Six and Six," *Time*, XXXII (July 4, 1938), 9.

Slichter, Sumner H. "Corporate Price Policies As a Factor in the Recent Recession," Academy of Political Science, *Proceedings*, XVIII (January, 1939), 142–155.

Smith, Blackwell. "Teamwork for Prosperity," *Dun's Review*, XLVII (May, 1939), 6 ff.

"So-Called Monopoly Committee, The," *Fortune*, XVIII (November, 1938), 72 ff.

"Steel's Brain Trust Tackles TNEC," *Business Week*, February 3, 1940, pp. 15–16.

Stern, Laurence. "Outline of a New Economic Order," *The Magazine of Wall Street*, LXII (September 24, 1938), 670–672.

Stigler, F. J. "Extent and Basis of Monopoly Studies by the TNEC," *The American Economic Review*, Vol. XXXII (June, 1942), Supplement, pp. 1–22.

Stone, I. F. "O'Mahoney Sums Up," *The Nation*, CLII (March 22, 1941), 315.

"These Are the Monopoly Investigators," *Business Week*, July 2, 1938, pp. 15–17.

"They Can't Do This to You, Can't They," *The Saturday Evening Post*, CCXII (September 16, 1939), 22 ff.

Thorp, Willard L. "Distrusting the Anti-Trust Laws," *Dun's Review*, XLVI (August, 1938), 22–24.

"TNEC Digs into Consumer Question As O'Mahoney Defends Advertising," *Printer's Ink*, CLXXXVII (May 18, 1939), 30–33.

"TNEC—Magnificent Failure," *Business Week*, March 22, 1941, pp. 22–31.

U. S. Commerce, Department of. 390 Bills, a Digest of Proposals Considered in Congress in Behalf of Small Business, 1933–1942. Washington, D.C., 1940.

U. S. Congress. House. "Debate in the House on S. J. Res. 300 to Create a Temporary National Economic Committee, June 14, 1938," *Congressional Record,* 75th Cong., 3d sess., LXXXIII, Part 8, pp. 9336–9341.

U. S. Congress. Senate. "Debate in the Senate on S. J. Res. 300 to Create a Temporary National Economic Committee, June 7, 8, and 9, 1938," *Congressional Record,* 75th Cong., 3d sess., Vol. LXIII, Part 7, pp. 8338–8340; Part 8, pp. 8497–8507 and pp. 8588–8595.

—— —— —— Special Committee to Study and Survey Problems of Small Business Enterprises. Hearings . . . 76th Cong., 1st sess., Parts 1–13, 1942.

—— —— —— Report: Industrial Prices and Their Relative Inflexibility, S. Doc. 13, 74th Cong., 1st sess.

U. S. Federal Trade Commission. Report to the President, November, 1934. Washington, D.C., 1934.

U. S. National Resources Committee. Consumer Incomes in the United States—Their Distribution in 1935–36. Washington, D.C., 1938.

—— —— The Structure of the American Economy. Parts 1 and 2. Washington, D.C., 1939.

U. S. President, 1933— (Franklin Roosevelt). Annual Message to Congress, January 3, 1938, Calling Attention to the Concentration of Economic Control. (H. Doc. 458) *Congressional Record,* 75th Cong., 3d sess., LXXXIII, Part 1, pp. 8–11.

—— Message to Congress, April 29, 1938, on Strengthening and Enforcement of Antitrust Laws. (S. Doc. 173) *Congressional Record,* 75th Cong., 3d sess., Vol. LXXXIII, Part 6, pp. 5992–5996.

U. S. Temporary National Economic Committee. Monographs. Washington, D.C.

    3. Gerhard Colm and Helen Tarasov. Who Pays the Taxes? 1940.

    9. Clifford Hynning and Gerhard Colm. Taxation of Corporate Enterprise. 1940.

   13. Federal Trade Commission. Relative Efficiency of Large, Medium-Sized, and Small Business. 1940.

   16. Walton Hamilton. Antitrust in Action. 1940.

   18. Charles Albert Pearce. Trade Association Survey. 1940.

   20. H. Dewey Anderson. Taxation, Recovery, and Defense. 1940.

   21. Clair Wilcox. Competition and Monopoly in American Industry. 1940.

   37. Oscar L. Altman. Saving, Investment, and National Income. 1940.

U. S. Works Progress Administration. Price Dispersion and Industrial Activity, 1928–1938. Washington, D.C., 1939.

"Untermyer Inquiry, The," *Review of Reviews,* XLVII (February, 1913), 137 ff.

Ware, Caroline F., and Gardiner Means. The Modern Economy in Action. New York, Harcourt, Brace, 1936.

Watkins, Myron W. "The Monopoly Investigation," *Yale Review,* XXVIII (December, 1939), 323–339.

"What Consumers Told TNEC," *Business Week,* May 20, 1939, pp. 44–45.

"What to Expect from the Monopoly Investigation," *Commercial and Financial Chronicle,* CXLVII (July 23, 1938), 481–483.

Whitney, Simon N. Trade Associations and Industrial Control. New York, Central Book Company, 1934.

Williams, Edward A. "Probes by Congress Check Government," *The Washington Post,* April 6, 1935, p. 7.

Yarros, Victor S. "Senator Borah and Monopolies," *The Christian Century,* LIII (February 12, 1936), 262–263.

INDEX

Administration, probes of conduct of, 379

Administrative commissions, temporary, 379

Advertising, role of restraint, 225-27; tooth paste, 226; use of material in schools: unreliability of claims, 310; role in concentration and monopoly neglected, 361

Agencies, government, *see* Government agencies

Agrarian economy replaced industrialized society, 92

Agricultural machinery, *see* Farm machinery

Aldrich Plan, 389

Aldrich-Vreeland Emergency Currency bill, 389

Altman, Oscar L., 68; on concentration in investment banking, 130

Aluminum, capital required to start production, 218

American Brass Company, 180 ff.

American Communications Association guaranteed severance pay, 309

American Dental Association, 227

American Petroleum Institute, preparation for hearings, 62, 99

American Roller Mill Company, separation allowances paid by, 309

American Standards Association, 303, 306

American Telephone and Telegraph Company, 111, 127; wealth controlled by, 11

American Trucking Association, 100, 169

"American way," 154

America's Capacity to Consume (Moulton), 13

America's Capacity to Produce (Nourse), 12

Anaconda Copper Mining Company, 321

Anchor Hocking Glass Corporation, 234

Anderson, Dewey, 337; quoted, 252

Annuities, uniformity in rates and commissions, 204

Antimonopoly campaign, *see* Monopoly investigation

Antimonopoly legislation, unethical practices after fifty years of, 356

Antimonopoly sentiment, ancient, 8; imbedded in our folklore, 365

Antitrust activities, 5; improvement of procedure, 359

Antitrust cases, FTC as a master of chancery in, 318, 347; suggested that a Government agency be empowered to render advance opinions, 320

Antitrust laws, administration of, 9; strengthening and enforcement advocated, 17, 21, 26, 318, 323; set aside under NRA codes, 150; modification advocated by U.S. Chamber of Commerce, 156, 157; intent of collusion to violate, 193; insurance companies' efforts to hide machinery of combination, 205; prohibit interlocking relations, 232; exporters plead handicap by, 234; "fair trade" laws denounced as antagonistic to, 327; enforcement recommended by TNEC: funds for enforcement, 342; legislative changes, 343-49; penalties for violating, 347; FTC as master in chancery, 347; *see also* Corporate mergers; Monopoly laws; Patent laws; Sherman Act

Armstrong Insurance Committee, 388

Armstrong Investigation, 299, 354, 373, 375, 388; excerpt from report, 122; exposed efforts of insurance companies to control legislation, 294

Arnold, Thurman W., 56, 277, 322, 331, 357, 358, 376; quoted, 37, 181, 202 ff. *passim*, 289; on TNEC: record and point of view, 43; on executive committee, 59; persistent advocate of antitrust action, 319, 323; recommended repeal of Miller-Tydings Act: denounced "fair trade" laws, 327

Arrow-Hart-Hegeman Electric Company, 281

Ashurst, Senator, 35

Association of Grocery Manufacturers of America, 19

Association of Life Insurance Presidents, 97; surveillance of and lobbying before state legislatures, 293, 294; method used to control legislation, 296 ff.

Association to stabilize prices, 185

Atlantic Refining Company, 233, 234

Austin, Senator, call for commission to study monopoly laws, 26; foe of TNEC, 29n, 31

Automatic gob feeding machine, 273

Automobile industry, social use of patents,

73